Community Care Practice and the Law

Two week loan

Please return on or before the last date stamped below.
Charges are made for late return.

CONTENTS

PART III: COMMUNITY CARE PROCESS

9. Assessment 136

10. Fairness and User Empowerment in Assessment 169

17. Housing Services 274

18. Charges for Services 293

19. Planning for Community Care 317

20. Information and Publicity 335

PART IV: REMEDIES

21. Summary of Remedies 355

22. Informal Remedies 357

23. Non-Legal Remedies 359

Disclaimer

Every effort has been made to ensure that the information contained in this book is cited correctly and interpreted reasonably. However, no book of this type is likely to be completely error-free.

Any views expressed are personal and do not represent the views of any past or present employer.

Acknowledgements

Thanks are due to the many individuals and organisations who have contributed advice informally on countless questions and problems which have arisen during the writing. These include lawyers, librarians, voluntary organisations, government departments (in their capacity as public information providers) and professional associations. Needless to say, none of these are responsible for any errors.

The final form of the book has benefited greatly from the advice and criticism of Professor Joel Mandelstam.

ABBREVIATIONS

AC	Appeal cases (law reports series)
ACC	Association of County Councils
ADSS	Association of Directors of Social Services
All ER	All England Law Reports
AMA	Association of Metropolitan Authorities
BMA	British Medical Association
CA	Court of Appeal
CCP	Community care plan
CHC	Community Health Council
CSP	Chartered Society of Physiotherapy
CI	Chief Inspector (Circular guidance)
CLAE	Commissioner for Local Administration in England
CLAS	Commissioner for Local Administration in Scotland
CLAW	Commissioner for Local Administration in Wales
CPA	Care Programme Approach (mental health)
CSDPA	Chronically Sick and Disabled Persons Act
CSDP(NI)A	Chronically Sick and Disabled Persons (Northern Ireland) Act
DC	District Council
DFG	Disabled facilities grant
DH	Department of Health (formerly DHSS)
DHA	District Health Authority
DHSS	Department of Health and Social Security (now divided into DH and DSS)
DLA	Disability Living Allowance
DLF	Disabled Living Foundation
DoE	Department of Environment
DP(SCR)A	Disabled Persons (Services, Representation and Consultation) Act
DSS	Department of Social Security (formerly DHSS)
EL	Executive Letter (Circular guidance)
ENT	Ear, nose, throat
FCR	Family Court Reports
FHSA	Family Health Services Authority
FHSL	Family Health Services Letter
FPC	Family Practitioner Committee (now FHSA)
GLC	Greater London Council (former)
HASSASSA Act	Health and Social Services and Social Security Adjudications Act
HB	Health Board (Scotland)
HC	Health Circular (replaced by HSG series)
HL	House of Lords
HN	Health Notice (Circular)
HRA	Housing Revenue Account
HRC	Health (Service) Reorganisation Circular
HSC	Health Service Commissioner (ombudsman)
HSCA	Health Service Commissioners Act
HSG	Health Service Guidelines (Circular guidance)
HSSB	Health and Social Services Board (Northern Ireland)
IHSM	Institute of Health Service Managers
ILEA	Inner London Education Authority
ILF	Independent Living Fund

IRC	Inland Revenue Commissioners
J	Justice (title of eg. High Court judge)
LA	Local authority
LAC	Local Authority Circular
LASSL	Local Authority Social Services Letter
LBC	London Borough Council
LBOTMG	London Boroughs' Occupational Therapy Managers Group
LGHA	Local Government and Housing Act
LGIU	Local Government Information Unit
LGR	Local Government Reports
LGRevReps	Local Government Review Reports
LJ	Lord Justice (title of a Court of Appeal judge)
MBC	Metropolitan Borough Council
MHA	Mental Health Act
MR	Master of the Rolls (most senior Court of Appeal judge)
MWA	Minor works assistance
NAA	National Assistance Act
NAHA	National Association of Health Authorities (now NAHAT)
NAHAT	National Association of Health Authorities and Trusts (formerly NAHA)
NAO	National Audit Office
NCC	National Consumer Council
NCVO	National Council of Voluntary Organisations
NHSE	National Health Service Executive (formerly NHSME)
NHSME	National Health Service Management Executive (now NHSE)
NISW	National Institute for Social Work
NFHA	National Federation of Housing Federations
NHSA	National Health Service Act
NHSCCA	National Health Service and Community Care Act
NLJ	New Law Journal
OPCS	Office of Population Censuses and Surveys
OT	Occupational therapist
PCA	Parliamentary Commissioner for Administration
PT	Physiotherapist
QBD	Queen's Bench Division (of the High Court)
RADAR	Royal Association for Disability and Rehabilitation
RCN	Royal College of Nursing
RCP	Royal College of Physicians.
RHT	Registered Homes Tribunal
RNIB	Royal National Institute for the Blind
RNID	Royal National Institute for the Deaf
SHHD	Scottish Home and Health Department (now SOHHD)
SI	Statutory instrument
SLT	Speech and language therapist
SOHHD	Scottish Office Home and Health Department (formerly SHHD)
SSD	Social Services Department
SSI	Social Services Inspectorate
STS	Speech therapy services
SWD	Social Work Department (Scotland)
SWSG	Social Work Services Group (Scotland)
TENS	Trancutaneous electric nerve stimulator
TNS	Trancutaneous nerve stimulator
WO	Welsh Office

PART I

INTRODUCTION

CHAPTER I

INTRODUCTION

HOW TO USE THE BOOK

This book can be used in different ways and at different levels depending on the reader. This Introduction describes how to use the book, who it is for, what its aim is and the approach which has been taken. It explains why community care is a complex system which is difficult to understand. It is recommended strongly that all readers look at this introduction.

The main components of the book are as follows:

(1) **Part I** The *Overview* is a systematic summary, giving the reader a condensed version of the whole book. It is particularly recommended to readers who are not very familiar with community care.

(2) **Part II** of the book contains five chapters containing themes basic to the whole book. *Uncertainties and resources in community care* explains the uncertainties and questions about resources which pervade the community care system.

Community care services lists community care services and their source in legislation.

The *Checklist: matching services with legislation* contains an alphabetical list of specific services ranging from wheelchairs to home help. Against each item, a key indicates the legislation under which that service can be provided. As far as the authors are aware, no such detailed list has been produced elsewhere.

The chapter about *Types and status of document* describes the basis for community care in terms of legislation and government guidance. It explains why it is important for all concerned to understand what these documents are and their significance.

Legal principles explains the concepts which underlie legal remedies. The chapter is written for non-lawyers to convey basic information to readers unfamiliar with these principles.

(3) **Part III** of the book describes and analyses the community care process in terms of legislation, guidance and practice. In addition to social services, health and housing services are included, even though they are not legislatively defined as 'community care services'. The broad plan of this part is as follows. Each chapter starts with a short explanation of *Key issues*. Each section within each chapter generally contains a *Summary* of the section; *Extracts* from legislation and guidance; followed by a *Discussion* of particular issues.

(4) **Part IV** deals with the remedies to be used when service users are dissatisfied with the decisions or actions of local authorities and health authorities.

WHOM THE BOOK IS FOR

The book has been written for:

- social services department, health service (and housing authority) purchasers and providers, both managers and practitioners;
- voluntary and advice-giving organisations;
- interested users and carers;
- lawyers;
- university lecturers and students.

AIM OF THE BOOK

The intention of the book is to provide practical assistance for readers. It aims to do this by bringing together a wide range of information and analysis relating to community care practice and law. By including many practical examples and using non-legal language, the book bridges the gap between law and practice.

Community care practice is based on legislation and guidance of various types. It is important for all concerned to be aware of this and what it means. Neither service providers nor service users can understand fully what they are doing without knowing what powers, duties, rights and remedies arise from the legislation.

Only a minute proportion of disputes ever become formal legal proceedings. Similarly, only a small proportion of grievances will find their way even to social services complaints procedures or to the ombudsmen. Therefore, although the book will assist people involved in formal legal disputes, its predominant aim is to give useful information about legislation and guidance at the 'lowest' level of confrontation as a way of avoiding, not just solving, disputes. For example, the statutory service manager who is well-informed is less likely to try to implement a legally dubious policy – whilst well-informed service users (or their representatives) are more likely to be able to challenge successfully, and perhaps informally, particular decisions or policies at the outset.

SCOPE OF THE BOOK

The book covers relevant social, health and housing services for elderly people, younger physically disabled adults and people with mental disorders. 'Community care services' as defined in legislation are provided by social services departments. However, in the sense that community care is about caring for people in their own homes or in residential accommodation, health and housing services are very much part of community care in a wider sense. Indeed, legislation places duties on social services departments to consult with health and housing departments about community care plans and to invite them to assist with individual assessments.

But apart from all this, there are practical reasons why all concerned need to know about the range of responsibilities across social, health and housing services. For example, a statutory authority might be planning services and demarcation of responsibilities between it and another authority (eg. between social services and the health service). It is clearly important that the authority is aware fully not only of its own legal powers and duties – but also those of the other authority. Conversely, for service users and their representatives or advisers, it is important to know the duties and responsibilities of different agencies. If one agency does not deliver a service, another might.

APPROACH OF THE BOOK

The book juxtaposes practice, policy and law in order to give readers a rounded picture of community care. The approach is 'descriptive' rather than 'prescriptive', and attempts to deal even-handedly with a number of controversial issues. **What the book does not do is make judgements about whether community care is 'working'**. There seem to be very different views about this and it is not the book's aim to comment one way or another. Thus, the many practice examples in the book are intended to illustrate what problems individual authorities or service users *can* face. Inevitably, these examples are often about things 'going wrong'. But this is not necessarily a criticism of the system: even in the best of systems, things go wrong. Whether those problems are faced by one in two, or one in a hundred local authorities or service users, the problems are very real to those authorities and those users. Disputes, whether solved informally, through reference to charters, through complaints systems or ultimately through formal litigation, are very much about individuals.

COMPLEXITY OF COMMUNITY CARE

'Community care' (other than for mentally ill people, for whom it existed previously) is, officially, a 'new' policy and is undoubtedly ill-understood. It is clear from reports emerging from different sectors that people's expectations, and their understanding of what community care is, vary widely. For example, some reports from the voluntary sector on the one hand, and the Department of Health on the other, describe apparently different worlds.

There are a number of reasons why community care is difficult to understand. One reason is that the 1990 community care legislation, for the main
part, only puts in place a framework for assessment. To find 'community care
services', one has to look to pre-existing legislation which is itself not always
readily comprehensible. This means that, in order to understand the legal and
policy basis for community care, a range of legislation and Circular guidance
stretching back decades (as far back as 1948) has to be identified.

In addition, the compatibility of these different pieces of legislation is not
always evident. One also finds, confusingly, that the same service (for example,
home help) might be available from social services under at least three different
pieces of legislation.

UNCERTAINTY AND DISCRETION IN COMMUNITY CARE

One way of understanding how the community care system works is to
recognise that it consists of a series of uncertainties. This is the underlying
theme of the book, because it is at these points of uncertainty that significant
decisions are made and actions taken. It is at these points too, that disputes arise
between service providers and service users; for example, when the service user's
idea of 'need' does not correspond with the authority's idea of it.

These uncertainties are probably inevitable in a welfare system. One could
refer to them in other terms, such as 'safety valves', 'discretionary elements',
'variables with unpredictable values' – and so on. Their function is to give the
system some flexibility, and to allow authorities to regulate the system according
to their resources and priorities. They can therefore be viewed as a mechanism
which allows authorities to ration services. Authorities will particularly wish to
do this when a scarcity of resources puts pressure on them and strains these
'safety valves'.

Two most important, related points arise from this situation. First, authorities
have great discretion to regulate the level of services which they provide and
to decide for whom they will provide them. Second, generally speaking, **service
users have few, if any, absolute legal rights or entitlements to services**.
Instead, the provision of services generally depends on the policies of authorities, the judgements of their staff – and crucially, on what money (resources) is
available for provision.

ALLOCATION OF SCARCE RESOURCES: RATIONING

The issue of resource allocation, priority setting, or rationing – whatever name
is chosen – is complicated. It is highly sensitive, not new, but now highlighted
by community care policy and guidance. The allocation of scarce resources is,
of course, a thankless task whether planned and executed by central or local
government – or even, at the other extreme, not planned at all but allowed to
develop in haphazard fashion or by lottery. It not only involves 'tragic choices'
but can also too easily bring opprobrium on rationing agents, such as government, whatever strategy or 'non-strategy' is adopted (Calabresi, Bobbitt 1978).

Describing, as this book does, a welfare system framed by uncertainties which allow authorities to ration services, is not to imply criticism. This might be an unavoidable feature of such systems. However, the system still needs to be described, so that both authorities and service users realise what is going on.

WHAT THE BOOK DOES NOT COVER

Because community care is such a large subject, both in breadth and depth, it is not possible to include everything about it. We have had to set some confines to the book. For example, the book covers only in outline the complicated system of charges for residential care and does not cover inspection of social services by either the Social Services Inspectorate or local authority inspection units.

There are also a number of other subjects and services which have been excluded. The book does not cover services for children for two main reasons. Firstly, community care legislation does not formally apply to children, who are instead covered by legislation such as the Children Act 1989 and the Education Act 1981. Secondly, children's services and needs are a large subject in their own right. Thus, although many of the principles of community care might apply to children, we could not possibly have done justice to the subject.

We have not given a detailed account of the benefits system, run by the Department of Social Security, although money is of course of paramount importance. Information about benefits is set out expertly in other publications, and there is little merit in providing what is already accessible elsewhere.

Similarly, the book might have covered the Social Fund (including community care grants and budgeting loans) operated by the Department of Social Security. This is a complex and unpredictable system in its own right which quite clearly is relevant to 'community care'. A summary of the system can be obtained in a guide for advice organisations published by the Department of Social Security. More precise details of the system are available in a looseleaf form (*Social Fund Officer's Guide*) from Her Majesty's Stationery Office.

So, too, the Independent Living Fund might have been included. It is a trust fund, which pays money to very severely disabled people who meet certain conditions. The money enables them to remain living in the community rather than enter residential care. The eligibility criteria are available from the Trust itself and are explained also in Department of Health Circular guidance (LASSL(93)6).

TYPES AND SOURCES OF INFORMATION

The book collates and analyses information from different types of material in order to try and give a rounded picture of community care practice in relation to the law. These include:

- Acts of Parliament;

- statutory instruments;
- directions and approvals made under Acts of Parliament;
- guidance (including policy guidance, practice guidance and Circular guidance);
- reports of law court cases;
- quotes from Hansard (House of Commons and House of Lords);
- ombudsman (local, health and Parliamentary) investigations;
- registered homes tribunal decisions;
- reported practice (books and journal articles).

The chapter on *Duties and Powers of Authorities* explains the significance of the different types of legislation and guidance.

EFFECTS OF SETTING PRIORITIES AND RATIONING

Amidst much talk and guidance about priorities, eligibility criteria, targeting those in 'greatest need', planning systems, efficiency – and so on – there might be a tendency sometimes to forget exactly how rationing, be it ever so 'rational', can affect people.

For example, bathing is traditionally classed as low priority and people might have to wait months and even years before they are assessed and assisted. Yet would many of 'us' do without a bath or shower for years – and regard it as a minor inconvenience and of low priority? Similarly, would we accept that we do not 'need' a stairlift or downstairs lavatory – but instead should have a commode in our living room? And, even in the case of the commode in the living room, how many of us would accept an authority's view that we do not 'need' (as opposed to 'prefer') a commode which at least looks like a piece of living room furniture (eg. with upholstery) – but only 'need' a basic commode?

These are difficult questions. However, neither the courts nor the ombudsmen can interfere with decisions unless they are taken illegally, unreasonably or unfairly; or unless there is bad administration involved. Therefore, these questions about priorities and rationing have, as the courts sometimes state, to be asked elsewhere (in Parliament) – and such considerations are beyond the scope of this book. Nevertheless, a spirit of enlightened self-interest might be appropriate all round, since many of us, even if not disabled at present, are likely to become disabled at some stage of our lives, in one form or another.

The following are just four examples drawn from ombudsman investigations to illustrate that people waiting long periods for services or deemed to be low priority do not necessarily have correspondingly minor needs. For example, a two year wait for a stairlift was suffered by a woman with arthritis who had to pull herself up and down the stairs several times a day. This caused swelling and pain; forced her to protect her hands with hand splints and take pain killers; caused depression; and forced her to remain upstairs sometimes because of the pain in coming downstairs (CLAE 91/A/1481). A child with severe learning difficulties, poor physical skills, epilepsy and double incontinence had to wait nearly two years for a downstairs extension (CLAE 91/C/1972,p.3).

A woman in her thirties with permanent spinal injury caused at work had to wait 15 months for an assessment. She could not move her head to the right, lift her right arm or hand, which intermittently became swollen and discoloured. She was advised by doctors that she would never work again, jolts or bumps to her right side were painful, and ordinary activities such as shopping, cooking and housework were restricted or impossible. She was placed in neither of the two priority categories, her need for a shower being judged low priority: she waited 15 months for an assessment. (The local ombudsman found that this wait was not maladministration because the local authority was entitled to make priorities: CLAE 92/A/1693.)

A hospital decided to discharge a patient to nursing accommodation (where he would have to pay the fees) on the grounds that he did not need active medical treatment but did need 'substantial nursing care'. The patient was doubly incontinent, could not eat or drink without assistance, could not communicate, had a kidney tumour, cataracts in both eyes and occasional epileptic fits. The health authority defended its position with reference to resources, priorities and national policy (the health service ombudsman made a finding in this case against the health authority: HSC E.62/93–94).

CHAPTER 2

OVERVIEW

This chapter provides a summary and overview of the contents of subsequent chapters.

PART II: SERVICES AND PRINCIPLES

Part II of the book contains five chapters relating primarily to services, and to the principles involved in community care.

Uncertainties and Resources in Community Care (Chapter 3)

This chapter explains a whole gamut of uncertainties which underlie the community care system from the referral stage right through to service provision, review and the handling of disputes by the law courts. These uncertainties act as 'safety valves' in the community care system, allowing authorities to deliver services within resources and escape otherwise oppressive obligations.

The chapter also explains the all important question of resources, its inevitable presence in a welfare system and how it affects authorities' legal powers and duties and depletes service users' rights.

Community Care Services (Chapter 4)

Community care services are defined by legislation to include social services provision of residential accommodation (with or without nursing care) and a range of non-residential services (such as personal care, day services, equipment and adaptations to people's homes). This chapter covers the legislation under which 'community care services' are provided.

Checklist: Matching Specific Services to Legislation (Chapter 5)

Many specific services, items of equipment and home adaptations are not mentioned in legislation. In addition, some services can be provided under more than one piece of legislation and by more than one type of authority (for example by a local authority or by a health authority).

This chapter lists a wide range of services and equipment provided by social services, health and housing authorities – and indicates the legislation under which each service might be provided.

This will be particularly useful for service users and their advisers, if it enables them to cite the appropriate, and where there is a choice, the most powerful legislation. For example, local authorities have the power (ie. they can but do not have) to provide practical assistance in the home for elderly people *in general* under the Health Service and Public Health Act 1968; but a *duty* to do so for *individual* disabled people under the Chronically Sick and Disabled Persons Act 1970.

Duties and Powers of Authorities (Chapter 6)

Community care services are based for the most part on a range of legislation and guidance issued by the Department of Health. Understanding the effect of this legislation and guidance is not always easy but is clearly important. Authorities need to know the extent and limit of their obligations, whilst service users and their advisers need to know what they might be entitled to and when they can reasonably challenge authorities' decisions.

Legislation gives both *duties* and *powers* to authorities. Authorities have a *duty* to provide some services – that is they must provide them. Other services, authorities have a *power* only to provide – that is they can provide them, but they don't have to. However, even in the case of duties, there is complication because there are different types of duty. For example, a duty can be towards *individual* people or it can be towards the local population in *general*. The first of these is normally the stronger type of duty.

A second complication exists because few duties of either type (individual or general) are 'absolute', since they are normally qualified by particular words and phrases. For example, a health authority might have a general duty to provide nursing services to the population, but only to the level 'necessary to meet all reasonable requirements' – whatever that might mean. The consequence of this is that authorities often have broad scope to interpret how to carry out such duties, and the law courts are therefore less likely to intervene against authorities. Even if the courts sometimes define terms (such as 'ordinarily resident'), they usually leave it to authorities to apply terms (e.g. to decide whether any particular person 'needs' a service).

In addition, the legislation on which services are based does not generally prescribe in detail what, and how, they should be provided. Perhaps by way of compensation, the Department of Health does issue abundant guidance. But one of the difficulties about this guidance is that its legal status is generally unclear and authorities cannot always be sure whether they have to follow it. Similarly, service users and their advisers will be uncertain about the extent to which they can rely on it when challenging authorities. Even the highest court in the country, the House of Lords, has disagreed in the past about the legal effect of guidance.

Legal Principles (Chapter 7)

This chapter explains, briefly, the main legal principles which apply to community care. A later chapter, *Using legal remedies*, summarises some of the practical aspects of employing these principles.

English law is divided into *public law* and *private law*. In the community care field, most disputes reaching the law courts will probably be public law cases.

In public law cases, claimants can seek *judicial review* of acts and decisions of public authorities, such as local authorities and health authorities. In public law, judges can examine whether authorities have acted *unreasonably*, *illegally* or *unfairly*. These concepts are not straightforward and it might be difficult to predict exactly how judges will interpret and apply them in any particular case.

Very basically, the following examples illustrate what these terms can mean:

- *unreasonableness*. In principle, an authority's behaviour would have to be very wayward indeed before it was found to be unreasonable. However, in practice, the courts do sometimes find that authorities have behaved unreasonably (e.g. when an authority failed to consult local home owners about proposed contracts which could have had the effect of closing most of the homes in the locality);
- *illegality*. An authority acts illegally if it does not adhere to the legislation under which it is meant to be acting. If an authority refused even to consider assisting disabled people with privately arranged holidays under disability legislation (CSDPA 1970), it would probably be following an illegal policy. This is because the legislation refers quite explicitly not only to holidays arranged by the local authority, but also to other holidays;
- *unfairness (procedural impropriety)*. judgements about unfairness and fairness reflect the courts' concern with the idea of *natural justice*. Aspects of fairness include *consultation* (e.g. consulting with residents when a residential home is about to be closed), the provision of *information* about decisions (e.g. not to provide home help), *absence of bias*, and *legitimate expectation* (ie leading people to expect certain services and then either not delivering them, or taking them away).

In public law, judges will not directly substitute their own opinion for that of authorities. It is most important that readers be aware of this fact. **Judicial review is not about enforcing directly individuals' rights to receive services; instead it is about ensuring that authorities make their decisions legally and properly.** This means that even if a court finds that an authority has acted unreasonably, illegally or unfairly in denying services to a person, the court cannot, normally, explicitly order that the person receive those services. Instead it orders that the authority re-take the decision and that this time the decision should be made legally and properly. The authority could still deny the services to the person – but it would have to do so for different reasons.

For example, an authority might have originally denied services to a person because it claimed he was not 'ordinarily resident' in the area of the authority. The court might then rule that the authority had used the wrong definition of 'ordinarily resident', that the person was an ordinary resident and that the authority should re-take its decision about providing services for the person. This time around, the authority could still deny services to the person but it would have to so on other grounds; for example, because it assesses that the person is not at sufficient risk to qualify for service provision. On the other hand, if the sole reason for originally denying services was on the basis of residence, then the authority might not have much room for manoeuvre when it re-takes the decision – and the new decision would probably be in favour of the claimant.

Thus, judicial review might only be an indirect method of enforcing provision of services, but it, or even just the threat of it, does at least place some limits on the wide discretion of authorities.

In *private law*, the position is different. Private law claims are for the enforcement of personal rights to services – so, in principle, the courts can provide remedies directly to claimants. For example, a judge could in principle order that a person receive home help; or award damages/financial compensation. However, in practice, private law has relatively limited application to community care. This is because neither of the two main grounds for claims, *breach of statutory duty* or *negligence* are well-established in this field.

Breach of statutory duty occurs when an authority does not perform its duty. However, in the community care field, judges are likely to deny claims based on such breaches of duty. They might state, for example, that duties in the legislation are so vague that it is not possible to say whether authorities really have breached their duties. Alternatively, the judges might find that even if authorities have breached their duties, it is clear from the legislation that Parliament never intended that individual service users should have a right to a private law remedy. (The House of Lords will consider some cases about breach of statutory duty from the local authority field in late 1994 – although it is not expected that the judges will break with past legal decisions.)

The other private law claim, *negligence*, is well-established in principle in the health care field (e.g. medical negligence) – although it can still be difficult to prove. It depends on individual practitioners (such as doctors) having an individual duty of care towards patients; breaching that duty by being careless; and thereby causing physical harm to patients. By contrast, negligence is not at present well-established in the personal social services and community care field, although the House of Lords will be considering the principle later in 1994.

However, as some health service tasks become increasingly redefined as social care tasks (see p.193), it might be likewise increasingly difficult (logically) to recognise the principle of negligence in the health service but not the social services field (e.g. it might be difficult for courts to distinguish between a community nurse (health service) who scalds a person in a bath and a personal care assistant (local authority social services) who does exactly the same thing).

PART III: COMMUNITY CARE PROCESS

Part III of the book covers the process of community care – how is works in practice.

Access to Assessment (Chapter 8)

The community care system revolves around assessment. It is assessment which is the new element introduced by the 1990 Act, since 'community care services' have long been provided under pre-existing legislation, some of it dating from 1948 (see Chapter 4).

Assessment is the gateway through which people have to pass in order to obtain services. Therefore, access to assessment is of paramount importance, since without assessment, people get no services.

Local authorities have a legal duty to assess people who appear to them to be in possible need of community care services. Then they have a separate duty to decide what services they should actually provide. This means that assessing people's needs for services is not the same as saying that those services will be provided. There is a separate decision involved.

Authorities do not have to assess people on request – that is, they do not have to assess everybody who asks for an assessment. It is in principle open to authorities to set their own definition of 'need'; they would not have to assess people who appear to fall outside that definition of need. It is unclear how restrictively authorities can, or are likely to, define 'need' at this stage.

It should also be noted that local authorities do not have a positive duty to identify all the people who might be in need of services and who therefore should be assessed. But they do have duties to find out how many disabled people there are locally and to keep a register of disabled people.

Before actually assessing people, local authorities decide whether people qualify for assessment at all, what sort of 'priority' they are, what sort of assessment they should get, and how quickly they should get it. Therefore some people might have to wait for an assessment. For authorities, such an initial 'screening' process is a powerful tool for controlling and channelling demand for services.

The local ombudsmen have investigated many cases where the priorities and resource problems of local authorities have led to long waits. Sometimes, the ombudsmen look unfavourably on long waiting times, even for people who are deemed to be 'low priority'; at other times they accept the inevitability of priority setting and waiting times. Much seems to depend on the facts of individual cases.

During assessments, local authorities have a duty to invite *health and/or housing authorities* to participate in assessments if it appears that people might have health or housing needs. Health and housing authorities are not under a duty to accept such invitations.

It is not clear to what extent health and housing authorities might explicitly refuse such invitations wholesale. Nevertheless the scale and speed of their participation will almost inevitably be influenced by their own priorities and available resources. Guidance states that local authorities must not make commitments about service provision on behalf of other authorities without agreeing those commitments with the other authorities first.

Assessment (Chapter 9)

Legislation states that assessment must be about what community care services the person needs. After that, authorities must decide which of those services, and to what level, they are actually going to provide.

However, some government guidance and advice suggests that the assessment should be 'needs-led'. This means in principle that service provision should be moulded to people's needs – rather than people's assessed needs moulded to whatever services happen to be available. However, one interpretation of 'needs-led' assessment seems to be that services should not be mentioned at all until after the assessment. Such practice would seem not to conform with the legislation which states clearly that assessment should be about 'needs for services', not just 'needs'.

Extra Duty Towards Disabled People

During the assessment, local authorities have a duty, if they think people are disabled, to decide what home welfare services (under disabled persons' legislation: the 1986 and 1970 Acts) they need – and to tell them about their rights under that legislation. Guidance states that disabled people should be offered 'comprehensive' assessments – although there is probably some confusion about the implications of this, because many people classed as disabled might not necessarily need comprehensive assessments. It is somewhat unclear from the legislation whether assessment under the disability legislation is meant to be part of the main community care assessment or separate from it.

Decision about Provision of Services

When local authorities have completed assessments, they have a duty to decide whether people's identified needs for services 'call for' services to be provided. Local authorities do not have a duty to provide all the services for which they have identified needs. For example, an authority might state that a person 'needs' a service, but say also that it is not necessary for the authority to provide the service, because the person does not fall into a 'high risk' category and so is outside the *authority's definition of need*. Equally, where a person is judged to need a service which an authority does not have a duty to provide (but can if it wants), then the authority is probably free not to provide it.

The distinction between a person's assessed needs, and the needs for which a local authority will provide, can become confusing. One solution proposed by the Department of Health was that authorities should distinguish between recording people's 'needs' (for which they must provide) and people's 'preferences' or 'desires' (for which they do not have to provide). However, this proposed solution itself created some confusion and controversy.

The confusion revolves around the opinion that, once a need for at least some services has been identified, they must be provided. For example, it is thought that if a need for services under the Chronically Sick and Disabled Persons Act 1970 has been identified, then those services must be provided because there is an absolute duty to do so. In fact, the position might not be quite so clear, because the duty under that Act is possibly not quite so 'absolute' as has been supposed – and it is not clear how far it persists if an authority simply does not have enough money to provide services in individual cases.

Nevertheless, whatever the legal position is, service users and their advisers might be well advised to exploit authorities' anxiety about the meaning of need and its consequences under the CSDPA 1970. Authorities, on the other hand, would be well advised to look closely at the various ways in which CSDPA duties are perhaps less than 'absolute' (see Chapter 11).

Criteria of Eligibility

Local authorities, when deciding whether they are going to provide any services for which they have identified a need, will probably employ criteria of eligibility. For example, these criteria might state that services will only be provided for people who are at some risk – that is, their safety is in question and there is danger to life and limb.

The idea seems to be that local authorities will develop criteria of eligibility and definitions of need in line with their resources and priorities. This would then allow just enough people to qualify within the criteria for the provision of services to fall neatly within budget. However, part of the ability to set criteria rationally depends on local authorities' being well-informed about needs amongst the local population. It is generally accepted that many authorities do not have good quality information of this type. Consequently, it will probably be difficult for authorities to develop criteria which regulate the flow of demand precisely in line with resources.

Once resources become unpredictably stretched, authorities might be increasingly forced to take of account of them when deciding what to provide following individual assessments. This in turn leads to anxieties for authorities about how to do this legally. As already explained, there is a strong view that at least in the case of some duties (e.g. under the CSDPA 1970), lack of resources might not legally justify non-provision of services which have been assessed as needed in individual cases. However, there is an alternative view which suggests that judges might be reluctant to rule against authorities simply because they do not have enough money.

There is concern that eligibility criteria should be applied fairly and consistently by authorities, especially if they wish to avoid ombudsman findings of maladministration or possibly even adverse judicial findings on grounds of fairness (see Chapter 7). However, the extent to which criteria are applied consistently and fairly in practice is not clear; nor is it certain how easy it is to accomplish. For example, actual application of criteria depends on professional judgements which in their very nature can differ from one another. In addition, and confusingly, criteria should not be applied too rigidly even though they should be applied consistently. This is because authorities must allow themselves scope to consider individual circumstances which might constitute the exception to the rule. Otherwise, authorities might offend against the principle of 'fettering of discretion' (see Chapter 7).

Care Plan

Following a decision about what services will be provided, guidance (but not legislation) states that a plan should be drawn up of what services a person is going to receive and how he or she will receive them. The form and complexity of a care plan will vary greatly depending on the level and types of service involved.

Review

Guidance states that care plans should be regularly reviewed. Clearly, if people's needs increase or decrease, then the level of services they receive might be varied. However, and rather confusingly, it is also possible for people's needs to remain the same, but for the level of services still to be varied. This can happen if an authority's policy and eligibility criteria alter, so that people no longer qualify for the same level of services, even though their own circumstances have not changed at all. Government guidance suggests that where this happens, people should at least be informed about what is happening, and be reassessed before services are altered or withdrawn.

Provision of information, explanation and reassessment in such circumstances is clearly good practice. Legally, the reason for such provision could be connected with 'fairness' – that is, people have a 'reasonable expectation' of continuing to receive services which they have been assessed as needing. Thus, before a withdrawal or reduction, there needs to be a process whereby people can readjust their expectations. Consultation and information-giving can also be requirements of procedural fairness (see Chapter 7). For example, the courts have ruled that a local authority should have at least consulted properly with the residents of a residential home before deciding to close it.

There might also be a legal concern (whether or not well-founded) that once authorities are providing services to people, they have a 'duty of care' to those people. If authorities breach their duty of care, and a person then suffers harm (e.g. he or she falls down the stairs), then authorities might be liable in negligence. However, this duty-of-care principle is clearer in the field of health care, where the law of medical negligence is well developed, than in the social services field where, at present, it is not (see Chapter 7). Nevertheless, reassessment is an obvious way of stating quite clearly that any such duty of care has come to end.

Fairness and User Empowerment in Assessment (Chapter 10)

This chapter gives a few examples of aspects of what *fairness* in assessment might require authorities to do (e.g. allowing people 'to be heard' through an interpreter); deals with a number of aspects of user empowerment (including its limits), a concept emphasised consistently in community care guidance; covers directions and guidance about people's choice of residential or nursing home – and the limits to that choice; and covers the assessment of carers.

Chronically Sick and Disabled Persons Act 1970 (Chapter 11)

Welfare services provided under s.2 of this Act are central to the community care system, because they assist people to remain in their own homes. These services can probably be defined formally as 'community care services' because they are an extension of s.29 of the National Assistance Act 1948. However, the NHS and Community Care Act 1990 does not make this clear and there appears to be some confusion about just how assessment for these CSDPA services relates to community care assessment.

Understanding the way in which the CSDPA has operated in the past is very instructive for both service users and authorities, since it has rehearsed many of the complications now central to community care as a whole (of which the CSDPA is a part). These complications include the defining of 'need', the making of priorities, waiting lists for assessment, criteria of eligibility for services – and so on.

The duty to provide CSDPA services is a 'strong' one towards individual people (see p.61). As already explained above, there is concern that, under this Act, authorities might find themselves with obligations which they cannot afford to meet. In fact, there are a number of ways in which the duty under s.2 of this Act is less than absolute:

(1) *definition of need:* the duty depends on people's 'need' for services; and need can be defined by authorities. Therefore, in principle, authorities should be able, by judicious planning and policies, to avoid acknowledging needs which they cannot afford to meet.

(2) *necessity to meet the need:* even when need has been identified, the Act does not state straightforwardly that authorities must meet it. Authorities have to decide whether in order for the need to be met, it is 'necessary' for them to make arrangements for services. This represents a separate decision-making stage, means that an authority can decide whether the needs can be met in some other way, and suggests that

acknowledgement of need might not automatically trigger a duty to meet the need.

(3) *making arrangements:* the duty is not about 'providing' services but about 'making arrangements' for provision. This need not be the same as direct provision: for example, authorities might assess people for long-handled reaching sticks or non-slip bath mats, before advising them to buy these items from a pharmacy.

(4) *lack of resources:* even where authorities have acknowledged need and said that they will provide for that need, they might still be able to plead lack of resources. Although there is a strong view that authorities would be on weak legal ground if they did this, it is possible that the courts might be very reluctant to rule against authorities *solely* on the grounds that they do not have enough money.

Uncertain Areas of Responsibility for Services (Chapter 12)

The delivery of 'seamless' services between agencies (e.g. social services, health and housing services) is a major stated aim of community care. 'Seamless' can be taken to mean 'non-fragmented'. The importance of this aim is emphasised by guidance precisely because of a long history of fragmented welfare services.

One of the difficulties in achieving seamless services is that a combination of imprecise legislation, rigid organisational structures and the complexity of people's needs can lead to gaps and overlaps between services. 'Grey' areas can result, where it is unclear which agency is going to provide which service under what conditions. At worst, these grey areas can lead to 'buck-passing' between agencies – that is, agencies will not take responsibility for certain types of provision, usually because of the costs involved. The result can be delay, and sometimes non-provision of certain services – as well as confusion amongst both service users and providers of services about who can, or should, provide what.

Another consequence of the existence of these 'grey' areas is that services are sometimes re-defined. For example, a person's need for help with baths at home, originally deemed to be a health need and to involve a community nurse, might be re-defined locally as a 'social' need to be met by a social services care assistant. One of the important consequences of such re-defining is that services provided by the NHS such as bathing or respite care must (by law) be provided free of charge; whereas if provided by social services departments, they can be charged for (following a means-test).

For authorities, the advantages of uncertain responsibilities is that expensive and unwanted services can sometimes be jettisoned – although, in this respect, one authority's gain might be another's loss, since 'buck-passing' by one authority is likely to increase pressure on another. There can also be disadvantages for authorities in planning activities, since agreement about demarcation of responsibilities might be difficult; especially given the fear that, at a later date, one authority might unilaterally withdraw from any agreement.

For service users, the disadvantages of this situation are obvious. Nevertheless, one possible benefit to users is that if one authority fails to deliver a service, then another can sometimes be approached. For example, if a housing authority fails to assist with a home adaptation, then in some circumstances the social services department can be approached for assistance.

Continuing (Long-Term) NHS Care (Chapter 13)

A particularly sensitive example of this re-defining of a service concerns the provision of continuing (long-term) health care. The health service is generally reducing the number of long-stay beds it is prepared to pay for, whether in hospital or elsewhere (e.g. in nursing homes). Consequently, where there is no (free) health service bed available, people have to enter a private nursing home where they will have to pay for the bed (unless they have very little money anyway) until they have used up most of their savings.

For service users, it has been unclear when they will be judged to 'need' NHS care rather than private nursing home care. This is because even if they are acknowledged to be in clinical 'need', NHS care might still not follow since its provision might depend on health authorities' local priorities and on available resources at a particular time.

The rights of a person to refuse to leave hospital – which would result in the need to enter a nursing home where he or she will have to pay the fees – have also been unclear. For example, the health service ombudsman has recently condemned a health authority's refusal to provide nursing care for a very disabled person. This decision has made health authorities more uncertain than ever about what constitutes a legal policy and has affected their ability to make priorities, plan services and allocate resources. In response, the Department of Health has issued draft guidance on the subject.

Draft Guidance

At the time of writing, draft Department of Health guidance has attempted to clarify the issue. It states that most NHS patients who require continuing care in nursing homes will not be paid for by the NHS: instead, social services departments will be responsible for means-testing people and placing them in nursing and residential homes. However, people with 'complex or multiple health care needs' who require 'continuing and specialist medical or nursing supervision' should remain the responsibility of the health service. The draft guidance also states that people who do not qualify for NHS care do not ultimately have a right to remain in hospital – this is a departure from previous guidance which had appeared to state the opposite.

Whether this draft guidance clarifies matters for individual service users and their families is open to question – although it does tend to confirm the wide discretion of health authorities. *First*, it remains for local health authorities to determine their own criteria of eligibility for continuing NHS care. This seems to invite considerable local variations in policy and practice, as well as disputes about what terms such as 'complex or multiple health care needs' really mean. *Second*, as the guidance also makes clear, any NHS responsibilities are subject to 'available resources'. Thus, authorities can alter their criteria from time to time; and even in the case of an individual who apparently meets the criteria, they could probably defend (legally) lack of provision on the basis of lack of resources. *Third*, the model of care which the guidance puts forward is one that has probably more or less existed *in practice* for some time – but which has not prevented disputes and confusion.

Nevertheless, the guidance does apparently support the recent decision of the health service ombudsman to the effect that a health authority should not have a rigid policy which systematically denied NHS continuing care to all people in severe need. This suggests that, although armed with great discretion to set priorities and levels of services, health authorities should not 'wash their hands' completely of long-term care provision.

Provision of Services in Residential and Nursing Homes (Chapter 14)

There is some confusion about what health services people should, or are likely to receive, in residential homes – and much greater confusion in the case of private nursing homes. Inevitably, much of this confusion reduces to who is going to pay for particular services: the home (as part of its integral services), the health service, or residents and their relatives. Neither legislation nor guidance sheds a great deal of light on the question: for example, Department of Health guidance emphasises the discretion which health authorities have in this area of provision.

In practice, the level and types of health services which people receive in homes – and who pays for them – are likely to vary greatly from home to home and from area to area.

For health authorities, residents of homes might appear to be a convenient 'low priority' group. This is because, under the care of an institution, they will be regarded generally as being at less risk than people living in their own homes. For residential and nursing home owners, there seems to be considerable latitude, since the legislation covering homes is vague about specific services (such as physiotherapy) and who should be providing and paying for them.

For residents, their relatives and their advisers, there can be great uncertainty; and this uncertainty has sometimes given rise to the fear that residents of homes are in danger of losing, in practice if not in principle, their 'rights' to NHS services. (Although see p.6 for a discussion about 'rights' to health services.)

Home Owners' Duties

This chapter also explains the duties which legislation places on home owners to provide certain services and facilities and summarises a number of Registered

Homes Tribunal decisions, which have considered provision of some of these services and facilities.

Discharge from Hospital (Chapter 15)
Hospital discharge involves decisions about where, how, and with whom a person is going to live. Of particular importance is whether suitable and effective arrangements have been made and whether people's needs and wishes have been taken into account.

People's needs when leaving hospital can be complicated, requiring consideration of many factors including physical ability, mental ability and attitude, social and environmental factors – and so on. There are sometimes many arrangements to make. Whether or not optimum arrangements are eventually achieved would appear sometimes to depend on chance, since there are many variable factors which influence the outcome of discharge. This makes the discharge process unpredictable and yet one more 'uncertainty' in the community care process.

Legislation does not mention hospital discharge, but in the face of evidence of unsatisfactory practice, central government guidance continues to emphasise the importance of improving practice. The health service ombudsman regularly investigates cases concerning hospital discharge. Although the ombudsman cannot question 'clinical' decisions, he investigates widely and sometimes finds fault with authorities on issues such as consultation, communication with patients and relatives, and decisions which have been made on the basis of inadequate information. The line distinguishing clinical from non-clinical decisions is sometimes difficult to draw and in any case a single complaint might cover both types of decision.

Sometimes, the pressure to clear hospital beds can lead to conflicts between different professions who might have different views about what is needed. On the one hand, there might sometimes be pressure to clear beds before appropriate arrangements have been made. On the other hand, community care assessments can delay discharge, especially where hospital social workers and other staff have to negotiate with different social services departments (with divergent procedures and criteria) for different patients.

Health Service Assessment and Provision (Chapter 16)
Social services authorities have a duty to consult health authorities about community care plans and to ask health authority staff to participate in community care assessments. Basically, however, the duties of health authorities remain unchanged and are not covered by the community care legislation. This is because health authorities and NHS Trusts do not have a duty to participate in community care assessments even when they are invited by local authorities to do so. **Therefore, health services are not officially, or legally, defined as 'community care services' – even though in practice they are essential to community care.**

This anomaly introduces a whole range of uncertainty. For example, it means that the essential and pivotal duty of community care, which is to assess people's needs, does not apply to health authorities and NHS Trusts. In addition, the legislation under which health services are provided is arguably even more vague and imprecise than the social services legislation.

Health authorities have general duties which include the provision of medical and nursing services as well as the prevention of illness, care of people who are ill, and after-care for people who have been ill. The duties are general duties only (towards the local population, but not towards individuals) and only extend to providing the services 'necessary to meet all reasonable requirements'. In addition, most specific health services (such as neurology, rehabilitation and physiotherapy) are simply not mentioned at all in the legislation.

Therefore, these duties to provide services are far from absolute and are carried out within the resources which authorities have available and according to priorities which authorities set. (Although there is no mention of resources in the legislation, both judges and government guidance are apt to supply the words 'within available resources' when interpreting health authority duties.) This means that the level of services such as physiotherapy or chiropody, and sometimes even the existence of specialist services, is decided locally.

From a practical point of view, it seems inevitable that authorities have to set priorities, in order to provide services within the resources they have available. In (legal) principle, such priorities should not be applied absolutely rigidly, since they need to be flexible enough to cater for exceptional circumstances and needs. This is so that authorities do not 'fetter their discretion' (see Chapter 7).

The effect of this general situation is that health authorities have very wide discretion indeed to regulate both what services they provide and at what level they provide them. So long as the priorities are set reasonably, legally and fairly (see Chapter 7), there seems little to fear, since the courts and, most of the time, the health service ombudsman, have upheld this wide discretion. It is true that the ombudsman has recently questioned the extent of this discretion in the context of long-term nursing care. However, by and large, health authorities and NHS Trusts seem to have more to fear from public opinion (about, for example, age discrimination) than from serious legal challenge.

For patients, the situation is one of considerable uncertainty. **Service provision can vary from authority to authority, which means that what services people get can depend on where they live.** Even within the same authority, provision can also vary from week to week and from month to month, depending on the resources and facilities available. For example, one person with particular needs might be admitted to an NHS bed one week. Two weeks later, another person with the same needs could be denied a bed on the grounds that there is over-demand and that other people's needs are greater.

Housing Services (Chapter 17)

Common sense would suggest that since the preferred aim of community care is to enable people to remain in their own homes, housing services would be particularly important. However, housing services are not defined legally as 'community care services', and so form yet one more uncertain piece of the community care system.

This chapter covers in particular the provision of home adaptations (through a number of different schemes) and the provision of welfare services in warden-assisted housing.

Charges for Services (Chapter 18)

Money is all important, of course, and charges for services are a critical part of community care. Charging can be one more way of regulating, or 'rationing', the provision of services. However, the system of charging is uneven. Local authorities have duties to charge for residential nursing home accommodation and can charge for most non-residential services if they wish (but do not have to), whilst health authorities and NHS Trusts can charge only for specified items and services. Further uncertainty attaches to this system of charging, because local authority charges can vary from place to place.

Charges for Residential and Nursing Homes Care

When local authorities place people in residential or nursing homes, they have a duty to assess people financially and charge according to the result of a legally prescribed means-test. Depending on what sort of needs people have, and thus what sort of home they need to go to, local authorities set a 'usual cost'. This is the maximum amount they are prepared to pay. These 'usual costs' can vary from authority to authority. If people are staying a short time (up to eight weeks) in residential care, local authorities have discretion how much to charge. They can apply the prescribed residential care means-test and charging system, or they can decide not to do so and charge much less. Practices vary.

Charges for Non-Residential Services

For non-residential services, local authorities can charge if they wish – although they do not have to – but only if it is 'reasonably practicable' for people to pay. Guidance states that people should not be charged for assessment, but otherwise government has encouraged authorities to make more charges for services. In practice, this seems to be what is happening. This change illustrates the flexibility built into the community care system, since no change in legislation has been required and authorities are simply making more use of existing legal powers. If people do not pay the charges for the services they have been assessed as needing, it is not clear that authorities could withdraw services legally. But authorities do have the power to recover the money owed as a civil debt.

One significant, and from users' point of view, worrying trend, is the re-defining of certain services as 'social' rather than 'health' care. Services such as bathing or respite care, previously provided free of charge by the health service, might now be provided by social services departments for a charge (following a mean-test).

Health Service Charges

The health service does not have the same wide powers as social services to make charges. Certain items can be charged for if specified in legislation – for example, equipment and drugs prescribed by general practitioners, as well as certain items supplied in hospitals, such as wigs, surgical brassieres, and spinal supports. But everything else, both services and equipment, which is not so specified, must be provided free of charge. This would seem to be a straight-forward situation, but in fact it is not. Health authorities and NHS Trusts sometimes make illegal charges – and a certain amount of confusion seems to exist.

One irony (possibly little appreciated) of this situation is that, whilst health authorities cannot charge for most services and equipment, they do have the discretion simply not to provide them at all. For example, incontinence pads cannot be charged for; but an authority could in principle decide not to provide them to certain groups of people, on the basis of local priorities. Similarly, for example, nebulisers (respiratory equipment) cannot be charged for, but hospitals might instead simply ask people to buy their own if they need them for more than a few months.

Planning for Community Care (Chapter 19)

Social services authorities have duties to consult about, and to publish, com-munity care plans. The form, clarity, detail and coverage of plans is likely to vary considerably, although government guidance does state what subjects should be covered.

Guidance states that a central ingredient of community care planning is meant to be knowledge about the local needs of the population. This is because such knowledge is the basis for setting local priorities, allocating resources, and setting criteria of eligibility and need. However, it seems that good quality information about local needs is not easily available to local authorities. This threatens to undermine basic community care policy that services should be planned and delivered within budget to those with the greatest needs.

Information and Publicity (Chapter 20)

Community care guidance (but not legislation) states that social services departments should make detailed information accessible to all potential users of community care services. Taken literally this is a difficult and probably over-ambitious task, though much hinges on what is meant by 'all' potential users, and by 'accessible'. Similarly, user empowerment, stated by guidance to be a function of information provision, does not necessarily follow simply from that provision. It is unclear in practice how effective such information provision is, since it is difficult to measure.

The Chronically Sick and Disabled Persons Act 1970 has long placed duties on social services to publish information generally about welfare services; and also to inform existing individual users of services about other available services. How effectively authorities have carried out these duties over the years is not evident, but a number of studies have pointed to general shortcomings in local authority information provision.

PART IV: REMEDIES

Part IV of the book covers the remedies available to people who feel that their needs have not been met.

Summary (Chapter 21)

Disputes can arise in any welfare system, no matter how well run it is. As already explained, there are many 'uncertainties' in the community care system, from the wording of legislation down to the variable practices of local authorities and health authorities. These uncertainties can give rise to disputes; for example, over whether a person really 'needs' a service or not.

When disputes arise, there are a number of remedies available. These can be divided into three categories: the informal, the non-legal and the legal (ie. involving the law courts). It is important to know not just what the remedies are, but when they can be used and – if there is a choice – which one to use. This knowledge is important both for authorities and for service users.

Informal Remedies (Chapter 22)

An 'informal remedy' is used in this book to indicate a dispute which never even 'gets off the ground' because well-informed service users or their representatives effectively challenge authorities decisions' at the outset; or, alternatively, because well-informed authorities know they are on firm legal ground and can demonstrate that from the outset. In either case, the potential dispute might be defused. It is to be hoped that if all concerned are better-informed – and if authorities' obligations and users' rights are better understood – then at least a proportion of disputes might be avoided. Nevertheless, it could be argued that the uncertainties (see Chapter 3) inherent in community care almost invite disputes.

An example of informal dispute resolution might concern a decision to discharge somebody from hospital without domestic arrangements planned and arranged, and without consultation with the patient and relatives. If patients or their representatives can refer to government Circular guidance on hospital discharge which covers these matters, then the hospital might think twice. Better still, showing actual copies of guidance or legislation to authorities' staff and managers can have a disconcerting effect.

Such is the confusion about some aspects of community care legislation and guidance, that it might be possible to worry an authority even if, in fact, there were nothing legally dubious about what the authority was doing. The authority might change its mind about a decision either because of legal anxiety (even if ill-founded), concern about the costs of litigation or simply because it wished to avoid bad publicity. Similarly, MPs and Local Councillors might take up constituents' cases not on compelling legal grounds but simply for benevolent or compassionate reasons. For example, it is not unknown for a councillor to approve social services priority criteria in committee one month, and the next month, to oppose them when one of the councillor's own constituents falls victim to the criteria.

On the other hand, from an authority's point of view, it is useful to be able to refer to central government guidance stating clearly that authorities have the power to make local priorities. For example, this could be useful to an authority if a resident of a nursing home complains that he or she is not receiving (adequate) NHS physiotherapy.

Resolving disputes informally is normally the preferable option; neither service user nor authority wishes to incur the time, trouble, stress and expense of engaging in a dispute. The possible souring of future relations between authority and user is also a significant consideration.

Non-Legal Remedies (Chapter 23)

Non-legal remedies involve the use of formal procedures, which are not, however, legal procedures – they do not involve courts of law.

Social Services Complaints Procedures

Social services complaints procedures are intended to cover most grievances of community care service users. There are time limits within which local authorities must respond to and resolve formal complaints, and where there is continuing disagreement, the dispute can be referred to review panels. There is a little uncertainty and concern about how authorities handle informal complaints, since the time limits apply only to formal complaints. In other words, there is scope for delay until a complaint is acknowledged to be formal.

Review panels are apparently able to investigate not just the way in which local authorities have dealt with complaints, but also the merits of disputed decisions. For example, it appears that panels can decide not just about the way in which assessments are conducted, but also about the result of assessments – for instance, whether a person is really in 'need' of home help or not. If this is so, review panels can generally explore issues more widely than the courts and the local ombudsman who are generally restricted to questioning the *way* in which authorities decide things, rather than *what* they actually decide.

The complaints procedure will therefore be the most suitable channel for the majority of disputes relating to social services.

Secretary of State's Default Powers

Another non-legal remedy is an appeals procedure which is contained in legislation. The Secretary of State has powers to declare both social services departments and health authorities 'in default' of their duties. In the case of social services, the default would not be declared if the authority had a 'reasonable excuse' for not complying with its duty. In fact no authority has ever been declared to be in default, although the Department of Health does make informal enquiries into possible 'default' cases. Sometimes, however, even these informal enquiries can take a long time.

Judges sometimes refer to this appeals procedure when explaining why they will not intervene in a dispute – they say that this procedure, rather than a court case, is the correct way of solving the dispute. However, the fact that the procedure has never been used means it is arguable that this 'default' remedy is scarcely a remedy at all. Therefore, this procedure is going to be, generally, unhelpful for users; and probably more 'helpful' for authorities, given that they are very unlikely ever to be declared in default.

Local Ombudsman

The local ombudsman investigates maladministration in local authorities and can recommend remedies, including financial compensation, where people have suffered injustice. From authorities' point of view, they receive bad publicity in the press when ombudsmen find maladministration. Although they do not have to accept an ombudsman's findings, they receive even worse publicity when they do not.

In common with judicial review by the courts, the local ombudsman investigates the way in which authorities act and make decisions rather than what those decisions and actions ultimately are. Nevertheless, under cover of maladministration, the ombudsman seems to operate far more freely than the courts and investigates in detail all sorts of local authority acts and decisions. For this reason (and for reasons of time, effort and potential expense), service users are well-advised to use, where possible, the ombudsman rather than the courts.

The local ombudsmen (there are several) have for many years investigated a number of issues relevant to community care: for example, waiting lists, the application of priorities and criteria of eligibility, communication between local authority departments – and so on. The cases are most instructive for both authorities and users who wish to understand how the ombudsmen are likely to view the acts and decisions of local authorities. They also give insight into the sorts of situations and difficulties which give rise to disputes in the first place.

Health Service Non-Legal Remedies

Within the health service, there are four main non-legal remedies. The first is the main *hospital complaints system*. The second covers *complaints about clinical judgement* (which are excluded from the main complaints system). It is sometimes known as the 'second opinion' procedure.

The third remedy is the *health service ombudsman* who can investigate health authorities and NHS Trusts in relation to maladministration, failure within a service and failure to provide a service (which there is a duty to provide). The ombudsman cannot directly question 'clinical judgement' – that is, the professional opinion of hospital staff such as doctors, nurses and therapists. However, this is not too restrictive, since the ombudsman can investigate the basis of, and circumstances surrounding, these clinical judgements. For example, the ombudsman might find that a doctor's decision was taken on the basis of inadequate information, or inadequate consultation, about the patient. The ombudsman is likely to carry out a thorough and thoughtful investigation, although one criticism has been that investigations take quite a long time.

Lastly, complaints about general practitioners, community dentists, community pharmacists, ophthalmic opticians and ophthalmic medical practitioners are dealt with through the *Family Health Services Authority (FHSA) complaints system*.

The health service complaints system as a whole has been criticised by a recent report, and there are likely to be changes in the near future.

Legal Remedies (Chapter 24)

There are two basic types of legal remedy: *private law* remedies (breach of statutory duty and negligence) and *public law* remedies (judicial review). The principles underlying these remedies are explained at length in a previous chapter – where it is also explained that most community care disputes will probably involve public rather than private law.

This chapter explains briefly the procedures for judicial review; what the advantages there are in principle of bringing a private law case (where this is possible); and a few aspects of judicial decision-making of which service users and authorities might find it useful to be aware.

PART II

SERVICES AND PRINCIPLES

CHAPTER 3

UNCERTAINTIES AND RESOURCES IN COMMUNITY CARE

AIM OF COMMUNITY CARE

The preferred, stated aim of community care is to enable people to remain in their own homes whenever, and for as long as, possible. Community care is concerned with elderly people, younger disabled adults (16–64 years old), and people with a mental disorder. Social services authorities (local authorities) have been given the leading role in community care, but both health and housing authorities have an essential role as well. However, health and housing services are not defined legally as 'community care services' and the community care legislation essentially leaves untouched the duties of health and housing authorities.

This book covers the provision of health and some housing services, as well as the formal 'community care services' provided by social services departments.

UNCERTAINTIES IN COMMUNITY CARE

A number of 'uncertainties' pervade the community care system and are to be found at every stage, from referral and access to assessment right through to review by the courts. As the following paragraphs show, these uncertainties tend to work in favour of authorities rather than service users. However, sometimes the uncertainties are such that there is general confusion amongst authorities, as well as service users, about what 'the law' really is – in which case well-informed users and their advisers might look to exploit this confusion by confronting authorities, more or less formally, with well-prepared arguments.

Essentially, these uncertainties, which originate in imprecise legislation, allow authorities flexibility in planning and delivering services. In particular, they allow authorities to carry out their functions within available resources – that is, within budget. These uncertainties give authorities very great discretion in deciding what services to deliver, at what level to deliver them, and for whom.

Such uncertainties, or 'safety valves' are probably necessary in any welfare system where resources are finite.

This collective flexibility or uncertainty in the community care system is an underlying theme of the whole book. This uncertainty includes, for example, how authorities define and apply concepts such as *need, priority, urgency, assessment, criteria of eligibility* – and how they make charges for services. The concept of need seems to be all pervasive. It is present from the time before people are assessed (they have to appear to be in need to get an assessment in the first place). And it persists right through to the review stage, where people's services can be increased, reduced or withdrawn, depending on the way in which authorities view their needs.

It is therefore at such points of uncertainty (and there are many) that crucial decisions are made by social services departments and health authorities in order to 'regulate' the system locally and maintain it within resources. Rationing is one way of referring to this. It is also at these points where disputes can arise; for example, when a service user disagrees with an authority's decision about personal 'need'; challenges the imposition of charges for a service; or challenges a hospital's decision not to provide long-term care.

The consequence of this discretion and uncertainty in the community care system is that, generally speaking, **individual service users do not have absolute legal rights or entitlements to services.** Instead, what they receive is generally determined by authorities' policies and by the professional judgement of staff. Thus, because two local authorities might define need differently, service users with similar needs but living perhaps a few hundred yards apart (in different authorities) might receive different (levels of) service.

Because of the prevalent uncertainty in the whole community care system, the law courts will often (but not always) be wary of intervening against authorities. Since there are so few identifiable, legal 'rights' for service users, the judges tend to tread cautiously. For example, service users can seldom expect to be able to win damages in private law cases from authorities. This is because claims for damages rely on the existence of enforceable rights; if such rights are unrecognised, private law cases for damages have no foundation. Therefore, as explained elsewhere, most community care cases will be judicial review cases, which are not really about enforcing users' rights to services, but more about enforcing legal and proper decision-making by public authorities. Even in judicial review, there is uncertainty, because the concepts on which such review is based are themselves uncertain – it is not easy to predict how the judges will define and apply them in different situations (see Chapter 7).

It is also important that both authorities and service users realise that, in any case, the application of the law by judges is not a simple, predictable, logical exercise. There are various factors which can influence the outcome, including the judges' wariness of becoming involved in issues of public policy; the circumstances and facts of the individual case before the court; and the approach of particular judges. Therefore, even the proceedings in a court of law can add yet one more aspect of uncertainty and unpredictability to the community care system.

Similarly, even the local ombudsmen who operate more flexibly than the courts – and who have explored parts of the community care field more widely (e.g. services under the CSDPA 1970) than the courts – are restricted in their investigations. They investigate maladministration which, in common with judicial review, concerns the way in which authorities have reached decisions, rather than what those decisions ultimately are (see p.370).

Examples of Uncertainty

Examples of these uncertainties abound. They are of various types and are to be found at every stage of the community care process, whether in legislation, guidance or practice. The wording of legislation is often undefined and vague. Public authorities can make it mean what they want; thus, health authorities have a duty to provide services to meet 'all reasonable requirements'. Social services authorities have duties to assess people's 'needs'; and to make charges for services which are 'reasonably practicable' for people to pay. All these terms are undefined by the legislation. Even social services 'assessment', around which the whole community care system is based, remains undefined. Locally, authorities develop their own definitions, policies, priorities and criteria of eligibility around these terms. The judges usually confirm this arrangement, by leaving most (though not all) of these words to be defined and applied by authorities rather than by the courts.

Much guidance is issued by central government to local authorities and to health authorities to fill the gaps left by legislation. An uncertainty about this guidance is that nobody seems quite sure of its status and legal effect – is it just advice, or must authorities follow it? For example, recently, a local authority thought it was obliged to follow guidance about childminders and the smacking of children – the High Court thought otherwise and told the authority that it was not rigidly bound by such guidance. Even more confusingly, this wealth of guidance itself falls into different categories.

Charging for services is another way of regulating the system. Recently, local authorities have been imposing higher charges for more services. This is a good example of flexibility within the system, arising not from any change in legislation but simply from authorities' financial difficulties and with encouragement from government guidance.

Yet another symptom of all this uncertainty is that many specific services are not mentioned at all in legislation. As a result, it is not always clear which type of authority is responsible for which service (see Chapters 5 and 12). For example, people at home might be assisted by social services to have a 'social' bath; or by the health service to have a 'health' bath. Some people receive long-term care from the health service; whilst others have to pay for it in private nursing homes. Such 'grey' areas of responsibility – and there are quite a number of them – allow, at best, for flexibility; but at worst for 'buck-passing' between authorities, particularly when resources are scarce.

RESOURCES

The issue of resources appears fundamental to many of the disputes which are likely to arise about community care. For example, resources can lie behind disputes about the length of wait for an assessment, whether somebody is in need of services or not, what level of service a person is going to get (e.g., a commode in the living room or a downstairs bathroom), whether and how much somebody should be charged for services – and so on. Such disputes are not always based on resources: for example, sometimes the downstairs bathroom is a totally unsuitable solution which will not deal with the problem. However, often these disputes are, fundamentally, about resources.

The problem facing service users, authorities, the ombudsmen and the courts, is how resources affect the duties of authorities to provide services. The basic question seems to be whether all duties are implicitly subject to resources. If they are, this means that no matter how clearly duties are stated in law, authorities only have to carry them out if they have enough money. If this is not the position, and some duties stand irrespective of resources, it means that authorities have to carry out these duties even if they do not have enough money. **Put simply, do authorities legally have to perform their duties even if they don't have enough money; or do they only have to perform them when there is enough money? In other words, are all duties undermined in the last analysis by the availability of resources?** If so, the notion of individual legal rights appears to dissolve.

This also raises the question of what 'lack of resources' really means. For example, the fact that the equipment and adaptations budget for one particular area of an authority is exhausted does not necessarily mean that it is exhausted authority-wide.

The question of resources can often affect (both through general policy decisions, and decisions in individual cases) whether people get services, what services they get, and how quickly they get them. Both the ombudsmen and the law courts have had to deal with cases about these issues. In the context of the health service, the law courts seem to have accepted that the duty to provide health services is subject to resources. Therefore, for example, people complaining about waiting times for orthopaedic treatment or 'hole-in-the-heart' operations lost their cases – even though they were clearly acknowledged by the health authorities involved to be in need of services. In one of the cases, the judge actually said that the words 'within the resources available' should be implied into the legislation (even though they were not actually written there) (see p.258). Similarly, recent draft guidance on long-term NHS care states as a matter of course that NHS responsibilities exist only so far as 'available resources' allow – even though no such words are to be found in the NHS Act 1977.

In the context of community care services, the position is slightly less clear because a view has developed that some community care duties persist in some circumstances even if the authority does not have enough resources. This view particularly concerns the duties to provide home welfare services under 1970 disability legislation, and to provide after-care under mental health legislation. (This latter duty also applies to health authorities.)

These are strong legal duties towards individual people which the law courts are likely to wish to enforce; but on the other hand, it is possible that the courts will be reluctant to rule against authorities who are defending a case on the grounds that they do not have enough money. In the absence of any legal cases decided on this point, it is not possible to give a definite opinion.

The findings of both the local ombudsman and the health service ombudsman seem unpredictable in this respect. For example, the health service ombudsman has often accepted health authority arguments based on lack of resources. On the other hand, he appeared not to accept such an argument in a recent case about the provision of long-term care. Similarly, the local ombudsman generally accepts that local authorities have to make priorities according to what money they have available, but may or may not find that it is consequently acceptable to keep people waiting a long time for an assessment.

DEFINING DISABILITY AND NEED

It is true that uncertainty seems 'built in' to the community care system by imprecise legislation and the resulting discretion which local authorities have to regulate services. But there are additional difficulties. Irrespective of this legislation and of any resource constraints, people's disabilities and needs are not always easily identified.

People with similar conditions may not have similar disabilities. For example, somebody with frequency of urine who has easy and quick access to a lavatory will not be deemed incontinent. But the same person who cannot get to the lavatory in time (because it is difficult to get to) might suddenly 'become' incontinent and require advice and assistance.

Solutions might be different too. For one person the solution might be the addition of a downstairs lavatory to their home. For another person, the solution might be much simpler: for example, a chair which the person can get out of easily and quickly when in need of the lavatory. A third solution, cheap, often socially unacceptable but probably not uncommon in practice, is to give people commodes in their living rooms.

When local authorities allocate people particular priorities, they often consider the risk and dependency of those people. But as the Office of Population Censuses and Surveys points out, this can be difficult to do: 'While dependency is often measured in terms of disability, it also affected by environment. Dependency is not a fixed attribute, it changes over time, it is related to environment and circumstances and it is affected by events. A person who is very dependent in his/her home due to lack of suitable aids/support may be considered independent in another more supportive environment' (Carey 1993,p.3).

CHAPTER 4

COMMUNITY CARE SERVICES

Community care services are defined in the NHS and Community Care Act 1990 (s.46) by reference to four pieces of previously existing legislation. These are:

(1) the National Assistance Act 1948, Part 3 (residential accommodation and welfare services).

(2) Health Service and Public Health Act 1968, section 45 (welfare of elderly people).

(3) NHS Act 1977, section 21 and Schedule 8 (home help and laundry facilities).

(4) Mental Health Act 1983, section 117 (after-care services).

(5) Chronically Sick and Disabled Persons Act 1970. Services under section 2 of this act are not mentioned explicitly in section 46, but there is evidence which suggests that they are community care services. (This is explained elsewhere in this book (see p.189).) They are therefore listed in this chapter.

N.B. Health and housing services, although covered by this book (see chapters 16 and 17), are not formally defined as community care services.*

I. NATIONAL ASSISTANCE ACT 1948, Part 3

(a) Residential (Including Nursing Home) Accommodation: General Duties And Powers

Under the National Assistance Act 1948 (s.21(1)): 'a local authority may with the approval of the Secretary of State, and to such extent as he may direct shall, make arrangements for providing...residential accommodation for persons aged eighteen or over who by reason of age, illness, disability or any other circumstances are in need of care and attention which is not otherwise available to them'

---

*   For ease of reference key words and phrases contained in the legislation appear in bold.

Directions (involving duties) and **Approvals** (involving discretionary powers) have been made by the Secretary of State under section 21 (they are attached to Circular LAC(93)10).

As a result, local authorities have a number of **duties and powers** 'to provide **residential accommodation** for persons aged 18 or over who by reason of **age, illness, disability** or any other circumstances are in need of care and attention not otherwise available to them':

- **duty:** toward people 'who are **ordinarily resident** in their area and **other persons** who are in **urgent need**...';
- **power** toward people 'with **no settled residence**'; and 'to such extent as the authority may consider desirable' for people who normally **live in another authority** (with the other authority's consent);
- **duty** to provide **temporary accommodation** for people who are in **urgent need** of it and where the need could not reasonably have been foreseen;
- **duty** toward people 'who are or have been suffering from **mental disorder**'; or for preventing mental disorder; and this includes people who are 'ordinarily resident' or people 'with no settled residence';
- **power** toward people – 'who are or have been suffering from **mental disorder**', or in order to prevent mental disorder – who are normally 'ordinarily resident' in another local authority but following hospital discharge are now resident in the local authority's area;
- **power** to meet the needs of people for the prevention of **illness**; the care of people suffering from illness and the aftercare of people suffering from illness.
- **power** toward people who are **alcoholic or drug-dependent**.

Further Directions place **duties** on local authorities to make arrangements for services for residents for:

- their **welfare**;
- supervision of **hygiene**;
- obtaining of **medical attention, nursing attention and NHS services** (but there is no requirement to provide anything normally provided under the NHS);
- provision of **board and other services, amenities and requisites** (but not anything the authority thinks is unnecessary);
- regular review of arrangements.

An Approval gives local authorities power to provide 'in such cases as the authority considers appropriate, for the **conveyance of persons** to and from' residential accommodation.

The local authority remains 'under a duty to continue to make arrangements to provide accommodation' for residents of what were local authority **homes which have been transferred** to other management (Secretary of State's

Approvals and Directions under section 21(1) of the National Assistance Act 1948: attached to LAC(93)10).

(b) Welfare services

Under the National Assistance Act 1948, s.29(1): 'A local authority may, with the approval of the Secretary of State, and to such extent as he may direct in relation to persons ordinarily resident in the area of the local authority shall make arrangements for promoting the **welfare** of persons to whom this section applies, that is to say persons aged eighteen or over who are **blind, deaf or dumb**, or who suffer from **mental disorder** of any description and other persons aged eighteen or over who are substantially and permanently **handicapped by illness, injury, or congenital deformity** or such other **disabilities** as may be prescribed'.

Under section 29(4) and under directions and approvals made under the section 29(1) of the Act, local authorities have the:

- **duty** to maintain **registers of people** to whom the section relates (ie. keep registers of disabled people who are ordinarily resident in the area);
- **duty (for ordinary residents) or power (for other people)** 'to provide a **social work service** and such **advice** and **support** as may be needed for people in their own homes or elsewhere';
- **power** to **inform** people of services available under section 29(1);
- **power** to **instruct** people 'in their own homes or elsewhere in methods of overcoming the effects of their disabilities';
- **duty (for ordinary residents) or power (otherwise)** 'to provide, whether at centres or elsewhere, facilities for the **social rehabilitation and adjustment** to disability including assistance in overcoming limitations of mobility or communication;
- **power** to help people dispose 'of the produce of their work';
- **duty (for ordinary residents) or power (otherwise)** 'to provide, whether at centres or elsewhere, facilities for **occupational, social, cultural and recreational activities** and, where appropriate, the making of payments to persons for work undertaken by them';
- **power** 'to provide **holiday homes;**
- **power** to provide free or subsidised **travel** for people 'who do not otherwise qualify' for travel concessions...';
- **power** to assist a person to **find accommodation** which will enable him or her 'to take advantage of any arrangements made under section 29(1)';
- **power** to contribute to the **cost of employing a warden** in warden-assisted housing;
- **power** to provide **warden services** in private housing;
- **power** to provide '**workshops** where such persons may be engaged (whether under a contract of service or otherwise) in suitable work, and

hostels where persons engaged in the workshops, and other persons to whom arrangements under [section 29(1)] relate and for whom work or training is being provided in pursuance of the Disabled Persons' (Employment) Act 1944 or the Employment and Training Act 1973 may live'.

(Secretary of State's Approvals and Directions under section 29(1) of the National Assistance Act 1948: attached to LAC(93)10).

2. NHS ACT 1977, S.21 AND SCHEDULE 8

(a) Home help and Laundry Facilities

Under Schedule 8 of the NHS Act 1977, local authorities have a **duty** 'to provide on such a scale as is adequate for the needs of their area, or to arrange for the provision on such a scale as is so adequate, of **home help** for households where such help is required owing to the presence of…a person who is suffering from illness, lying-in, an expectant mother, aged, handicapped as a result of having suffered from illness or by congenital deformity…and every such authority has **power** to provide or arrange for the provision of **laundry facilities** for households for which home help is being, or can be, provided…'.

(b) Prevention of Illness and Care of People Who are Ill or Have Been Ill

Under Schedule 8 of the NHS Act 1977, local authorities have the:

- **power** to make arrangements to provide '**centres or other facilities** for training them or keeping them suitably occupied and the equipment and maintenance of such centres'; together with the provision of 'ancillary or supplemental' services;
- **duty** towards people who are, or have been, 'suffering from **mental disorder**':
  - to make arrangements to provide '**centres** (including training centres and day centres)…';
  - to appoint **sufficient approved social workers**;
  - to exercise their functions towards people received into **guardianship** under Part 2 or 3 of the Mental Health Act 1983;
  - to provide '**social work and related services** to help in the identification, diagnosis, assessment and social treatment of mental disorder and to provide social work support and other domiciliary and care services to people living in their homes and elsewhere
- **power** to make arrangements for the **provision of meals** at centres and other facilities and meals-on-wheels for housebound people for people not already provided for under other legislation;
- **power** to make arrangements for the **payment** of people 'engaged in suitable work at centres or other facilities';
- **power** to make arrangements for the provision of 'social services (including advice and support) for the purposes of **preventing the**

impairment of physical or mental health of adults in families where such impairment is likely, and for the purposes of preventing the break-up of such families, or for assisting in their rehabilitation';

- **power** to make arrangements for the provision of **night sitter services; recuperative holidays;** facilities for **social and recreational activities;** services specifically for **alcoholic or drug-dependent people.**

(Secretary of State's Approvals and Directions under paragraphs 1 and 2 of schedule 8 to the NHS Act 1977: attached to LAC(93)10).

3. HEALTH SERVICES AND PUBLIC HEALTH ACT 1968
Welfare of Old People

Under section 45 of the Health Service and Public Health Act 1968, local authorities 'may with approval of the Secretary of State, and to such extent as he may direct shall, make arrangements for promoting the welfare of old people'.

Approvals (in DHSS 19/71) give local authorities the power to make arrangements 'for any of the following purposes to meet the needs of the elderly':

- 'to provide **meals and recreation** in the home and elsewhere';
- 'to **inform** the elderly of services available to them and to identify elderly people in need of services';
- 'to provide facilities or assistance in **travelling to and from the home** for the purpose of participating in services provided by the authority or similar services';
- 'to assist in finding suitable households for **boarding** elderly persons';
- 'to provide **visiting and advisory services and social work** support';
- 'to provide **practical assistance** in the home, including assistance in the carrying out of works of **adaptation** or the provision of any additional **facilities** designed to secure greater **safety, comfort or convenience**';
- 'to contribute to the **cost of employing a warden** on welfare functions in warden assisted housing schemes';
- 'to provide **warden services** for occupiers of private housing'.

4. MENTAL HEALTH ACT 1983
After-Care

Under section 117 of the Mental Health Act 1983, social services and health authorities have a duty to provide after-care for people to whom sections 3, or 37, or 47 and 48 apply: 'It shall be the duty of the District Health Authority and of the local social services authority to provide, in co-operation with voluntary agencies, after-care services for any person to whom this section applies until such time as the District Health Authority and the local social services authority are satisfied that the person concerned is no longer in need of such services'.

5. CHRONICALLY SICK AND DISABLED PERSONS ACT 1970
Welfare Services

Local authorities have a **duty** to provide services under section 2(1) of the CSDPA 1970.

'Where a local authority having functions under section 29 of the National Assistance Act 1948 are **satisfied** in the case of any person to whom that section applies who is ordinarily resident in their area that it is **necessary in order to meet the needs of that person for that authority to make arrangements** for all or any of the following matters, namely-

(a) the provision of **practical assistance** for that person in his home;

(b) the provision for that person of, or assistance to that person in obtaining, **wireless, television, library** or similar recreational facilities;

(c) the provision for that person of lectures, games, outings or other **recreational facilities** outside his home or assistance to that person in taking advantage of **educational facilities** available to him;

(d) the provision for that person of facilities for, or assistance in, **travelling to and from his home** for the purpose of participating in any services provided under arrangements made by the authority under the said section 29 or, with the approval of the authority, in any services provided otherwise than as aforesaid which are similar to services which could be provided under such arrangements;

(e) the provision of assistance for that person in arranging for the carrying out of any works of **adaptation** in his home or the provision of any **additional facilities** designed to secure his greater **safety, comfort or convenience;**

(f) facilitating the taking of **holidays** by that person, whether at holiday homes or otherwise and whether provided under arrangements made by the authority or otherwise;

(g) the provision of **meals** for that person whether in his home or elsewhere'

(h) the provision for that person of, or assistance to that person, in obtaining, a **telephone** and any special equipment necessary to enable him to use a telephone,

then...it shall be the duty of that authority to make those arrangements in exercise of their functions under the said section 29'.

CHAPTER 5

MATCHING SPECIFIC SERVICES WITH LEGISLATION

KEY ISSUES

Non-Specific Legislation

Social services, health and housing authorities can provide a very a wide range of specific services, types of equipment and home adaptations which can be provided. The A–Z list of services in this chapter begins to give an idea of this range.

However, relatively few of the services are mentioned in legislation and this can make it difficult for service users and their advisers, as well as practitioners and managers, to know which legislation applies to which services. Even where a service is mentioned such as 'practical assistance in the home', the legislation does not go on to specify what services this term might cover in practice (eg. personal care, home help, cleaning, shopping, cooking).

Services Provided by Different Authorities

A further explanation is that, as pointed out elsewhere in this book, a significant number of services can be provided by more than one authority under different legislation. For example, bathing and respite care can be provided by either health or social services authorities. Alternatively, gaps can exist where particular services fall between legislation and between agencies.

Services Provided by the Same Authority Under Different Legislation

This is further complicated by the fact that even if a service can only be provided by one type of authority, it can sometimes be provided under more than one piece of legislation. For service users, this can be important to know. For example, the duty of social services to provide home help under the NHS Act 1977 is a weaker duty than the duty to provide it under the Chronically Sick and Disabled Persons Act. Similarly, social services provision of home adaptations for elderly people under the Health Service and Public Health Act 1968 is only a power (ie, authorities can provide if they want to, but they don't have to, whereas under section of the CSDPA 1970, provision of adaptations is a duty towards individual people.

Disabilities and Conditions

The list of services does not include reference to the large number of people's needs, disabilities and conditions. However, the government has made it clear that community care is intended to assist people in need – more or less irrespective of the condition or disability which has caused that need. For example, during the passing of the NHS and Community Care Bill, the government made it clear that the definition of disability under section 29 of the National Assistance Act 1948 'is cast in broad terms with the aim of being as inclusive as possible and related to a degree of severity rather than to a particular condition' (H91 1990).

HOW TO USE THE CHAPTER

The following section consists of a list of the main legislation relevant. Each item is numbered and contains the following information (where appropriate):

- the legislation   eg. (CSDPA 1970,s.2);
- what it is about   (welfare services);
- duty or power   (duty to individuals);
- authority affected   (social services departments);
- essential words/phrases   ('need', 'satisfied', 'necessary' etc.).

Chapter 6, *Duties and Powers of Authorities*, explains the different types of duty and how words and phrases affect, qualify, and sometimes, weaken duties.

Following this legislation key is a second key, listing services in alphabetical order. Each item is followed by one or more numbers which relate to the legislation key.

Chapter 4, *Community care services*, gives details of specific powers, duties and services relating to those services defined as 'community care services' – and should be used in conjunction with this chapter.

LEGISLATION LIST

Each entry consists of one or more of the following elements:

(a) the Act and section;

(b) reference (if appropriate) to Directions (implying duties) or Approvals (implying discretionary powers only)

(c) what services the legislation is about;

(d) whether there is:
- a **duty toward individuals** and therefore a stronger duty;
- a **general duty** (ie., to the population generally) and therefore a weaker duty;

- or whether there are just **powers** (the authority can provide but doesn't have to);

(e) which type of authority the duties or powers apply to;

(f) key words and phrases which surround the duty or power.

1a **National Assistance Act 1948, s.21 (and s.26)** (including Directions)
About placing people in residential or nursing homes (and 'less dependent' people in other homes where board is provided)
Duty (general): local authorities (social services).

1b **National Assistance Act 1948, s.21 (and s.26)**
(including Approvals)
About placing people in residential or nursing homes (and 'less dependent' people in other homes where board is provided)
Power: local authorities (social services).

1c **National Assistance Act 1948, s.29** (including Directions)
About non-residential welfare services
Duty (general): local authorities (social services)

- applies to people with/who are 'blind, deaf or dumb', 'mental disorder', or who are 'substantially and permanently handicapped by illness, injury, or congenital deformity';
- applies to people aged eighteen years or over;
- applies to ordinary residents.

1d **National Assistance Act 1948, s.29** (including Approvals)
About non-residential welfare services
Power: local authorities (social services)

- applies to people with/who are 'blind, deaf or dumb', 'mental disorder', or who are 'substantially and permanently handicapped by illness, injury, or congenital deformity';
- applies to people aged eighteen years or over;
- certain services are available to non-residents as well as residents of the local authority's area.

1e **National Assistance Act 1948, s.47**
About the compulsory removal of people from their homes (not otherwise covered in this book)
Power: local authorities (social services)

- people who 'are suffering from grave chronic disease, or being aged, infirm or physically incapacitated, are living in insanitary conditions' and;
- 'are unable to devote to themselves, and are not receiving from other persons, proper care and attention'.

2 **Health Service and Public Health Act 1968, s.45** (including Approvals)
About welfare services for elderly people
Power: local authorities (social services).

3a **Chronically Sick and Disabled Persons Act 1970, s.2**
About home welfare services
Duty (to individuals): local authorities (social services)

- people must 'need' services;
- authorities must be 'satisfied' that for the needs to be met, it is 'necessary' for them to 'make arrangements' for the provision of services;
- duty applies to people who are 'ordinarily resident'.

3b **Chronically Sick and Disabled Persons Act 1970, s.1**
About providing existing service users with information about other relevant services, including those provided by other organisations and authorities
Duty (to individuals): local authorities (social services)

- 'relevant to his needs';
- in the authority's 'opinion';
- relates to services the authority knows about: 'particulars are in the authority's possession'.

3c **Chronically Sick and Disabled Persons Act 1970, s.1**
About publishing information about available services provided under the National Assistance Act 1948,s.29 (see above)
Duty (general): local authorities (social services)

- 'from time to time';
- 'appropriate general information'.

4 **Local Government and Housing Act 1972, s.137**
About incurring expenditure for the benefit of the local population
Power: housing authorities.

5a **National Health Service Act 1977, s.3(1)(a–c)**
About health authority and NHS Trust provision of medical, nursing, dental and ambulance services; also of hospital and other accommodation
Duty (general): health authorities

- services to be provided 'to such extent' as are considered 'necessary to meet all reasonable requirements'.

5b **National Health Service Act 1977, s.3(1)(e)**
About various facilities in relation to illness
Duty (general): health authorities

- for 'the prevention of illness, the care of persons suffering from illness and the after-care of persons who have suffered from illness';
- and which health authorities consider 'are appropriate as part of the health service'.

5c National Health Service Act 1977, s.28
About provision by local authorities of a social work service to hospitals
Duty (general): local authorities (social services)

- 'make available to health authorities' local authority employees, 'so far as is reasonably necessary and practicable to enable health authorities to discharge their functions'.

5d National Health Service Act 1977, s.28A
About health authority payment of money to social services departments, housing associations etc.
Power: health authorities.

5e National Health Service Act 1977, s.5(2)
About health authority provision of 'invalid carriages'
Power: health authorities.

5f National Health Service Act 1977, Part 2 (generally)
About general practitioners, dentists, pharmacists, opticians
Duty (general): family health services authorities.

5g SI 1992/635 (Regulations containing GP terms of service)
About GP annual offer of consultation to patients at least 75 years old, and duty to assess particular aspects of their health. Also giving advice by GPs to their patients about how to benefit from social services;
Duty (individual): general practitioners

5h Drug Tariff (made under SI 1992/662/NHS Act 1977, s.41)
Determines what GPs can prescribe and pharmacists dispense.

5j General practice-based therapists, chiropodists, nurses (according to a variety of arrangements)

5k National Health Service Act 1977, Schedule 8, para 2 (including Directions)
About prevention of illness, care of people who are ill, and about after-care
Duty (general): local authorities (social services) (applies to mental disorder).

5m National Health Service Act 1977, Schedule 8, para 2 (including Approvals)
About prevention of illness, care of people who are ill, and about after-care
Power: local authorities (social services).

5o National Health Service Act 1977, Schedule 8, para 3
About home help
Duty (general): local authorities (social services)

- 'provide' or 'arrange' on a 'scale adequate for the needs of their area'

- for various people including people who are ill, 'aged', 'handicapped'.

5p National Health Service Act 1977, Schedule 8, para 3
About laundry facilities
Power: local authorities (social services)

- 'provide or arrange'; for 'households for which home help is being, or can be provided'.

6 Health and Social Services and Social Security Adjudications Act 1983 (Schedule 9, Part 2, para 1)
About meals and recreation for old people in their own homes or elsewhere
Power: housing authorities

- 'power to make such arrangements as they may from time to time determine'.

7 Mental Health Act 1983, s.117
About after-care for mentally ill people
Duty (to individuals): health authorities and social services

- 'shall be the duty';
- 'to provide after-care services for any person to whom this section applies' until the authorities are 'satisfied that the person concerned is no longer in need of such services'.

8a Registered Homes Act 1984: regulations (SI 1984/1345, r.10)
About provision of facilities and services in and by residential homes
Duty (general): home owners

- 'having regard to the size of the home and the number, age, sex and condition of residents';
- many of the items mentioned are to be provided to an 'adequate' level.

8b Registered Homes Act 1984: regulations (SI 1984/1578, r.12)
About provision of facilities and services in and by nursing homes
Duty (general): home owners

- 'having regard to the size of the home and the number, age, sex and condition of the patients';
- many of the items mentioned are to be provided to an 'adequate' level.

9a Housing Act 1985, s.11A
About provision of welfare services in sheltered housing
Power: housing authorities

- 'may provide in connection with the provision of housing accommodation by them...as accord with the needs of those persons'.

9b Housing Act 1985, s.9
About alteration, enlargement, repair or improvement to council housing stock
Power: housing authorities.

10a Disabled Persons (Services, Consultation and Representation) Act 1986, s.4

About assessing, when requested, people for services under the CSDPA 1970

Duty (to individuals): social services (local authorities)

- when requested by a disabled person or his or her carer, a local authority 'shall decide' whether his or her needs 'call for' the 'provision' of CSDPA 1970 (s.2) services.

10b Disabled Persons (Services, Consultation and Representation) Act 1986, s.9

About having regard to the carer when assessing a disabled person for welfare services

Duty (to individuals): social services (local authorities)

- the local authority must 'have regard to the ability of that other person to continue to provide such care on a regular basis'.

10c Disabled Persons (Services, Consultation and Representation) Act 1986, ss.5,6

About cooperation between social services and education departments for purposes of assessing disabled people who are leaving school (not otherwise covered in this book).

11a Local Government and Housing Act 1989, s.114

About disabled facilities grants for home adaptations (mostly for access purposes)

Duty (towards individuals): housing authorities

- adaptations must be 'necessary and appropriate'; and 'reasonable and practicable';
- the housing authority must 'consult the welfare authority';
- the application must be approved if it is for one of the purposes prescribed in the section.

11b Local Government and Housing Act 1989, s.114

About disabled facilities grants for home adaptations – which there is. not already (see above) a duty to provide

Power: housing authorities

- 'for the purpose of making the dwelling…suitable for the accommodation, welfare or employment of the disabled occupant'.

11c Local Government and Housing Act 1989, s.131

About minor works assistance for elderly people receiving state benefits

Power: housing authorities.

12a NHS and Community Care Act 1990, s.47(1)

About assessment of people in possible need and decision about services

Duty (to individuals): local authorities (social services)

- 'appears to a local authority';
- a person who 'may be in need of community care services';
- a person 'for whom they may provide or arrange for the provision of community care services';
- assessment to be about 'his needs for those services'

12b NHS and Community Care Act 1990, s.47(1)

About specific duty to decide what services a person is going receive
Duty (to individuals): local authorities (social services)

- 'having regard to the results of that assessment, shall decide whether his needs call for the provision by them of any such services'.

12c NHS and Community Care Act 1990, s.47(2)

About specific duty to assess disabled people (for CSDPA services)
Duty (to individuals): local authorities (social services)

- if during the community care assessment 'it appears to a local authority that he is a disabled person';
- 'shall proceed to make a decision as to the services he requires' under s.4 of the DP(SCR)A 1986 (ie. referring to CSDPA, s.2 welfare services);
- 'shall inform him that they will be doing so' (ie. deciding about CSDPA services) 'and of his rights under that Act' (ie. under the DP(SCR)A 1986).

A–Z LIST OF SERVICES: KEY TO LEGISLATION

The following is a list of services, relevant to community care, provided by local (social services) authorities, health authorities and housing authorities. The number(s) against each item refers to the legislation key set out immediately above. **When using the list, the following should be noted:**

- because of the uncertainties described (throughout this book) affecting the provision of services and equipment, the following cannot in any sense be a precise guide. It is, however, likely to be a very useful starting point;
- there are generally few absolute rights to services or equipment – even if the services or equipment are notionally covered by a 'duty';
- sometimes items are mentioned explicitly in the legislation, but often they are not. For example, laundry facilities are mentioned in the NHS Act 1977; but are not mentioned in the CSDPA 1970 nor in the Health Service and Public Health Act 1968. However, they could in principle be provided under all three Acts;
- there is a fine line sometimes in deciding whether a service is mentioned 'explicitly' in legislation: for example, if 'advice' is mentioned in the legislation, does that *necessarily* include the provision of 'information'?;
- equipment provision is a particularly complex and unpredictable system (see: Mandelstam 1993);

- some of the following services and equipment are available through other statutory channels such as employment and education. These avenues are not covered in the following list.
- the following list does not cover assistance with, or provision of, services and equipment which voluntary organisations can sometimes offer.

N.B. (*) An asterisk indicates that the item is mentioned explicitly in legislation. In the absence of an asterisk, we are making an inference that a particular service is likely to be covered by that particular piece of legislation.

( ) Items are bracketed to indicate a reduced likelihood that the service is available through that particular legislation

Adaptations	SEE Home adaptations
Adult placement schemes	1a, 1b, 1c, 1d, 2
Adult training centres (learning disabilities)	5k*, 5m*
Advice	1c*, 1d*, 2*, 5g*, 5m*
After-care of ill people	5b*, 5k*, 5m*, 7*
Alarms (see also Community alarm systems)	2, 3a, 9b, 11a, 11b, 11c
Alcohol related services	1b*, 5m*
Ancillary/supplemental services in centres	5m*
Approved social worker services (mental) health)	5k*
Artificial limbs	5a, 5b
Assessment (community care)	12a*
Assessment (of disabled school-leavers)	10c*
Assessment (disability)	10a*, 12a, 12c*
Bathing/baths (assistance with/ equipment)	2, 3a, 5b
Bathrooms (extensions)	SEE Home adaptations
Bed equipment/materials	2, 3a, 5b
Boarding/placement of adults (not residential/ nursing care)	1a, 1b, 1c, 1d, 2*
Car equipment (eg. car hoists)	2, 3a
Care of ill people	5b*, 5k*, 5m*
Carers (having regard to – during assessment for welfare services)	10b*
Cars for disabled people (repair, replacement, maintenance – but not provision	5e*
Centres for social rehabilitation and adjustment to disability	1c*, 1d*
Centres for keeping people occupied	5k*, 5m*
Centres for training	5k*, 5m*
Chiropody/foot services/appliances	(2), (3a), 5a, 5b, 5h, 5j
Cleaning in the home	2, 3a, 5o
Clinical psychology	5a, 5b
Commodes	2, 3a, 5b
Communication aids/equipment	2, 3a, 5a, 5b
Community alarm systems	2, 3a, 4, 9a, 9b,

Community care assessment	12a*
Community care/housing for former long-stay hospital patients (mental health/learning disability)	5d
Community care services (decision about provision)	12b*
Community nursing services	5a, 5b
Compulsory removal from own home	1e
Contact lenses	5a, 5f
Continuing care (nursing)	1a, 1b, 5a, 5b,
Cooking (assistance with)	2, 3a, 5o
Counselling	1c, 1d, 2, 5a, 5b, 5k, 5m
Crutches	5b
Cultural activities (facilities for)	1c*, 1d*
Cushions (eg. pressure relief)	2, 3a, 5b
Daily living equipment	2, 3a, (5a), (5b)
Day centres	1c*, 1d*, 3a, 5k*, 5m
Day hospitals	5a, 5b
Dental services	5a*, 5f*
Diabetes services/equipment	5a, 5b, 5h*
Disabled facilities grants	11a*, 11b*
Disposal of produce of work (assistance with)	5k*
Domiciliary facilities for training or occupation	5k*
Domiciliary services	1c, 1d, 2, 3a, 5b, 5k*, 5m, 5o, 5p, 9a
Downstairs extensions	SEE Home adaptations
Dressings/bandages	5a, 5b, 5h*
Dressing equipment	2, 3a
Drop-in centres	1c, 1d, 5k, 5m
Drug related services	1b*, 5m*
Eating and drinking (assistance with)	2, 3a, 5o
Educational facilities (assistance to use)	3a*
Elastic hosiery	5a, 5h*
Elderly care (NHS)	5a, 5b, 5g*
Environmental controls (for severely disabled people)	2, 3a, 5a, 5b
Equipment (disability)	2, 3a, 5a, 5b, 7h
Extensions (to dwelling)	SEE Home adaptations
Facilities for safety, comfort or convenience	2*, 3a*
Facilities for social rehabilitation and adjustment to disability	1c*, 1d*
Finding accommodation (assistance with)	1d*, 2*
Foot supports/pads/materials	5a, 5b,
Footwear (surgical, special)	5a, 5b
Games	2, 3a*
Getting up/putting to bed (assistance)	2, 3a, 5b
GP-prescribed equipment/drugs	5h*
GP services	5f*, 5g*, 5h*

Health visiting (for elderly people)	5b
Hearing aids (bodyworn)	5a, 5b
Hearing aids (environmental)	2, 3a, (5a), (5b);
Hearing therapy	5a, 5b
Hoists	2, 3a, 5b, 9b, 11a, 11b, 11c
Holidays	1d, 3a*, 5m*
Holiday homes	1d*, 3a, 5m
Home adaptations (generally)	2*, 3a*, 9b*, 11a*, 11b*, 11c*
Home adaptations (renal dialysis)	5a, 5b
Home help	2, 3a, 5k, 5o*
Home nursing equipment	5b
Home personal care	2, 3a, 5b
Hospital accommodation	5a*
Hospital discharge arrangements	5a, 5b, 5c
Hostels	1d*
Household equipment (disability)	2, 3a
Hygiene in residential accommodation	1a*
Incontinence equipment/services	1a, (2), (3a), 5a, 5b, 5g*, 5h*
Information about services	1c, 1d, 2*, 3b*, 3c*, 5g
Instruction for overcoming effects of disability	1d*
Interpreter services	1c, 2
Invalid carriages	5e*
Laundry (ordinary)	2, 3a, 5p*
Laundry (incontinence)	2, 3a, 5b, 5p*
Lectures	3a*
Library facilities	3a*
Lifting (assistance with)	2, 3a, 5b
Lifts (stair)	2, 3a, 9b, 11a, 11b, 11c
Lifts (through-floor)	(2), (3a), 9b, 11a, 11b, (11c)
Low vision aids (hospital eye service and specialist opticians)	5a, 5b, 5f
Lunch clubs	2, 3a, 5m, 6
Meals	2*, 3a*, 5m*, 6*
Medical attention in residential accommodation (obtaining not providing)	1a*
Medical services	5a,* 5b, 5f*
Medicine administration (injections)	5a, 5b, 5f
Medicine administration (applications)	2, 3a, 5a, 5b, 7
Mental health resource centres (SSD)	1c, 1d, 5k
Minor works assistance	11c*
Mobility assistance (equipment/ rehabilitation)	1c*, 1d*, 2, 3a, 5a, 5b, 5e
Nebulisers	5a, 5b, 5h*

Night sitter services   2, 3a, 5m*
Nursing attention in residential accommodation
   (obtaining not providing)   1a*
Nursing care at home   5b
Nursing care in nursing homes (basic)   8b*
Nursing care in nursing homes (specialist/advice)   5a, 5b
Nursing care in residential homes   5a, 5b
Nursing home accommodation   1a*, 1b*, 5a, 5b
Nursing home services and facilities   5b, 8b*
Nursing services (generally)   1a, 5a*, 5b, 8b*
Occupational activities   1c*, 1d*, 5k*, 5m*
Occupational therapy (assessment)   2, 3a, 3b, 5a, 5b, 5j, (5k),
                                                             11a, 11b, 11c

Optical services   5a, 5f*
Ostomy equipment   5a, 5b, 5h*
Outings   2, 3a*
Oxygen concentrators   5a, 5b, 5h*
Oxygen cylinders   5a, 5b, 5h*
Payments for work   1c*, 1d*, 5m*
Pension (drawing for housebound person)   2, 3a, 5o
Personal care at home   2, 3a, (5b), 5k
Pharmacy services   5a, 5f*, 5h*
Physiotherapy   (2), (3a), 5a, 5b, 5j
Practical assistance in the home   2*, 3a*, 5k, 5o
Practice nurses (in GP surgeries)   5j
Pressure relief equipment   (2), (3a), 5a, 5b
Prevention of illness   5b*, 5k*, 5m*
Psychiatric nursing   5a, 5b
Radio   2, 3a*
Recreational activities (facilities for)   1c*, 1d*, 2*, 3a*, 5m*
Register of disabled people   1c*
Rehabilitation services (NHS)   5a, 5b
Removal from own home, compulsory   1e
Representation   1c, 2, 5k, 5m
Residential care   1a*, 1b*
Residential home (provision of health services)   5b
Residential home services & facilities   1a*, 8a*
Respiratory equipment   5a, 5b, 5h*
Respite care (including holidays)   1a, 1b, 1c, 1d, 2, 3a, 5a,
                                                             5b, 5m 5b

Shopping   2, 3a, 5k, 5o
Short-term breaks   SEE Respite care
Social activities (facilities for)   1c*, 1d*, 2, 3a, 5m*
Social education centres (learning disabilities)   1c, 1d,
Social work service   1c*, 1d*, 2, 5k*, 5m*
Social work support   1c*, 1d*, 2*, 5k*, 5m*
Spectacles (including special low vision)   5a, 5b, 5f

Speech aids/equipment	2, 3a, 5a, 5b
Speech and language therapy	(2), (3a), 5a, 5b, 5j
Stoma care equipment	5a, 5b, 5h*
Surgical supports	5a, 5b, 5h*
Telephone-related equipment	2, 3a*
Telephones	2, 3a*
Television	2, 3a*
Temporary accommodation	1a*
Therapy services	2, 3a, 5a, 5b, 5j, (9b), (11a), (11b), (11c)
Training centres	5k*, 5m*
Transport to and from residential accommodation	1b*
Travel assistance	1b*, 1d*, 2*, 3a*
Visiting services	1c, 1d, 2*, 5k
Walking aids	2, 3a, 5a, 5b
Warden services (contribution to cost of in warden-assisted housing)	1d*, 2*
Warden services in private housing	1d*, 2*
Washing (assistance with)	2, 3a, 5b
WCs/adaptations to WCs	2, 3a, 9b, 11a, 11b, 11c
Welfare (generally)	1a*, 1c*, 1d*, 2*, 3a, 9a*
Welfare of residents	1a*
Welfare services (in warden-assisted housing	9a*
Wheelchairs (assessment)	(2), (3a), 5a, 5b, 5e
Wheelchairs (provision, manual)	(2), (3a), 5a, 5b
Wheelchairs (provision, powered)	(2), (3a), 5a, 5b, 5e
Wigs	5a, 5b
Wireless	2, 3a*
Workshops	1d*
Writing aids/equipment	2, 3a, (5b)
Writing letters (assistance with)	2, 3a, 5o

CHAPTER 6

DUTIES AND POWERS OF AUTHORITIES

KEY ISSUES

Throughout the book, references to documents indicate their status: for example, legislation, policy guidance, practice guidance, Circular guidance – and so on. Readers will find it useful to refer back to this chapter which explains the significance of these different types of document.

Familiarity with these types of document is essential if service users or authorities are to understand how the community care system – with all its uncertainties – functions.

Community care law and policy is to be found in a range of documents ranging from Acts of Parliament to 'advice' notes. The significance of these different types of document can be bewildering. In addition, the precise effect of these documents depends on their wording, and the context in which are they considered.

For example, **legislation sometimes places duties on authorities – that is authorities have obligations to do certain things. Sometimes, however, legislation simply gives powers to authorities – that is, authorities can do certain things if they want to, but they don't have to do them.**

But even these duties can be of various types; some of them are stronger duties towards individuals, whilst others are weaker because they are duties towards the local population generally rather than to individuals in particular. In addition, duties are often qualified or 'weakened' by surrounding wording, which effectively gives authorities a 'way out' of what might be otherwise oppressive obligations. Another way of putting this is that although authorities have duties, many of them are carried out only after authorities have made decisions about what the duties really entail, who precisely should benefit from them, and how.

Much of the legislation relevant to community care contains imprecise wording; and social services and health service practice is determined also by abundant guidance issued by the Department of Health. The legal status and effect of guidance is somewhat unclear, and the position is further complicated because there are different types of guidance.

Although there is an order of precedence for these documents (with Acts of Parliament at the top and Circulars some way down the order), the particular context in which they are considered can be all-important. For example, the health service ombudsman might focus his findings in a hospital discharge investigation not on the NHS Act itself (which is vague) but on Circular guidance (which specifically deals with discharge) – thus elevating the significance of the guidance in that particular investigation.

LEGAL PRECEDENCE OF DOCUMENT

The following is a rough guide to the importance and precedence of different classes of document. However, in practice this order of precedence is not necessarily definitive.

Broad Guide to Precedence

Broadly, the order of precedence of documents is as follows. It must be emphasised that the context in which documents are cited is all important (see below). Duties place obligations on authorities (ie., they have to do them). Powers do not place obligations on authorities (authorities can do what the wording says, but don't have to).

(1) **Acts of Parliament** ('primary' legislation). Can place duties or powers on authorities;

(2) **Statutory instruments** (sometimes known as Regulations; they are secondary, or delegated, legislation). Can place duties or powers on authorities;

(3) **Directions** made under an Act of Parliament (another form of delegated legislation). Place duties on authorities.

(4) **Approvals** made under an Act of Parliament (another form of delegated legislation). Place powers on authorities.

(5) **Guidance and codes of practice** Some guidance is made explicitly under an Act of Parliament. This is potentially the strongest form of guidance, but the extent to which even this imposes duties and obligations is a little unclear. Community care policy guidance is made explicitly under legislation. However, for example, a recent case about childminders and smacking resulted in a judge ruling that the local authority was not rigidly bound by Department of Health guidance (issued under the same legislation) – whereas the local authority had thought that it was bound.

Department of Health guidance explains that codes of practice fall 'between regulations and guidance notes. They may be 'statutory' in that they are required by legislation and are laid before Parliament. They therefore carry more weight than other departmental guidance, but they are not law in the way that regulations are law. As with section 7 (LASSA 1970) guidance, courts expect detailed justification for not following codes of practice, but some flexibility to suit the needs of a particular case is allowed and expected' (DH 1990a, p.2).

Other guidance is not made explicitly under an Act of Parliament. Generally, such guidance is thought not to impose duties and obligations on authorities even if it uses words of obligation such as 'should'. Nevertheless there is considerable uncertainty about guidance. There has been disagreement in the highest of law courts (the House of Lords) about its legal effect.

In addition, whatever the precise legal status of guidance, courts sometimes regard it as a strong indication of government policy. Thus one judge has referred to Circular guidance when he was interpreting what a community care assessment should be about. In another area of law (immigration), a court ruled that guidance created a 'legitimate expectation' that people would be treated in a certain way – and should be so treated. In the health service sphere, the health service ombudsman seems to regard Circular guidance about hospital discharge as imposing obligations on health authorities.

Department of Health guidance (DH 1990a) explains 'the differences between the requirements of these various offjcial documents like this: Regulations say "*You must/shall*"; codes say "*You ought/should*". When guidance explains regulations in setting out good practice, it conveys the message that "*It is highly desirable to...*" or "*Unless there is good reason not to, you should...*" rather than "*You must*" (pp.2–3).

Usefulness of Documents in Different Contexts – and As 'Bargaining' Tools

The usefulness of a document might vary depending on the context in which it is considered.

Although the order of precedence (see above) of different types of document is important, it is not necessarily decisive. For example, the health service ombudsman has sometimes criticised health authorities for not following hospital discharge Circular guidance. In this particular context, referring to Circular guidance has been actually more useful for the complainant than referring to the vague duties in legislation (which do not mention hospital discharge). This is because the ombudsman has not been afraid to use the guidance as imposing some obligations on a health authority.

Furthermore, because all these types of document normally represent government policy, they can be powerful, informal, 'bargaining' tools locally, whether used by an authority to justify difficult decisions about priorities, or by service users and their advisers to question those decisions.

Of course the uncertainty about the legal effect of guidance, or the meaning of wording surrounding a duty, can also be very unhelpful both to service users and authorities. On the other hand, this very uncertainty can also be exploited.

For example, if an authority is not clear about the effect of a piece of guidance, it might decide to accede informally to a well-argued challenge, rather than risk going to court.

ACTS OF PARLIAMENT

Acts of Parliament are 'primary' legislation and state what the law is.

Powers and Duties

Legislation places both duties and powers on local social services, health and housing authorities. Analysing what these powers and duties might mean is essential for authorities in order to gauge the likely extent of their obligations; and for service users in order to try and ascertain what entitlements they might have.

Duties are mandatory: that is authorities are under an obligation to carry them out. Duties are often evident in the use of the imperative word 'shall'. For example, this word governs social services' duty to carry out assessment of people's needs for community care services under section 47 of the NHS and Community Care Act 1990.

Powers are discretionary: that is authorities do not have to exercise them. Powers are often signalled by use of the word 'may'. For example, local authorities can provide welfare services for elderly people under section 45 of the Health Services and Public Health Act 1968 – but they don't have to provide them. Or, for example, housing authorities have the power to assist elderly people to stay in their own homes through a 'minor works assistance' scheme under section 131 of the Local Government and Housing Act 1989. In fact, it has been reported that some housing authorities choose not to exercise this power and so do not provide minor works assistance at all.

The Difference Between Duties Towards Individual People and 'General Duties'

Duties are not all of the same type and effect. First, some duties can be viewed as directed towards individuals, whereas others are more general duties towards a local population as a whole. Those directed towards individuals are generally 'stronger' duties than more general duties. This means that, in principle at least, it is less easy for public authorities to avoid duties directed towards individuals.

Examples of duties towards individuals in the context of community care include:

- social services assessment of people who might be need of community care services (NHS and Community Care Act 1990, section 47: refers to 'any person');
- making of arrangements by social services for various welfare services under section 2 of the Chronically Sick and Disabled Persons Act 1970 (for 'any person');

- health service and social services duty to provide after-care for people discharged from hospital under section 117 of the Mental Health Act 1983 (which refers to 'any person').

Examples of general duties include:

- the provision by health authorities of health services to the general population (NHS Act 1977, s.3);
- the duty of local authorities to provide home-help for the area (s.21 and Schedule 8, NHS Act 1977).

The distinction between duties towards individuals and general duties in these examples, is that in the cases of duties towards individuals, the legislation uses the term 'any person'. In the case of the general duties there is no such term. Section 3 of the NHS Act 1977 refers to provision not to 'any person' but to provision 'throughout England and Wales'. The duty to provide home help under the NHS Act 1977 is similarly a duty, towards a population (here a local one), not to individuals, to provide 'on a scale as is adequate for the needs of their area'.

Qualification of Duties

Duties are qualified in another way. As already explained the word 'shall' usually denotes the existence of a duty. However, surrounding wording will often qualify the duty.

Under the NHS Act 1977, s.3, the Secretary of State has a general duty (delegated to health authorities) to provide various services – but with the following qualification: 'to such extent as he considers necessary to meet all reasonable requirements'. In practice, it is this qualification, added to the fact that the duty is only a 'general' one anyway (to the population, not to individuals), which allows health authorities to exercise so much discretion in deciding what to provide – and what not to provide. There is a view amongst some lawyers that so broad is this discretion that, in respect of any one specific health service or level of service, health authorities have a power or discretion only, rather than a duty.

Sometimes, if judges wish to explain why authorities do not really have absolute duties, they will not only make use of qualifying wording but possibly 'add' some wording of their own. For example, in one health service case about waiting times for orthopaedic treatment, a judge in the Court of Appeal suggested that the duty to provide health services 'necessary to meet all reasonable requirements' was further qualified by the words 'within the re-sources available' – even though these last words do not appear in the legislation (*R v Secretary of State for Social Services, ex p. Hincks 1979*). More recently, in a case about provision of after-care (a community care service) under the Mental Health Act 1983, the judge was prepared to find that the duty was a strong one – but he explicitly did not consider what effect lack of resources would have on the duty (*R v Ealing DHA, ex p. Fox 1992*).

Extent and Degree of a Duty

There is another way in which duties are qualified. Even if a court accepts there is a particular duty to do something, it might say that the decision about the type and level of service to be provided is up to the authority. For example, the court is likely to be very reluctant to substitute its opinion for that of a health authority over the allocation of resources – even when the result has been long waiting times (*Re Walker's Application 1987*).

Where priorities and waiting times are at issue, there might be a fine line between deciding whether an authority is doing its duty but doing it slowly, or whether it is failing to do its duty altogether. For example, the local ombudsman, when investigating cases about waiting times, sometimes accepts the need for priorities and waiting times; but at other times states that authorities have not done their duty because they have failed to assess people who have been waiting. Where the line is crossed for the ombudsman, between slow performance and non-performance of duty, seems unclear and to vary from case to case.

The strength of duties is similarly qualified if expert professional judgement is involved. For example, the courts will not generally interfere with the clinical decisions of doctors (*eg. Re J 1992*) or other professionals; the health service ombudsman is legally unable to question clinical decisions; and the local ombudsman cannot question professional judgements.

Similarly, in a case concerning s.2 of the CSDPA, the judge ruled that it was for the local authority to decide about a person's needs: the court could only intervene if the authority's decision was 'perverse or irrational' (*R v DHSS, ex p. Bruce 1986*).

Defining and Applying Imprecise Language

Community care and health service legislation contains *subjective language* at 'key' points in it. These terms generally indicate that it is for a local authority to decide how exactly to carry out its duty. Examples of such language include whether people *appear* (ie to the authority) to be in *need* of community care services (NHSCCA 1990, s.47); whether people's needs *call for* services (NHSCCA 1990, s.47); whether an authority is *satisfied* that it is *necessary* to provide services (CSDPA 1970, s.2); and whether a health authority's provision of services is *necessary to meet all reasonable requirements* (NHS Act 1977, s.3).

Generally speaking, the courts are unlikely to dictate to authorities what these terms mean *objectively*. For example, the courts are likely to be reluctant to state what conditions have to be met for a person to appear to be in need; or for a person to satisfy an authority that it is necessary to provide services; or for a health authority to show that it is meeting reasonable requirements. Instead it will be left up to authorities to define what these terms mean; and to decide who qualifies under those definitions.

In a recent Court of Appeal case about child care, one of the judges systematically analysed how imprecise language in legislation precluded the court ruling against the authority. This language included: 'If it *appears* to a local authority'; 'the *general* duty' (as opposed to specific duty); 'take *reasonable* steps'; 'have *reasonable* cause'; where 'a local authority *conclude*' (*M v Newham LBC 1994*: our italics to emphasise imprecise terms).

Adhering to Legal and Proper Procedure

However, the courts do have the power to intervene in a number of ways – if they so wish. First, there are certain limits to authorities' discretion to decide what a term means. If an authority is acting unreasonably, in bad faith, on improper grounds (Wade 1988, p.446) or illegally, then the court might intervene (see Chapter 7). For example, if the authority decided that community care services were 'called for' (NHSCCA 1990, s.47) only for people who were less than six feet tall (rather than on the basis of their assessed needs) – then this might be deemed illegal or unreasonable by the courts. A second example might be when a court finds that an authority could not have made a proper decision about whether, for instance, it was 'satisfied' because it had not taken into account the relevant facts (for this principle, see eg. *Secretary of State for Education and Science v Tameside MBC 1976*). In the community care context, this principle might apply if an authority declared itself not 'satisfied' that a person needed assistance in the home (under the CSDPA 1970), without having undertaken an assessment or possessing any information on which it could have come to the decision.

The term 'satisfied' is used also in housing legislation; authorities have to satisfy themselves that applicants are homeless and in priority need. The courts have not directly defined the circumstances in which an authority should be satisfied; but have established a number of procedural conditions about enquiries which must be met before an authority could declare itself 'satisfied'. For example, the authorities should consider medical opinion (which may be conclusive) and should make all other necessary enquiries (*R v London Borough of Lambeth, ex p. Caroll 1987*; see also Gordon 1993, p.16). It is a question of the courts developing ways to penetrate 'behind the ostensible "satisfaction" or "appearance" and deal with realities' (Wade 1988, p.446).

Terms Defined by the Courts

Second, some terms in legislation *are* defined by the courts. For example, the term 'ordinarily resident' in community care legislation (NAA 1948, CSDPA 1970), is a condition of receiving some services. It is not defined in the legislation and the courts state what it means. Therefore, it is not for the local authorities *subjectively* to decide what they mean by 'ordinarily resident' (see Chapter 8) but for the courts to do so *objectively* (see eg. *R v Barnet London Borough Council, ex p. Shah 1982*). Terms from other fields which the courts are prepared to define include 'illegal immigrant' (see eg. *R v Home Secretary, ex p. Khawaja*

1984); 'gypsy' (*R v South Hams DC, ex. p. Gibb 1993; R v Dorset CC, ex p. Rolls 1994*); 'applicant' to a housing department (*R v Tower Hamlets LBC, ex p Begum 1993*).

Some of these terms which the courts define are themselves completely undefined in the legislation ('ordinary resident'); whereas others are defined already in legislation and the courts try and give further meaning to particular parts of the definition. For example, legislation (Social Security Act 1975) states that a person qualifies for attendance allowance if he or she is severely disabled. The definition of severe disability in this context includes the phrase 'frequent attention throughout the day in connection with his bodily functions'. But the courts, rather than the legislation, have further defined that phrase to include the act of guiding a blind person (*Mallinson v Secretary of State for Social Services 1994*). Similarly, the courts have stated what the word 'nomadic' should mean within the definition of 'gypsy', which is already contained in legislation (*R v South Hams DC, ex p. Gibb 1993*).

However, it is important to realise that although the courts may define such terms, they will not always state whether a person actually is an illegal immigrant, gypsy etc. This is because, as already stated (see Chapter 7), judicial review involves the courts ensuring that authorities make decisions properly and legally – but it does not involve the courts' taking decisions for authorities. In other words, courts may *define* terms but they will not usually *apply* them.

Nevertheless, sometimes the courts do apply the term as well as define it; for example they did so in the *Khawaja* (immigration) case. This approach is likely to be rejected in other circumstances by the courts (see eg. the *South Hams* case about the term 'gypsy' and the *Begum* case about a homeless 'applicant'), but the line between defining and applying a term can be fine.

For example, in cases about ordinary residence (which can affect people's eligibility for some community care services), it is not always clear whether the courts are, strictly speaking, just defining the term – or whether they are defining *and* applying it. The House of Lords stated (in *R v Barnet LBC, ex parte Shah 1983*) that it was for the education authority, 'and it alone', to determine whether 'as a matter of fact' the students (applying for grants) were ordinary residents. However, the judge (Lord Scarman) went on to state that not only had the authorities 'misdirected themselves in law' (ie applied the wrong definition) but also that the students were ordinary residents. A similar approach has been taken in other ordinary residence cases (*R v Waltham Forest LBC, ex p. Vale 1985; R v London Borough of Redbridge, ex p. East Sussex CC 1992*).

Many terms central to community care, such as 'need' are very vague – and, as government guidance (DHSS 12/70) suggests, might ultimately be determined by local resources, rather than by any objective considerations relating to people's individual circumstances. Such terms are likely to be generally difficult for the courts to grapple with – although in one recent case, a court did seem to confirm that the term 'need' in s.47 of the NHSCCA 1990 refers to 'future' needs as well as immediately present needs (*R v Mid-Glamorgan County Council ex p. Miles 1993*). And in another community care case, the judge did express his agreement with a complains review panel that 'in law need is clearly capable of including psychological need' (*R v Avon CC, ex p. M 1993*).

It is possible in the future that even if the courts do not become enmeshed in trying to define precisely some of the vague terms in community care legislation, they could still state what procedures might be associated with those terms. For example, they might specify what sort of enquiries or what sort of factors should be taken into account before an authority decides whether somebody is 'in need'.

Thus, in principle, it could be argued by service users that where the legislation includes terms which are not qualified by expressions such as 'appears to the local authority', or 'the local authority is satisfied that', then the courts could define and apply these terms. This has happened in the case of 'ordinarily resident' and could possibly happen in the future with other terms. Examples could include 'disabled' (DP(SCR)A 1986, s.4), or 'adequate' staff (LASSA 1970, s.6) or provision of 'after-care' (Mental Health Act 1983, s.117) – since surrounding wording in the legislation does not indicate that it is up to authorities to arrive at their own definitions and views. There are no qualifying phrases such as 'if it appears', or 'in the view of the authority'. In other words, the argument might be, a person either is or is not disabled, an ordinary resident or eligible for after-care – it is not a question of opinion. For example, it has been suggested that a court might hold that an authority could not argue that it had adequate staff, if its own committee minutes showed that for years the committee had been aware of staff shortages but done nothing about them (see Clements 1992 on: *R v Hereford and Worcester CC, ex p. Chandler 1991*).

Duties but no Remedies

Another way of qualifying, and weakening, duties is for the courts to state that although there might be a duty, it does not give individuals a right to remedies when the duty is not carried out. The judges might say that by reading the legislation, it is clear that Parliament never intended there to be any remedies for breach of the duty (eg. *R v ILEA, ex p. Ali and Murshid 1990; R v Mid-Glamorgan CC, ex p. Greig 1988*).

STATUTORY INSTRUMENTS

Statutory instruments are secondary, or delegated, legislation and also state what the law is. The authority for making them stems from powers given by an Act of Parliament. For example, the test of resources (means-test) used by social services to assess people for residential or nursing home care is laid down in a statutory instrument which is made under section 22(5) of the National Assistance Act 1948.

They too can place powers or duties (see above) on authorities.

DIRECTIONS AND APPROVALS

Directions (and Approvals) are another form of delegated legislation, and are used extensively in the administration of the NHS (Wade 1989, p.856). For example, the Secretary of State for Health is authorised expressly to make various Directions under the NHS and Community Care Act: about community care plans (s.46), assessment (s.47); or under the Local Authority Social Services Act 1970 about social services functions (s.7A).

Directions place duties on authorities; Approvals give powers – that is, authorities can do what the Approval suggests, but are not obliged to.

Examples of community care Directions include:

(a) the complaints Directions, made under s.7B(3) of the LASSA 1970 which state: 'A local authority shall comply with any directions...'.

(b) Choice of residential accommodation Directions, made under s.7A of the LASSA 1970 which state: 'every local authority shall exercise their social services functions in accordance with such directions as may be given...'.

GUIDANCE IN GENERAL AND CODES OF PRACTICE

The legal significance of 'guidance' in general is unclear, and to make matters more complicated there are different types of guidance. Community care guidance includes:

- policy guidance;
- codes of practice;
- practice guidance;
- Circular guidance (of which there are various types);
- advice.

Generally, the precise legal status and strength of each of these types of guidance is nebulous. Even the courts can disagree about the legal import of guidance. The issue is important because much of the detail of the community care system is provided by guidance.

One distinction is between guidance made explicitly under legislation (eg. community care guidance made under s.7 of the LASSA 1970 which local authorities must 'act under') and other guidance which authorities need, perhaps, only 'have regard to'. The former imposes greater obligation than the latter – but neither impose, it seems, legally binding obligations.

Even if guidance does not impose legally binding obligations, it is still important evidence of government policy and is likely to be used in disputes. For example, the health service ombudsman is prepared to criticise health authorities and NHS Trusts when they do not follow Circular guidance on hospital discharge.

The courts might also refer to guidance. For example, in recent case (*R v Avon County Council, ex p. M 1993*) the judge referred to Circular guidance in order to support his interpretation of what the local authority's duty to assess consisted of. The guidance stated that: 'Services should be planned on an individual basis'. The judge concluded therefore: 'I take this to mean that the residential services provided should be suitable for the needs of the individual applicant, and it is this that the Local Authority must assess'.

On the other hand, again confusingly, a court might state that, despite the existence of guidance, an authority is not absolutely bound by it and does not always have to follow it. This occurred in a recent case about child-minding and the smacking of children – and was especially significant because the guidance was of relatively 'strong' status, since it was of the type made explicitly under an Act of Parliament.

Guidance and the NHS and Community Care Act

During the passing of the NHS and Community Care Bill through Parliament, government opposed a number of proposed amendments by stating that they were better taken account of in guidance than in the Act itself. The ensuing discussions about the status of guidance illustrate some of the uncertainty and dissatisfaction surrounding the whole subject.

Responding to such questions, for example, Baroness Hooper for the government distinguished between guidance and guidelines: 'My under-standing is that the use of the word "guidance" is different from the use of the word "guidelines". "Guidance" apparently has some significance in that, if an authority fails to observe guidance, the Secretary of State can enforce the suggestion by means of directions. Therefore, the effect of guidance is quite strong' (H85 1990).

Similarly, Baroness Hooper stated that 'guidance carries a great deal of clout... If not complied with it is for the Secretary of State to enforce the guidance by giving the necessary directions'. She explained that the Bill provided the 'necessary legal framework', whilst the 'various forms of guidance' would 'flesh out the framework of care' (H86 1990).

The guidance carrying 'clout' was probably what was to become the main community care policy guidance document (DH 1990). However, more than one type of guidance was referred to during the passage of the NHS and Community Care Bill. For example, an amendment, which would have made health authority incontinence services mandatory, was resisted by the govern-ment (Baroness Blatch) by referring to a 1988 health notice which mildly invited authorities 'to consider' provision. As Baroness Seear put it: 'it is not enough to say that a circular should advise people to consider it. One can do damn all in response to that kind of instruction. If we say, "There must be a district-wide incontinence service: get on with it", we shall get what the House wants' (H87 1990).

Baroness Masham voiced similar concerns, observing that people look at Acts of Parliament but 'forget everything else. They forget about White Papers and Green Papers and also, with the hurly-burly and the rush which ensue, they forget about the circulars issued by the Department' (H88 1990).

Community Care Policy Guidance

The main guidance underlying community is called 'policy guidance' (DH 1990) and was issued explicitly under legislation: the LASSA 1970 (s.7) (see EL(90)M5/LAC(90)12). This places a duty on local authorities to 'act under the general guidance' of the Secretary of State.

It is clearly a major policy document, although the terms in which it describes itself leave plenty of room for flexible interpretation: it sets out:

> 'WHAT is expected of health authorities and local authorities to meet the Government's proposals on community care. It provides the framework within which the delivery of community care should be planned, developed, commissioned and implemented locally. It leaves maximum scope for innovation and flexibility at local level, whilst being sufficient to enable Ministers to monitor and review progress towards national policy objectives' (DH 1990, para 1.4).

The possible uncertainty about this guidance is illustrated by the example given below concerning guidance about the Children Act 1989, which is issued under the same legislation (LASSA 1970, s.7). A further point of uncertainty is that the community care policy guidance is addressed to both social services department and health authorities – yet LASSA 1970 (s.7) concerns only social services departments. This would seem to mean that the guidance places a greater degree of obligation on social services than on health authorities.

Nevertheless, in a community care case about the provision of respite care under s.29 of the National Assistance Act 1948, the judge ruled against a local authority because it had breached two paragraphs of the community care policy guidance (DH 1990). These paragraphs state that local authorities should take account of people's preferences during assessment. This the authority failed to do in this particular case. Consequently, the judge stated that, despite the difficult circumstances in obtaining the person's preferences, it 'must follow that the decision was unlawful in the sense that it was made in breach of paragraphs 3.16 and 3.25 of the Policy Guidance'. This judgement would appear to strengthen the contention that such guidance imposes firm legal obligations on authorities (*R v North Yorkshire CC, ex p. Hargreaves 1994*).

Code of Practice Under the Mental Health Act 1983

This code is made under s.118 of the Mental Health Act 1983. The Secretary of State has a duty to 'prepare, and from time to time, revise, a code of practice'. It has to be laid before, and approved by, Parliament. The code is 'for the guidance' of various professions and managers (Mental Health Act 1983, s.118).

The Code itself (DH/WO 1993) states that the 'Act does not impose a legal duty to comply with the Code but failure to follow the Code could be referred to in evidence in legal proceedings' (p.1). The Secretaries of State 'warmly commend the new Code. It is an essential guide for all those involved in caring for people with a mental disorder. We look to them to make the fullest use of it' (p.iv).

The *Encyclopaedia of Social Services and Child Care Law* explains that the code 'is not mandatory in that professionals ...are not legally obliged to follow the advice contained in it. A failure to have regard to the Code could be used in legal proceedings as prima facie evidence of bad practice although the effect of non-compliance will largely depend upon the nature of the provision in the Code that has not been followed' (vol.3, E1– 287).

Homelessness Code of Practice

Under s.71 of the Housing Act 1985, in connection with homelessness, 'a relevant authority shall have regard in the exercise of their functions to such guidance as may from time to time be given by the Secretary of State', who 'may give guidance either generally or to specified descriptions of authorities'.

The Department of Environment, Department of Health and Welsh Office publish 'Homelessness: code of guidance for local authorities' (3rd edition) under this section. Issued to both housing and social services authorities in England and Wales, its status is explained in the following terms: 'In discharging their responsibilities under Part III of the Act, such authorities must have regard to this guidance. The Code is not, however, a substitute for the legislation. It gives guidance on how authorities might discharge their duties and apply the various statutory criteria in practice' (DoE,DH,WO 1991, p.5). The law courts have confirmed that the code is not to be regarded as 'binding statute'; and that although authorities must 'have regard' to it, they can 'depart from it' if they think fit (*De Falco v Crawley CC 1980*).

Children Act Guidance

An example of the uncertainty of the status of guidance, even when made expressly under an Act of Parliament, reached the courts recently. It concerned the smacking of children by childminders. It had been assumed that volume 2 of the Department of Health's guidance on the Children Act 1989 actually proscribed smacking. The guidance is made, as is the community care policy guidance, under s.7 of the LASSA 1970.

The High Court held that the guidance, which stated that smacking 'should not be used by any other parties within the scope of this guidance', was not absolutely binding. This was because neither the guidance, nor the legal duty to 'act under the general guidance of the Secretary of State', obliged the authority to adopt an inflexible, blanket policy. The effect of such guidance was, for example, in contrast to regulations (in a statutory instrument) which did prohibit strictly corporal punishment in children's homes (*Sutton London Borough Council v Davis 1994*).

CIRCULAR GUIDANCE

The term 'Circular guidance' has been used in this book to refer to a series of documents generally known as Circulars. Their titles are abbreviated: for example, *HSG* (health service guidelines), *LAC* (local authority circular), *LASSL* (local authority social services letter), *CI* (chief inspector) *HN* (health notice), *EL* (executive letter) and so on. Health and social services authorities are sent an abundance of Circular guidance each year. Some Circulars have a long life: for example, some Circulars from the early 1970s are still valid.

Legal Effect of Circular Guidance

The status of Circular guidance seems as unclear as it is important.

For example, the debate about when people have a right to an NHS longstay bed includes a much quoted point that people cannot be forced to leave hospital and go into a nursing or residential home where they or their relatives will have to pay the fees. But this statement seems to emanate from a booklet which was issued with a Circular on hospital discharge in 1989. What is the legal status of the booklet? (This guidance might anyway be cancelled shortly: see Chapter 13).

Whatever its status, Circular guidance is evidence of government policy and so useful to authorities when planning and defending their policies; to service users when challenging authorities; and even to judges when they are trying to interpret the implications of legislation.

One view is that Circulars 'themselves...have no legal effect whatever, having no statutory authority' (Wade 1989, p.860). However, this is not quite the whole picture. For example, the status of Circular-type guidance was considered by the House of Lords in the case of *Gillick v West Norfolk and Wisbech Area Health Authority 1986*. The Law Lords disagreed about whether the 'memorandum of guidance' (about contraceptive advice given by GPs) had been issued under statutory authority or not (Wade 1989, p.862).

In fact, it is arguable that most community care guidance is issued under s.7 of LASSA 1970, although often this is not made clear because much of the guidance does not state whether or not it is issued under this section. However, a Department of Health guide (about Children Act guidance) does state that documents and Circulars are 'usually issued' under s.7 of the LASSA 1970 (DH 1990a, p.2).

Even if of no formal legal force, it is possible that the courts might hold that a Circular gives rise to a reasonable or legitimate expectation. For example, in one 1984 immigration case, the Court of Appeal held that a Home Office Circular 'afforded the applicant a reasonable expectation that the procedures it set out...would be followed' (Parker LJ in *R v Secretary of State for the Home*

Department, ex p. Khan 1984). More recently, a judge referred to Circular guidance in order to interpret what the local authority's assessment should have been about (*R v Avon County Council, ex parte M 1993*).

Whatever the exact legal effect of Circulars, the health service ombudsman has criticised health authorities for failing to follow Circular guidance about hospital discharge procedure. For example: 'None of the hospital staff was aware of – nor did Infirmary policy apparently provide for – the requirement in the guidance...to set out in writing, before discharge to a nursing home, who would pay the fees. I criticise that significant omission' (HSC E62/93–94).

Circulars Containing Directions and Formal Guidance

Sometimes, however, and confusingly, Circulars are used as a vehicle to carry material of binding legal force; for example, Directions (see above), which do place duties on authorities, might be physically attached to a Circular.

Alternatively, Circulars sometimes expressly declare that they carry guidance made under a section of an Act of Parliament (see above). For example, Circular LAC(94)16 (about local authority inspection units) states that it is issued under section 7 of the LASSA 1970 and that it 'builds on and develops' the earlier policy guidance (DH 1990). The Under-Secretary of State for Health explained during the passing of the NHS and Community Care Bill that: 'General directions could be embodied in circulars, although we do not intend to issue circulars as directions. Most of the content of circulars would be guidance' (H89 1990).

Different Functions of Circular Guidance

A further and complicating factor is that there are different Circular series which have, in principle, slightly different functions. For example, health service Executive Letters (ELs), seen as communications between the NHS Management Executive and health authorities and trust managers, have little long-term significance. More long-term guidance for the health service, would normally be contained in Health Service Guidelines (HSGs).

Similarly, for social services communications, Local Authority Circulars (LACs) aim to be more significant, in terms of action and long-term policy, than Local Authority Social Services Letters (LASSLs) which tend to relate more to information provision and short-term actions. Letters from the chief inspector of the (CIs) are generally meant to be about good professional practice rather than policy.

Cancellation of Circulars

Sometimes Circular guidance carries a cancellation date. The effect of this is to nullify the Circular. In principle, if the message of the Circular is to continue, it has to be resurrected or continued in another Circular.

For example, health service executive letters (ELs), as already explained, are intended to have a short life only. Similarly, for some other Circulars: for example, social services LASSLs carrying details of annual grants, might be cancelled one year after issue. Sometimes longstanding Circulars might be cancelled: for example, LAC(93)10, concerning arrangements under the National Assistance Act 1948, cancelled a number of Circulars going as far back as 1974.

It is not always clear why a Circular is cancelled or what the effect of the cancellation is. For example, the fact that EL(92)20, about NHS equipment charges, was cancelled on 31st March 1993 does not mean that the message of the Circular is obsolete. This is because the Circular was essentially stating an interpretation of the law (NHS Act 1977): and the law has not changed.

Occasionally, the matter is even less clear. For example, an SSI Chief Inspector letter (CI(92)34) on community care assessment was cancelled on 31st March 1994 and has not been replaced or explicitly modified. The Circular carried advice on community care assessment and caused some controversy. However, despite the cancellation, it is to be presumed that the message in the guidance is not suddenly made obsolete only 13 months after it was issued. Therefore, it can probably still be relied on as at least sound evidence of government policy – until the particular messages contained in it are explicitly overruled or modified.

PRACTICE GUIDANCE

Community care practice guidance includes practice guidance for managers (SSI/SWSG(MG) 1991); for practitioners (SSI/SWSG(PG) 1991); and complaints procedure guidance (SSI 1991). The introductions to this guidance state that it is designed to 'help authorities to decide HOW to implement good practice locally'; whereas the policy guidance (see above) 'describes WHAT authorities need to do'.

Such guidance does not impose clear legal obligations on authorities, though presumably constitutes evidence of government policy, even though it is called 'practice' rather than 'policy' guidance. If this guidance is issued under s.7 of the LASSA 1970 – and it is not clear whether or not it is – then authorities have a duty to 'act under' it.

GUIDE AND ADVICE NOTE

An SSI (1991) document on information provision, called 'Getting the message across', refers to itself as a 'guide'. This is not issued explicitly under legislation, but still serves as an indication of government policy.

Long awaited guidance on charges by social services came in the form of brief guidance contained in a Circular (LAC(94)1), followed by more extensive advice in an SSI (1994) 'advice note'. The advice note is an indication of government policy but would seem to impose no legal obligations. This advice note has not been issued under s.7 of the LASSA 1970, because that section does not apply to the legislation (HASSASSA 1983) which gives authorities the power to charge.

SOCIAL SERVICES INSPECTORATE STANDARDS

The Social Services Inspectorate is a branch of the Department of.Health. It carries out inspections of local authority services, inspecting the quality of, and management arrangements for, services. The SSI has adopted a standards-based approach to inspection. The standards do not have a formal legal status, but are drawn variously from legislation, government policy, 'achievable best practice supported by research', and 'beliefs and values current in social services' (SSI 1993g, p.14).

SSI standards would seem to have no legal force in themselves. However, various consequences could flow from an SSI inspection using these standards. For example, the Secretary of State could order an inquiry as a result of concern raised by an inspection.

For local authorities it is clearly important to be able to distinguish which standards are based on legislation and guidance and which are simply proposed as good practice but with no statutory basis. The Association of Directors of Social Services (ADSS News 1994) has pointed to the possible confusion when on the one hand SSI measures performance against guidance, but on the other the courts rule that guidance is discretionary only (for example, the *Sutton* childminding and smacking case: see above).

HEALTH SERVICE: PATIENT'S CHARTER

The Patient's Charter is already in existence; there are currently proposals to introduce community care charters (DH 1994c).

The status of charters, generally, seems uncertain. For example, it has been stated of charters generally that the 'precise status of these documents is difficult to ascertain. Formally they are of no legal effect, being merely aspirational, but they could be characterised as customer service documents or customer guarantees...' (Barron, Scott 1992). The uncertain legal status of these documents has not prevented ample reference to the 'rights' arising from charters.

Circular guidance (HSG(92)36, annex 1, para 6.1) explained some 'common terms' in relation to the NHS Patient's Charter:

- **right:** 'a level of service to which the patient is entitled and which must always be delivered';
- **guarantee:** 'a right which is non-negotiable and met in every case, ie, if it becomes apparent that a provider is not going to deliver a guarantee then the purchaser will be expected to take immediate action';
- **standard:** 'a level of service which the patient can expect to be delivered other than in exceptional cases';
- **target:** 'a level of service which authorities are aiming to meet but which the patient cannot always expect to receive now. Targets can also be used as staging posts on the way to the full achievement of a standard';
- **performance:** 'a measure (in hard or soft data terms) of the level of achievement against agreed standards'.

QUOTES FROM PARLIAMENT

The book carries quotes from Parliament (proceedings of which can be read in a series called Hansard). There are two main reasons for carrying these quotes.

Parliament's Legislative Intention

Where the quoted person is a promoter of a Bill, the statements can shed light on what Parliament intended certain words and phrases to mean. This is particularly significant, since the House of Lords ruled in November 1992 that the law courts could refer to Hansard. Before this date, in theory at least, the courts could not do so. Certain conditions have to be met, before a court will allow reference to Hansard:

(1) 'legislation is ambiguous or obscure, or leads to an absurdity'; and

(2) 'the material relied on consists of one or more statements by a minister or other promoter of the Bill together if necessary with such other parliamentary material as is necessary to understand such statements and their effect'; and

(3) 'the statements relied on are clear' (Lord Browne-Wilkinson in *Pepper v Hart 1992*).

Useful Information about Policy

Quotes by members of the government, whenever made (before, during or after the passing of an Act) are an indication of government policy and sometimes convey useful information.

CHAPTER 7

LEGAL PRINCIPLES

KEY ISSUES

This chapter outlines the main legal principles referred to throughout this book. Practical use of these principles is dealt with in Chapter 24 on using legal remedies. It has been written for non-lawyers in an attempt to explain (at a basic level) concepts, of which many people – whether local/health authority staff or service users and their representatives – may have little experience or understanding.

It should again be emphasised that the definitions of some of these principles, as well as their application by the courts in the community care context (and other contexts), are to some extent unclear – thus adding to the uncertainties within the 'community care system as a whole' identified throughout this book.

In English law, cases can be brought either in *public law* or *private law*. There is sometimes confusion about the division between these two types of law; and sometimes uncertainty about which of them to use in particular circumstances. In the context of community care, the uncertainty is exacerbated because private law remedies such as negligence and breach of statutory duty (when an authority fails to perform its duty) are anyway not well-established in the personal social services field. Nevertheless, understanding the distinction between public and private law is important, because depending on the circumstances there can be advantages in using private law (see Chapter 24).

It is likely that **most community care court cases which reach the courts will involve public law rather than private law**. Public law in this context involves *judicial review* by the courts of decisions made by public authorities, such as local authorities or health authorities. Judicial review is used to decide whether an authority has reached a decision illegally or improperly (ie. whether it has made a decision based on *unreasonableness, illegality or unfairness (procedural impropriety)*). If decisions have not been properly or legally made, the courts do not directly overturn authorities' decisions but instead ask them to make the decisions again – this time properly or legally.

For example, if an authority decides a person is not entitled to attend a day centre for elderly people because he or she had red hair, a judge might find that the decision was unreasonably and probably illegally made. However, the judge would not rule that the person was entitled to attend the day centre, but would instead rule that the authority must take the decision again. The authority could still reach the same decision and deny the person access to the day centre, but would have to reach this decision on proper grounds – for example, that the person did not have a high priority need.

Therefore, judicial review is not directly about people's legal rights to services, but about their rights to legal and proper decision-making by authorities.

The courts can also make declarations. These are statements which can clarify legal questions (on which service provision can depend); for example, whether a person is 'ordinarily resident' in the area of an authority, or whether a proposal by an NHS Trust to sell walking frames is legal.

Private law remedies, in contrast to judicial review, are about people's explicit legal rights to services and to compensation for poor or non-delivery of those services. For the purposes of this book, there are two main grounds on which people could try to enforce private law rights: *negligence* and *breach of statutory duty*. Negligence involves the breach of a common law duty of care by an authority; whilst breach of statutory duty occurs when an authority does not perform its duty as laid down in legislation.

For example, a nurse who fails to read treatment notes and consequently administers too many injections which damage a person's cranial nerve might be negligent (*Smith v Brighton and Lewes HMC 1955:* see Brazier 1992). An authority which finds a homeless person to be in priority need, but then fails to provide housing for that person, might breach its statutory duty – since the legislation imposes a specific duty to provide housing in such circumstances.

However, apart from claims relating to negligence in the health care field (for example, concerning medical negligence), neither of these two private law remedies are well-established in the community care field.

PUBLIC LAW (JUDICIAL REVIEW)

This section explains the concepts of unreasonableness, illegality and procedural impropriety (unfairness).

Unreasonableness

Generally speaking, an authority would in principle, have to behave very waywardly in a very blatant manner in order for a court to rule that it has behaved unreasonably. This is because the authority would had to 'have come to a conclusion so unreasonable that no reasonable authority could ever come to it' (*Associated Provincial Picture Houses Ltd v Wednesbury Corporation 1947*). This is of course a circular and unhelpful – though famous – phrase. Sometimes the term 'irrational' is used instead by the courts; for example, an irrational decision 'is so outrageous in its defiance of logic or of accepted moral standards that no sensible person who had applied his mind to the question could have arrived at it' (Lord Diplock in *CCSU v Minister for the Civil Service 1984*).

Put yet another way, in a more recent case directly relevant to community care about provision of welfare services under the CSDPA 1970, the judge stated that an authority would act unreasonably if 'no local authority, properly discharging their duty and having regard to the facts before them, would have' acted in that particular way (*R v DHSS, ex p. Bruce 1986*). In another case against a health authority which had postponed the operation on a baby with a hole in its heart, the Court of Appeal accepted that the postponement was due to finite resources. The court also stated that it would only interfere if the authority had allocated its funds in an 'unreasonable' way (*In re Walker's Application 1987*).

It might seem that authorities could never be found by the courts to be unreasonable, unless they had 'taken leave of their senses'. However, in practice, the courts do find unreasonableness (Wade 1988, p.409). Recently, for example, a court found that a local authority had behaved unreasonably when it did not consult, and if necessary negotiate with, local residential home owners about the terms on which the authority would make contracts with them. In particular, the authority had behaved unreasonably because the proposed terms were more onerous than they had been in the past; because the consequence of them would be that most homes in the area would have to close down; and this would have defeated the purpose of the NHSCCA 1990 (*R v Cleveland County Council, ex p. Cleveland Care Homes Association 1993*).

It has also been suggested by a judge that if a person suffered epilepsy attacks with 'intense regularity' then it would be to 'fly in the face of reality' to suggest that the person was not 'vulnerable' (and therefore not in priority need) under homelessness legislation (Housing Act 1985, s.59). This might have been unreasonable if no other authority could have reasonably come to the same conclusion on the same evidence (see the discussion in: *R v Wandsworth BC, ex p. Banbury 1986*).

Illegality

Illegality occurs when an authority acts *ultra vires* – this means that it acts outside the legislation which determines its powers and duties. Obvious examples might be where an authority is under a duty to assess people who might have needs for community care services; but instead assesses all people (whether or not they need services) whose surnames have more than three syllables.

Another, real, example in the community care field occurred when the court ruled against an authority which had refused as a matter of policy even to consider assisting a disabled person with a privately arranged holiday. This was not a legal policy, because the legislation (CSDPA 1970) specifically refers not only to holidays arranged by local authorities but also to other (ie. privately arranged) holidays as well (*R v London Borough of Ealing, ex p. Leaman 1984*). As the judge explained, the authority had in effect excised certain words from the legislation: this was wrong. Thus, the authority's rigid policy was not based on the wording of the legislation – as it should have been.

However, as the judge also emphasised, he was not stating that the person should have been assisted with the holiday by the local authority but that the authority should have at least considered his application: 'it was quite wrong for them to deprive themselves of the opportunity of asking that question'. This illustrates judicial review well: judges do not directly enforce individuals' entitlements to services, but simply ensure that authorities make decisions for the right reasons and in a proper manner.

Unfairness

Fairness is another uncertain concept which the courts use – and is perhaps more difficult to explain than the basic concepts of unreasonableness and illegality. The local ombudsman and health service ombudsman also seem to apply considerations of fairness when reaching their findings. There are several different aspects to fairness (see below).

It is difficult to predict what standards of fairness courts might insist on in the community care field, since standards and approaches to fairness vary from situation to situation (Wade 1988, p.532). The right to natural justice seems to be based on a notion that a person's property and personal rights should be protected from unfair administrative decisions (*Ridge v Baldwin 1984*: see Wade 1988, p.529). One basic principle, however, is that the more important the issue to the claimant, then the more fairness the courts are likely to insist on. For example, if a community care dispute involved possible sale of a person's home (to pay for care), then the courts might insist on greater fairness. Or, for example, in the case of *R v Cleveland County Council, ex p. Cleveland Care Homes Association 1993*, one of the reasons the judge gave for finding that the local authority should have consulted (about its proposed new contracts for residential homes) was that the consequence of not doing so might have involved closure of many of the homes. This could have been disastrous to both home owners and residents alike.

(1) 'Legitimate Expectation'

Broadly, this applies when an authority has led people to believe that they are going to get certain services – and then changes its mind so that they do not get what they had been led to expect.

This principle is potentially relevant to many stages of community care. For example, if an authority publishes criteria of eligibility which state that people with certain needs will get a telephone then people who have those needs will have an 'expectation' of getting the telephone. Another example would be if local authorities state that they will assess people within certain time-limits and then fail to do so. Similarly, sudden and unexplained removal of services from people is likely to dash their expectations. Past practice might also give rise to legitimate expectation (ie, of two people with similar needs, the second might expect to be treated the same as the first was a month previously).

Community care guidance urges that authorities should give people plenty of information about assessment, services and eligibility. But if authorities follow this guidance incautiously, they could be at risk of creating 'rods for their own backs' – by making rash and unqualified 'promises' which they are unable to keep.

However, the rulings of judges about legitimate expectation are probably unpredictable, varying from case to case and from context to context (eg. immigration, prisons). The courts might sometimes rule more favourably on the principle (eg. *R v Secretary of State for the Home Department, ex p. Khan 1984; R v Liverpool Corporation, ex p. Liverpool Taxi Fleet Operators' Association 1972; Hong Kong v Ng Yuen Shiu 1983*); sometimes less so (*Re Findlay 1984; R v Torbay BC, ex p. Cleasby 1990; R v Knowsley BC, ex p. Maguire 1992*). For example, in the *Khan* case (about immigration), the court stated that the Minister could not withdraw from a statement or undertaking made to an individual (in a Circular letter) – without giving the person a hearing, and anyway only if overriding public interest required the withdrawal. On the other hand, in the *Maguire* case (about Taxi licences), the judge stated that even if a policy had been set out in a letter to an individual, and appeared to specify conditions, it should not be regarded as a contract to which the authority would be bound. It was merely an accurate representation of council policy at the time.

One important question is whether the judges will recognise not just procedural but also 'substantive' expectations (see eg. Wignall 1994). For example, a local authority might have a published policy stating that it will assess whether a person in need was living alone and – if so – then provide home help. The *procedural expectation* would be that the authority take into account whether the person is living alone; the *substantive expectation* would be that the person will actually get the home help, assuming he or she qualifies under the policy. The judges are more likely to uphold procedural than substantial expectation, since otherwise they run the risk of accusations of excessive intervention in local authority decision-making.

It will probably be rare for the courts to force authorities to adhere to their representations (eg their published information) as binding promises for the future, since otherwise authorities would find it very difficult to break with past conduct and to change their policies. But a court might not approve when an authority arbitrarily and informally departs from its policy (see eg. *R v Leeds CC, ex p. Hendry 1993*). However, it would be good practice for authorities to inform people promptly of changes in policy, and the local ombudsman might find maladministration where this does not happen: for example, if an authority has changed its policy about which types of houses (occupied or unoccupied) will be given priority for renovation grants (CLAW 92/741).

There are anyway safeguards for authorities. For instance, an authority could introduce words such as 'normally', or 'most of the time' when referring to who qualifies under its criteria of eligibility, or when stating the time-limits for assessment. For example, the recent draft document about community care charters suggests that standards could be about 'normal' performance and state that 90 per cent of letters will be answered within 10 working days (DH 1994c).

So as to be able to withdraw or reduce services – with less chance of offending against the principle of legitimate expectation – an authority could give people (when first in receipt of services) full information that service provision might in the future be subject to changing policies. People could not then claim to be surprised when, at a later date, reduction or withdrawal of services is proposed. At that later date, the authority could give full information about precisely why, when and how the services will be reduced or withdrawn. This would probably go some way to satisfying the legal principles of fairness and good administration.

In addition, although the courts are unlikely even to contemplate that any contractual obligations arise from local authority policies, cautious authorities could make it quite clear that their policies do not create any legal relations.

(2) 'Fettering Discretion'

This concept is a little confusing since it seems to contradict the idea of legitimate expectation. Legitimate expectation is about adhering to policies consistently; but at the same time authorities should not 'fetter their discretion'. This means that they must not be absolutely bound by policies and must be prepared to consider exceptions to those policies. In other words, an authority must not 'allow its policy to take its decisions for it' (Emery,Smythe 1986, p.195).

For example, in community care an over-rigid policy might mean that an authority never charges a particular category of user for services. (Central government, for example, might wish to challenge this on the grounds that the authority had fettered its discretion.) Another example might be an authority which never, as a matter of policy, provided facilities for people's comfort or convenience (a duty under the CSDPA 1970, s.2).

In the health service, a fettering of discretion might occur if a health authority decides never to provide continuing care for people with a neurological condition who are under 60 years old (see Chapter 13).

An instance of fettering of discretion occurred in a recent case concerning government guidance about the smacking of children. The local authority had thought it was bound absolutely by the guidance and so adopted a rigid policy which prevented it from deciding reasonably whether a particular childminder was a 'fit person'. The court ruled that the policy should not have been applied so strictly and automatically (*Sutton LBC v Davis 1994*).

(3) Consultation

Sometimes, judges will find that fairness requires that authorities should consult in certain circumstances. For example, a judge might find that if an authority is going to close a residential home, it has a duty to consult the residents before it does so. Sometimes the courts might not only state when there is a duty to consult but also what the consultation should consist of (*R v Durham CC, ex p Broxson 1992; R v Secretary of State for Health, ex p. US Tobacco International 1990*). For example, in the *Broxson* case, the court held that the elderly residents of a home should have been consulted at a reasonably early stage – not just five days before the proposed closure. At other times the courts might be less willing to prescribe the nature of the consultation (*R v Secretary of State for Social Services, ex p AMA 1986*).

Fair consultation has been held to include, for example:

- asking for views at the proposal stage (ie, before a final decision has been made);
- providing adequate information and time to respond in the circumstances, conscientiously considering the response;
- giving a fair opportunity to criticise constructively the proposal and to express preferences (see eg. *R v Brent LBC, ex p. Gunning 1985; R v LB Sutton, ex p. Hamlet 1986*).

(4) Procedural Fairness Generally

This might entail people having a right to:

(a) a *'fair hearing'* (eg, supplying people who cannot speak, or who cannot speak English, with interpreters or other means of 'speaking' such as electronic communication equipment);

(b) *information about decisions which affect them* (eg, the right to be told about how long they will wait for an assessment; and to be told if the expected length of waiting time alters);

(c) *information which the authority is using to reach an unfavourable decision* (eg, if an authority has seen somebody, who is meant to be housebound, walking down the road and on this basis decides not to provide services);

(d) *reasons for a decision* (eg, where a person is assessed as needing no services);

(e) *an absence of bias.* Fairness requires not only that decision-makers should not be biased but also that they should not *appear* to be biased, even if they are not *in fact* biased. (For example, this could occur if an assessor were related to the person being assessed.)

(5) Giving of Reasons for Decisions

Procedural fairness as a whole is an uncertain concept because, as already mentioned, it is difficult to predict what sort of standards of fairness the courts will apply in different circumstances and contexts. For example, the courts have stated firmly in 1993 that 'the law does not at present recognise a general duty to give reasons for an administrative decision' – but that the duty can be implied in 'appropriate circumstances' (*R v Secretary of State for the Home Department, ex p. Doody 1993*).

Thus, whether or not the courts would insist that reasons must be given for community care decisions is not wholly clear – but generally speaking, authorities would probably be well-advised to have reasons to hand.

If a dispute went to judicial review, the court would probably expect sufficiently full reasons to be given to enable it to decide whether any procedural errors had been made (see, for example, *R v Lancashire CC, ex p. Huddleston 1986*); so the presence of reasons from the start would give an authority better prospects in court. Without them, the charge of arbitrary or faulty decision-making might be more difficult to refute.

There are a number of cases from other fields of law which suggest that reasons should generally be given in some circumstances. One involved the Civil Service Appeal Board (*R v Civil Service Appeal Board, ex p. Cunningham 1991*). In another (*R v Higher Education Funding Council, ex p. Institute of Dental Surgery 1994*), the judge stated that reasons must be given where the interest at stake is so important that fairness dictates that reasons must be given. For instance, in community care, an important interest might arise when the selling of a person's house is at stake in a dispute about financing residential care. It has also been stated by a judge that there is a general duty to give reasons whenever 'the statutorily impregnated administrative process is infused with the concept of fair treatment to those potentially affected by administrative action' (*R v Lambeth LBC, ex p. Walters 1993* – about homelessness). In another case about homelessness (where the legislation (Housing Act 1985, s.64) imposes a duty on authorities to give reasons for adverse decisions – it should be noted there is no similar duty in community care legislation – the court stated that the giving of reasons was a valuable discipline; enabled applicants to understand why they were unsuccessful; and enabled an assessment to be made of whether an appeal or judicial review might be successful (*R v Islington LBC, ex p. Trail 1993*).

The reasons would probably have to deal with the points which have been raised in the case; would not necessarily have to be long; but should be more than just a paraphrase of the words in the legislation (Emery, Smythe 1986, p.211). For example, if an authority had to give reasons why it was not 'satisfied' (under s.2 of the CSDPA) that a person needed welfare services, its reasons for not providing services should not simply refer to the fact that it was not satisfied. Similarly, under the housing homelessness legislation (HA 1985,ss.59,64), simple recital of the four 'priority routes' to qualify for accommodation would fail to meet the duty to give reasons (*R v Islington LBC, ex p. Trail 1993*).

Even if the courts continue to debate when reasons should be given, the local ombudsman is clear that good administration requires that reasons be given for adverse decisions (see eg. CLAE 1993 on axioms of good administration).

(6) Identification of Procedures Required by Fairness

Where legislation describes not only duties but also procedures, then it is easier for the courts to apply an idea of fairness. They can simply refer to the legislation (eg the Directions about the complaints procedures). In addition, even where legislation does lay down procedures, the judges might choose to add their own requirements if they think necessary (Wade 1988, p.533).

However, most community care procedures have been created by guidance which does not impose statutory duties on authorities. Nevertheless, judges, looking for indications of fair procedures in community care might still look to this guidance – but it will be difficult to predict in what circumstances the judges will do this. For example, the courts might think that guidance about provision of a written care plan simply states good practice only, but think that other guidance, stating that people with communication difficulties should be able to participate in assessment (see eg. DH 1990, para 3.21), constitutes legally fair procedure.

PRIVATE LAW

The grounds for private law remedies in the community care field might, in principle, be either *negligence* or *breach of statutory duty*. These principles are explained below. However, neither of these remedies are well-established in the community care (social services) field, and so are not, at present, likely to succeed. (Negligence is established in the health care field: for example, medical negligence.)

The reason for this is that private law claims depend on the existence of identifiable and potentially enforceable legal rights – and, to date, the courts have not generally recognised such private law rights in the personal social services (community care) field.

However, it is important for all concerned to be aware of these remedies because they remain possible channels of redress; and because there can be advantages in using private instead of public law.

Negligence

Negligence claims are private law matters and are based on 'common law', rather than on 'statute law'. In other words, a negligence claim depends on a general 'duty of care' which a practitioner has towards service users.

A claim in negligence depends on somebody (eg a doctor) owing a 'duty of care' to somebody else; the first person 'breaching' that duty of care (ie, being careless); and the second person suffering harm as a result of the carelessness. People can be awarded damages in money if they win negligence cases. This book does not deal with this subject to any depth, since it is covered already by many other books.

Negligence Not Well-Established in Community Care

It should be noted that the principle of negligence is not well-developed in the area of social services, compared to the health care field where the negligence principle applies to a wide range of services and practitioners, including doctors, nurses, therapists, pharmacists and so on (Nelson-Jones 1990, p.25). For example, in the child care field, the courts have argued recently that neither individual local authority staff, nor the authority itself, have a duty of care to service users. The argument was that *local authority 'clients' are not the same as health service 'patients'*, because the former have had services 'thrust upon them' – and that *the duty of care owed by the local authority staff is not to the clients but to the local authority*. This particular argument then went on to deny that the authority had a duty of care because:

- the duty of care must exist either in 'common law' or in the legislation;
- it does not exist in the common law because local authorities do not have 'by the common law any right or duty to interfere in the lives of children within its area';
- it does not exist in the legislation (in this case, child care legislation);
- *therefore*, the authorities have no duty of care (see eg. *M v Newham LBC and Others 1994; P and others v Bedfordshire CC 1994*).

Sometimes the courts might also take a similar approach to that taken in breach of statutory duty cases (see below). If there is an *alternative remedy*, such as an appeals procedure in the legislation (compare the community care complaints procedure), the courts might deny a claim in negligence (*Jones v Department of Employment 1988*).

Possibility of Negligence Claims in Community Care

Although, as stated above, negligence does not seem established in the community care field, it is not necessarily ruled out.

For example, in a recent case against an education authority (*E v Dorset CC and other actions 1994*), the Court of Appeal stated that a negligence claim was at least possible in principle against the authority. The court thought that local authority staff such as psychologists, teachers and officials receiving reports and making decisions could, *in principle*, have a duty of care to the people they assess. The position is unclear and the House of Lords is to consider this case (and others about the same issue) towards the end of 1994.

One of the arguments used in court was that a psychologist interviewing and advising a child was acting much like a doctor. This argument was therefore apparently attempting to make a link with the established principle of negligence in the health care field. This is most relevant to community care since, for example, an increasing amount of personal care is being delivered by social services departments. Therefore, it might be difficult for courts to distinguish between a community nurse (health service) who scalds a person in a bath and a personal care assistant (social services) who does exactly the same thing.

Similarly, in another case involving a baby injured by a childminder, the Court of Appeal did not find that the authority had acted negligently by not having previously deregistered the childminder. However, it did find the local authority and the particular officer concerned liable for a *negligent misstatement*; the nursing/childminder adviser had in effect recommended the childminder even though he knew, or should have known, that the baby would be at risk (*T v Surrey CC 1994*). Some years ago, negligence was established in another case when damage to property near a children's community home was caused after a social worker had failed to warn the home of a child's tendency to start fires. The court found negligence on the basis that the social worker's behaviour had *not* been part of the local authority's administrative, decision-making powers (with which the court would have been reluctant to interfere) (*Vicar of Writtle v Essex CC 1979*).

In the context of the CSDPA 1970 and National Assistance Act 1948, an earlier Court of Appeal case also suggested that development of negligence in the social services area is possible. The case (*Wyatt v Hillingdon LBC 1978*) is often cited as limiting people's rights to challenge authority's decisions – and it did deny that people could sue authorities for breach of statutory duty (see below) under the legislation. However, the judge did suggest that a negligence case might have been possible if a home help had dropped a person and injured her; or if the authority had provided a defective bed which collapsed and caused injury.

(The question of local authority liability generally (ie, not just in the social services/community care field) is to some extent uncertain and complex. In the past, the courts have sometimes been more likely to consider liability when the negligence is about *implementing decisions* (for example, installing a hoist badly), rather than *making decisions* (for example, whether people with a certain level of need qualify for hoists at all). This is because the courts do not like to interfere with the discretion of authorities to make decisions in the light of local needs, priorities and resources.

One distinction between decision-making and decision-implementing was described (*Anns v Merton LBC 1978*) as the difference between *policy* and *operational* actions and decisions. However, this distinction itself can be difficult to make in individual cases; and more recently it seems that the judges might not put so much store by the distinction. They might instead decide on grounds of public policy whether or not there should be a duty of care – rather than on the grounds of whether the act was of the operational or policy type (*Rowling v Takaro Properties 1988; Hill v Chief Constable fo West Yorkshire 1988*; and see eg. Dugdale, Stanton 1989,pp.145–151; Buckley 1993, p.245). For example, they might simply not wish to interfere with the statutory functions and discretion of local authorities, and so decide that there can be no duty of care (see section immediately above)).

Aspects of Negligence Claims

Negligence claims can be difficult to win, even in the health care field where negligence is well-established in principle. There are a number of possible complications when suing in negligence, and it is necessary to confirm:

- *whom to sue* (this can be complicated where there are purchasers, providers, contractors, sub-contractors, ordinary employees – some of whom may be blaming each other for the accident: for example, a slippery floor in hospital (Brazier 1992, p.142));

- *questions of vicarious liability* (for example, an employer is generally liable for employees', but much less strictly so for independent contractors', negligence (see eg. Jones 1991, pp.252–273)). This is particularly relevant in a health service and social services of ever more purchasers, providers and 'contracted out' services;

- *carelessness/negligence* (for professionals, it has to be shown that they have acted carelessly; that is that they have breached their duty of care by acting beneath the standard of 'the ordinary skilled man exercising and professing to have that special skill. A man need not possess the highest expert skill; it is well established that it is sufficient if he exercises the ordinary skill of an ordinary competent man exercising that particular art' (*Bolam v Friern Hospital Management Committee 1957*));

- *expert evidence* (in establishing whether a professional has breached his or her duty of care, expert evidence is likely to be required; this can lead to protracted, expensive and inconclusive disputes: see eg. Brazier 1992, p.155);

- *causation* (ie, showing that the carelessness caused the harm (eg a doctor might negligently turn away a person with arsenic poisoning who then dies; however, if the expert evidence is that the person would have probably died anyway, then the doctor is not liable because his or her negligence did not cause the death: *Barnett v Chelsea v Kensington Hospital Management Committee 1969*). Proving causation can be very difficult and complicated (see eg. Jones 1991, pp.124–160, Balen 1994));

- *type of harm* (negligence claims are strongest where personal injury or damage to property has been caused. They are less strong where the harm is only economic/financial, or where the person has suffered 'nervous shock' which leads to a medically recognised mental or physical illness. The law is complicated in this area.)

Breach of Statutory Duty

Breaches of statutory duty occur when authorities have not performed their duties in law. The present position seems to be that, in the main, it will be very difficult to obtain private law remedies for breach of statutory duty in the community care field. The main reason for this is that claimants have to establish that the relevant legislation actually creates legal 'rights' for individuals and that these rights are based on authorities' 'absolute' duties to do certain things. The judges are unlikely, it seems, to recognise such rights and absolute duties in the community care field.

For example, in the case of *Wyatt v Hillingdon LBC 1978* (concerning the National Assistance Act 1948 and the CSDPA 1970 in relation to home help), the judge (Lane LJ) stated emphatically that a 'statute such as this which is dealing with the distribution of benefits – or, to put it perhaps more accurately, comforts to the sick and disabled – does not in its very nature give rise to an action by the disappointed sick person. It seems to me quite extraordinary that if the local authority, as is alleged here, provided, for example, two hours less home help than the sick person considered herself entitled to that that can amount to a breach of statutory duty which will permit the sick person to claim a sum of monetary damages by way of breach of statutory duty'.

Similarly, in the health service field, where a shortage of hospital facilities caused orthopaedic patients pain and suffering through waiting for treatment, the court found it 'impossible to pinpoint anywhere a breach of statutory duty…it all turns on the question of financial resources. If the money is not there then the services cannot be met in one particular place'. The duty was only to provide services to such extent as was necessary (*R v Secretary of State for Social Services, ex parte Hincks 1979*: quoted in Finch 1994, p.154).

The availability of private law actions (resulting in damages) for breach of statutory duty is a complicated field of law – especially outside of the health and safety field where such actions are relatively well-established in principle (Jones 1991, p.274; Stanton 1986; Wade 1988, p.772; Emery, Smythe 1986, p.265). It seems to be accepted that breach of statutory duty is a very unlikely ground for a successful private law action in the community care field, although this does not stop people continuing to bring legal actions on these grounds. In fact, the House of Lords is due to consider the issue again in late 1994 in cases from the local authority field.

Lack of Absolute Duties and Enforceable Private Law Rights in the Community Care Field

In the community care field, there is generally little indication that Parliament intended to give, or that the courts are likely to find, absolute duties and rights which could give rise to private law actions for breach of statutory duty. For example, when the NHS and Community Care Bill was passing through Parliament, the government resisted successfully amendments designed to enforce service provision by authorities once people's needs had been assessed – thus probably precluding claims that the legislation was creating absolute rights to services (H95, 1990).

Therefore the community care legislation seems no exception to other local authority legislation in which the judges are likely to find imprecise duties couched in 'subjective' language. This means that such duties are triggered by local authorities' discretionary decision-making – and so the courts cannot, or choose not to, identify absolute individual rights in the legislation. For example, the duty to assess (under the NHSCCA 1990, s.47) is qualified by the fact that a person must *appear* to the authority to be in *need*. There is no absolute right to the assessment – it is up to the authority to decide. Alternatively, the courts might state that the duty on an authority is to the population in general, rather than to particular individuals (see Chapter 6) – and so presume generally that people do not have individual, enforceable rights (eg. *R v ILEA, ex p. Ali and Murshid 1990; R v Mid-Glamorgan CC, ex p. Greig 1988*).

Nevertheless, in the past the courts have sometimes recognised individual, enforceable, private law rights – if it has appeared to the judges that Parliament intended to benefit particular individuals (see eg. *Meade v Haringey 1979, Bradbury v Enfield 1967*). However, the courts have now stated that even evidence of Parliament's intention to benefit or protect particular individuals is not enough – there must be additional evidence that Parliament intended that *individual legal rights of action* be given to those individuals (eg. *Hague v Deputy Governor of Parkhurst Prison 1991*).

For example, it has been stated in 1994 (in two child care cases heard together) by the Court of Appeal that even if it is clear that the legislation was designed for the 'protection of the interests and welfare of children', this is not enough to infer that Parliament intended to give individual children or their parents rights of legal action against authorities. (The two cases were about an authority not investigating facts concerning child abuse properly; and about an authority not placing children on the child protection register or taking other action, in the face of overwhelming evidence that the children were at risk.)

The judge's reasoning was two-fold:

- 'the duties imposed on local authorities were framed in *terms too general and unparticular* to lend themselves at all readily to direct enforcement by individuals';
- 'the local authorities were accorded *so large an area* for the exercise of their *subjective judgement* as to suggest that direct enforcement by individuals was not contemplated' (our italics). (*M v Newham LBC and others/P and others v Bedfordshire CC 1994*, Sir Thomas Bingham MR).

In another similar case (where an authority failed to deregister a childminder who then apparently injured another child), the judge approved the statement that 'only in certain exceptional circumstances' would a person (or a representative) be able to claim damages for a breach of statutory duty – even if the person had been badly injured as a result of the authority failing to do its duty. In this case, the duty in the legislation was to ensure that only people who were fit to look after children under five years old should be registered as childminders (*T v Surrey CC and Others 1994*: approving statement in *R v Mid-Glamorgan Council, ex p. Greig 1988*).

Even if a court were to find that an authority had breached its duty, it is likely to deny a person a right to claim damages; at most it might make an order ensuring that the authority do its duty (see eg. *E v Dorset CC 1994*).

Alternative Remedies to Breach of Statutory Duty Claims

Another major obstacle to the recognition of private law claims for breach of statutory duty is that the courts tend to presume that if there is an *alternative remedy* in the legislation then Parliament must anyway have intended to exclude private law rights. For example, in community care, alternative remedies include the complaints procedure and the powers of the Secretary of State to declare an authority in default of its duty (see Chapter 23). The courts might state that people have to use these remedies and that they cannot bring private law legal action.

Two earlier cases involving the National Assistance Act 1948 and therefore relevant to community care illustrate this principle. For example, in the case of *Wyatt v Hillingdon LBC 1978* (concerning the National Assistance Act 1948 and the CSDPA 1970 in relation to home help and practical assistance in the home), the judge (Lane LJ) stated emphatically that an action for damages on grounds of breach of statutory duty was not appropriate, but that the default powers were the appropriate remedy.

An earlier case (*Southwark LBC v Williams 1971*), about providing accommodation to people in urgent need under the NAA 1948, s.21, demonstrates the same approach by the courts. Here the judge (Lord Denning) stated that: 'It cannot have been intended by Parliament that every person who was in need of temporary accommodation should be able to sue the local authority for it'.

The courts have also stated that just because legislation does *not* contain an alternative remedy for breach of statutory duty, it does not follow that an individual has a right to damages (*T v Surrey CC 1994*). Thus, one more obstacle is placed in the way of individuals seeking damages for breach of statutory duty.

Possible Identification of Private Law Rights

As already stated, a private law action for breach of statutory duty would have to identify clear, individual, enforceable rights. Generally, these cannot be found in welfare legislation. However, there are some *possible* arguments in favour of finding private law rights in the welfare field.

For example, s.47(2) of the NHS and Community Care Act 1990 refers to people's 'rights' under s.4 of the DP(SCR)A 1986, concerning request for assessment for welfare services. A judge has held that aftercare services under the Mental Health Act 1983 are mandatory; and in the education field, mandatory duties have been recognised by the courts to the extent that authorities must arrange for the provision of what has been recorded on statements of educational needs (see eg, *R v Secretary of State for Education and Science, ex p. E 1992*).

The courts are now formally allowed to look at Hansard to divine what Parliament's intention might have been when an Act of Parliament was passed. In relation to the CSDPA 1970, this could be useful for service users, since various statements made at the time might support the intended existence of 'rights'. For example, Alf Morris MP (the author of the bill) spoke of the 'mandatory' nature of what is now section 2 of that Act (H96); whilst its sponsor in the House of Lords, the Earl of Longford, stated that CSDPA services would in the future 'be available as of right. I cannot say that too often. We are going a long way to establish the mandatory instead of the permissive principle. No longer will the disabled have to go round cap in hand...The benefits will belong to them as a matter of law' (H97). Even so, a question remains about whether such statements might be interpreted as referring to *individual* disabled people's private law rights, or merely to benefits *generally* for disabled people as a whole.

Community care legislation does not actually state that private law actions cannot arise; and in response to the argument that other remedies exist, it might be possible to argue that neither the Secretary of State's default powers nor the complaints procedure, are designed to deal with breach of statutory duty.

Failure to Implement a Decision and Breach of Duty
The courts have sometimes attempted to distinguish between authorities' decisions and the implementation of those decisions. The decision-making has been held to be a public law matter; the decision-implementing to be a private law matter (ie, giving private law rights to a person).

For example, in the housing (homelessness) field the courts have stated that a local authority's decision about whether a person should get services (housing) was a *public law matter*. However, once the authority had made the decision in favour of the person, then the authority had a duty to implement the decision – and this, second and derivative, duty was a *private law* matter (*Cocks v Thanet DC 1982; Thornton v Kirklees BC 1979*). In the health care field, the courts have also identified private law rights very close to public law issues. The case concerned a GP's right to payment from the local Family Practitioner Committee. The Court of Appeal found that if the Committee had failed to include the GP's name on its list, then the issue would have been in public law; but that the GP's claim for payment was based on a private law contractual right (*Roy v Kensington & Chelsea and Westminster FPC 1992*. For the above, see McLeod 1993, pp.62–64).

A community care example might – there has not been an actual case on this issue – occur in relation to s.2 of the CSDPA 1970 (see p.156). If an authority had decided that a person needed assistance with a holiday and that it was necessary for the authority to provide it, then failure to assist with the holiday might give rise to a private law right. This would be because the authority would not have performed its duty to implement the decision. However, failure to decide in the first place whether the person needed the holiday would be a public law matter because it would be about *decision-making* (see eg, *R v London Borough of Ealing, ex p. Leaman 1986*); as opposed to decision-implementing.

For example, the duty to assess people under s.47 of the .NHS and Community Care Act 1990 involves *decision-making* by the local authority. This is because the duty depends on whether it 'appears' to the local authority that a person is in 'need' – that is the authority has to *decide* whether a person is in need. Therefore, the judges would probably state that a challenge about this duty would be a public law matter.

(However, in theory at least, if the duty was simply to assess any person at all – whether or not the authority thought he or she was in need – then it might be argued that the person had a right in private law, since there would be no decision involved. For example, in a case involving the Inner London Education Authority (*Ettridge v Morrell 1986*), the Court of Appeal found that the ILEA's failure to perform its duty (by not providing election candidates with rooms for meetings), gave individuals private law rights. There was no decision-making involved (Wade 1988, p.682)).

Thus, once an authority had decided that it was necessary for it to provide services under s.2 of the CSDPA 1970 – and then did not provide them – a private law action for breach of statutory duty might arise. It should be borne in mind, however, that even in such circumstances, there might be a defence for the local authority if it were to argue lack of resources (see p.154). This defence might maintain that the authority's breach of duty is part of its decision-making and discretionary powers (here, allocation of resources); and therefore the courts should not interfere (except in the extreme circumstances of unreasonableness, illegality or unfairness).

DECLARATIONS

Declarations are available generally in both private and public law (Wade 1988, p.597). However, where public authorities are concerned, the courts are likely to treat an application for a declaration as a public law matter.

When making a declaration, the court can, for example, state what a person's qualification, status or rights are – for example, whether he or she is 'ordinarily resident' within a particular authority's area. Or the court could state whether an authority's action, or proposed action, is authorised in law (Wade 1988, p.595); for example, it could declare that an NHS Trust's proposal to charge for surgical footwear would be illegal.

Although the declaration might not seem to be a dramatic remedy in itself, its consequence might be that the dispute is resolved because the legal position (and the inevitable outcome of any dispute) has been made clear to both parties. For instance, in the example above, it would be that the NHS Trust cannot charge for the footwear because the NHS Act 1977 does not authorise it.

Nevertheless, the public law courts might stop short of using declarations to state explicitly that a particular person is entitled to services. For example, in a case about education grants and ordinary residence, the court found that the students were ordinary residents, but it would not declare that they were entitled to grants – because, on judicial review principles, it was for the authority and not the court to take that decision (*R v Barnet LBC, ex p. Shah, 1983*). On the other hand, in a more recent case (*R v London Borough of Redbridge, ex p. East Sussex CC 1992*) about provision of residential accommodation for two children with learning disabilities, the judge appeared to go one step further and state not only where the children were resident, but also which local authority had the duty to provide the accommodation.

Part III

Community Care Process

CHAPTER 8

ACCESS TO COMMUNITY CARE ASSESSMENT

KEY ISSUES

The NHS and Community Care Act 1990 (NHSCCA) makes assessment a duty and a service in its own right. This assessment service is pivotal to the provision of a number of community care services, including both residential and non-residential care services. A full list of services can be found in Chapter 4 Thus, access to assessment is a crucial part of the whole community care process.

In order to gain access to assessment there are a number of considerations which control who will be assessed, when they will be assessed and what sort of assessment they will get. The legislation states that the local authority has to decide whether a person appears to be in possible need of community care services (if not, there is no duty to assess). In practice, the authority is likely to go on to decide whether a person:

- is a high priority (if not, the person might have to wait for an assessment);
- needs a high or low level of assessment (this will determine how comprehensive and wide-ranging the assessment is).

The way in which local authority staff operate initial screening is not legally prescribed, but such screening can act as a powerful filter. This is particularly so because (within fairly wide limits) local authorities can create and apply their own definitions of terms such as 'need', 'priorities', 'levels' of assessment, 'urgency' – and so on. Thus, although almost only a 'pre-assessment' stage, screening can determine what happens to people. It is a tool which authorities can use to regulate both the amount and level of demand made on them.

These considerations, regulating access to assessment, amount to some of the 'uncertainties' identified in the introduction to the book. As also pointed out there, such uncertainties sometimes give rise to disputes. For example, the local ombudsman has frequently investigated the long waits which can result when people are deemed 'low priority'.

How restrictively an authority can define what it means by need at this pre-assessment stage is a little unclear. In principle, so long as the policy is not unreasonable or illegal, there may be little problem. In practice, it might be more difficult to set a restrictive definition since the duty is triggered by the word 'appears' which is broad; and because authorities are confronted with the vicious circle that people's needs cannot really be 'known' until they have been assessed.

BASIC DUTY TO ASSESS

Local authority assessment is a duty and service in its own right. It is the process around which the whole community care system revolves. Legislation states that if a person appears to be in need of community care services which a local social services authority can provide, then there is a duty to assess that person. If a person does not appear to be in such need, social services can refuse to make the assessment.

There is probably some uncertainty about the exact circumstances in which a local authority can, and in practice is likely to, refuse assessment. Generally speaking, refusal is unlikely in most circumstances but if a person is judged low priority and put on a long waiting list (see below), this might be tantamount to a refusal to assess. Uncertainty about a person's ordinary residence might in practice give rise to a reluctance to assess (see below), although guidance states that this should not happen.

Authorities can temporarily provide services for people they think are in urgent need without carrying out an assessment.

EXTRACTS

Legislation (NHS and Community Care Act 1990,s.47) states that:

> **(duty to assess)** 'where it appears to a local authority that any person for whom they may provide or arrange for the provision of community care services may be in need of any such services, the authority – (a) shall carry out an assessment of his needs for those services...' (s.47(1)(a)).

> **(urgent assessment)** 'Nothing in this section shall prevent a local authority from temporarily providing or arranging for the provision of community care services for any person without carrying out a prior assessment of his needs in accordance with the preceding provisions of this section if, in the opinion of the authority, the condition of that person is such that he requires those services as a matter of urgency' (s.47(5)).

Policy guidance states that where:

> 'an individual's care needs appear to fall entirely outside the responsibility of the local authority it will usually be sufficient to refer the person to the appropriate agency and to notify that agency accordingly. A record should be made of such

referrals. Care should be taken that individuals are not repeatedly referred from one agency to another' (DH 1990, para 3.34)

DISCUSSION
Appearance of Need
The duty to assess seems to be broad, since only an 'appearance' of possible need is required. The duty falls short however of 'assessment on request'.

Circular guidance (CI(92)34) states that: 'authorities do not have a duty to assess on request, but only where they think that the person may be in need of services they provide' (para 5). During the passage of the NHS and Community Care Bill, the government resisted making 'assessment on request' a duty; since where 'the local authority deems that there is no case to take the assessment further, it may choose not to do so'. To impose a duty to assess on request would be to impose a 'wholly unrealistic burden' on local authorities (H17 1990).

Even so, Baroness Blatch added that the duty was 'virtually' assessment on request, since the clause 'requires any local authority to carry out an assessment of any person for whom it appears the authority might arrange community care services. The provision was intended to be as wide-ranging as possible and not to deny anybody making a request for an assessment the opportunity to have one' (H18 1990).

Defining a High Level of Need at Planning and Policy Level
The term 'need' is left undefined by the legislation. In principle, it is therefore open to authorities to set a level of need which controls how many people are eligible for assessment – in effect, how many people appear to be in need of services.

For example, the Health Committee (1993,vol.1,p.xxi) has reported its concern that assessment can be restricted by authorities: some 'local authorities have limited access to assessments so that only those with a certain level of need will be assessed. This is done through the application of criteria which assign individuals to particular categories depending on their level of need... Very strict criteria could lead to an apparent very high level of success in meeting assessed needs, whereas if the criteria are broader and thus the gateway to assessment wider, it is less likely that the authority will appear to be meeting all the needs of those it assesses'.

Nevertheless, the courts have ruled that 'need' includes future need; and, in another case, that if a person with learning difficulties is being assessed, then the authority must assess the individual needs of the person (*R v Avon CC, ex p. M 1993*). In this latter case, the court also held that 'psychological need' can be part of a person's needs.

In the first case, a local authority refused to assess on the grounds that the person did not need community care services but only had 'a possible need for services at an unspecified time in the future'. It concerned a prisoner who could not gain parole from the Parole Board without a prior assessment – but the authority would not assess. Eventually, the parties came to an agreement before the hearing. The court approved the agreement that the authority should carry out the assessment. The effect of this was that the authority had to assess for possible future need as well as for present need (*R v Mid Glamorgan County Council ex p Miles: see Clements 1994*).

Limits to Definition of Need

How restrictively an authority can define what it means by need at this pre-assessment stage is unclear. Apart from blatantly unreasonable or illegal (see Chapter 7 for the meaning of these terms) definitions, it would be difficult to challenge authorities on the principle of a restrictive definition. For example, it would be unreasonable to state that only women can be in need; and it would be illegal to consider need for only some, as opposed to all, of the community care services defined in the Act. However, a policy which stated that only people who appear to be at (high) risk would be deemed to appear to be in need, might be more difficult to challenge.

However, there may be a practical, rather than a theoretical, difficulty for authorities in setting a restrictive definition of need. This is because of the existence of a vicious circle: before assessment has taken place, it is difficult to tell what people's needs actually are and just how much risk they are at. It might therefore be a bold authority which stated, even before assessment, that large numbers of people did not even appear to be in need – especially if most other authorities employed much broader definitions of need.

On the other hand, it would not be surprising to find that, as a system of rationing develops, definitions of need become (over the next few years) relatively more restrictive as a matter of normal practice in authorities.

Resources and the Duty to Assess an Individual

There is a question about whether a local authority can take account of resources, at an individual's level (as opposed to policy and planning level: see above), when faced with the duty to assess.

An authority might wish to take account of resources in two ways: first, to refuse assessment altogether; second, to determine the type or level of assessment. There is a view (Gordon 1993,p.15) that a local authority cannot legally take account of resources to refuse assessment to an individual. However, it is possible that the courts might be reluctant to rule against an authority solely because it doesn't have enough money. On the other hand, the local ombudsman has on occasion explicitly rejected lack of resources as a reason for non-assessment under the DP(SCR)A 1986 and CSDPA 1970 (eg. CLAE 92/C/0670,p.7).

In any case, it is possible that, most of the time, authorities will not explicitly deny assessment to people but instead will put them on waiting lists (see eg. SSI 1994g,p.16).

In practice, there is some evidence that resources are in fact taken into account when, for example, individuals 'are frequently being told that they can't have an assessment because there is no money to pay for the services they might need' (NFHA 1993,p.12). What is also at issue is at what point a long waiting time for assessment becomes, in effect, a refusal to assess. The implications of waiting times are explained below.

Wait for Assessment

Authorities are likely to set priorities for assessment, which means that people who are deemed to be of lower priority might have to wait some time for an assessment. It is unclear at what point a long wait for assessment becomes a refusal to assess, and the local ombudsman has regularly considered this question: examples of investigations are given later in this chapter.

Groups of People to Whom Community Care Services Apply

Legislation does not refer to specific groups of people covered by community care services: for example, people dependent on drugs or alcohol, with HIV/AIDS, or vulnerable due to domestic violence or physical and sexual abuse. A reason for doing so would have been to ensure that these groups are not neglected in favour of other groups. The reason for *not* actually doing so, given by government during the NHSCCA 1990s Parliamentary passage, is that 'the policy objectives of the White Paper are to help to improve services to all vulnerable people... We should be loath to write in the specific groups for which services shall be provided, because we are considering the overall, comprehensive range of services for those who need community care' (H19 1990)

HEALTH AND HOUSING AUTHORITY PARTICIPATION IN COMMUNITY CARE ASSESSMENT

When a local authority is assessing a person for community care services and it thinks that the person might need health or housing services, then it must notify the health or housing authority (or both) and invite it to assist in the assessment. However, neither the health or housing authority has a duty to accept the invitation.

(Health and housing services are not defined legally as 'community care services'. The legislation does not state that health and housing authorities must accept the invitation. This sums up the elusive position of health and housing services in the community care legislative framework – they are both present and 'not present').

EXTRACTS
Legislation states:

(community care assessment) 'If at any time during the assessment of the needs of any person under subsection (1)(a) above, it appears to a local authority':

(health service) '(a) that there may be a need for the provision to that person by such District Health Authority as may be determined in accordance with regulations of any services under the National Health Service Act 1977, or'

(housing authority) '(b) that there may be a need for the provision to him of any services which fall within the functions of a local housing authority (within the meaning of the Housing Act 1985) which is not the local authority carrying out the assessment';

(notification) 'the local authority shall notify that District Health Authority or local housing authority'

(invitation) 'and invite them to assist, to such extent as is reasonable in the circumstances, in the making of the assessment; and, in making their decision as to the provision of services needed for the person in question, the local authority shall take into account any services which are likely to be made available for him by that District Health Authority or local housing authority' (NHSCCA 1990, s.47(3)).

Policy guidance states:

'the aim of assessment should be to ensure that all needs for care services are considered. Collaboration with health authorities and local housing authorities will therefore be of particular importance. Section 47(3) of the Act will require SSDs to bring apparent housing and health care needs to the attention of the appropriate authority and invite them to assist in the assessment. Arrangements for assessment and care management need to be addressed jointly by local agencies and roles and responsibilities agreed within those arrangements. As well as considering health and housing needs, staff from the local housing and health authorities may be able to offer expert advice on, and contribute to, the assessment of community care needs... All relevant agencies should be involved in the assessment process before commitments are made...' (DH 1990, paras 3.32–3.33).

DISCUSSION
Appearance and Need

The local authority's (social services) duty to notify health and housing authorities is subject to two judgements about 'appearance' and 'need'. The first governs whether the local authority assesses a person for community care services at all. The second governs whether, during that assessment, it then 'appears' (for a second time) to the local authority that there might be a 'need' for health or housing services (NHSCCA 1990, s.47(3)). There are then two judgements which local authority staff have to make; the first is about 'social services' needs, but the second is about needs for other types of services (health and housing).

This second judgement depends on local authority staff knowing what other authorities can provide and consider to be 'needs'. It also depends on local authority staff being able to recognise these needs. For example, Age Concern has expressed its concern to the House of Commons Health Committee (1993) about the effectiveness of this part of the legislation. First, social services would need to be aware of relevant medical problems and how to respond to them, and not, for example, assume that incontinence is just a fact of life, fail to identify depression, or misdiagnose confusion. If it was not aware in this way, it might simply fail to notify the health authority. Second, it is not clear what happens in practice even when other agencies are informed about the problem: 'in fact, it then falls off the cliff, no one else has to do anything' (vol.2,p.170).

Invitation to Health and Housing Authorities

The local authority makes an 'invitation' only (NHSCCA 1990, s.47(3). Health and housing authorities are not obliged by the legislation to accept the invitation. Furthermore it is an invitation to assist in assessment only 'to such extent as is reasonable in the circumstances'. This appears to give considerable discretion to the invited authorities, in terms of whether they respond, or on what scale and with what speed. Indeed, an amendment to the NHS and Community Care Bill, making the cooperation of health and housing authorities mandatory, failed (H19 1990).

It has been suggested (Gordon 1993,p.17) that where a housing or health authority declines unreasonably to assist, a local authority could seek judicial review, claiming that it could not come to a decision.

INITIAL SCREENING FOR COMMUNITY CARE ASSESSMENT

'Screening' is a powerful, non-statutory (ie, not based on legislation) filter which can control the demand made upon authorities' resources and services. It can determine what happens to people; for example, whether they should be assessed at all, at what level and with what priority. It is not totally apparent whether or not this 'screening' is meant formally to be part of statutory 'assessment' or not. The legislation is of no assistance, since it does not define what assessment is.

What policy guidance calls 'initial screening' seems to be envisaged as the 'gateway' to formal assessment. In practice, screening plays a crucial role. At one extreme, a decision might be made to refer a person to another agency because the apparent, possible need is nothing to do with social services. At the other, a person might be allocated a comprehensive community care assessment. Because of the crucial role of such screening, some local authorities have trained staff specially for the role.

It seems to be recognised that, for screening to work well, the information received must be of sufficient quality to enable reasonable and equitable decisions to be made.

Such screening is not in principle new for social services departments. For example, in the past, referrals to occupational therapy or disability services have often been screened in order to determine priorities and waiting lists.

EXTRACTS

Legislation is silent about the screening of people.

Policy guidance refers to 'initial screening' as included in assessment arrangements:

> 'Assessment arrangements should normally include an initial screening process to determine the appropriate form of assessment. Some people may need advice and assistance which do not call for a formal assessment, others may require only a limited or specialist assessment of specific needs, others may have urgent needs which require an immediate response. Procedures should be sufficiently comprehensive and flexible to cope with all levels and types of need presented by different client groups' (DH 1990, para 3.20).

Practice guidance goes on to identify processes of information-gathering leading to assessment allocation decisions. Processes listed include:
- receive enquiries;
- give and gather information;
- encourage the full participation of the appropriate people;
- develop triggers for identifying other significant needs;
- designate responsibility for the allocation of the assessment response;
- set criteria for decision-making;
- identify levels of assessment;
- agree priorities for assessment allocation (SSI/SWSG(PG) 1991,p.37).

Practice guidance seems to portray initial information gathering as a pre-assessment rather than an assessment process. Trigger questions might aim to identify the following types of circumstance and associated risk and priority level:
- recent hospital discharge;
- recent move to independent living/change of accommodation;
- recent bereavement;
- living alone, experiencing loneliness and isolation;
- living on or below income support level;
- deteriorating health: eg. problems with continence, memory, falling;
- history of drug or alcohol abuse;
- carers' request for support;
- carer's or person's chronic loss of sleep;
- carer under stress (based on examples given in practice guidance, SSI/SWSG(PG) 1991,p.40 and in an SSI review: SSI 1991c, p.10).

DISCUSSION

Initial Screening: Part of Community Care Assessment?

Where no assessment for community services is judged to be needed, policy guidance (DH 1990, para 3.20) states that referral elsewhere will involve 'advice and assistance'. Practice guidance too refers to the 'information and advice' to be given in response to 'inappropriate enquiries' (SSI/SWSG(PG) 1991, p.38). Policy guidance seems to envisage screening as part of assessment arrangements, whereas practice guidance appears to see it as a pre-assessment process. Legislation is silent about what constitutes assessment (no directions have been made under NHSCCA 1990, s.47(4)).

The policy guidance (see above) seems to differentiate between informal assessment (screening) and formal assessment, but leaves unclear whether informal assessment is part of what the legislation refers to as 'assessment' of people's needs for services. There is no clear picture of what assessment really is, since legislation defines neither the term itself nor any associated procedures. For example, in practice it is possible that a few 'cursory' questions asked over the telephone might constitute 'assessment' (Age Concern 1994a,pp.16–17).

During the House of Lords Committee stage of the NHS and Community Care Bill the government tried to explain: 'a person presents himself to a social services department and asks what can be done for him. At that stage the social services department does not know whether he will turn out to need community care. Obviously further preliminary inquiries are needed to determine whether this is likely to be the case. If the person's needs turn out not to be for community care services then the preliminary inquiries may in fact amount to the assessment and this may be a perfectly reasonable way of dealing with the request' (H20 1990). The 'initial sift' would have a two-fold purpose: to identify those people who do not need a more 'detailed assessment' as well as those 'making unreasonable or vexatious' requests. Second, to decide on the 'most appropriate form of assessment' (H21 1990)

Initial Screening: Practice

Whether or not screening functions in practice as part of 'assessment' is also unclear. For example, a Joseph Rowntree project reports that administrative staff 'saw their task as to weed out enquiries which did not fit with their under-standing of services available within the department. In taking referrals, they would record only such information as they thought 'relevant' to the range of specialist teams. Consequently, referrals for a 'general assessment' would not be accepted but translated into a specific request' (Ellis 1993, p.17). Arguably, this means that assessment takes place already at the preliminary referral stage.

One local community care plan refers to initial screening as a type of assessment: 'Everybody has the right to receive at least an initial 'screening' assessment of their needs so, if at first sight, people feel they might not meet the relevant criteria, they should enquire regardless' (Kent County Council Social Services 1993,para 1.4).

The importance of high quality initial screening and informed decision-making is underlined on the one hand by community care guidance on the importance of appropriate assessment response (SSI/SWSG(PG) 1991,p.37; and see CI(92)34, para 9); and on the other by recognition that in the past this has not always happened. For example, the provision of some services in the past has depended more on chance and haphazard referral patterns than on people's needs (SSI/DLF 1992,p.6). Authorities might train and appoint staff to handle enquiries and conduct initial screening (eg receptionists, customer service officers, information and access officers (SSI/NHSE 1994e,p.18)).

Adequate Information Available on Referral

In practice, the screening process – and subsequent care management arrange-ments – will be affected by the quality of referral information (SSI/NHSE 1994e,p.29). For example: 'forms officially notifying the department of people newly registered as blind were automatically placed on a 5 month waiting list in one authority precisely because insufficient information was provided for an informed judgement about the urgency of individual circumstances to be made'. There may be little incentive for overworked staff to change such practices (Ellis 1993,p.18).

The screening ('trigger') questions themselves might be inadequate. Age Concern (1993) has expressed its concern: '"Can you get yourself out of bed; and can you make a cup of tea". If the answer to these is yes, they are told that social services cannot do anything for them. Is this really an assessment?' (p.11).

One (SSI/NHSME 1994a, p.8) study on community care implementation reports that some staff were wary of over-reliance on written referral informa-tion, and felt speech contact improved the quality of information; telephone conversations might be preferred (see also SSI/NHSE 1994e,p.30).

Past local ombudsman investigations have exposed instances of inadequate referral information in relation to assessment and services under the CSDPA 1970. For example, in one case an occupational therapist 'was unable to give the case its proper priority initially because she did not have the necessary information to help her make the decision'. The decision was made about a woman who had suffered a stroke; was partially paralysed and mainly bedridden downstairs; and was unable to climb the stairs or have a proper bath or shower. This led to delay in assessment, though the ombudsman did not criticise the council for it, since the therapist involved did all she could (CLAE 91/C/0121,p.7).

In another local ombudsman case, the practice of identifying priority applications was described by staff as 'hit and miss', since the forms did not contain sufficient information to facilitate informed decisions about priority. The ombudsman noted that a new form was being designed but found maladministration because of the inadequate basis for evaluating priority (CLAE 92/C/0670,p.7).

It is possible that if the law courts were to examine how authorities screen people, they might look to the housing/homelessness field where the courts have made a number of rulings about what proper enquiries should consist of. These include, for example, taking account of all relevant factors; at least considering medical evidence; giving users full opportunity to explain their circumstances and taking into account language difficulties (see eg. Gordon 1993,p.16). However, it should be pointed out that the duty to make enquiries about people's homelessness is stated explicitly in the legislation (Housing Act 1985,s.62). There is no such reference to enquiries in s.47 of the NHS and Community Care Act 1990.

The consequence of the lack of any sort of duty placed on health and housing authorities even to respond to the invitation to assess – let alone provide services – is illustrated by a recent court case. This involved a county council (social services department) asking a district council (housing authority) to provide accommodation for a family. The power to make the request is contained in s.27 of the Children Act 1989 and that section also states that the authority which has been requested 'shall comply with the request if it is compatible with their own statutory or other duties and obligations and does not unduly prejudice the discharge of any of their functions'.

Yet the court confirmed that in principle the housing authority was not under any absolute duty to accede to the request; it could refuse, for example, if it had no available accommodation or if provision would create a damaging financial burden on it (*R v Northavon DC, ex p. Smith 1994*). This ruling appears to give authorities considerable discretion in the child care context to refuse such requests despite the legislative wording; how much more latitude for health and housing authorities in the community care context, given that the NHSCCA 1990 is silent both about compliance with the request for assessment and about provision of services by health and housing authorities .

IDENTIFICATION OF PEOPLE WHO ARE IN NEED

The NHS and Community Care Act places no positive duties on local authorities to seek out individuals potentially in need of community care services, nor even to measure local needs in general. Policy and practice guidance does urge the importance of measuring local population needs, but is also silent about the identification of individuals.

This does not mean, however, that authorities can 'bury their heads in the sand'. People can bring themselves, or be brought by others (relatives, carers, professionals etc.), to the attention of local authorities.

In addition, there are other relevant duties under previous legislation:

(1) Local authorities are under a duty to keep registers of disabled people under section 29 of the National Assistance Act 1948. People do not need to be registered in order to receive services and can refuse· registration. It is likely that, whatever their planning value, registers are in practice inadequate identification tools. It is difficult to keep them current and comprehensive.

(2) Section 1 of the CSDPA 1970 places duties on local authorities to find out how many disabled people (as defined in section 29 of the NAA 1948) there are in their area, but does not mention identification of individuals. Circular guidance of over 20 years ago is hesitant about whether this should involve 100% identification of individuals. It is noteworthy that the equivalent 1978 Northern Ireland Act does extend the duties to individual identification of disabled people so far as 'reasonably practicable'.

These duties are, in principle, central to community care, since many people in need of community care services are disabled; and since the preferred aim of community care is to enable people to remain in their own homes. Nevertheless, it seems clear that in Great Britain as a whole, the duties have never been exercised so as comprehensively to identify individual disabled people.

EXTRACTS
(1) Community Care Legislation and Guidance
Legislation (NHSCCA 1990) says nothing about whether local authorities should actively identify individuals who may be in need of services, or indeed whether they should identify even general patterns of local need.

Policy guidance states that community care plans should identify:

> 'the care needs of the local population taking into account factors such as age distribution, problems associated with living in inner city areas or rural areas, special needs of ethnic minority communities, the number of homeless or transient people likely to require care' (DH 1990, para 2.25).

(2) National Assistance Act and Guidance: Registers of Disabled People
Legislation (National Assistance Act 1948, Part 3 (services under which are defined as 'community care services' in s.46 NHSCCA 1990)) refers to the power of local authorities to maintain and compile 'classified registers' of disabled people to whom arrangements for welfare services under section 29(1) 'relate' (s.29(4)(g)).

Directions convert this power into a duty (Directions attached to LAC(93)10 (Append 2,para 2(2)):

'The Secretary of State hereby directs local authorities to make the arrangements referred to in section 29(4)(g) of the Act (compiling and maintaining registers) in relation to persons who are ordinarily resident in their area'.

Circular guidance explains that the purpose of registration under the NAA 1948, s.29 is twofold. First, it is necessary for certain statutory purposes (eg visually impaired people's benefits depend on registration). Second, registration is described as needed for planning and providing services. The form of the registers is not prescribed, and is left open. It is emphasised that provision of services under NAA 1948,s.29 and CSDPA 1970,s.2 is not dependent on registration, and that people are entitled to request that they not be registered (LAC(93)10, Append 4, paras 2–3).

(3) Chronically Sick and Disabled Persons Act
Legislation (CSDPA 1970,s.1(1)) makes explicit reference to identification of local need:

'It shall be the duty of every local authority having functions under section 29 of the National Assistance Act 1948 to inform themselves of the number of persons to whom that section applies within their area and of the need for the making by the authority of arrangements under that section for such persons'.

Circular (1971) guidance (DHSS 45/71) stated that the 'ultimate task' of local authorities is to identify 'everyone who both needs and wants a service'. This might only be achievable after various steps had been taken over time, such as sample surveys, the development of services, the creation and maintenance of lists of disabled people. Nevertheless 'comprehensive identification' is to be the eventual aim (paras 11–12).

An earlier Circular (DHSS 12/70) was also cautious:

'It is not a requirement of the Section that authorities should attempt 100 per cent identification and registration of the handicapped. This would be a difficult, expensive and time consuming exercise, diverting excessive resources from effective work with those who are already known, involving a restrictive and artificial definition and likely to be counter-productive' (para 5).

DISCUSSION
Extent of Duty
There seems to be no duty actually to identify individual people who might be in need of community care services.

The closest reference to a duty appears in section 1 of the CSDPA. However, it is generally accepted that the duty extends only to finding out about the numbers of disabled people locally, rather than their identity. This can be seen by comparing the duty with its equivalent in the Northern Ireland version of the Act: the CSDP(Northern Ireland) Act 1978. This contains additional words (italicised): 'The Department of Health and Social Services for Northern Ireland shall inform itself of the number of and, *so far as reasonably practicable, the identity of persons...*' (s.1(1): our italics).

The 1978 Act seemed to acknowledge the possible loophole in the original 1970 Act; or least as Baroness Phillips (during the passing of the 1978 Act) explained, it was making explicit what she had believed was always the intention of the 1970 Act: individual identification. The purpose of such identification was to 'ensure that the Department has a continuing duty to identify handicapped people, and that it cannot be content with, what one might term, a one-off operation' (H22 1978). She did add, however, that even in the 1978 legislation there were 'too many words like "practicable" and "reasonable" in the Bill for some of us to be happy' (H23 1978).

Therefore, the 1970 Act, contrasted with the 1978 Act, would seem to be about anonymous, rather than individual identification of disabled people. Indeed, even when the author of the CSDPA 1970 became a Minister in the new Labour government of 1974, he did not give instructions to local authorities about individual identification (Topliss, Gould 1981,p.93).

In 1983, two unsuccessful CSDP(Amendment) Bills attempted to bring the CSDPA 1970 into line with the Northern Ireland version. The government justified its resistance by referring to the expense of establishing the identity of every disabled person, because frequent and extensive house-to-house surveys would be required (H24 1983).

Significance for Community Care of CSDPA Duties

The duties to keep registers and identify numbers of disabled people are, in principle, most significant for community care. This is because, first, practice guidance states that the 'majority of adults who appear to have community care needs are affected by some form of disability' (SSI/SWSG(PG) 1991,p.44). Second, the preferred aim of community care, enabling people to remain in their own homes (DH 1990,para 3.24), means that domiciliary welfare arrangements under the National Assistance Act 1948, s.29 (extended by the CSDPA 1970,s.2) are at least potentially relevant to all such people.

Nevertheless, it has been pointed out that people are more likely to be entered on the register (see above) after application and receipt of services rather than before. In which case, registers do not function as an identification tool (Topliss, Gould 1981,p.100).

PRIORITIES FOR COMMUNITY CARE ASSESSMENT

Local authorities do not have the staff and resources to assess all applicants immediately and in depth. Therefore they have to decide, at the initial screening stage, how urgent people's needs probably are; how long they will have to wait for assessment; and what sort of assessment they will get.

Practice guidance draws a sometimes complex picture about how people's priority for assessment might be decided. It lists 'decision-making criteria'; assessment allocation priorities; and factors to be taken account of when making those allocation priorities.

Legislation does not clarify the guidance since it does not refer at all to the screening process and the application of priorities. It is perhaps not surprising that there are some reports of local authority screening systems which are complex and ill-defined. There is also concern about the principles on which priority criteria should be drawn up; and that they should work consistently and equitably. For example, the local government ombudsman has in the past found maladministration, when priority criteria have been applied inconsistently. Unpredictable and arbitrary application of criteria might also offend the law courts' idea of fairness (see Chapter 7); for example, about people's 'legitimate expectations' and their right to be given information about what is happening, or is going to happen to them. Authorities might therefore be well-advised to qualify published information about priorities with words such as 'normally', or 'generally' or 'resources allowing'.

Equally, and confusingly, authorities have to make sure that they do not offend against another legal principle, 'fettering discretion' (see Chapter 7) – that is, an authority's policy must not be applied be so rigidly that it cannot take account of individual circumstances.

In practice, high priority is likely to be accorded to those people deemed to be *at risk*. The making of priorities sometimes leads to waiting lists. In some localities, waiting lists have long been a 'fact of life'; for example, for assessment for equipment and home adaptations.

EXTRACTS

Legislation does not mention assessment priorities.

Practice guidance states that the initial screening and information-gathering process is followed by 'allocation of the appropriate assessment response' (SSI/SWSG(PG) 1991,p.40). It lists three sets of criteria. It is not wholly clear how they relate to one another.

(1) **Decision-making criteria.** The practice guidance states that the assessment allocation decisions 'should **consistently apply the same criteria** which should:

- reflect the policies and priorities set out in the published information on assessment practice;
- judge the urgency of the required response;
- take account of the assessment resources available in terms of the number of administrative, vocationally or professionally qualified staff relative to demand;
- weigh the options available to meet specific needs which will affect the level and complexity of the assessment required;

- use the assessment to make cost-effective use of the available resources' (SSI/SWSG(PG) 1991,pp.40–41).

(2) Assessment allocation priorities. Guidance states that: 'most referrals for assessment will fall into four categories that can be related to the basic objectives of community care. There are those:

- for whom community living is no longer a possibility or who are at risk, for example, people with intensive care needs;
- reliant on others for survival, requiring help with, for example, feeding, toileting;
- reliant on others for support, requiring help with, for example, cleaning, shopping;
- whose functioning or morale is reduced, for example, as a consequence of depressive illness...

Most cases requiring statutory or crisis intervention are likely to fall in the first two categories. In each of the four categories, people may be rated as having a low, medium or high level of need' (SSI/SWSG(PG) 1991,p.43).

(3) Factors to take into account when allocating assessment priorities: 'Any judgement of the appropriate assessment response and level of priority will have to take account of such factors as:

- severity or complexity of needs;
- degree of risk or vulnerability of user or carers;
- the level and duration of the projected resources required (whether immediately or in the future);
- the degree of stress experienced by user, carers or other agencies;
- the necessity of co-ordination with other care agencies, for example, about hospital discharge or housing transfer;
- the length of time already spent on a waiting list, for instance, a higher priority response should be triggered after a specified period on a waiting list' (SSI/SWSG(PG) 1991,pp.43– 44).

DISCUSSION
'Statutory or Crisis Intervention'

The practice guidance suggests that the first two of the four main categories of priority (see the criteria in (2) immediately above) are likely to require 'statutory or crisis intervention'. The meaning attaching to 'statutory' is not clear. Presumably what is meant is 'statutory duty', since provision of cleaning or shopping (in the third category above) are 'statutory' services insofar as they can be provided under statute (eg. under NHS Act 1977,Schedule 8,para 3 (home help)).

This seems to imply that people in the third and fourth categories (in (2) above) are likely to be low priority, and so drop down the waiting list.

Basis for Priority Categories

However, a person can easily move from one category to another, and there is anyway a question about the principles and policies on which priority criteria should be based. In addition, lack of information about people's needs (before they are assessed) can mean that people are wrongly given a low priority.

For example, a person, arguably in the third category (cleaning and shopping help) and therefore low priority, may not be able to continue 'community living' (a part of the first category) if that help ceases – and so immediately become higher priority. This raises the question of to what extent criteria should reflect a policy of prevention.

The Alzheimer's Disease Society has illustrated to the Health Committee (1993, vol.1,p.xxv) how 'low priority' needs can escalate: 'an hour of care a week...for someone with Alzheimer's Disease who is in the early stages may be enough to keep that person out of hospital for a very long time, but if they have no care at all initially because they are not considered to be severely in need, then you are always in a state of crisis management, so...there is a real conflict in the idea of rationing and in assessment between focusing all your care on crisis management and none of your care on the preventative work which actually all of us want' (vol.1,p.xxv). In similar vein, the RNIB pointed out that timely assessment may actually result in less expenditure by statutory services if it enables people to remain independent (vol.2,p.139).

Priorities and the CSDPA 1970, Section 2

One view put forward by a local authority solicitor (as reported by the local ombudsman) attempted to justify the local system of priorities and why some people, judged to be low priority, had to wait for assessment. This was that since – under the National Assistance Act 1948,s.29 and CSDPA 1970,s.2 – there was a duty to assist people who are 'substantially' disabled, 'the Council might be failing in their legal duty to those persons who are permanently and substantially handicapped if their needs are not met in a reasonable time because resources are being expended on persons who do not have substantial handicap'.

In fact, a vicious circle was conceded in the same case by the local authority: it did not know whether the woman, whose assessment it was delaying, was 'substantially and permanently' disabled or not. This was precisely because she had not yet been assessed. The woman had suffered several strokes, used a wheelchair and could not use the bath. The resulting delay of two years was found to be maladministration (CLAE 91/C/1852; see also CLAE 91/C/0831).

In addition, there is a possible legal complication to using high risk as a measure of priority. The effect of doing so can be that some people, with serious, but not life-threatening, problems might be given a lower priority. For example, five month waits for a woman with a progressive illness and only able to mount and descend the stairs on her hands and knees; and for an older man smelling offensive because his son was unable to bath him (see Ellis 1993, p.17). Risk and safety might seem to be rational and defensible priority criteria.

However, the local ombudsman has pointed out that under section 2 of the CSDPA 1970, the law 'makes no distinction between the Council's duty to make an assessment in 'urgent' and 'non-urgent' cases. Any disabled person is entitled to request an assessment and to expect that the request is met within a reasonable time' (CLAE 1992, 91/A/0482,p.21). Under section 2, people's need for facilities and adaptations is referred to as being for 'safety', 'comfort' or 'convenience'. A policy based on high risk ('safety') factors alone – which therefore denies assessment for people's comfort or convenience – could possibly be illegal and so challengeable. This same point would also apply *after* assessment has been carried out and authorities are using criteria of eligibility to decide what services to provide.

Manipulation of Priority Criteria

A report on community care by the National Federation of Housing Associations (1993) found that criteria could be manipulated in order to gain access to priority assessment. For example: 'One agency was emphasising aspects of the individual's mental health history when making a referral for assessment, rather than their homelessness. In a hostel for ex-offenders, funding was being agreed if the agency could prove that residents were additionally vulnerable in some way, through age, physical or mental illness for example. Callers felt they were being forced to play games with the local authority over criteria, but it had proved an effective approach' (p.13).

Complexity of Systems of Priorities

Criteria defining access to different stages of the whole service process are reported to be confusing staff (SSI/NHSME 1994a,p.8). For example, it might be difficult to distinguish between criteria as applied right through the community care process: getting an assessment, type or level of assessment, speed of assessment response, priority of need, accessing resources (financial allocation), and particular services.

Furthermore, false correlation between different types of eligibility can occur. For example, just because an assessment is simple, it doesn't follow that it is not urgent: the provision of a commode might be 'simple' but could well be very urgent (SSI/NHSE 1994e,p.30).

Consistent Application of Priority Criteria: Ombudsman Investigations

Priority criteria are a necessary fact of life for some services. Practice guidance states that they must be applied consistently (see above). The local ombudsmen are unlikely to criticise priority criteria in principle, but might find maladministration if they are applied inconsistently. They have investigated a considerable number of cases relating to social services' duties under the CSDPA 1970 (section 2) and the DP(SCR)A 1986 (s.4). The following investigations referred to mainly concern one or both of these Acts, and give examples of both non-findings and findings of maladministration.

For example, the local ombudsman will not find fault solely because some delay is caused (in home adaptation assessment) by application of a priority policy; and generally will not criticise professional opinions even though recognising that they 'may differ on the assessment of individual needs' (CLAE 91/A/3602,p.18).

A six month delay for home adaptation assessment was not criticised since the local authority had 'applied a system of priorities which took into account the sort of factors which might be important when such time scales were involved. Within this system [the applicant's] priority was relatively low. I have considered whether the...application should have been given priority because of the reason of the transfer, but in my view this would have been unfair to other residents awaiting adaptations' (CLAE 91/A/3466,p.13).

A 15-month delay was not deemed by the ombudsman to be maladministration because the authority had 'adopted a policy of priority categories for the allocation of referrals, as they were entitled to do, and my investigation has shown that [the applicant's] referral was dealt with properly according to the policy'. In addition, taking into account the council's 'particular resource and staffing difficulties' the delay was not 'so unreasonable as to amount to maladministration in this case' (CLAE 92/A/1693,p.25).

Similarly, where 'there are restrictions on the resources available to a Council and on the number of staff who can be employed in assessing needs, I do not see that I can be critical of a Council for employing a practice of giving greater priority to those in greater need'. This, even where the resulting wait for an assessment amounted to two years (CLAE 92/C/1403,p.7).

Apart from variations in waiting times between local authorities, there are sometimes discrepancies within the same local authority. The local ombudsman might find maladministration since it 'cannot be fair or reasonable that an applicant for a renovation grant in one part of the Borough has an application dealt with in a matter of weeks, whilst others...wait for years' (CLAE 91/A/3911,p.18). In another finding of maladministration, one of the 'serious failures' was that a person who had waited four years and eight months for an assessment might have waited only five months had she lived a few hundred yards away in the same authority (CLAE 91/A/0482,p.20).

The local ombudsman has also found maladministration where an initial visit, but no 'proper assessment', was carried out following an application for a shower. A letter sent to the complainant following the visit and explaining why no help could be provided was 'erroneous' since it stated that showers could not be provided in principle, when in fact they could. The woman consequently had to wait a total of four years for the shower despite the fact that her doctor had pointed out that her epilepsy made bathing dangerous and she had difficulty washing her father. She could not have a proper wash for those four years (CLAE 91/A/2523).

Another investigation found that a council had been misapplying its priority criteria: five people in a sample of 45 cases had been given priority incorrectly ahead of the particular complainant. The case illustrated the difficulties facing local authority staff such as occupational therapists. The reasons for the 'incorrect' decisions included 'soft-heartedness' in the case of a woman with asthma, emphysema and osteoarthritis who could just about manage indoor steps and stairs indoors. A second person 'had great difficulty getting up from a sitting position, and could not bathe without aids, was unable to get in and out of the bath, and lived alone'. Two sisters, aged 82 and 81, with various problems including Crohn's Disease, arthritis, osteoarthritis in spine, hips and knees were both unable to bathe. They should not have been given priority – but were, probably because of their joint needs and previous requests. Yet still, the misapplication of priority criteria amounted to maladministration (CLAE 92/A/1693).

Professional Judgement in Allocating Assessment

However detailed criteria are, their eventual application is usually a matter of professional judgement. Professional judgements can vary, and just as the health service ombudsman cannot by law question 'clinical judgements', so the local ombudsman will not directly challenge professional judgements – since, in principle, they are outside the scope of maladministration. However, like the health service ombudsman, the local ombudsman can question the factors surrounding such decisions: for example, lack of information on which a decision is based.

For example, the ombudsman found maladministration where a decision about the priority of an elderly man, unsteady on his feet after four strokes, was taken on the basis of inadequate information. The ombudsman identified in particular the fact that a GP's medical certificate was given less weight than an incomplete OT assessment carried out over six months earlier. An assessment visit had been made by an officer who was neither professionally nor medically qualified. Other professionals involved, such as the district nurse, had not been contacted for information. A further communication by the GP that the applicant's condition had deteriorated was not investigated and therefore the decision not to raise his priority made without evidence and not in accordance with procedures (CLAE 91/B/0254,p.18)

In another investigation, within a finding of maladministration on a number of counts, the ombudsman considered an occupational therapist's decision not to support an application for home adaptations as 'almost incomprehensible'. The decision, following which the file had been closed, left the applicant 'in a house completely unadapted for her needs, in particular with no bathing facilities which she could use at that time' (CLAE 194/A/86).

Fluctuation of Priority Given to a Person's Needs

Since local authorities are forced to make priorities in the light of demand for services and resources, the priority accorded to a particular individual might fluctuate not because of his or her 'objective' circumstances, but because of changes in other people's circumstances and needs. Although this might seem unfair, it seems to follow logically from the existence of priority criteria.

For example, in one case the local ombudsman noted that it 'might take eight months for a lower priority client to receive a visit; there were some eight or nine hundred clients on the waiting list, but a client's position could change if new urgent cases came on the list or if existing clients' needs became more or less urgent'. The ombudsman did not criticise such a system of priorities (CLAE 91/A/3466,p.13).

To avoid possible challenges where fluctuation of priority might occur, authorities might be well-advised to keep people well-informed, and not to commit themselves absolutely to particular timescales. This might avoid accusations of maladministration because of lack of information; or disappointing the 'legitimate expectation' of a person (see Chapter 7).

LEVELS OF COMMUNITY CARE ASSESSMENT

Legislation is silent about assessment 'levels'. However, community care practice guidance describes how, following a decision about urgency of assessment, a further decision should be made about the level of assessment which an individual should receive. The guidance suggests six levels of assessment. In practice, it seems that local authorities adopt fewer levels, corresponding broadly to the type of staff required to do the assessment. Guidance states that disabled people should be offered a comprehensive assessment, although there is probably some confusion about the implications of this.

EXTRACTS

Legislation (NHSCCA 1990) is silent about assessment levels.

Policy guidance states:

'Assessment arrangements should normally include an initial screening process to determine the appropriate form of assessment. Some people may need advice and assistance which do not call for a formal assessment, others may require only a limited or specialist assessment of specific needs, others may have urgent needs which require an immediate response. Procedures should be sufficiently comprehensive and flexible to cope with all levels and types of need presented by different client groups' (DH 1990, para 3.20).

Practice guidance provides an example model, consisting of six levels of assessment. Each level is illustrated in terms of the needs, services, agency and staff likely to be involved (SSI/SWSG(PG) 1991,p.42). The model is not prescriptive: 'Agencies will want to determine their own levels of assessment according to their policies, priorities and available personnel' (p.41).

Examples of Levels

Assessment levels, together with examples of service outcome might be:
- simple (bus pass, disabled car badge);
- limited assessment (low-level domiciliary support);
- multiple assessment (assistance with meals, chiropody, basic nursing);
- specialist assessment: simple (simple disability equipment);
  complex (home adaptation);
- complex assessment (speech therapy);
- comprehensive assessment (family therapy, substitute care or intensive domiciliary support) (p.42).

DISCUSSION

Linking Assessment Level to Criteria

Community care monitoring (SSI/NHSME 1993) has found that although many authorities distinguish between simple and complex assessments, their basis might be unsatisfactory since they might not be linked to 'fully worked-out eligibility criteria' (para 3.4). In other words, authorities might be making, or least be in danger of making, arbitrary and possibly inequitable decisions. Joint SSI/NHSME (1993) monitoring found 'instances in which a number of levels of priority of need were combined with a number of levels of complexity of assessment to produce systems which were almost impossible to work into practice' (para 3.5).

In practice therefore, it seems that many authorities might operate no more than three levels of assessment based on the staff needed to carry them out: simple (administrative/auxiliary staff); specialist (auxiliary/qualified/specialist staff); comprehensive (qualified/multi-agency staff) (SSI/NHSME 1994a,p.9).

'Fast-track' assessment might exist for 'emergency, high-risk cases, or cases involving people who misuse drugs or alcohol'. However, some other 'fast-track' applications, such as hospital discharge might be 'ways of introducing priorities into the system which do not necessarily relate to the intrinsic urgency of the case' (SSI/NHSME 1993, para 3.7).

ASSESSMENT LEVEL AND DISABILITY

The NHS and Community Care Act 1990 states that if, during an assessment, the local authority thinks a person is disabled then it must decide if he or she needs home welfare services available under s.2 of the Chronically Sick and Disabled Persons Act 1970.

Overall, community care guidance seems a little unclear about the implications of this. It states that disabled people should be offered a comprehensive assessment; that many people in possible need of community care are disabled; but that comprehensive assessments should form only a minority of assessments because they are time-consuming and expensive. These points seem inconsistent; but the point is important because of the level of resources which comprehensive assessments demand.

Disability is defined by s.29 of the National Assistance Act 1948 and associated guidance.

EXTRACTS

Legislation states:

'If at any time during the assessment of the needs of any person…it appears to a local authority that he is a disabled person, the authority - (a) shall proceed to make such a decision as to the services he requires as is mentioned in section 4 of the Disabled Persons (Services, Consultation and Representation) Act 1986 without his requesting them to do so under that section; and (b) shall inform him that they will be doing so and of his rights under that Act' (NHSCCA 1990, s.47(2)).

(Section 4 of the Disabled Persons (SCR) 1986 states that, if requested, local authorities must decide if a person needs any of the services under s.2(1) of the CSDPA 1970).

Policy guidance reinforces this:

'if at any time during their assessment, an individual is found to be a person to whom section 29 of the National Assistance Act 1948 applies, the authority must so inform them, advise them of their rights and make a decision as to their need for services, as required by Section 4 of the Disabled Persons' (Services, Consultation and Representation) Act 1986' (DH 1990, para 3.30).

Circular guidance states:

'A full scale assessment of all needs should be offered to individuals appearing to be disabled, as prescribed by Section 47(2) of the NHS and CC Act' (CI(92)34,para 9 now formally cancelled: see p.401).

Practice guidance states that where:

'The type of assessment response will normally be **related as closely as possible to the presenting need.** However, there is one legally prescribed exception. Where a person appears to be 'disabled' under the terms of the Disabled Persons (SCR) Act 1986, the local authority is required to offer a comprehensive assessment, irrespective of the scale of need that is initially presented' (SSI/SWSG(PG) 1991, p.43).

DISCUSSION

Appearance of Need

It seems that in order to progress to assessment for CSDPA 1970,s.2 services, the individual needs to pass through two gateways of 'appearance'. The first governs access to an NHSCCA 1990,s.47(1) assessment; the second governs access to the decision about whether the person needs any of the 1970 Act services. At that point, the local authority has a duty to tell the person what it is doing and what the person's rights are under the 1986 DP(SCR)A.

Offer of Comprehensive Assessments for Disabled People

Practice guidance states that the 'majority of adults who appear to have community care needs are affected by some form of disability' (SSI/SWSG(PG) 1991, p.44). The legislation states that if a person is getting a community care assessment and it appears that he or she is disabled, then a decision must be taken about the need for services under the 1970 Act. The practice guidance states that disabled people must be offered a comprehensive assessment (p.43). This would appear to be stating that there will be many comprehensive assessments.

(It is not clear why the practice guidance states that comprehensive assessment for disabled people is a 'legally prescribed exception'. None of the legislation mentions 'comprehensive' assessment. Furthermore, the statement in the guidance (see immediately above) that such an offer must be made irrespective of the scale of need would seem in principle to corrode the whole notion of a needs-based system of priorities and assessment levels).

On the other hand, Circular guidance urges that comprehensive assessments are 'both time consuming and expensive. They should be reserved for the minority of users with the most complex needs' (CI(92(34),para 9). On the face of it there is inconsistency here.

In practice, the inconsistency might be resolved if many people are offered, but some do not accept, a comprehensive assessment. From the point of view of speed, a simple assessment might have distinct advantages for service users. Alternatively, it is possible that an authority might define disability under s.29 of the National Assistance Act 1948 at a high threshold, thus 'reducing' the number of disabled people. However, it is to be noted that the longstanding Circular guidance on the definition of disability encourages a broadly inclusive approach to disability and not a narrow, exclusive approach (see below).

Offer of Comprehensive Assessment for Minor Disability

A further consequence of having to offer comprehensive assessments to people who appear disabled, is that the offer might apply to people who might not appear to be 'high risk' or to have the greatest needs. For example, services under the CSDPA s.2, include those 'additional facilities designed to secure his greater safety, comfort or convenience'. Yet 'comfort' and 'convenience' scarcely fall within urgent, risk or safety considerations.

There seems to be further complication. The practice guidance provides examples of different levels of assessment. The need for simple disability equipment or a home adaptation is put at level 4 which might require a 'specialist', but not necessarily a 'comprehensive', assessment (p.42). This is not consistent with the notion that comprehensive assessments must be offered to all people deemed to be disabled. This is because provision of disability equipment and home adaptations is normally made under the CSDPA 1970,s.2 – to disabled people, defined as such as under s. 29 of the National Assistance Act 1948 (p.43).

Practice: Complex Assessments

In fact, early reports have found relatively high numbers of complex, comprehensive assessments, taking up excessive time and resources – caused by, for example, 'threshold criteria at too low a level' (SSI 1993k,p.9).

SSI/NHSME (1993) monitoring found that complex assessments were more numerous than had been anticipated, and were sometimes being given priority over simple assessments, 'leading to delays and possibly distortions' (para 3.5). Similarly, comprehensive assessments might be carried out (perhaps inappropriately) whenever more than one agency is involved – which means that the complexity is determined more by the type of service response than by an individual's need (SSI/NHSE 1994e,p.32).

Nevertheless, it has been pointed out in the Health Committee (1993) that by emphasising the need for simple assessment in many if not most cases, there is a danger of simply perpetuating a service-led, rather than a needs-led approach (vol.2,p.31). An example of this might be when a person asks for a non-slip bath mat or for a reaching stick. The simple assessment response might be simply to provide the item or even advise the person to buy it from a pharmacy. The difficulty for local authorities is knowing, in such cases, when there might be a host of hidden needs which would justify a more comprehensive, 'needs-led' assessment.

DEFINITION OF DISABILITY

Home welfare services under the National Assistance Act 1948 and the CSDPA 1970 depend on people being disabled. Disability is defined in section 29 of the National Assistance Act 1948.

The definition is further explained in longstanding Circular guidance which has recently been reproduced. The approach advocated by the guidance, and by the government during the passing of the NHS and Community Care Act 1990, appears to be a generally inclusive one, thus discouraging local authorities from setting narrow definitions of disability in order to exclude people from eligibility.

The 1948 definition (in its amended version) applies to the:

- NHS and Community Care 1990 (assessment for CSDPA services during a community care assessment: see above);
- Chronically Sick and Disabled Persons Act 1970 (home welfare services);
- Disabled Persons (Services, Consultation and Representation) Act 1986 (request for assessment for CSDPA services);
- Local Government and Housing Act 1989 (grants for home adaptations).

Nevertheless, though the Circular guidance does give advice on how to define disability, it explains that precise guidance cannot be given. It is therefore for local authorities both to define what they mean by disability and also to decide whether particular individuals are in fact disabled under that definition.

EXTRACTS

Legislation The National Assistance Act 1948, s.29, applies to people 'aged eighteen or over who are blind, deaf or dumb, or who suffer from mental disorder of any description and other persons aged eighteen or over who are substantially and permanently handicapped by illness, injury or congenital deformity or such other disabilities as may be prescribed by the minister'.

Circular guidance advises on eligibility under section 29. It states:

'As indicated above, once it has been established that a person comes within the scope of section 29, the matter or registration in no way affects eligibility to receive help – in other words the material question in determining that eligibility is whether, for the purposes of section 29, the person is to be regarded as having a hearing, vision or speech impairment or is substantially and permanently handicapped by illness, injury or congenital deformity' (LAC(93)10, appendix 4,para 5).

In summary:

- **Visual impairment:** there are well established procedures for certification of blindness or partial sight.
- **Hearing impairment:** 'There are no formal examination procedures for determining whether a person is deaf or hard of hearing for the purposes section 29, and there is no intention of introducing any new procedure in this respect' (para 7).
- **General disability:** 'It is convenient to continue to use the term "General Classes" to apply to those persons within the scope of section 29 whose primary handicap is neither visual nor auditory. It has not proved possible to give precise guidance on the interpretation of the phrase "substantially and permanently handicapped". However, as hitherto, authorities are asked to give a wide interpretation to the term "substantial", which the Department fully recognises must always take full account of individual circumstances. With regard to the term "permanent", authorities will also wish to interpret this

sufficiently flexibly to ensure that they do not feel inhibited from giving help under section 29 in cases where they are uncertain of the likely duration of the condition' (appendix 4,para 8).

Categories of Disability

The Circular guidance asks local authorities to keep registration data under three main headings:

- very severe handicap;
- severe or appreciable handicap;
- and other persons (for example, including people with a less severe heart or chest condition or with epilepsy (para 10).

The first two of these categories are themselves further explained.

Very severe handicap includes those who:

(1) 'need help going to or using the WC practically every night. In addition, most of those in this group need to be fed or dressed or, if they can feed and/or dress themselves, they need a lot of help during the day with washing and WC, or are incontinent';

(2) 'need help with the WC during the night but not quite so much help with feeding, washing, dressing, or, while not needing night-time help with the WC need a great deal of day-time help with feeding and/or washing and the WC';

(3) 'are permanently bedfast or confined to a chair and need help to get in and out, or are senile or mentally impaired, or are not able to care for themselves as far as normal everyday functions are concerned, but who do not need as much help' as the above two categories (annex 1 to appendix 4).

Severe or appreciable handicap includes those who:

(4) 'either have difficulty doing everything, or find most things difficult and some impossible';

(5) 'find most things difficult, or three or four items difficult and some impossible';

(6) 'can do a fair amount for themselves but have difficulty with some items, or have to have help with or two minor items'.

DISCUSSION

Interpretation of Definition of Disability (NAA 1948,s.29)

The Circular guidance, dealing with general disability, asks local authorities to give a wide interpretation to the term 'substantial' and a flexible interpretation to 'permanent' – so, in the latter case not to deprive people of services.

An inclusive approach to the definition is further confirmed by the categories listed immediately above, under which local authorities are asked to register disabled people. These categories cover both severe and less severe disabilities, thus indicating that the term 'substantial' in section 29 does not necessarily equate with 'very severe' or even 'severe'.

During the passing of the NHS and Community Care Bill, Baroness Hooper for the government explained that the definition of disability under section 29 of the National Assistance Act 1948 'is cast in broad terms with the aim of being as inclusive as possible and related to a degree of severity rather than to a particular condition'. This made unnecessary the amendment being considered which would have extended the definition of disability specifically to people dependent on alcohol or drugs, people with HIV/AIDS, mental disorder including Alzheimer's Disease (H91 1990).

DELAY IN ASSESSMENT AND WAITING TIMES

Waiting lists have been a longstanding problem for at least some local authority services: for example, assessment for daily living equipment and home adaptations. It appears that waiting lists still persist – at least for some services in some localities. What constitutes a reasonable response time, from time of referral to time of assessment, remains obscure and judicially undetermined. Therefore, it is unclear how long a local authority can delay assessment before that delay in effect becomes a refusal to assess.

Government has urged authorities to set target response times; this is helpful for users. However, if local authorities do this, they would be well advised to qualify any promises – so as to avoid challenges on the basis of people's 'legitimate expectations' (see above).

Waiting lists might not in principle be the 'fault' of local authorities. Many have followed good practice in trying to reduce them, for example, by setting up self-assessment clinics, staff recruitment and retention packages (to overcome staff shortages), and workload reorganisation.

Local government ombudsmen have investigated many cases of delay in assessment, especially in relation to the CSDPA 1970 and the DP(SCR)A 1986. The reports of their investigations give insight into both local authorities' and service users' standpoints. It is not easy to state a definitive rationale governing the ombudsmen's decisions since so much seems to depend on individual facts and circumstances. For example, they have not laid down a universal limit to waiting times.

In general, they have often found maladministration where waiting times are at issue. On the other hand, depending on the particular circumstances of the case, the ombudsmen might accept the explanations of local authorities that priority systems are necessary and waiting times inevitable. However, even where the ombudsmen accept this, they may invoke another aspect of good administration: for example, the giving of information to people to let them know what is happening to them.

Some of the particular issues investigated by the ombudsman concern how long people should wait, whether they are classed as high or low priority; staff shortages causing waiting times; very long waits (years); whether practice reflects policy; excessively long waits; the closing of waiting lists; and the giving of information to people about waiting times.

The law courts might occasionally intervene when a public body delays doing its duty (eg. R v Home Secretary, ex p. Phansopkar 1976: an immigration case); but generally, they are likely to be reluctant to interfere with how quickly duties are performed (Gordon 1993,p.41).

EXTRACTS

Legislation is silent about waiting times, and does not place a time limit within which assessment must be carried out.

Circular guidance states that readily understandable, published information should include:

'any standards against which the assessment arrangements will be measured, including the estimated length of time between referral and the completion of an assessment' (CI(92)34, para 6 now formally cancelled: see p.401).

Practice guidance states that as:

'a point of good practice, local authorities should publish their guidelines on timescales for responding to referrals. These guidelines should be monitored and adjusted to keep waiting lists for assessment to a minimum' (SSI/SWSG 1991(PG), p.41).

Consultation document on proposed community charters states that authorities should specify a range of response times including time:

- between initial contact and first response;
- between that response and start of assessment;
- for completion of different types of assessment;
- between completion of assessment and start of services;
- taken to refer people to other services (DH 1994c).

DISCUSSION

Time Limits
An unsuccessful amendment to the NHS and Community Care Bill attempted to ensure that authorities assess 'within a reasonable period of time'. The government responded that the need for assessments to be carried 'without due delay is stressed in our guidance' (H25 1990).

Community care guidance similarly does not define unacceptable delay, but suggests that timescales should be set. Even if there are agreed 'response' times, the definition of 'response' can vary between authorities, for example, from referral to assessment, to completion of assessment, or to service delivery (SSI 1993n,p.7). Where response times are set, staff can struggle to meet them; although policies on response times are not necessarily published (SSI 1994g,p.15).

A code of practice published on behalf of seven county councils discussed acceptable and unacceptable assessment delay under s.4 of the Disabled Persons

(SCR) Act 1986. The code includes the following comments on delays in assessment: 'There is no specific and absolute time limit regarding waiting list delays. Therefore the matter legally rests on a test of 'reasonableness'... Waiting lists seem to be a fact of life for most social services departments. The Act is not clear when a delay in awaiting assessment becomes a refusal to assess. Professional advice is that a delay in excess of 6 months is unacceptable and that most Local Authorities should be working to a 3 month limit' (Devon Social Services 1989,p.2).

Waiting Lists for Assessment

Delay has characterised some local authority services for many years, meaning that people might have a long wait, especially those accorded 'low priority'. One report on community care indicates that in some places, 'only users in the higher dependency bands were receiving an assessment, and...waiting lists were occurring for people with lower dependency needs, (SSI 1993j,p.9).

It seems that occupational therapy and disability services often command waiting lists. Social services departments receive many referrals about disability equipment and home adaptations. For example, it has been reported that nearly 50% of referrals of older people were for equipment (SSI 1991f,p.2; see also SSI/NHSE 1994e,p.22) whilst another report (SSI 1994a,p.9) found a figure of 23% of total (all client groups) referrals to social services. Yet occupational therapy services 'continue to fall short of the increasing demands made on them' (p.37).

It is notable that early reports on community care implementation refer to continuing problems involving equipment, adaptations, occupational therapists and waiting lists (RADAR SSI 1993h,p.13; SSI 1993e,p.16; SSI 1994e,p.18), the last of which stand sometimes at unacceptable levels (SSI 1994a,p.10).

The problem is not new. Past reports have referred to periods of ten months between referral and allocation (and a further six months for service provision) (SSI 1991a,p.13); any period between 11 days and over a year (SSI 1991b,p.11); three to nine months for those 'regarded as lower priority' (London Borough of Barnet 1987,p.5). Waiting lists as large as 1500 people and never less than 600 may be the subject of complaints to local authority councillors for a decade and more (CLAE 92/A/1693,p.8) – though delay caused to an individual because of this might not in itself constitute maladministration (p.25).

Agreed policies and waiting times for assessment are one thing: practice sometimes another. The ombudsmen might find maladministration where a joint social services/housing department assessment should, according to policy, have been made within 7 days from receipt of referral – but instead took place 6 weeks later (CLAE 91/A/1481). Sometimes, simple administrative inefficiency is found by the local ombudsman: for example, where a request by a registered blind person (also at risk of falling and with a rare degenerative disease) for equipment was not passed to the sensory impairment team by an

Assistant Director of social services. A nine month delay resulted (CLAE 92/A/3725,p.22).

Staff Shortages and Demand on Services

One reason often pleaded by local authorities (under the CSDPA 1970, s.2 and Disabled Persons (SCR) Act 1986,s.4) for delayed assessment is the shortage of occupational therapists, experts in daily living assessments. The local ombudsman has investigated this issue on a number of occasions and is generally, but not always, unsympathetic to local authorities who plead this excuse.

For example, the ombudsman has commented that if authorities 'are unable to provide an assessment within a reasonable period of time, then they should look at other ways of providing the assessment' (CLAE 91/C/3108,p.12).

In cases of staff shortages, the ombudsman might look at how councils have attempted to carry out their duties under LASSA 1970,s.6 to ensure that there are 'adequate' staff to assist Directors of Social Services 'in the exercise' of their functions. The legal advice of a local authority solicitor, reported in an ombudsman investigation, was that 'the word "adequate" can be taken to refer to both quantity and quality (ie training, qualifications and experience)'. Maladministration might be found where problems have long since been reported to, and known by, the Social Services Committee, and yet 'wider failure' in service delivery has continued, including a lack of monitoring and inadequate records of waiting lists (CLAE 92/A/4108,pp.2,17).

(It has been pointed out (Clements 1992) that social services committee minutes, showing unsuccessful requests by the director of social services for adequate staff, could constitute objective evidence of significant understaffing. This could form grounds for application for judicial review, even though the duty under LASSA 1970,s.6(6), to provide adequate staff, has usually been regarded as one of 'imperfect obligation' and scarcely enforceable).

On the other hand, if councils face 'particular resource and staffing difficulties' and have made attempts to remedy the situation, the ombudsman might not find maladministration. For example, where a council has offered a recruitment and retention package for staff, set up a special assessment clinic, and seconded health authority staff (CLAE 92/A/1693).

Even so, a three month wait for assessment, for day centre attendance by a 19-year-old woman seriously ill with Asperger's Syndrome (a form of autism), was found to be maladministration. The ombudsman did not 'consider that staff shortages or a departmental reorganisation can ever justify a failure to respond to repeated requests of this seriousness for help' (CLAE 93/C/0005). Similarly, a ten month delay in assessing a woman unable to use her upstairs bathroom was maladministration. Shortage 'of money, communication and administration problems do not absolve the Council from their statutory duty' (CLAE 92/C/0670, p.7).

A failure to assess for 21 months was deemed maladministration: in the absence of professional OTs, the council 'should have sought other means to ensure that people did not wait an acceptable length of time for an assessment'. When 'disabled people ask the Council for assistance in providing adaptations to their homes, they have the right to expect that assistance is provided with reasonable speed' (CLAE 91/C/2038,p.4; see also CLAE 91/C/3210; CLAE 91/C/0729).

The ombudsman has stated that there 'may be many fields of activity where the Council – or one of its citizens – would prefer in an ideal world to act only on the advice of a professional person. That ideal is not always achievable either because of cost or because of the shortage of suitable professionals. Postponing action for a year or more may be one option but is certainly not the only alternative. If the action required is to fulfil a statutory duty then postponement for a year should not even be an option'. The ombudsman did not challenge the authority's use of priority criteria, but found maladministration because it failed 'to find a different way (as they have now done) for dealing with those applicants for whom they did not feel able to make early use of their occupational therapists' (CLAE 88/C/1048,pp.6–7).

In one authority, by the end of 1991, disability services were receiving 500 referrals per month and had over 1000 people awaiting assessment. Reorganisation and recruitment recommendations, made in a report to the Social Services Committee, were thwarted shortly afterwards by a moratorium on recruitment of non-qualified staff imposed on financial grounds. Industrial action added to the three year delay the complainant suffered. Despite all these events, the ombudsman found maladministration in that the local authority should have addressed both the resourcing problems and staffing levels long before (CLAE 91/A/3911).

Waiting Times for 'Lower Priority' People

The longer waiting times tend to be experienced by people deemed to be 'lower priority'.

For example, in one local authority, the waiting times for the highest priority was some four months; for priorities 2 and 3 up to three years. A woman aged 86 applied for adaptations. She suffered from arthritis, asthma and sciatica and had fallen and broken her hip. She had not been able to use the bath for two of the three years she had awaited assessment. The ombudsman's finding was maladministration, the delay being 'totally unacceptable' even though it was a 'relatively low priority' application. The assessment should have started within 6 months of the first approach to the local authority (CLAE 92/A/4108).

The local ombudsman has stated that it is 'not acceptable that a client may wait up to two years for an assessment, whatever the outcome of that assessment'. This was maladministration, though she did commend the council for implementing a system of gathering information at an early stage so as to determine quickly whether it could assist the person (CLAE 91/C/1852,p.7).

Even allowing for shortage of staff, and the fact that a person does not fall into the 'at risk' category, the local ombudsman might find that 'it cannot be acceptable for a client in need to face a two year wait before their needs are even quantified' (CLAE 91/C/0729,p.9).

Waiting Times for 'Higher Priority' People

Sometimes even people categorised as higher priority may have unacceptably long waits. For example, one ombudsman investigation concerned an 88-year old woman with arthritis, dizzy spells, obesity and cataracts in both eyes, osteoarthritis, and high blood pressure. She had to crawl up the stairs, and only walked (with the aid of a stick) when she went to the lavatory. Placed initially in the second and then first priority category, she had to wait 20 months for an assessment. This was 'totally unacceptable' to the local ombudsman and was maladministration. Of further concern was that the problem was not exceptional: 'delays in assessments have been widespread – there is evidence of long delays being suffered by many applicants and of large backlogs of applicants awaiting assessments in all categories' (CLAE 92/A/1173).

Very Long Waiting Times

There exist cases where very much longer waits occur. For example, the local ombudsman has investigated the case of a woman who had suffered a serious spinal injury and experienced considerable pain when sitting, standing or walking. She had to spend most of her time lying in a horizontal position. This meant that she had difficulty with, or was unable to cope with, the lavatory, taking baths, putting on socks and shoes, washing dishes at the sink, lifting a kettle, the door and window security locks (in case of fire). The wait for a full assessment for equipment and adaptations was four years and eight months, during which time her condition had worsened. This woman was not alone in waiting a long time in this local authority; the ombudsman noted a number of other people who had been waiting excessively and found maladministration (CLAE 1992 91/A/0482).

Closing of Waiting Lists and 'Never' Seeing People

In one case, the local ombudsman found that demand for occupational therapy services was such that 'non-urgent' waiting lists had been closed indefinitely. The ombudsman pointed out that the 'law makes no distinction between the Council's duty to make an assessment in "urgent" and in "non-urgent" cases. Any disabled person is entitled to request an assessment and to expect that the request is met within a reasonable time. In my opinion the Council may be failing to discharge its duties under the Chronically Sick and Disabled Persons Act' (CLAE 91/A/0482, p.21).

The local ombudsman might recognise the national problem of shortage of occupational therapists to carry out assessments, and even commend the practice of establishing priorities. However, "it can not be acceptable that those with the lowest priority may never be seen by an OT and thus never have their case considered" (CLAE 89/C/1114,.16).

Information about Waiting Times

The local ombudsman has found maladministration because of lack of clear information given to the person about waiting time. For example, a woman with an ileostomy and difficulties in bathing and showering had to wait two years for an assessment. The ombudsman accepted the council's system of priorities, but criticised the non-provision of 'clearer information' about how long she would have to wait. The injustice caused was the consequent uncertainty and inability to plan (CLAE 92/C/1403).

ORDINARY RESIDENCE

Some local authority obligations to provide community care services (both residential and non-residential) depend on whether a person is 'ordinarily resident' in the authority's area. If a person is not ordinarily resident, then the duties do not exist – or are converted to 'powers' – that is authorities can provide the services if they want to but don't have to.

Local authorities' duty to assess only applies to people for whom they 'may' provide community care services – and a government minister has said that a person denied assessment on those grounds (that an authority may not provide services) could challenge the decision in the law courts (but not via the social services complaints procedure). This is probably referring to the fact that the question of 'ordinary residence' is to be determined by the courts.

Should a dispute arise about where a person really lives, Circular guidance makes it clear that assessment and service provision should anyway not be delayed or prevented. The decision about which of two authorities is responsible should be made afterwards. In any case, Directions state that if a person's need is urgent, a local authority cannot refuse to provide residential accommodation on grounds that the person is not 'ordinarily resident' in its area.

If a person has housing needs and a housing authority becomes involved as well as the social services department, there is some scope for uncertainty because the social services and housing tests for 'ordinary residence' differ.

1. Ordinary Residence: Social Services

EXTRACTS

Legislation which is affected by the 'ordinary residence' condition includes the:

- National Assistance Act 1948 (s.21: provision of residential accommodation; and s.29: welfare services);

- the Chronically Sick and Disabled Persons Act 1970,s.2: welfare services).

What might be a duty towards an 'ordinary resident' might be a power (discretion) only towards a non-resident of the area.

DISCUSSION

Disputes Affecting Service Provision

Uncertainty and disputes between authorities about ordinary residence sometimes arise. However, Circular guidance states that delay in assessment and service provision should not occur: 'If there is a dispute about the ordinary residence of a person in need of services it should be debated after the care assessment and any provision of service' (LAC(93)7,Summary and para 3).

Additional Circular guidance about drug and alcohol misusers states that arrangements between local authorities should ensure that people not ordinarily resident in an authority can nevertheless be assessed there; and that people who have no 'settled residence' are not denied assessment because they have not been long enough in a particular locality to qualify for assessment (LAC(93)2,para 14).

Meaning of 'Ordinarily Resident'

There is no fixed definition of 'ordinarily resident' and it seems that it is ultimately for the courts to decide what it means.

Circular guidance states: 'There is no definition of "ordinarily resident" in the [National Assistance Act 1948] and the term should be given its ordinary and natural meaning subject to any interpretation by the Courts. The concept of ordinary residence involves questions of fact and degree, and factors such as time, intention and continuity, each of which may be given different weight according to the context, have to be taken into account' (LAC(93)7, para 2).

A number of court cases which have considered 'ordinary residence' are cited (paras 12,13):

- *R v London Borough of Barnet, ex p. Shah 1983:* "'abode in a particular place or country which he had adopted voluntarily and for settled purposes as part of the regular order of his life for the time being, whether of short or long duration'" (Lord Scarman);
- *Levene v IRC 1928:* 'residence in a place with some degree of continuity and apart from accidental or temporary absences';
- *R v Waltham Forest London Borough Council, ex p. Vale 1985* and *R v London Borough of Redbridge ex p. East Sussex County Council 1992* (re: people with learning difficulties making choices as to residence);

Urgent Need

Directions state that local authorities have a duty to provide residential accommodation for people who are in urgent need, whether or not they are ordinarily resident in the authority (National Assistance Act 1948, s.21(1)(a); Directions, LAC(93)10, appendix 1,para 2). For example, Circular guidance stresses the importance of 'rapid assessment procedures for drug and alcohol misusers' whose needs might be so urgent that they will need immediate residential care. It also suggests that other vulnerable people who are homeless might require urgent assessment responses: for example, because of frailty, physical disability or mental disorder (LAC(93)2,paras 26–27).

Provision of Accommodation for a Person Ordinarily Resident in Another Authority

Legislation states that a local authority can provide for such people if they have the consent of the other authority (in which the person is ordinarily resident) (NAA 1948, s.21(1)(a); Directions, LAC(93)10, appendix 1,para 2).).

People in Hospital, Nursing Homes, Prison and Similar Establishments

Legislation states that people in hospital are to be regarded as ordinarily resident in the area (if any) they were ordinarily resident in before entering hospital (NAA 1948,s.24(6); see LAC(93)7,para 2).

Circular guidance suggests that local authorities 'could reasonably apply this approach when considering responsibility for people leaving prisons, resettlement units and other similar establishments without a permanent place to live who will require social services involvement at the time of their discharge. No case law exists however, and any dispute must be resolved in the light of the specific circumstances' (LAC(93)7, para 14).

Placement of a Person in a Home in Another Authority's Area

Circular guidance states that a person 'will not as a general rule become ordinarily resident in the other local authority's area'. The other authority should be informed of the placement by the original authority.

The original authority 'should also ensure that satisfactory arrangements are made before placement for any necessary support services, such as day care, and for periodic reviews, and that there are clear agreements about the financing for all aspects of the individual's care'.

Likewise, 'no host authority should alter the accommodation or services provided for that person to a significant degree without consulting in advance the responsible local authority' (LAC(93)7,para 8).

Voluntary Move to Residential Accommodation Without Social Services Involvement

Circular guidance states that if a person moves into residential accommodation situated in another area without any social services involvement, then he or she will 'usually' become ordinarily resident within that new area. Any subsequent need for social services should be sought in the new area (LAC(93)7).

Resolution of Disputes

Circular guidance states that disputes about ordinary residence under Part III of the National Assistance Act can be determined by the Secretary of State under section 32(3) of the National Assistance Act 1948. Disputes might be about non-residential, as well as residential services.

The guidance states that each case has to be considered on its own facts; that the Secretary of State's decision is final subject only to judicial review; that the question of establishing ordinary residence is essentially a legal one; and that authorities must have agreed provisional liability for service provision before the dispute is referred to the Secretary of State (LAC(93)7, paras 24–25). The guidance describes the procedure to be followed by local authorities (paras 27–28).

Mental Health

The Secretary of State's powers of dispute resolution under section 32 of the National Assistance Act 1948 do not apply to section 117 of the Mental Health Act 1983 (after-care for discharged patients) (LAC (93)7, para 24).

2. Ordinary Residence: Health Service

Health authorities are normally required to give consent before a person is placed by social services in a nursing home.

EXTRACTS

Legislation is referred to in the following discussion.

DISCUSSION

Identification of Health Authority for Giving Consent to SSD Placements in Nursing Homes

Legislation (statutory instrument) governs how health authorities, responsible for giving consent for an individual to enter a nursing home, are to be identified by local authorities (SI 1992/3182 as amended by SI 1993/582).

The rules appear straightforward. In case of doubt the local authority should accept the address given by the person as the address at which he usually lives. If the person doesn't give such a usual address but gives instead his or her most recent address, then that address should be accepted. If the person gives neither a usual nor a most recent address, then the responsible health authority is identified simply by wherever the person is at the time.

Responsible Health Authority for Health Care

The same method is used also to identify the responsible health authority for providing health care (in general) to people (SI 1991/554; see also LAC(93)7, para 18).

Responsible Health Authority for Health Service Provision for People in Residential/Nursing Homes

Circular guidance states that if a person is placed permanently in residential accommodation outside the person's usual DHA, then responsibility transfers to the DHA in whose area the home is situated. If the placement is temporary then the original DHA normally retain responsibility (LAC(93)7, para 20).

This could mean then that whilst people's social services authority remains the same (ie the original placing authority), their health authority does not.

Dispute Procedure: Health Authorities

Disputes between health authorities should be referred to the appropriate regional health authority (LAC(93)7,para 18).

3. Ordinary Residence and Homelessness

Social services and housing authorities apply different tests to establish the 'ordinary residence' of homeless people. There is some concern that without good cooperation between housing and social services departments, this could lead to confusion.

EXTRACTS

Legislation does not explicitly compare social services and housing tests for ordinary residence.

Circular guidance states:

(social services): 'When a person states that he has no settled residence or describes himself as NFA (no fixed abode) the social services authority where he presents himself should normally accept responsibility. For a person in urgent need, the social services authority of the moment cannot argue that the possible existence of a "local connection" elsewhere excuses it from the duty to assess and provide any necessary social services; decisions on where the responsibility for the funding of such services rests, based on ordinary residence, should be decided subsequently. Rules for determining responsibility under Housing Acts should not be used to identify ordinary residence for social purposes. Any outstanding ordinary residence questions should be clearly recorded in social services records at the time they arise. Failure to do this may prejudice subsequent consideration' (LAC(93)7,para 16).

(housing) '"Local connection" for housing purposes (defined in section 61 of the Housing Act 1985, and discussed further in the statutory Homelessness Code of Guidance for Local Authorities, 3rd edition) may be established by present or past settled residence in an area, by employment in that area, by family connections, or other special circumstances. Where the test of "local connection" results in the transfer of responsibility for securing accommodation to another housing authority, the social services authority will wish to consider where "ordinary residence" then rests. The homelessness legislation provides that, where a person has no local connection, the duties to provide accommodation rest with the housing authority to whom he first applies. Even if a housing authority suspects that a person may have a local connection elsewhere, this does not absolve it from an initial duty to provide temporary accommodation if the immediate circumstances require it, pending the transfer of responsibility to another housing authority' (para 17).

Application of Different Definitions

There is concern therefore that housing authorities and social services departments assess ordinary residence for homeless people under different definitions and criteria. The result might be that 'it is perfectly possible for a homeless person with care needs to be eligible for community care services such as domiciliary support because they are "ordinarily resident" but for there to be no responsibility on the housing authority to provide accommodation because they have no "local connection" (Health Committee 1993 vol.1,p.xxxii: evidence given by the Specialist Information Training Resource Agency for Single Person Housing).

In practice, there is some evidence that at least some authorities are collaborating so as to 'reconcile conflicts of interpretation and to facilitate smooth cross-referral' (SSI 1993k,p.23).

CHAPTER 9

Assessment

KEY ISSUES

The concept of 'need' goes to the heart of community care assessment. If people are not acknowledged by authorities to be in need, then they will not qualify for services. It is also a very uncertain term. It is essentially for each local authority to define and is consequently an unpredictable element. At the planning and policy level, authorities can define need in the light of the resources they have available, and also alter that definition from time to time. Consequently, people's 'needs' (together with the services they receive) can fluctuate not just according to their own changing conditions and circumstances, but also as a result of authorities' changing policies.

The uncertainty about 'need' seems to operate on a number of different levels. For example, there is confusion about whether local authorities should be assessing people's 'needs-for-services' (which is what the legislation appears to say); or assessing people's needs 'in-the-abstract' without mentioning services at all at the assessment stage (this seems to be suggested by government guidance).

Another dimension of uncertainty is that even when people's needs have been assessed and acknowledged by authorities, the consequences of the assessment are not straightforward. This is because once people's needs (for services) have been established, there is a further decision to be made by authorities about whether those services are 'called for' or are 'necessary'. Authorities are likely to apply criteria of eligibility to decide this – and perhaps, for example, only people 'at risk' will qualify for service provision.

These criteria themselves are often an uncertain element; it is not always clear on what basis they have been developed (because useful information about the needs of the local population might not be available); nor always clear how consistently and fairly the criteria are applied.

If these criteria of eligibility are not set to a level which ensures that only the 'right' number of people qualify for services, local authorities' budgets are likely to be strained unpredictably. This then raises another large and uncertain legal issue about when, and whether, local authorities can take account of resources in deciding how to respond to particular individuals' assessments – either by deciding about the level of service to be provided, or even by denying provision altogether.

Yet further difficulty arises because community care services are provided under different pieces of legislation. There is a strong view that if 'need' is identified under some (e.g. the Chronically Sick and Disabled Persons Act) – but not all – of this legislation, then authorities do actually (and automatically) have legal obligations to provide services to meet that need. Government guidance suggests that local authorities could avoid such obligations by distinguishing between people's 'preferences' and their 'needs'. This guidance has itself caused confusion and controversy.

(The tension between preferences and needs is further highlighted by the fact that guidance urges 'user empowerment' in assessment, but acknowledges that decisions about need and about what to provide lie ultimately with authorities and the professional judgements of their staff. This is dealt with in the next chapter.)

The overall significance of this elastic and elusive concept of 'need' is that local authorities generally have very considerable discretion to determine who should receive what services. On the other hand, service users and their advisers might be advised to exploit the confusion which exists about use of the term 'need' and about the legal consequences which follow once it has been acknowledged in individual cases. Thus, in a recent case about residential care, the judge accepted professional advice about a person's needs – and dismissed the authority's argument that the needs only amounted to a preference and that it could therefore take resources into account. This judgement appears to represent a straightforward approach to the concept of need.

ASSESSMENT: A SERVICE IN ITS OWN RIGHT

Community care assessment is a statutory duty and a service in its own right. Legislation states that local authorities must assess a person's needs for community care services if it appears that he or she might be in need of such services. Following the assessment, authorities then have a duty to decide which services they are going to provide. The assessment, and then the decision about provision, are two separate duties.

Legislation does not state what form assessment should take – this is left to what an authority might 'consider appropriate'.

EXTRACTS

Legislation states:

'where it appears to a local authority that any person for whom they may provide or arrange for the provision of community care services may be in need of any such services, the authority...shall carry out an assessment of his needs for those services; and…having regard to the results of that assessment, shall then decide whether his needs call for the provision by them of any such services' (NHSCCA 1990,s.47(1)).

Policy guidance states that:

'assessment is a service in its own right and can be distinguished from the services that are arranged as a consequence' (DH 1990, para 3.15).

Directions. Under section 47(4) of the NHS and Community Care Act 1990, the Secretary of State has power to make Directions about 'the manner in which an assessment under this section is to be carried out or the form it is to take but, subject to any such directions and to (section 3 of the Disabled Persons (SCR) Act 1976: unimplemented)…it shall be carried out in such manner and take such form as the local authority consider appropriate'.

No such Directions have been made.

DISCUSSION
Form of Assessment
During the passing of the NHS and Community Care Bill, the Secretary of State for Health, resisting an amendment to prescribe the form of assessments, referred to the 'cumbersome and time-consuming' assessment of special educational needs by education authorities, and indicated that similar formalities should be avoided in community care. She explained: 'The Government will not prescribe how local authorities should make the essential assessments. The challenge to local authorities will be to tackle that task within their resources'. Rule books were not the answer (H26 1990).

This means that the process of assessment, pivotal to the whole community care system, remains legally undefined: local authorities are free to adopt their own approaches to it.

COMMUNITY CARE SERVICES: POWERS AND DUTIES

Community care assessment is about assessing people's needs for community care services. Community care services are defined in section 46 of the NHS and Community Care Act 1990 which refers to other, previously existing, legislation. This previous legislation defines a number of duties and powers governing the provision of a number of services. These are described fully elsewhere in this book (see Chapter 4).

NEEDS-LED ASSESSMENT

The NHS and Community Care Act 1990 does not refer to how assessment should be carried out, nor has the Secretary of State used her power to make Directions specifying the form of assessment. In the absence of such Directions, both policy and practice guidance do refer to assessment and advocate 'needs-led' assessment. This seems to mean assessing people's needs first, almost 'in the abstract', before considering what services they require and what services they can be provided with. This principle of assessing people's 'real' needs fully, rather than solely in terms of available services ('service-led' assessment), is a model welcomed in principle by many people.

Practice guidance points out that such an approach requires local authorities to break with past practices of 'service-led' assessments. It is reported that social services staff are sometimes finding it difficult to assess without reference to services.

EXTRACTS

Legislation is silent about the form of assessment, and neither the term 'needs-led' nor the concept (expressed in other words) appears to be clearly stated.

Policy guidance states that the 'needs-led approach pre-supposes a progressive separation of assessment from service provision' (DH 1990,para 3.15).

Circular guidance states that 'the assessment of need and decisions about the services to be provided are separate stages in the process' (CI (92)34,para 5).

Practice guidance states that assessment systems should be 'consistent with a needs-led, rather than a service-led, approach' (SSI/SWSG (MG) 1991, p.43).

DISCUSSION

Service-Led Approach in the Past

The needs-led approach is viewed as breaking significantly with past practice. Practice guidance states:

> 'the assessment of need will require a significant change in attitude and approach by most practitioners. They will have to make conscious efforts to treat the assessment of need as a separate exercise from consideration of the service response...few practitioners currently make that distinction, nor are they encouraged to do so by the assessment procedures they are required to operate' (SSI/SWSG 1991(PG), p.47).

This past state of affairs was confirmed by SSI research published in 1991 (SSI 1991c, p.39). More recently, Ellis (1993, p.17) in a Joseph Rowntree report found the same pattern:

> 'administrative staff saw their task as to weed out enquiries which did not fit with their understanding of services available within the department. In taking referrals, they would record only such information as they thought "relevant" to the range of specialist teams. Consequently, referrals for a "general assessment" would not be accepted but translated into a specific request.'

Early reports on community care implementation suggest that in some areas, staff, users and carers are struggling with the needs-led approach (eg. SSI/NHSME 1994a, p.11; SSI 1994g, p.18). For example, where resources are limited and services have to be provided quickly (eg. on hospital discharge) it might be difficult to adhere to the 'needs-led' approach (SSI 1994d, p.26). For example, the local ombudsman has found maladministration when an authority was applying a two-hour-per-week maximum to home help services; this inhibited the 'proper assessment of each individual's needs' (CLAE 93/A/2071).

NEEDS-LED ASSESSMENT: FOR 'NEEDS', OR FOR 'NEEDS FOR SERVICES'

The NHS and Community Care Act 1990, section 47, describes a twofold process. First, a person's 'needs for services' are assessed. Second, a decision is made about what services the local authority will provide.

However, there has been some suggestion that assessment be 'needs-led' to the extent that services are not mentioned in the assessment at all. It is only after the assessment that the results of the assessments are to be 'translated' (e.g. via criteria of eligibility) into a plan about service provision (corresponding with the second part of legislative process: the decision about services).

It is not certain that such needs-led assessment is consistent with the wording of the legislation in section 47(1)(a), which talks about assessment of 'needs for services' – not just 'needs'. It could be argued that a person cannot be assessed for services without those services being considered and mentioned in the assessment itself. A further point to make is that if no mention of services and criteria of eligibility is made in the assessment, then it is difficult to see how users can participate fully in the assessment (guidance states that they should, see Chapter 10; see RADAR 1994, p.27; SSI/NHSE 1994f, p.27; SSI/NHSE 1994; p.38). It might also be argued that the legal principle of fairness (see Chapter 7) is being contravened if people are not told about how services and criteria relate to the assessment – since they are then being denied crucial information about how the whole procedure is working.

In this connection, some anxiety has arisen in central and local government about the effect of section 2(1) of the Chronically Sick and Disabled Persons Act 1970. Under that Act, local authorities are thought to have a 'strong' duty (towards individuals) to provide or arrange welfare services for people assessed as needing them. Local authorities now have a duty towards disabled people, when carrying out a community care assessment, to decide if they need any of the services under section 2(1) of the 1970 Act. The concern has been that local authorities will find themselves legally committed, beyond their resources, to providing services under the 1970 Act – and yet not be able to plead lack of resources.

There seems to be a view in some quarters that the needs-led approach to assessment could avoid the problem, because if services are not mentioned in the assessment, then s.2 duties to provide those services cannot be triggered.

However, a reading of s.47(2) (see below) would seem to make it quite plain that, during (not after) an assessment for CSDPA services, an authority has to identify a person's needs for the services mentioned in the 1986 Act (the services mentioned are those in s.2 of the CSDPA 1970). If this is what the Act says, then it would seem not to be open to authorities to fail to mention services during assessment for CSDPA services.

EXTRACTS

Legislation describes the local authority's duty to assess as:

> 'an assessment of his needs for those services' (NHSCCA 1990, s.47(1(a)). It goes on: 'having regard to the results of that assessment, [it] shall then decide whether his needs call for the provision by them of any such services' (s.47(1)(b)).

Legislation (NHSCCA 1990, s.47(2) states:

> 'If at any time during the assessment of the needs of any person under subsection (1)(a) above it appears to a local authority that he is a disabled person, the authority-
>
> (a) shall proceed to make such a decision as to the services he requires as mentioned in section 4 of the Disabled Persons (Services, Consultation and Representation) Act 1986 without his requesting them to do so under that section; and
>
> (b) shall inform him that they will be doing so and of his rights under that Act.'

Policy guidance states:

> 'Assessment does not take place in a vacuum: account needs to be taken of the local authority's criteria for determining when services should be provided, the types of service they have decided to make available and the overall range of services provided by other agencies, including health authorities' (DH 1990, para 3.15).

Policy guidance also states:

> 'Once an individual's need for welfare services, specified in Section 2 of the Chronically Sick and Disabled Persons Act 1970, has been established, the authority must make the necessary arrangements to meet it' (DH 1990, para 3.30).

Practice guidance states:

> 'The needs should have been defined at the assessment stage but more detail may be required to specify the service requirements. The aim of the care planning stage is to target any intervention as precisely as possible on the identified needs' (SSI/SWSG 1991(PG), p.62).

Practice guidance also states that initial assessment response 'does not presuppose the service outcome' (SSI/SWSG 1991(MG), p.43).

DISCUSSION
Assessment of 'Need for Services'
A straightforward interpretation of the NHSCCA 1990,s.47(1) would be that the statutory duty to assess is the duty to assess an individual's needs for services. This seems to be what the words say. The legislation goes on state that the local authority must then decide which services actually to provide or arrange.

Baroness Blatch (H59 1990) explained during the Committee stage of the NHS and Community Care Bill.

> 'Assessment will identify needs for services. However, [the subsection] requires that, following assessment, local authorities must decide, having regard to the results of the assessment, whether there is a need for them to provide services. Therefore, the local authority is required to decide which of the needs it will meet taking account of duties under Section 2 of the Chronically Sick and Disabled Persons Act 1970. Apart from that, it is not obliged to meet all needs and will wish to take into account its priorities and resources.'

Both the legislation (s.47(1) and (2)), and Baroness Blatch's statement seem to indicate distinctly that assessment will identify people's needs for services – but that not all those needs have to be met.

Assessment of Need Not Specifying Services
Nevertheless, policy and practice guidance seem to suggest removing reference to services altogether from the assessment. For example, policy guidance states: 'The needs-led approach pre-supposes a progressive separation of assessment from service provision' (DoH 1990, para 3.15). Community care practice guidance gives an example of this. Assessment proformas should '**focus the assessment on needs, without categorising those needs in terms of services**' (SSI/SWSG(PG) 1991, p.56).

'Triggering' of Statutory Duties
As already observed, the needs-led approach to assessment might in principle satisfy many people's notions of good practice: the finding out of people's 'real' needs. However, a possible consequence of not referring to services in the assessment is that certain duties, for example, under s.2 of the CSDPA 1970, would never be triggered by assessment alone. The following paragraphs explain this approach, although as already explained (see above), it is not clear whether such an approach to assessment is consistent with the NHSCCA 1990.

The Audit Commission tried to explain this approach to the House of Commons Health Committee (1993,vol.2). If local authorities

> 'say to people, "We have assessed you for home care, we think you qualify but we cannot provide it", then they are at risk of laying themselves open to being legally bound by that decision. If they assess people, people's mobility, their capability

to undertake basic daily living tasks and so on and provide people with that sort of assessment and then say: "You may need help with some of these, our eligibility criteria are these, and therefore we can provide help with those but you still need help with other activities", then I think they sit on the right side of the law' (vol.2, p.8).

A 1993 SSI letter to directors of social services in London spelt out a similar message. It referred to the

'legal ambiguity as between the Chronically Sick and Disabled Persons Act 1970 which is service-led and the Disabled Persons Act 1986 and the NHS and Community Care Act 1990 which are needs-led...It is this 'service-led' definition of need which leads lawyers to be cautious. It reinforces the requirement to develop a "needs-led" language, which leaves open the selection of the appropriate level and type of service response' (in: Health Committee 1993,vol.2,pp.44–45).

Indeed, it is reported that this is just what some local authorities are attempting to do (AMA 1993). They might, for example, attempt '"to distinguish in...assessment procedures between the recording of a general description of help needed, eg. help with domestic activities in the home, help during the day etc., from the final Care Plan which identifies specific services that could be provided for an individual"'. Another example quoted in the AMA trawl seems blatantly not to conform with what the legislation states (about assessing 'needs for services'): '"We are assessing need and then offering services to relieve that need, but we are not assessing for services; hence we do not record need for services"' (p.4).

There might in any case be a question about just how sustainable the distinction is between need-in-the-abstract, and a need for services. For example, 'practical assistance in the home', a service under s.2 of the CSDPA 1970, is already a broad term covering anything from basic housework to personal care. How non-specific, in this example, must the language of assessment be, in order to avoid words which will automatically trigger the duty to provide such practical assistance? The Audit Commission (see above) suggests using the language of functional needs. A substitute, in this example, might be: 'difficulties with daily living functions'?

As already explained above, it is anyway arguable that the 'needs-led' approach is not consistent with the legislation.

NEED AND CRITERIA OF ELIGIBILITY

The NHS and Community Care Act lays down a two stage process consisting of assessment for services and then a decision about what services will be provided by the local authority. Legislation does not state how such a decision should be reached, but both practice and Circular guidance explain that priorities and criteria of eligibility should be applied in reaching the decision.

Local authorities have a discretion to set their own eligibility criteria and definitions of need.

Eligibility criteria are envisaged by guidance as a tool for deciding whether a person is in sufficient need to qualify for services from the local authority. The idea behind such criteria seems to be two-fold: (a) that they will enable authorities to target their resources on those most in need; and (b) that authorities will be able to do this without exceeding their budgets.

There are a number of difficulties. Formulation of criteria reflecting the levels of local needs depends on prior possession of adequate information about the needs of the local population; and there is evidence that local authorities do not generally possess this (see Chapter 19). Without such information, criteria are unlikely to reflect local needs, or to ensure that assessed 'needs' do not outstrip resources available. In other words, the criteria might let too many people through the 'gate' and put authorities in danger of attempting to provide more services than they can afford.

If this occurs, there is in turn a risk that authorities, might make arbitrary and inequitable decisions in individual cases about what, or at least what level of, services people can have. Such decisions might run the risk of findings of maladministration by the local ombudsman; and possibly unfavourable rulings by public law courts if authorities have behaved very unreasonably or unfairly (see Chapter 7).

At the same time, Circular guidance reminds authorities that such criteria cannot be applied absolutely rigidly, because there must always be scope to take account of individual circumstances. Legally, this is because local authorities must not 'fetter their discretion' (this is explained in Chapter 7). For example, a policy never to provide facilities for 'comfort' or 'convenience' under the CSDPA 1970 might be a fettering of discretion – or in other words a rigid, 'blanket' policy which could be challenged.

The application of criteria at this stage is just one more hurdle, centred on concepts such as 'need' and 'priority'; which people have to get over in order to receive services; and which authorities can use to regulate services in line with resources. Thus, criteria are a powerful tool for authorities. On the other hand they are difficult to set and apply, and so service users and their advisers might be able to challenge authorities on grounds, for example, of inconsistent or arbitrary application of criteria. In addition there are sometimes ways of manipulating the presentation of people's needs, so that they 'fit' in with the criteria.

Thus, government guidance envisages an elastic concept of need. However, a recent community care case about residential care limited an authority's ability to manoeuvre. The judge took a straightforward approach to need and its consequences by stating that a person's needs could include his psychological needs; and that the authority had a duty to meet those needs. The judge appeared to dismiss the authority's contention that the person's 'needs' were really only his 'preferences' and that therefore it could take account of resources.

Legislation states that the local authority,

'having regard to the results of that assessment, [it] shall then decide whether his needs call for the provision by them of any such services' (NHS and Community Care 1990,s.47(1)(b)).

Practice guidance states that the response to assessment can be partly based on priority groups, such as those

'users with complex needs or those requiring significant levels of resources...Whatever groups are targeted, the **criteria for selecting** them should be understood by all staff, the other care agencies and by the public at large' (SSI/SWSG 1991(MG), p.64).

Circular guidance states:

'Authorities will still have considerable discretion, both with regard to their eligibility criteria for these services, and in respect of how assessed needs should best be met' (CI(92)34,para 4 now formally cancelled, but see p.401).

Circular guidance states that, in deciding the service response to assessment:

'Authorities can be helped in this process by defining eligibility criteria ie a system of banding which assigns individuals to particular categories, depending on the extent of the difficulties they encounter in carrying out every day tasks and relating the level of response to the degree of such difficulties. Any "banding" should not, however, be rigidly applied, as account needs to be taken of individual circumstances. Such eligibility criteria should be phrased in terms of the factors identified in the assessment process' (CI(92)34, para 14).

Elasticity of 'Need'
Eligibility criteria are effectively about defining 'need' – in terms of what, for whom and in what circumstances a local authority is or isn't going to provide services. The term 'need' is highly elastic, is used in a number of different ways and is capable of causing confusion and disagreement.

Practice guidance (SSI/SWSG(PG) 1991) states that it uses the term as 'shorthand for the requirements of individuals to enable them to achieve, maintain or restore an acceptable level of social independence or quality of life, as defined by the particular care agency or authority' (p.12). This statement emphasises that it is the local authority which ultimately determines need – not the individual who is being assessed. This means that a person deemed to be 'in need' in one local authority, might not be in need if they lived (perhaps only several hundred yards away) in another.

The guidance further explains that the meaning of need might vary in time even within one local authority because of changes in the law, in local policy, the availability of resources and the patterns of local demand (p.12). This means that a person deemed to be in need one year, might not be the next.

Eligibility criteria are not a 'new' concept for social services. For example, social services occupational therapists have long operated local criteria for the assessment and provision of daily living equipment and home adaptations. The London Boroughs Occupational Therapy Managers Groups has distilled these 'common criteria' for London in two sets of guidelines (LBOTMG 1992; LBOTMG 1988), which are probably used extensively outside of London as well.

Nevertheless, the courts have tackled the issue of 'need' in a case about provision of residential care under s.21 of the National Assistance Act 1948. The judge dealt straightforwardly with the issues by finding:

- an obligation to provide residential accommodation to the person concerned under s.21 of the NAA 1948;
- that assessment under s.47 of the NHSCCA 1990 should be appropriate to the particular needs of the individual – and that this was confirmed by Circular guidance (LAC(92)15) which states that services for people with learning disabilities 'should be planned on an individual basis';
- that the local authority's complaints procedure review panel had made a 'crucial finding of fact' (based on expert professional opinion) that the person's 'entrenched position' (insistence on going to particular, more expensive accommodation) was 'part of his psychological need' and not a mere preference;
- unconvincing the authority's argument that the person's position was mere preference which, as the authority put it, could not be allowed to 'override everything else including resources' and thus create unwanted precedent which the authority would be obliged to follow.

The judgement appears to dismiss two important arguments used by authorities; the plea of lack of resources linked to exploitation of the distinction between 'needs' and 'preferences' (see below). The judge concluded his reasoning by stating: 'the law is clear. The Council have to provide for the Applicant's needs' (*R v Avon CC, ex p. M 1993*).

Eligibility Criteria and Rationing

Rationing is not a freely used word for obvious reasons. Nevertheless, eligibility criteria are in effect a rationing tool. An Audit Commission (1992b, p.26) report referred to 'tough decisions on priorities and eligibility criteria' with local authority Members and senior managers having to 'take the decisions about rationing'. A local community care plan points out that whilst eligibility criteria are sometimes criticised as 'a backdoor route to rationing', rationing has, to an extent, 'always existed' (Kent County Council Social Services 1993, para 1.4).

Discretion to Set Local Eligibility Criteria

Local authorities have discretion to set local eligibility criteria. The logic of this would seem to be that, so long as it is done reasonably and legally, there are no restrictions. For example, one authority could set a low threshold of need and appear to be a generous provider; another could set a very high threshold and appear to provide little.

In written evidence to the House of Commons Health Committee (1993), the Department of Health explained:

'The setting of eligibility criteria is a matter for each local authority in the light of local circumstances including the availability of resources. As in all things, authorities must act reasonably, and the setting of eligibility criteria cannot exempt them from meeting their statutory duties or exercising their discretion properly'.

'It is most unlikely that the Secretary of State would wish to intervene in the setting of eligibility criteria. However, she does have powers generally and in cases of default, and she will therefore consider on their merits any cases in which it appears that an authority has manifestly failed to exercise its statutory functions without reasonable excuse' (vol.2, p.44).

A judge has stated that an applicant, contesting a refusal by two local authorities to make provision for him under the CSDPA 1970 (s.2), would have had to show that 'the refusal to meet the identified or contended for need was irrational in the accepted sense of the term in this jurisdiction'. Neither the court nor the Secretary of State's powers to intervene could arise unless the authority's decision was 'perverse or irrational' (*R v Kent County Council and Others, ex p. Bruce 1986*). This might suggest that eligibility criteria defining need would have to be very wayward before judges will intervene.

In broader but similar vein, asked about the 'acceptability of national minimum standards for care in the community', the government replied that it 'is the responsibility of local authorities to manage the implementation of community care. We will continue to monitor progress closely and offer guidance and direction as is considered necessary' (H60 1994).

Clearly then, the use of eligibility criteria to determine (level of) service provision is likely to vary, and perhaps sometimes strain, the meaning of the term 'need'. For example, one Department of Health-commissioned study of elderly people discharged from hospital found that 'over half the sample remained housebound and severely disabled twelve weeks after their discharge from hospital. In the researchers' views, they required more intensive and frequent care with a wider range of tasks than current levels of mainstream home help provision could provide, given the constraints on resources' (Neill, Williams 1992, p.140). This is an obvious example of differing interpretations of people's 'needs'.

Criteria might in some circumstances be manipulated to 'create' the appropriate 'need'. For example, a woman recovering from major surgery might require help with the housework, but the criteria rule out 'housework only' requests. To circumvent the criteria, the home care organiser persists by describing the woman's need as 'help with cooking'. This need then falls within the criteria and can thus be the vehicle for help with the housework – although the woman can actually manage cooking herself (Ellis 1993, p.37).

It might well be that public opinion rather than legal obstacle might curtail the stringency of eligibility criteria. It has to be remembered, however, that elderly and severely disabled people are vulnerable and many are unable or unwilling to publicise their plight.

Objectivity of Need?

As explained, authorities can set their own definitions of need. In addition, they might be able to argue that, even when they appear to treat two people with similar conditions differently, 'no two cases are the same'. They could argue this because people's individual circumstances can vary greatly. Thus, authorities might not only be able to set their own definitions of need, but also to some extent be able to 'get away' with inconsistent application of those definitions.

From service users' and their advisers' point of view, the aim might be to bring some objectivity to an authority's definition of need and its criteria of eligibility. One way of doing this is to pool local knowledge of how an authority is treating individual people – so as to be able to point to any radically inconsistent decisions by the authority. Another method of bringing some objectivity to the idea of need is for people to obtain medical opinions from doctors – these have traditionally held some sway in social services and housing departments.

Standards and the CSDPA 1970

The question of setting national minimum standards has been long considered in the context of the CSDPA 1970, an Act central to community care's main aim of enabling people to remain in their own homes. Furthermore, the principles involved and the objections raised are of general interest and application.

Sometimes widely varying services from authority to authority might seem to conflict with the intention of the author (Alfred Morris) of the CSDPA 1970. Introducing the Bill, he explained (what was to become) section 2 as meaning that 'provisions for the disabled which are now permissive would be mandatory upon local authorities. The whole Clause is intended to standardise local provision on the basis of the best existing practice' (H61 1969). This was why it was mandatory (H62 1970).

By contrast in 1983, when asked about 'any proposals for ensuring the attainment of nationally determined standards by local authorities in implementing' the CSDPA, the government replied that the implementation 'is the responsibility of local authorities, which are best placed to judge the provision necessary to meet the needs of disabled people in their particular area' (H63 1983).

The government has further explained why it is opposed to standards for the CSDPA 1970:

'detailed guidance prepared by a Government Department, however well-inten-tioned, would not be an adequate substitute for on-the-spot decisions by the authorities that are closest to the needs of the individual and the services which exist in his area. More important, there is always a risk that minimum standards – in practice that is all that we could sensibly talk about – would be treated in some cases as maximum standards and would inhibit some of the developments we would wish to see. They would restrict rather than enlarge the scope for flexibility and innovation...However, to acknowledge that local authorities are the best judges of local needs is not to absolve them of their statutory duties under the Act' (H64 1985).

Consistent Application of Eligibility Criteria in Practice

The task of applying eligibility criteria is reported to be giving local authorities difficulties (SSI/NHSE 1994e, p.6). Criteria might be ill-defined, unclear to service users and interpreted variably by local authority staff (Smith 1994, p.20). The danger alluded to by the Audit Commission (1993, p.4) is that if 'criteria are too vague they will produce arbitrary and variable results which will reduce equity and may not control expenditure if they are too tight they will limit creativity'. Nevertheless, there is also a pragmatic view that the 'initial fuzziness' of eligibility criteria could help rather than hinder authorities to achieve strategic policies which target people most in need (Jeffrey 1994).

An SSI letter to London Directors of Social Services has pointed out that if assessment outcomes do not relate to published eligibility criteria, then local authorities could face charges of maladministration (see: Health Committee 1993,vol.2, p.45). A study (SSI/NHSME 1994a, p.9) of six local authorities found a 'lack of a clear relationship between eligibility criteria and information collected in the assessment proformas. Therefore, there was little or no means of monitoring how, if at all, these criteria were being applied and with what degree of consistency'.

A RADAR project (1994) reports that adverse assessment decisions might be made on the basis of informal, orally communicated policies and eligibility criteria – which might not be available in documentary form. The consequence might be that there is no 'formal means whereby clients, the public, new staff and elected members could be properly informed' about such policies and criteria (p.33).

The potential problem is not new. A RADAR (Cook 1982) report about the CSDPA 1970 gave an example of how one local authority, surveying its own home help service, found large disparities between different divisions within the authority. People in one division might receive up to twice the amount of services as people with the same level of disability in another division (p.22).

Nor will the local ombudsman condone inconsistent and inequitable application of eligibility criteria. In one case involving home adaptations, delay occurred in placing an order because of insufficient financial resources. This was

> 'no justification for delay. Once the Council became aware of their financial position they should have instituted procedures to ensure that adaptation works were prioritised on a borough-wide basis. Instead it appears that whether a need was met depended on competing demands on the local repairs budget for a particular week. I cannot therefore be certain that people with similar needs were dealt with in a similar way' (CLAE 91/A/1481, p.17).

In another case, the local ombudsman investigated services provided (under CSDPA 1970,s.2) to a person discharged from hospital. Following a review of the person's needs, the letter stated that social services would not advocate for him with the housing department or DSS.

> 'Such responsibility cannot be evaded by stating that Social Services have no managerial responsibility for Housing or DSS. Instead the decision whether or not to advocate should have been based on objective criteria of the client's need and the Council's resources. I hope that the provisions of the 1990 Act which have recently come into force...will eliminate such examples of lack of clarity in decision-making' (CLAE 92/A/1374).

Consistent Application of Criteria over Time

An obvious question which arises is how often authorities can change their policies and eligibility criteria on the one hand, but on the other be seen to apply them consistently and fairly. Community care plans are published annually and it is perhaps on this basis that the Department of Health has stated that eligibility criteria should not be altered in mid-year. However, one director of social services has pointed out that, whilst it is easy for ministers to say this,

> 'it seems only realistic to work out how many complex care packages and/or placements we can afford to buy, and then set up budget controls for this on a monthly or quarterly basis throughout the year...In that way, practitioners will become involved in deciding who gets what, and when, if demand outstrips supply' (Jeffrey 1994).

This practical approach carries with it the implication that what people get could vary from month to month depending on demand. The question then remains, at what point, if any, such an approach becomes inequitable, if not in any legal sense, at least in the sense of maladministration which the local ombudsman might find. To vary provision in this way would apparently be contrary to government guidance – yet this does seem to be what happens in the health service sometimes, when access to an NHS bed might vary depending on demand from one month to the next. One question to be asked is what happens if authorities inform people clearly that provision is continually subject to the resources available – and that overall this is the most effective, and therefore, ironically, overall the most equitable way of handling provision. This would clearly satisfy some aspects of fairness such as information-giving and legitimate expectation: ie, people are told exactly what to expect.

Rigidity of Criteria and 'Banding'

If criteria need to be consistently applied, nevertheless the Circular guidance (above) states that the consequent 'banding' of priorities 'should not be rigidly applied' because individual circumstances must be taken account of. This is connected to the legal principle that authorities should not 'fetter their discretion' (see Chapter 7). It is a little difficult to understand because it would seem almost to contradict the idea of applying criteria consistently.

Under this principle, for example, 'policy decisions to remove some sorts of service from the catalogue of need – the most notable being cleaning in the home' (Health Committee 1993, vol.2, p.161) may be questionable in law if applied in rigid, 'blanket' fashion, rather than based on individual circumstances and assessment. Hence, more recently, the concern expressed in the House of Commons that the Secretary of State for Health had said 'without any suggestion of criticism, that some local authorities had now withdrawn cleaning-only home help services altogether. If so, then *ipso facto* such services are no longer available to any disabled person in their areas, irrespective of need and the requirements of the law' (H90 1991 and see RADAR 1994, p.8).

A Parliamentary ombudsman investigation notes (in passing) DHSS legal advice on this issue. A local authority had, because of financial pressures, withdrawn financial assistance for holidays for disabled people. The DHSS letter to the local authority stated that the s.2 duty 'placed an obligation on the local authority to assess the needs of all relevant persons for the service in question and sought an assurance that the Council were continuing to assess the needs of each individual and to take appropriate action where need was accepted' (PCA C.799/81 1981–1982).

The local ombudsman has commented on the taking account of irrelevant factors in determining need. For example, one local authority had developed a policy which was to provide telephone equipment ('minicoms') only to deaf people who already had a telephone installed in their home. The ombudsman agreed with the voluntary organisation that the prior existence of a telephone was irrelevant to need for the minicom (CLAE 90/C/2203, p.1). This view of the situation was reiterated by the government in Parliament when answering a question about duties to assess individual needs for telephones and associated special equipment (H39 1993).

RADAR (1993, p.19) reports the withdrawal at a stroke by one local authority of telephone rental payments to 273 disabled people. Two particular complaints were made that this had been done without reassessment and where need for the service had not diminished. RADAR and the British Polio Fellowship challenged the legality of this, and the director of social services agreed to reassess all the people concerned and reinstate the service where necessary. RADAR reports that the service for all 273 people was reinstated.

As one local community care plan puts it: the 'use of eligibility criteria is not an exact science, so care managers and social workers must have some flexibility about how the criteria are interpreted and applied' (Kent County Council Social Services 1993,para 1.4). This is discussed further in the specific context of the CSDPA 1970.

One way of avoiding over-rigidity and fettering of discretion would be, for example, for assessors to ignore priority ratings and criteria which are clearly unsuitable for certain groups of people. For example, the priorities/criteria might be 'overly rigid, focusing on immediate or urgent needs rather than ongoing and changing needs' – and so be perceived to be inappropriate for people with learning disabilities (reported in SSI/NHSE 1994f, p.25).

Basis for Criteria of Eligibility

The basis for criteria has already been discussed when priorities are made before assessment is carried out (see Chapter 8). The same principles apply after assessment – for example, should an authority concentrate its resources on fewer people at high risk, or spread its resources more widely, so as to prevent people deteriorating and entering (at a later date) the high risk category? To do so could, for example, lead to disagreement with health service staff about effective domiciliary care (SSI/NHSE 1994e, p.45). Similarly, there is a question of whether providing only for people at risk is inconsistent with part of s.2 of the CSDPA, which imposes a duty not just with respect to people's safety but also their comfort and convenience.

The additional point has been reported that practitioners might be sceptical about priorities and criteria if they have not been tested against past spending patterns for various needs. This is because the priorities cannot then serve either as a rationing or a planning tool (SSI/NHSE 1994e, p.31).

Waiting Lists

Waiting times might occur for both assessment and service provision itself. Waiting times have long been a feature of some services central to community care. For example, a Parliamentary ombudsman investigation (PCA C.12/K 1975–1976) in the 1970s noted (in passing) the view of the DHSS that some local authorities were placing people on waiting lists *after* assessment under the CSDPA 1970 simply because they were short of money.

The local ombudsman has commented on one local authority's claim about CSDPA 1970,s.2, 'that although they may be under an obligation to provide a facility they do not consider that they have an obligation to provide the facility immediately. Thus, they argue some delay is acceptable'. The ombudsman stated that 'whether or not any particular delay is so excessive as to constitute maladministration will depend on the facts of the individual case' (CLAE 90/C/2203, p.2).

In the field of housing law, where there was a duty 'to secure that accommodation becomes available', the judge ruled that the duty was not necessarily to produce a house immediately – and that putting a person on a waiting list sufficed (*R v Brent LBC, ex p. Macwan 1994*). The housing law duty here, 'secure that accommodation becomes available', could be regarded as comparable to the CSDPA 1970 (s.2) duty, to 'make arrangements' for the provision of services.

Professional Judgement

Inevitably, no matter how many explicit criteria are laid down, there is a point at which professional and personal judgements are decisive. For example, the local ombudsman is likely to decline to challenge professional judgements about what is or what is not needed unless it is 'utterly unreasonable' (CLAE 91/B/2154, p.23).

In one Scottish investigation, a social work department and housing department were disputing about which was responsible for replacing windows. A disabled couple who could not open their windows were living in an increasingly damp (through condensation) house. The ombudsman was 'faced with two technical judgements: ie that the windows were satisfactory as far as the Housing Authority were concerned and that the replacement of the windows was not necessary as far as the Social Work Authority were concerned. Both of these decisions were taken as a result of visits by both authorities to the house and I found no reason to criticise them'. (Nevertheless, he urged the authorities to review their procedures for joint action, and agreement for joint funding was finally reached) (CLAS 101/81, p.10).

Although it is not the business of the ombudsman 'to criticise decisions of a council, providing those decisions were properly made', they may not always be so made. For example, in one case assessment had been made by an experienced and qualified officer. Her decision was in effect overruled by her manager on the grounds that the decision was not consistent with other comparable cases. The ombudsman found both no evidence for those grounds and that they were anyway disputed by another officer – and thus that the overruling of the original decision was 'inconsistent' and constituted maladministration (CLAE 91/B/0254, p.19).

Where problems arise because of conflict between apparent need and, for example, safety standards, the local ombudsman cannot 'tell the Council what decision to make, as that is a matter for them. What they should do, however, is to put all the facts to Members who will then be in a position to come to a proper reasoned decision'. This had not happened, there had been delay and not all the options had been properly examined. This was maladministration (CLAE 88/A/303, pp.14–15).

TAKING ACCOUNT OF RESOURCES WHEN RESPONDING TO ASSESSED NEEDS

Local authorities have to operate within limited resources and this inevitably affects provision of services. Nevertheless, exactly how to regulate services appears at times to be a confused issue.

Resources might in practice be taken account of at two levels. At the planning and policy level, definitions of 'need' can be set, so that only if people are assessed as being in need, according to the definition, do they get services. For example, Circular guidance on the CSDPA 1970 made it quite clear that criteria of need were to be determined according to resources.

Second, at the individual level, there is the question of whether resources can be taken account of when responding to an individual's assessment.

There is a strong view shared, it seems, by central government and some lawyers, that for mandatory services, involving a duty to an individual (under the CSDPA 1970,s.2 and Mental Health Act 1983,s.117), resources cannot legally be taken account of in order to deny a service, once a need for it has been assessed and provision deemed to be necessary. (At most, perhaps, resources could be taken account of to decide the level and type of service provided – but not to deny a service altogether. However, if this is so, authorities still have considerable latitude, since, for example, the difference in cost between provision of a commode and a downstairs bathroom is immense – but in both cases a service is still being provided.)

This strong view, though, appears not to be based on any judicial ruling made in connection with either of the two Acts. There is a contrary view that even if a statutory duty arises under s.2 of the CSDPA or s.117 of the MHA 1983, the courts might possibly be reluctant to rule against public authorities on the sole grounds that they do not have enough money.

EXTRACTS

Legislation is silent about determining need in line with resources at planning and policy level; and about whether authorities can take account of resources when responding to an individual's assessment.

Policy guidance states:

'local authorities also have a responsibility to meet needs within the resources available and this will sometimes involve difficult decisions where it will be necessary to strike a balance between meeting the needs identified within available resources and meeting the care preferences of the individual' (DH 1990, para 3.25).

Practice guidance states:

'Wherever possible, the practitioner responsible for assessing needs should carry on to relate those needs to the available resources. This will help to ensure that assessment does not become a theoretical exercise but is firmly rooted in practical reality' (SSI/SWSG 1991(PG), p.61).

Circular guidance (formally cancelled, but see p.401) states:

> 'An authority may take into account the resources available when deciding how to respond to an individual's assessment', but 'once the authority has indicated that a service should be provided to meet an individual's needs and the authority is under a legal obligation to provide it or arrange for its provision then the service must be provided. It will not be possible for an authority to use budgeting difficulties as a basis for refusing to provide the service' (CI(92)34, para 13).

DISCUSSION
Determining Criteria of Need in the Light of Resources

Taking account of resources to determine levels of need at the planning and policy level (as opposed to the individual level when individual needs have already been assessed) is not a new principle or practice. For example, at the outset of the operation of the CSDPA 1970, Circular guidance stated that: 'Criteria of need are matters for the authorities to determine in the light of resources' (DHSS 12/70,para 7).

The issue is also present in the practice, in special education, of recording only those needs of a child which can be met from resources (see eg. CLAE 1994, p.24; NAHA 1988a, p.8). This can result in conflicts between staff's professional standards and their duties to employers (Bhuttarcharji 1992).

Setting criteria of need successfully however, might be a hard task. As the Audit Commission (1993,pp.4–5) explains, authorities 'should aim to set criteria to allow through just enough people with needs to exactly use up their budget (or be prepared to adjust their budgets)'. Nevertheless, this view presupposes that the application of eligibility criteria is an exact and simple science; there is a contrary view that both professional and user input precludes the use of strict criteria, which can be interpreted variably even when highly specific (Kenny,Edwards,Stanton 1994,pp.11–12). What is more, the Audit Commission's statement presupposes that local authorities have very exact information about local needs on which they can base rational eligibility criteria. There is little evidence that authorities generally possess such information.

A reason why authorities not only may, but possibly must, take resources into account when planning services is because of their 'fiduciary duty' (that is a duty to use money wisely) to council tax payers. For example, the courts ruled that the GLC had such a duty when planning a transport policy (*Bromley LBC v GLC 1981*).

In a case about provision of transport (though involving legislative wording comparable to the CSDPA 1970), the judge ruled that a county council could lawfully take resources into account, so long as it did not eliminate the service altogether (*R v Hertfordshire County Council, ex p. Three Rivers District Council 1992*).

In a case drawn from the education field, a local authority decided to withdraw music from the school curriculum, make it an optional extra and charge parents for it. The judge ruled that faced with scarce resources, the authority was not breaching its duty and had made a reasonable decision that 'something would have to go' (*R v Hereford and Worcester LEA, ex p. Jones 1981*).

View That Lack of Resources is No Defence for Non-Provision for Some Services Once Individual Needs Have Been Assessed

The following three statements, made during the passage of the NHS and Community Care Bill, seem to concede that some needs for services will be identified which cannot be met and that this is acceptable and inevitable. However, two of them also suggest that authorities are under a duty to meet all individual needs identified under s.2 of the CSDPA.

However, this view, though much quoted (it appears even in community care policy guidance) is not actually based on any court cases – and it is just possible that courts might be reluctant to rule against authorities which argue lack of resources.

(1) Baroness Hooper, resisting an amendment to the NHS and Community Care Bill in the House of Lords, stated that apart from needs for day and domiciliary care local authorities would not 'be under a specific duty to meet all conceivable needs for community care across the board'.

She explained that 'the aim of assessment should be to arrive at a decision on whether services should be provided by the local authority and in what form. Decisions must take account of what is available and affordable...Where high priority needs are identified which cannot be met within the resources available, information flowing from the assessment process will need to feed back into the local authority's planning process so that a view can be taken about whether new provision is necessary'. She went on to explain that it would not be realistic to expand the type of specific duty, which local authorities had under s.2 of the CSDPA, to all community care needs and services in general (H65 1990).

(2) The Secretary of State for Health said much the same thing, stating that 'decisions must take into account what is available and what is affordable' – except in the case of domiciliary and day care for disabled people when local authorities 'will be expected to provide the services for which the assessment calls' (under the CSDPA 1970) (H66 1990).

(3) The Parliamentary Under-Secretary of State for Scotland also stated: 'Although I have no doubt that every effort will be made to meet individuals' needs more systematically, it would be unrealistic to make the immediate fulfilment of each and every need a statutory requirement' (H67 1990).

This view that resources cannot be pleaded for non-provision of services to meet need assessed under the CSDPA 1970, s.2 relies in part on a High Court case (*R v Ealing London Borough Council, ex p. Leaman 1984*). In fact, this case

would seem not seem to support the view one way or another. It involved a
local authority which as a matter of policy no longer assisted people with
privately arranged holidays under the CSDPA, s.2. The judge ruled that this
policy was illegal, not because of any question of resources, but simply because
the legislation (see Chapter 4) places a duty on local authorities to assist with
privately arranged holidays. Therefore the authority's policy was inconsistent
with the legislation.

It is true that the view had gained ground even before this case. For example,
a Parliamentary ombudsman investigation had noted, in passing, that the DHSS
had received legal advice to the effect that a 'local authority could not plead
lack of money as a reason for not meeting need, but that they had discretion
as to the means employed to meet it' (PCA C.12/K, 1975–1976).

The position is not wholly clear. For example, in one case about the provision
of after-care under s.117 of the Mental Health Act 1983 (a community care
service) the judge ruled that the duty on health and local authorities was a strong
one towards individuals. However, when he interpreted the nature of this duty,
he had made it clear that his comments did not apply to the situation where an
authority failed to do its duty because of lack of resources (*R v Ealing DHA, ex
p. Fox 1992*).

A more recent case involved a local authority which had acknowledged a
person's need for intensive personal care which was not then provided. The
decision was challenged on two grounds: that the authority could not plead
lack of resources under the CSDPA, and that it was not employing adequate
staff (under s.6 of the LASSA 1970). The judge gave 'leave' (ie, permission) for
the case to go ahead as a judicial review case – at which point the authority
settled the case out of court (*R v Hereford and Worcester CC, ex p. Chandler 1991*).
However, the judge did not give reasons for his decision, so it is not clear
whether he thought that both grounds of the challenge were of merit. However,
this case does illustrate that whatever the legal position, authorities are likely
to be anxious about pleading lack of resources under the CSDPA – and faced
with this uncertainty might rather settle out of court than risk proceeding
further through the courts.

Level of Service

The *Encyclopaedia of Social Services and Child Care Law* takes the view that even
in the case of an inescapable duty to meet individual needs, 'it is submitted that
the authority has a discretion in identifying the level and precise nature of the
service to be provided given resource constraints' (at E1–295). This gives
authorities considerable latitude – for example, there is a big difference in
expense between giving somebody a commode in their living room and a
stairlift enabling them to get to the lavatory.

In addition, from the point of view of consistent and equitable provision
(see above), authorities can argue, at least up to a point, that different levels of

provision – for people with apparently similar needs – can be accounted for by differing individual circumstances: 'no two cases are quite the same'.

Discretionary Services

There is little dispute that where discretionary services are concerned (ie, where authorities have no duty to provide a particular service, but can do if they want) then local authorities certainly can take account of resources and decide not to provide a service. For example, in one case (not about community care services, but comparable) it was ruled that district councils were free to decide not to provide transport at all, since they only had a power, and not a duty, to provide it (*Three Rivers* case above).

Local Ombudsman

However the courts might react to the question of resources, the local ombudsman might sometimes not accept that lack of resources absolves a council from its duty to meet acknowledged need. Where it had assessed the need for a stair lift but delayed ordering it for nearly two years, the ombudsman stated that 'insufficient financial resources is no justification for delay' (CLAE 91/A/1481). At other times, the ombudsman might accept the operation of priorities and the delay which results, thus seemingly accepting the plea of lack of resources for (sometimes long) delay in assessment (see Chapter 8). Again, ombudsman findings do not always seem predictable and much would seem to depend on the particular circumstances of each investigation.

Level of an Authority at Which There is a Lack of Resources

It is not always clear what 'lack of resources' really means. For example, in an ombudsman case where lack of resources was held to be no defence for delay in providing a stairlift, the ombudsman went on to explain that the authority should have 'instituted procedures to ensure that adaptation works were prioritised on a borough-wide basis. Instead it appears that whether a need was met depended on competing demands on the local repairs budget for a particular week' (CLAE 91/A/1481). In other words, the local repairs budget might have been short of money – but the whole borough was not.

USER NEEDS, PREFERENCES AND UNMET NEEDS

Local authorities have a duty under the NHS and Community Care Act 1990 to assess people's needs for services and then decide what services to provide.

Community care practice guidance states quite explicitly that for various reasons assessed needs for services might not always be met by local authorities. When this happens, any 'unmet needs' should be recorded so that improvements could be made in services. After this guidance was issued, concern apparently grew in central government that if such 'unmet need' related to mandatory services (under s.2 of the CSDPA 1970), then local authorities could be challenged legally. This was probably largely because of the view, discussed above, that local authorities cannot plead lack of resources in individual cases under that Act.

As a result, subsequent Circular guidance (and in fact the policy guidance from the start) has referred to a distinction between recording 'unmet need' and 'unmet preferences'. The basis for this approach is that it is only the word 'need' which triggers duties under s.2 of the CSDPA 1970. This guidance was met by both criticism and cynicism. However, its substance is in fact not so controversial, at least in principle. It seems merely to be emphasising the point that the term 'need' can be defined by local authorities at the planning and policy level; and that any assessment should only record 'need' if it falls into this definition. Anything else is not 'need' as defined by the local authority and so should be recorded under a different heading, such as 'choice' or 'preference'.

The Circular guidance in effect was suggesting the introduction of yet one more 'uncertainty' or 'escape' route to protect local authorities from committing themselves to more service provision than they can afford.

EXTRACTS

Legislation is silent about recording people's needs or preferences.

Policy guidance states (of care plans):

> 'The aim should be to secure the most cost-effective package of services that meet the user's care needs, taking account of the user's and carer's own preferences...However, local authorities also have a responsibility to meet needs within the resources available and this will sometimes involve difficult decisions where it will be necessary to strike a balance between meeting the needs identified within available resources and meeting the care preferences of the individual' (DH 1990,para 3.25).

Circular guidance (CI(92)34 formally cancelled, but see p.401) states:

> **(unmet preferences)** 'Procedures will be needed which enable assessment staff to identify when the care packages actually provided do not accord with the preferences of users, either in terms of type, quantity, quality, cost, availability or cultural acceptability. A useful distinction might be drawn between those preferences which can be met within existing criteria of eligibility and those which would require some revision of the current policy' (para 24)

> **(individual or 'aggregate' recording of unmet preferences)** 'Authorities should consider whether such information for planning purposes is best provided on the basis of individual assessments or as aggregate returns in respect of each practitioner's total assessments. If individual feedback is recorded, it should be borne in mind that, even though it may not form part of the user's assessment or care plan, it might still be accessed by users, under the terms of the access to information legislation, if the data identifiably relates to them. Practitioners will, therefore, have to be sensitive to the need not to raise unrealistic expectations on the part of users and carers...' (para 25)

(**statutory obligations**) 'For their part, authorities will want to ensure that their actual service responses are in full compliance with their statutory obligations and that the identification of alternative responses does not imply any failure to meet these obligations...' (para 26).

Practice guidance (SSI/SWSG(PG) 1991) states:

(**recording of unmet need**) 'Having completed the care plan, the practitioner should identify any assessed need which it has not been possible to address and for what reason'. A care plan should contain 'any unmet needs with reasons – to be separately notified to the service planning system' (pp.66–67). The guidance refers explicitly to the possibility of the assessment of need which cannot be met. It refers to different categories of unmet need including those:

- 'statutory obligations, for example, those included in the Disabled Persons' (SCR) Act;
- defined as entitlements under local policies, for example, failure to provide services within defined timescales;
- new needs, identified by assessing staff but falling outside current policies or criteria, for example, the emerging needs of those with HIV/AIDS' (p.66).

As practice guidance points out, there may be a number of reasons for unmet needs including lack of resources, irrelevant or unacceptable quality and type of service, conditions of service (p.67).

DISCUSSION
Needs and Preferences
Policy guidance differentiates between needs and preferences and does not mention 'unmet needs'. By contrast, the practice guidance freely uses the term 'unmet need'. Subsequent circular guidance (CI(92)34) referred to unmet 'preferences' rather than unmet needs, clearly anxious about the view that 'once the authority has indicated that a service should be provided to meet an individual's needs and the authority is under a legal obligation to provide it or arrange for its provision then the service must be provided. It will not be possible for an authority to use budgeting difficulties as a basis for refusing to provide the service' (para 13).

Recording of Need in Practice
An AMA (1993) report on local authorities' response to the SSI Circular guidance (CI(92)34) found evidence of 'euphemistic' terminology being employed to avoid reference to 'unmet need'. For example, alternatives included: 'issues/tasks causing problems'; 'issues identified'; 'could have been met in a more desirable or satisfactory manner' (p.3); 'service shortfalls' (Neate 1994); or 'service preference deficit' (SSI 1994g, p.27). The term 'unmet need' might be used but in aggregate (ie. anonymous) form (SSI 1994d, p.40). Nevertheless, some authorities might *not* worry about such euphemisms – by stating, for example, that needs should be listed and objectives stated whether or not resources are available (SSI 1994g, p.27).

Asked in Parliament to rescind the Circular (CI(92)34) which the questioner interpreted as saying that 'the extent of a person's needs should not be assessed unless those needs could be met', the government denied the guidance had said any such thing (H68 1993). In fact the guidance could be so interpreted, since this is precisely the effect of setting exact eligibility criteria to define need, and calling everything else 'preference'. The government has stated that it 'is a matter for the authority if, for the purposes of planning its services in the longer term, it wishes to keep some record of needs which it would be desirable to meet but which it is not necessary to meet immediately' (H69 1993). Similarly, an SSI letter to London directors of social services suggested use of the term '"unmet choice", possibly differentiating between choices that fall inside and outside the current eligibility criteria' (in: Health Select Committee 1993, vol.2, p.45).

An SSI (1993e) inspection report found that authorities were struggling with the difference between 'preferred choice' and 'unmet need'; and were aware of the importance of distinguishing, for recording purposes, between not meeting people's mere wishes and not providing 'necessary or highly desirable services'. Authorities were considering how to record information about unmet need in 'aggregate fashion'; though at least one authority was not planning to do this (p.26).

The information 'trawl' by the Association of Metropolitan Authorities disclosed the following examples of local authority recording devices. Service user files might have a 'confidential module' to record 'service gaps'; the keeping of 'service deficiency/ improvement forms' which were not accessible to users and were used for 'aggregated' information. One authority would not produce care plans which 'spell out to clients that they have specific needs which we are not specifically addressing'. Another authority's care plans did 'not cover alternatives to those services offered or services which are not available to meet the assessed needs' (AMA 1993, p.3).

Nevertheless, a 1993 court case about provision of residential accommodation showed that there are limits to the manipulation of the concepts of 'need' and 'preference'. The judge accepted the view of the authority's complaints procedure review panel that the person had particular 'needs'. This view was based on expert professional advice and the judge did not accept the authority's view that the person's 'psychological needs' (especially where the person has learning difficulties) amounted to preferences only (*R v Avon CC, ex p. M 1993*).

RECORDING AND COMMUNICATION OF ASSESSMENT AND OF NEEDS FOR SERVICES

Guidance states that the result of assessment should be communicated to users. This would be good practice and failure to do so could, for example, amount to maladministration.

EXTRACTS

Legislation is silent about the communication of assessment results.

Policy guidance states that:

'local authorities will need to have in place...arrangements for communicating the outcome of assessments and decisions on service provision to applicants and carers and those participating in the assessment process' (DH 1990, 3.56). This appears to refer to both the assessment and care plan (since it is the care plan which refers explicitly to services).

Circular guidance (formally cancelled, but see p.401) states:

(care plan) 'As far as individual users are concerned, their care plans (of which they should receive a copy) should spell out the extent to which their needs qualify for assistance under the terms of the eligibility criteria. Care plans should also define the contribution to be made by each agency and professional towards the meeting of those individuals' needs' (C1(92)34, para 15)

Practice guidance states:

(recording of assessment and care plan) 'All assessments are likely to be recorded on some kind of proforma...A copy of the assessment of needs should normally be shared with the potential user, any representative of that user and all the people who have agreed to provide a service. Except where no intervention is deemed necessary, this record will normally be combined with a written care plan (the next stage of the management process) setting out how the needs are to be addressed...' (SS1/SWSG (PG) 1991, p.56).

DISCUSSION

In the case of simple needs, guidance states that the outcome of the assessment and care planning process may be communicated on a 'verbal basis' (presumably oral is meant). However, if a continuing service has been offered, the outcome should 'normally be communicated in writing in the form of an individual care plan' (SSI/SWSG(PG) 1991, p.46).

Nevertheless, good administration demands of authorities that even if decisions are communicated orally, a written record of the assessment and the decision will be kept.

PROVISION OF CARE PLANS

Legislation is silent about care plans. Policy guidance states that care plans should follow assessments and it lists, in order of preference, a number of types of care packages, from support for people in their own homes to institutional long-term care.

Only the practice guidance (see below) states explicitly that users should receive copies of their care plans. It is therefore not clear whether the courts would see this as a legal obligation, although the local ombudsman might see it as a matter of good administration. In practice, there is some evidence that service users might not receive care plans (see eg. SSI 1994h, p.26; SSI/NHSE 1994j, p.38).

EXTRACTS

Legislation (NHSCCA 1990 (s.47(1)) states that after assessment:

'having regard to the results of that assessment, shall then decide whether his needs call for the provision by them of any such services'.

Policy guidance (DH 1990, para 3.24) states that:

'Once needs have been assessed, the services to be provided or arranged and the objectives of any intervention should be agreed in the form of a care plan. The objective of ensuring that service provision should, as far as possible, preserve or restore normal living implies the following order of preference in constructing care packages which may include health provision, both primary and specialist, housing provision and social services provision:

- **support for the user in his or her own home** including day and domiciliary care, respite care, the provision of disability equipment and adaptations to accommodation as necessary;
- **a move to more suitable accommodation,** which might be sheltered or very sheltered housing, together with provision of social services support;
- **a move to another private household** (ie, to live with relatives or friends or as part of an adult fostering scheme);
- **residential care;**
- **nursing home care;**
- **long-stay care in hospital'.**

Practice guidance states that: 'All users in receipt of a continuing service should have a care plan' (SSI/SWSG 1991(PG), p.61) and a copy 'should be given to the user' (p.67).

MAKING THE DECISION ABOUT SERVICES TO BE PROVIDED BY OTHER AUTHORITIES

Legislation states that the local authority must take account of what services are likely to be provided by other services, such as health or housing. Policy guidance states that agreement must be reached before other agencies' resources are committed.

There are a number of points to bear in mind. First, health and housing authorities do not have a duty to participate in community care assessments, and if they do not, then social services staff might be 'guessing' at what might be provided by the other authorities. Second, health authorities anyway have great discretion (see Chapter 16) about what services they provide and for whom, so such guessing might be difficult.

EXTRACTS

Legislation states that:

> 'in making their decision as to the provision of the services needed for the person in question, the local authority shall take into account any services which are likely to be made available for him by that District Health Authority or local housing authority' (NHSCCA 1990, s.47(3)).

Policy guidance states:

> 'Decisions on service provision should include clear agreement about what is going to be done, by whom and by when, with clearly identified points of access to each of the relevant agencies for the service user, carers and for the care manager. No agency's resources should be committed without its prior agreement. However, where the agencies have agreed as a result of the assessment and care planning process to provide a service, they will be expected to deliver it' (DH 1990, para 3.26).

REVIEW OF PEOPLE'S NEEDS

Legislation does not mention reviewing people's needs. However, guidance states that care plans should be regularly reviewed. Clearly, if people's needs increase or decrease, then the level of services they receive might be varied. However, and rather confusingly, it is also possible for people's needs to remain the same, but for the level of services still to be varied. This can happen if an authority's policy and eligibility criteria alter, so that people no longer qualify for the same level of services, even though their own circumstances have not changed at all. Government guidance suggests that where this happens, people should at least be informed about what is happening, and be reassessed before services are altered or withdrawn.

Provision of information, explanation and reassessment in such circumstances are clearly good practice. Legally, the reason for this could be connected with 'fairness' (see Chapter 7) – ie, people have a 'reasonable expectation' of continuing to receive services which they have been assessed as needing. Thus, before a withdrawal or reduction, there needs to be a process whereby people can readjust their expectations. Consultation might be part of this process as well. For example, the courts have ruled that a local authority should have at least consulted with the residents of a residential home before deciding to close it.

There might also be a legal concern (whether or not well-founded) that once authorities are providing services to people, they have a 'duty of care' to those people. If authorities breach their duty of care, and a person then suffers harm (eg, they fall down the stairs), then authorities might be liable in negligence. However, this duty-of-care principle is more likely to apply in the case of the health service, where the law of medical negligence is well developed, than in social services where, at present, it is not. Nevertheless, reassessment is an obvious way of stating quite clearly that any such duty of care has come to an end.

EXTRACTS

Legislation does not mention review.

Policy guidance states:

> **(regular reviews)** 'Care needs, for which services are being provided, should be reviewed at regular intervals. This review, especially where it relates to complex needs, should wherever possible, be undertaken by someone, such as a care manager, not involved in direct service provision, to preserve the needs-led approach. The projected timing of the first review should be stated in the original care plan. However, reviews may take place earlier if it is clear that community care needs have changed...'

> **(purpose of review)** 'The purpose of the review is to establish whether the objectives, set in the original care plan, are being, or have been met and to increase, revise or withdraw services accordingly. Reviews should take account of any changes in need or service delivery policies...' (DH 1990, para 3.52).

Practice guidance identifies the following purposes:
- review of the achievement of care plan objectives;
- examine the reasons for success or failure;
- evaluate the quality and cost of the care provided;
- reassess current needs;
- reappraise eligibility for assistance;
- revise the care plan objectives;
- redefine the service requirements;
- recalculate the costs;
- notify quality assurance/service planning of any service deficiencies or unmet needs;
- set the date for the next review;
- record the findings of the review (SSI/SWSG 1991(PG),pp 84–85).

Practice guidance goes further by explaining that not only are individual:

> **(policy review causing change in services to users)** 'needs subject to change but so are the policies of the authority or agency. The increasing emphasis on

targeting will mean that reviews not only confirm or increase services, they will also sanction their reduction and withdrawal. Where the level of assistance is adjusted, the reasons for that change should be **explained to the user** or their representative' (SSI/SWSG(PG) 1991, p.85).

Circular guidance explains that the:

(reassessment before adjustment of services) 'care plans of all users should be subject to regular review. For frail people in the community, frequent reviews and adjustments of their care plans are likely to be needed. Before any changes in services are made for existing users, they should be re-assessed. In those cases, where assessments have been undertaken, particularly under section 2(1) of the CSDP Act 1970, authorities must satisfy themselves, before any reduction in service provision takes place that the user does not have a continuing need for it. So long as there is a continuing need, a service must be provided although, following review, it is possible that an assessed need might be met in a different way' (CI(92)34, para 31 formally cancelled, but see p.401).

DISCUSSION
Difficulty of Reviewing
The high profile of the reviewing process afforded in the guidance is in contrast to some past practice. Some local authority services have in the past been unable to conduct reviews adequately. Practice guidance acknowledges that reviewing 'has traditionally been afforded a low priority' (SSI/SWSG(PG) 1991, p.83) and subject to delay where it has taken place. This might account for a continuing to tendency to treat monitoring and review as 'rubber stamping exercises' (SSI/NHSE 1994a, p.34); or concern at the workload implications of comprehensive review systems (SSI 1994g, p.31).

Frequency of Review
An unsuccessful amendment to the NHS and Community Care Bill sought to make mandatory a reassessment six weeks following initial assessment, and then every six months after that first reassessment. The government replied that whilst it wanted regular reviews, it 'would be wrong to enshrine such reviews in legislation in the inflexible way that has been called for. It must be right to leave local authorities to decide upon the practice' (H71 1990).

Changes in Service Provision to Individuals Following Review
The implications of the practice and Circular guidance (above) seems to be as follows. Once a need has been assessed and a care plan made, services cannot be reduced, withdrawn or otherwise changed without the change being explained to people; or (according to the Circular guidance) a reassessment taking place.

It is clearly suggested also that 'need' can fluctuate not just as a result of an individual's particular circumstances changing, but as a result of policy change.

Thus an individual's needs could remain ostensibly the same, but the authority's response might change according to shifting priorities and definitions of need.

This suggestion in the guidance would appear to mark a shift from the type of answer which has been given in the past concerning withdrawal of service under the Chronically Sick and Disabled Persons Act 1970. Specifically, for example, in 1991 Alfred Morris MP sought to confirm that 'for provision of a telephone to be withdrawn is unlawful without diminution in the need in any particular disabled pensioner's case'. In reply, the government stated: 'The right hon. Gentleman has correctly interpreted the law on the responsibilities of local authorities...' (H72 1991). How one interprets this answer depends on whether 'diminution in the need' refers to the person's own circumstances only or whether it can also refer to an authority's re-definition of somebody's needs on the basis of altered policy.

In this vein, Circular guidance described 'review' in a broad sense which envisages the regular review of 'criteria of eligibility for services to take account of: new policy objectives; more efficient targeting of resources; newly available resources; changing volumes and types of assessed needs and user preferences; available resources' (CI(92)34,para 28).

The local ombudsman has accepted that a person's needs might fluctuate in the judgement of the local authority. For example, in one case, a severely disabled person using a wheelchair, with limited use of arms and living with a full-time carer was assessed for a second ramped access to his accommodation. Originally told he did 'need' it, then told he did not, and then told he did after all 'need' it, the ombudsman found that the local authority 'was entitled to change its view of the situation'. However, it did not communicate such these changes of view to the person: this was maladministration (CLAE 91/C/0565).

Information about Change in Service and Reassessment

Government guidance (above) states that people should be informed about a change in services. It also states that people should be reassessed before services are withdrawn or reduced. Failure to inform and explain to people what is happening to them could offend basic principles (such as legitimate expectation, information-giving and the giving of reasons, and of fairness, see Chapter 7) and invoke adverse rulings from the local ombudsman and the courts. Authorities might also be advised to state from the outset (eg. in a care plan) that the provision of services is subject to changing policies and priorities from time to time (see eg. CLAE 1993a, p.22 on axioms of good administration).

Reassessment would also reflect concerns about fairness already explained: for example, if people have legitimate expectations that authorities will provide for their needs, then they need to be told that they no longer have needs (according to the authority's definition of need) – before services are withdrawn. Another concern might relate to a 'duty of care' which authorities might have once they are providing services to people. The concern might be that authorities should withdraw cautiously from such a duty of care and make it quite clear that the duty of care has come to an end (because a person has been reassessed and no longer 'needs' services).

This is because if a person were to suffer harm from a sudden withdrawal of services, the authority might be open to a claim of negligence – although as explained (see Chapter 7) elsewhere the law of negligence is undeveloped in social services (by contrast with the health service).

The local ombudsman has found maladministration when psychotherapy was suddenly withdrawn from a person by the local authority. This was because (amongst various reasons) although the authority 'was entitled to reduce or stop the funding, and to consider its financial position in doing so', the person's needs should have been properly assessed; the authority knew the psychotherapist's view of the harm which might be caused by sudden withdrawal; and had the authority carried out an assessment, a 'phased reduction over at least a year could reasonably have been expected' (CLAE 93/A/0523, pp.16–17).

Continuity of Provision

During the passing of the NHS and Community Care Bill, Lord Kilmarnock unsuccessfully proposed an amendment to cover the situation where a person changed residence: 'any existing assessment shall apply in whichever local authority the person becomes resident for a period of 28 days in default of a new assessment'. The government resisted the amendment because it would be burdensome on local authorities and cause 'automatic continuation of treatment' even if inappropriate. Nevertheless, Baroness Blatch recognised that 'continuity of provision is essential' and that 'urgent treatment could be invoked if the person required care as a matter of urgency' (H70 1990).

CHAPTER 10

FAIRNESS AND USER EMPOWERMENT IN ASSESSMENT

KEY ISSUES

This chapter begins by explaining how the legal concept of 'fairness' might apply to community care assessments. It goes on to examine the idea of user empowerment in assessment; how conflicts of opinion between service users and practitioners might arise and are resolved; and other aspects of assessment and provision such as weighing up risk, self-assessment and cash payments to service users.

The chapter then explains the legislation (Directions) concerning people's choice about which homes they wish to enter and what limits there are to that choice. Finally it describes the position of carers in community care assessment.

LEGAL FAIRNESS IN ASSESSMENT

As already explained, the form of assessment is not prescribed in the legislation. Instead, the mass of guidance on community care contains many statements about what assessment should consist of. Because of its volume, it is not quoted here. Reference should be made to the policy guidance (DH 1990), and two sets of practice guidance (SSI/SWSG(PG) 1991; SSI/SWSG(MG) 1991); and to Circular guidance (CI(92)34), although this last guidance is officially cancelled. When looking for what might constitute fair procedures, the courts might look to this guidance; on the other hand it might be difficult to predict how and when they will distinguish between guidance which contains good practice only; and guidance which is relevant to legally fair procedures. For example, the courts might regard guidance about provision of a written care plan simply as good practice; but guidance to the effect that people with communication difficulties should be able to participate in the assessment process as associated with fairness (see eg. DH 1990,para 3.21).

However, apart from this guidance, the general legal concept of fairness should be considered. It should be emphasised that the judges are likely to impose different standards and forms of fairness depending on the circumstances.

Legal fairness covers a number of considerations, described in Chapter 7. The following are a few examples which might apply in the specific context of assessment. For instance, people should be able to correct preliminary impressions which an assessor might have formed. Assessors should not rely on information which they are not prepared to share with the people they are assessing (eg. if an assessor reaches a conclusion unfavourable to a person because he or she has been told that the 'housebound' person has been seen running down the street, the assessor should raise this with the person concerned). Thus, in a homelessness case, it was procedurally unfair for an authority not it disclose information which it had obtained when making enquiries about the applicant (*R v Poole BC, ex p. Cooper 1994*).

The right to be heard could mean that if a person who cannot communicate for one reason or another (eg. language or disability), is denied an interpreter or other means (eg. an electronic communicator), then the assessment/decision-making process could be challenged on the grounds of fairness. For example, in this context, policy guidance states that assessment procedures must be accessible to all potential service users and carers and that decisions about service provision 'must be, and be seen to be, non-discriminatory' (DH 1990, para 3.21).

Fairness might require that reports, including experts' reports which have been relied on, be disclosed – although some reports might carry immunity on grounds, for example, of legal professional privilege or public interest.

The giving of reasons is another aspect of fairness. It is not absolutely clear from existing, relevant court cases (from other fields) that authorities have to give reasons for community care decisions (see p.82). However, in the light of these cases, authorities would be well-advised to make sure that decisions do not appear 'aberrant' and that short reasons, clearly relating to policies, are given. Both service users and authorities should probably also be aware of the unimplemented s.3 of the DP(SCR)A 1986. Though not in force, it does represent procedure for disabled people approved by Parliament – and part of it concerns the giving of reasons for assessment decisions.

There are also helpful legal precedents from the housing field which suggest what sort of enquiries authorities need to make when they are assessing people's needs (see p.107).

The local ombudsman too is likely to insist on adequate enquiry systems, for example, for renovation grants (see eg. CLAW 92/741), especially as Circular guidance urges the establishment of 'effective preliminary enquiry' systems (DoE 12/90, para 14). The carrying out of a 'sufficient investigation so as to establish all the relevant and material facts' is also one of the general axioms of good administrative practice published by the Commission for Local Administration (CLAE 1993a,p.13).

USER EMPOWERMENT

Legislation is silent about user empowerment and increased choice for users, but these considerations are referred to in policy and practice guidance. Early reports suggest that some authorities are attempting to implement the spirit of this guidance. However, a number of limiting factors remain. Differences of opinion are sometimes inevitable and final decisions about needs and services are, as guidance makes clear, for local authorities to make; whilst advocacy, promoted by community care guidance, still lacks the statutory basis which the unimplemented s.3 of the Disabled Persons (SCR) Act 1986 would supply. Cash payments by local authorities to people remain illegal – even though they could enable some disabled people to live more independent lives. It is recognised that, even with the 'best will in the world', local authorities can only react within restricted budgets to user and carer needs.

In a recent community care case about respite care, the judge ruled against the authority because it came to a decision after obtaining the preferences of the carer – but not the preferences of the service user (the carer's sister). This meant that the authority's decision was 'unlawful' because it had breached paragraphs 3.16 and 3.25 of community care policy guidance (*R v North Yorkshire CC, ex p. Hargreaves 1994*).

EXTRACTS

Legislation is silent about empowering users.

Policy guidance (DH 1990) states that users and carers should:

> **(choice and participation)** be enabled 'to exercise genuine choice and participation in the assessment of their care needs' (para 3.18). Also, the 'individual service user and normally, with his or her agreement, any carers should be involved throughout the assessment and care management process. They should feel that the process is aimed at meeting their wishes. Where a user is unable to participate actively it is important that he or she should be helped to understand what is involved and the intended outcome' (para 3.16).

It also states that:

> **(availability to all potential users/carers)** 'Assessment procedures must be readily accessible by all potential service users and their carers. Decisions on service provision must be, and be seen to be, non-discriminatory. Authorities will need to take positive steps so that people with communication difficulties arising from sensory impairment, mental incapacity or other disabilities can participate fully in the assessment process and in the determination of service provision. Authorities

also need to ensure that assessment is accessible to people from black and minority ethnic backgrounds. They may wish to make information about assessment and services available in braille, on tape and in appropriate ethnic minority languages. Staff may need to be recruited from a range of racial or ethnic backgrounds' (para 3.21).

(cultural background) 'Because of their cultural background, some users may need services of a special type or kind; service geared to the requirements of the majority may not always be appropriate' (para 3.22).

(interpreters) 'Authorities should promote the involvement of people who can assist service users and carers during assessment, including interpreters, both to help with communication and to explain cultural needs' (para 3.23).

(preferences, resources and decisions) 'The aim shall be to secure the most cost effective package of services that meets the user's care needs taking account of the user's and the carer's own preferences. Where supporting a user in a home of their own would provide a better a quality of life, this is to be preferred to admission to residential or nursing home care. However, local authorities also have a responsibility to meet immediate needs within the resources available and this will sometimes involve difficult decisions where it will be necessary to strike a balance between meeting the needs identified within available resources and meeting the care preferences of the individual' (para 3.25).

Practice guidance reinforces the importance of user and carer participation in the assessment process, but concludes:

(need defined ultimately by local authorities) 'Need is unlikely to be perceived and defined in the same way by users, their carers and any other care agencies involved. The practitioner must, therefore, aim for a degree of consensus but, so long as they are competent, the users' views should carry the most weight... Ultimately, however, having weighed the views of all parties, including his/her own observation, the assessing practitioner is responsible for defining the user's needs' (SSI/SWSG 1991(PG),p.53).

Practice guidance states that:

(advocacy) 'Users and carers should be given every assistance and opportunity to represent their own interests. Where it is clear, however, that a user or carer would benefit from independent advocacy, they should be given information about any schemes funded by the authority or run locally...it is consistent with aims of basing service provision on the needs and wishes of users that those who are unable to express their views, for example, those with severe learning disabilities or dementia or those who have been previously disadvantaged, for example, those from minority ethnic groups should, as a matter of priority, be supported in securing independent representation' (SSI/SWSG(PG) 1991,p.51).

Restricted Resources and Decision-Making

Ultimately, as the guidance makes clear, it is for local authorities to make final decisions about need and services.

The SSI/NHSME (1994b) has reported on obvious limits to user choice: 'Users and carers also commented that the combination of tight eligibility criteria and charging policies were precluding the effective take-up of services by those in need and resulting in a continued over reliance on carers. It is difficult to see how Authorities can respond to this criticism given their need to ration resources' (p.46).

[handwritten margin note: see c-care article on c-c+ Resource]

A NISW study (Smale *et al* 1993,p.62) reported: 'Painful decisions have to be made and people will often not be able to have what they want, sometimes through lack of resources, sometimes because their needs conflict with others, sometimes through irretrievable loss of a person or personal capacity and often through some combination of all of these factors'.

Self-Assessment

There are some areas of social services provision where large demand and waiting lists (eg. SSI 1988a, p.6) have led to the introduction of 'self-assessment' services. For example, where people need simple items of equipment which are deemed not to have safety or risk implications. Such developments have been identified as good practice by an SSI/NHSME (1994,p.iv) report.

Representation and Advocacy: Unimplemented Legislation

Statutory provisions concerning representation and advocacy for disabled people remain unimplemented (s.1–3 of the Disabled Persons (SCR) Act 1986).

Briefly, people would have the right to an authorised representative; the authorised representatives would themselves be given rights; disabled people would have the right to make representations and have their views taken into account. They would also have the right to a written statement and the right of review of an assessment outcome.

An attempt to introduce similar provisions into the NHS and Community Care Bill failed, on the grounds, explained by the Secretary of State for Health, 'that the assessment should be informal' and that local authorities should not be given an additional formal burden (H27 1990). In the House of Lords, the government explained that three sections of the 1986 Act 'were the most complex and potentially the most expensive of all the Act's provisions.

Baroness Masham, in response, pointed to the logical consequence of non-implementation of those sections of the 1986 Act which after all had been accepted by Parliament four years previously. She queried

'how one undertakes an assessment without taking into consideration a person's views. It is most extraordinary. I cannot understand it. If a person has a view and can express himself and that view is not taken into consideration, he is being treated like an animal. When one assesses a pig or cow one cannot ask them, but with a human being one can' (H28 1990).

People from Minority Ethnic Groups

During the passage of the NHS and Community Care Bill, an amendment sought to make mandatory assessments which would 'take account of the needs of people of ethnic minority origin'. The Parliamentary Under Secretary for Wales explained this was not necessary because both social services departments and health authorities 'should have full regard to the needs of ethnic minority and national interests'. They would 'live up to…professional guidance because they will have helped to draw it up' (H29 1990).

Conflict of Interests and Opinions

Practice guidance recognises that conflict of interests might render local authority staff unsuitable to take on an advocacy role (see above).

In practice there is sometimes a danger that people who are aware of their entitlements, express preferences or challenge practitioners' decisions might, on that account, be stigmatised by local authority staff as 'demanding', 'grabbing', 'fussy' or 'manipulative' (Ellis 1993,p.22).

The local ombudsman sometimes investigates conflicts of opinion. One case involved the discharge of a 43-year-old man with learning difficulties and epilepsy to ordinary housing in the community run by the social services. The parents of the man wished for him to live still in either hospital or a similar institution, with a higher level of care. The ombudsman was not prepared to find maladministration simply on the basis that the parents disagreed with the decision that their son be discharged. The father had been invited to meetings with the hospital consultant and a review team – and so there was no finding of lack of consultation.

On the question of choice of accommodation: 'the Council need to seek the best provision… They believe they have done so and I have not questioned that decision. I see no cause to suppose that they have improperly excluded an alternative favoured by [the parents]. Once again, the fact that the Council and the parents disagree is not sufficient to conclude that the Council have acted with maladministration' (CLAE 91/C/0553). This case was investigated before the Direction on choice of accommodation had been passed. This Direction does introduce additional considerations and at least one court case has considered the question of choice of accommodation (see 178).

Risk

Decisions about acceptable risk can be difficult. On the one hand, is the view that risk is a part of everyday life. On the other hand is the concern of staff and managers not to infringe health, safety and good practice standards for fear both of accidents to users and of litigation.

Evidence of such tensions emerged in one local ombudsman investigation. The complainant, suffering from motor neurone disease, had been subjected to delay in obtaining a lift for his home. The applicant lived with his adult children and with his wife, who was the only member of the family without major problems. Consideration of safety standards had precluded a decision about provision of a lift. Yet, all this time, the applicant's family was incurring daily risk by carrying him up and down the stairs; and the applicant had been prepared to sign any disclaimer requested by the council.

The ombudsman concluded that: 'Given the Council's stated policy that people should, as far as possible, be allowed to remain in their own homes, the Council need to give very careful consideration to those cases where another aspect of their policy contradicts this. I am not satisfied that the Council adequately thought through the consequences of such a clash'. The council had delayed in reaching a decision and had, by its own admission, not examined all the options at the outset. This was maladministration (CLAE 88/A/303, pp.14–15).

Understanding the Assessment

One SSI report on community care implementation referred to anecdotal evidence that 'in many places users and carers still find the bureaucracy difficult to deal with and have problems understanding complex assessment processes' (SSI 1993h,Summary). An SSI/NHSME monitoring of community care for younger disabled adults found that though there were examples of good practice involving independent advocacy services, elsewhere the concept of advocacy did not feature in policy and practice documents (SSI/NHSME 1994,p.14).

Users and carers might find the process of assessment over-bureaucratic, especially, for example, where they have to sign seven times during an assessment. Yet they might still have no clear recollection of the choices offered them and completed assessments might bear all the hallmarks of prescribing particular services rather than recording agreed objectives (SSI/NHSME 1994a, pp.25–26).

Payment of Money to Service Users to Purchase Services

Long seen as a device for giving service users more choice, this remains illegal under both the National Assistance Act 1948, s.29 and section 45 of the Health Service and Public Health Act 1968. Unsuccessful attempts have been made to amend the law in order to make such payments possible: for example, the Disabled Persons (Services) Bill 1992, presented by Andrew Rowe MP; and a failed amendment to the NHS and Community Care Bill (H30 1990).

During the passing of the NHS and Community Care Bill, the government explained that it had 'concluded that it is not possible to find a formula to enable payments to be simple and unbureaucratic for local authorities and recipient clients, on the one hand, and which, on the other, can prevent expenditure from running out of control' (H31 1990). Three days earlier, the Secretary of State for Health had admitted the logic to payments in some circumstances and had held out some hope of a government amendment – though nothing ever came of this (H32 1990).

The Health Committee of the House of Commons (1993,Vol.1,p.xv) has noted the potential benefits of cash payment, particularly to younger disabled people and recommended a government review of the issue. The Griffiths report, foundation for the 1990 community care changes, did not recommend cash payments, but did suggest that Social Fund community care grant money should be transferred to social services (Griffiths 1988,p.14). This has not happened.

The separate Independent Living Fund scheme for severely disabled people makes cash payments to people so that they can purchase their own care services. It might also be possible where an intermediary, voluntary organisation is funded by the local authority to make cash payments (see: Health Committee 1993,vol.2, p.10); or where the money is placed in an independent trust (p.100).

In some areas there are schemes whereby local authorities do pay money to users via a third party (George 1994). The strict legality of this is probably a little unclear. For example, one such scheme 'tops up' the difference between a person's personal assistance needs and his or her financial resources (having claimed maximum benefits available) (Fiedler 1988,p.42). Another reported scheme gives people control of a budget by cheque book, without any cash flowing from authority to user but effectively giving the user power to purchase services (Wiggins, Carpenter 1994).

CHOICE OF RESIDENTIAL OR NURSING HOME

Directions ('delegated' legislation, which places duties on authorities) have been made about choice of residential or nursing home. Basically, people can allow the local authority to choose for them, can themselves choose from a preferred list (if there is such a list) or can choose any accommodation which the authority thinks is suitable for their needs. There are however restrictions which confine choice to some extent: for example, the varying level of home fees which different local authorities are prepared to meet; the availability of suitable local accommodation; and local authorities' willingness to fund accommodation outside of their area.

EXTRACTS

Directions (delegated legislation) issued under s.7A of the LASSA 1970 state that:

> **(duty to grant choice):** following a community care assessment which identifies a need for residential care under the NAA 1948,s.21, a local authority, subject to the provisos below, 'shall...make arrangements for accommodation pursuant to section 21 for that person at the place of his choice within England and Wales...if he has indicated that he wishes to be accommodated' there.

> **(provisos):** a 'local authority shall only be required to make or continue to make arrangements for a person to be accommodated in his preferred accommodation if':

(needs): '(a) the preferred accommodation appears to the authority to be suitable in relation to his needs as assessed by them';

(usual level of cost) '(b) the cost of making arrangements for him at his preferred accommodation would not require the authority to pay more than they would usually expect to pay having regard to his assessed needs';

(availability) '(c) the preferred accommodation is available';

(terms and conditions) '(d) the persons in charge of the preferred accommodation provide it subject to the authority's usual terms and conditions...'

(third party contributions). The Directions also make it clear that authorities have a duty to place people in preferred more expensive accommodation if a third party is prepared to pay the difference between the actual cost and what the local authority usually pays (National Assistance Act 1948 (Choice of Accommodation) Directions 1992: in LAC(92)27 and in LAC(93)18).

Circular guidance elaborates:

(presumption of choice) 'As with all service provision, there should be a general presumption in favour of people being able to exercise choice over the service they receive. The limitations on authorities' legal obligation to provide preferred accommodation set out in the direction are not intended to deny people reasonable freedom of choice, but simply to ensure that authorities are able to fulfil their obligations for the quality of service provided and for value for money...'

(justification for not granting choice) 'Where for any reason an authority decides not to arrange a place for someone in their preferred accommodation it must have a clear and reasonable justification for that decision which relates to the criteria of the direction' (LAC(92)27,para 7).

DISCUSSION
Inability of People to Exercise Choice
The Circular guidance states that there

'will be cases in which prospective residents are unable to express a preference for themselves. It would be reasonable to expect authorities to act on the preferences expressed by their carers in the same way that they would on the resident's own wishes, unless exceptionally that would be against the best interests of the resident' (LAC(92)27,para 13).

Single Rooms
In evidence to the Health Committee (1993) the Department of Health has stated: 'If the client believes that a single room is an over-riding consideration as far as he/she is concerned, then I think it is clear from the statutory direction that they have a right to choose a home which provides the facilities they need'. Nevertheless, in the same context the Department of Health stated also that the Direction on choice 'does not specifically enable a person to choose a single room if that is what they prefer' (vol.2,p.40). Age Concern expressed the precise

point that choice of room type would be subject to the limits on the local authority's usual costs (vol.1,p.xiii).

Residential Care Outside the Local Authority's Area

It is reported that in practice some local authorities might restrict choice by operating policies which rule out residential care support outside of their own area. It might be unclear whether this is consistent with the Department of Health's Directions. Such policies can certainly act to the detriment, for example, of people with visual or hearing impairment by denying them access to specialist homes (Health Service Committee 1993, vol.2,p.227).

Costs Paid by Local Authority

This is covered in the chapter on finance and charging.

Difference Between a Person's Choice and Needs

A recent court case demonstrated the difference between 'choice' and 'need'. A person with Down's Syndrome was determined that he needed to go to a particular home. The local authority denied that this was a need, stating that it was a preference only which it was not obliged to meet. It wanted to send him to a cheaper home. His wish to go to a particular home was deemed by the local authority's Review Panel, and by the judge, to be part of his psychological needs. The wish was therefore not just a preference, and the local authority had to treat it as a 'need' (*R v Avon County Council, ex p. M 1993*). This prevented the authority from referring to its 'usual cost' level as a factor limiting a person's choice – since the 'usual cost' is meant to be a limiting factor on people's preferences but not on their assessed needs.

ASSESSMENT OF CARERS

The NHS and Community Care Act 1990 does not mention carers, although policy guidance states that carers can request assessments. In practice, local authorities might assess carers.

The Disabled Persons (SCR) Act 1986, does place duties on local authorities to 'have regard' to carers of disabled people when they are assessing people under welfare legislation. Considerable concern has been expressed about the needs of carers, especially since their needs can conflict sometimes with those of the people they are caring for.

EXTRACTS

Legislation (NHS and Community Care Act 1990) is silent about the assessment of carers. However, the Disabled Persons (SCR) Act 1986, under which local authorities must assess for welfare services (under the CSDPA 1970,s.2) if they are assessing a disabled person under the 1990 Act, states (s.8) that where:

(substantial care) 'a disabled person is living at home and receiving a substantial amount of care on a regular basis from another person (who is not a person employed to provide such care by any body in the exercise of its functions under any enactment), and'

(assessment) 'it falls to a local authority to decide whether the disabled person's needs call for the provision by them of any services for him under any of the welfare enactments,'

(ability of carer) 'the local authority shall, in deciding that question, have regard to the ability of that other person to continue to provide such care on a regular basis'.

Policy guidance states that:

'Carers who feel they need community care services in their own right can ask for a separate assessment. This could arise if the care plan of the person for whom they care does not, in their view, adequately address the carer's own needs' (DH 1990,para 3.29).

Circular guidance (LAC(87)6,para 6) states that although section 8 of the Disabled Persons (SCR) 1986:

'places no specific requirement on the local authority to provide services or support for the carer, authorities will no doubt continue as part of normal good practice to have regard to the possible need for such services and to the desirability of enabling the disabled person to continue living at home for as long as possible if this is what he or she wishes to do'.

DISCUSSION
Duties under the 1986 Act

Although the NHSCCA 1990 is silent about carers, the duty to 'have regard' to carers under the DP(SCR)A 1986 (s.8) may apply in many community care assessments, since the duty under s.8 applies to assessments under the NAA 1948, s.29; the CSDPA 1970, s.2; and the NHS Act 1977, Schedule 8 (see s.16 of the DP(SCR)A 1986).

Conflicts Between Users and Carers

There is concern that separate assessment of carers is essential in some circumstances, where, for example, carers have their own needs and even more so where those needs conflict with the needs of the person being cared for.

In evidence to the Health Committee (1993,vol.1,p.xxii), the Institute of Health Services Management made the point that there were no 'widely disseminated protocols for managing conflicts between a user and a carer'. For example, the need for separate carer assessments to resolve conflicts may arise because 'in a climate of tight resources the needs of carers might be subordinated to those of users; for example, a programme of closure of long stay institutions might continue in spite of little account being take [sic] of the resulting additional pressure on carers'.

A House of Lords amendment to the NHS Community Care Bill (Committee stage) failed to make assessment of carers a statutory duty. Baroness Hooper for the government explained that, whilst she accepted the 'spirit of the amendment', it was not appropriate to put it 'on the face' of the legislation, but rather would be included in guidance on assessment dealing with consultation of carers (H33 1990).

In practice, local authorities sometimes anyway provide separate community care assessments for carers whose separate needs sometimes do conflict with those of 'users' (SSI 1993k,p.20). On the other hand, it is reported that many carers might find it difficult to obtain separate assessments (Warner 1994,p.48).

Respite Care

Respite care (short-term breaks), is often primarily in the interests of carers. There is some concern about possible changes to the pattern and provision of respite care. An unsuccessful amendment to the NHS and Community Care Bill sought to ensure that authorities would consider 'the particular need for respite care if requested to do so by the person being assessed or by a person who has the responsibility of caring for the person being assessed'. The government responded that highlighting in the legislation one particular form of care would be unhelpful and could discourage innovation (H34 1990).

CHAPTER 11

CHRONICALLY SICK AND DISABLED PERSONS ACT (CSDPA) 1970

KEY ISSUES

Services available under s.2 of the Chronically Sick and Disabled Persons Act (CSDPA) 1970 are central to community care objectives, since those services assist people to remain in their own homes. They include services such as practical help in the home, equipment and home adaptations, educational facilities, telephone and radio, holidays. They are available to people whom the authority defines as disabled and who are 'ordinarily resident' within the authority's area.

Many of the legal and practical uncertainties afflicting community care now have been rehearsed since 1970 through the working of the CSDPA. For example, questions about flexible definitions of needs, the role of resources, the pleading of lack of resources for non-provision of services, priority criteria and waiting lists have all been considered and argued. The local ombudsman has conducted many investigations into aspects of the CSDPA and the law courts also have considered, to a limited extent, some of the issues.

The importance of the CSDPA continues to be demonstrated by central government concern that local authorities' obligations under that Act could make excessive demands on authorities' resources. The concern about the effect of the CSDPA s.2 duties seems to be that they might be 'absolute' duties. That is, once need has been acknowledged for s.2 services, then the authorities must provide the services, even if they don't have the money to do so. However, there are a number of qualifications to the duty which, when added together, suggest that the duty is not absolute, and that authorities might have slightly more room for manoeuvre than is sometimes supposed.

What does some clear is that the undoubted strength of the section 2 duty, combined with the evident anxieties of both central and local government about this duty, invites exploitation by service users and their advisers.

BASIC DUTY AND SERVICES UNDER SECTION 2 OF THE CSDPA 1970

S.2(1) of the CSDPA 1970 places strong duties on local authorities to meet individuals' needs by providing a range of home welfare services.

Some of the services are to be provided for people's safety, comfort or convenience. The duty applies equally to these three aspects of people's needs. The legality of priority policies (based on high risk), which meet people's safety needs but not their comfort and convenience needs, might be open to challenge.

EXTRACTS

Legislation: s.2(1) of the CSDPA 1970 states that if a local authority is 'satisfied' that it is necessary for it to make arrangements in order to meet the needs of a person, then it has a 'duty' to do so. The person must be ordinarily resident within the local authority's area. The arrangements include practical assistance in the home; telephone; wireless; television; educational facilities; travelling arrangements; adaptations and facilities for greater safety, comfort and convenience; holidays; meals. S.2(1) is reproduced in full on page 44.

DISCUSSION

Urgency, Risk and the CSDPA 1970: Safety, Comfort, Convenience (Facilities and Home Adaptations)

It is noteworthy that duties under s.2(1)(e) of the CSDPA 1970, refer to the provision of adaptations and the 'provision of any additional facilities to secure his greater safety, comfort or convenience'.

The duty to make arrangements applies to all of the categories (safety, comfort, convenience) equally: the latter two categories are not discretionary powers. Yet priority criteria sometimes not only relegate 'comfort and convenience' to a low priority, but exclude them altogether. For example, 1989 internal guidance from one local authority stated: 'Priority 4: needs unlikely to be met (clients who require assistance and support to fulfil potential role in society – including advice on leisure time activities, employment preparation; clients whose quality of life could be improved to 'care, comfort and convenience' standards' – eg. adaptations to allow access to hobby areas)' (cited in Mandelstam 1993, p.40).

It is not clear how consistent with the legislation such a priority system is, because it appears to dismiss needs relating to 'comfort and convenience'. Perhaps in related vein, the local ombudsman has pointed out that the law (CSDPA 1970) 'makes no distinction between the Council's duty to make an assessment in "urgent" and "non-urgent" cases. Any disabled person is entitled to request an assessment and to expect that the request is met within a reasonable time' (CLAE 1992, 91/A/0482). Indeed the legislation does not state that the three terms form an order of priorities (and in fact, during the passing of the Act in 1970, the term 'safety' was only added at a late stage).

DUTY TO ASSESS FOR CSDPA SERVICES WHEN REQUESTED UNDER THE DISABLED PERSONS (SCR) ACT 1986

The duty to provide or otherwise arrange for the provision of services under s.2 of the CSDPA is strengthened by s.4 of the Disabled Persons (Services, Consultation and Representation) Act 1986. If a disabled person or his or her carer asks the local authority for an assessment, the local authority has a duty to assess whether the person needs any of the services listed in s.2. The local authority has a duty also to 'have regard' to whether a carer can continue providing regular care.

EXTRACTS
Legislation states:

> **(request for assessment)** 'When requested to do so by (a) a disabled person' or '(c) any person who provides care for him in the circumstances mentioned in s.8 [local authorities taking account of carers' abilities], a local authority shall decide whether the needs of the disabled person call for the provision by the authority of any services in accordance with s.2(1) of the 1970 Act (provision of welfare services)' (DP(SCR)A 1986, s.4) (our insertion in square brackets).

> **(carer assessment)** 'Where: (a) a disabled person is living at home and receiving a substantial amount of care on a regular basis from another person (who is not a person employed to provide such care by any body (in the exercise of its functions under any enactment), and (b) it falls to a local authority to decide whether the disabled person's needs call for the provision by them of any services for him under any of the welfare enactments, the local authority shall, in deciding that question, have regard to the ability of that person to continue to provide such care on a regular basis' (DP(SCR) 1986, s.8(1)).

(Disability is defined by s.29 of the National Assistance Act 1948)

DISCUSSION
Assessment on Request: Sealing of 'Loophole' in the Legislation

Circular guidance (LAC(87)6) explains that s.4 of the DP(SCR)A 1986 is designed to close a possible loophole in s.2 of the 1970 Act. The suspected loophole was that s.2 of the CSDPA does not refer to assessment and so 'does not make it explicit whether a local authority has a duty to determine the needs of a disabled person...'

> 'It was suggested in the course of debates in Parliament...that as the duty to "make arrangements" could be interpreted as applying only after the local authority are satisfied such arrangements are necessary in order to meet particular needs, local

authorities might refuse to come to a view as to what are those needs are as a means of avoiding the obligation to "make arrangements". It has never been the Government's view that s.2(1) should be interpreted in that way, and it is clear that this is shared by the vast majority of local authorities. However, it was agreed that the matter should be put beyond doubt' (para 3).

Thus, the local ombusman investigating almost a year's delay in assessing a man with multiple sclerosis, found maladministration in the 'failure by the Council to attempt even a partial assessment of the needs' of the applicant: 'when the Council were made aware of Mrs. Brown's disability they were under a duty to decide whether her needs called for their services. I do not believe this duty was fulfilled within a reasonable period' (CLAE 88/C/0814,p.15).

The one possible loophole left is that the duty to assess on request depends on a person being disabled; the definition of disability under s.29 of the NAA 1948 is capable of at least some manipulation (see p.122).

DUTY TO ASSESS FOR CSDPA SERVICES AS PART OF A COMMUNITY CARE ASSESSMENT

The duty in the 1986 Act to assess on request has been strengthened by the NHS and Community Care Act 1990.

If, under the NHSCCA 1990 (s.47), local authorities are assessing people who appear to be disabled, then authorities have, automatically, to decide whether the person needs any of the services mentioned in s.2 of the CSDPA. People do not have to make requests for this to happen.

EXTRACTS
Legislation (NHSCCA 1990, s.47(2) states:

'If at any time during the assessment of the needs of any person under subsection (1)(a) above it appears to a local authority that he is a disabled person, the authority

(a) shall proceed to make such a decision as to the services he requires as mentioned in s.4 of the Disabled Persons (Services, Consultation and Representation) Act 1986 without his requesting them to do so under that section; and

(b) shall inform him that they will be doing so and of his rights under that Act.'

Policy guidance states:

'if at any time during their assessment, an individual is found to be a person to whom s.29 of the National Assistance Act 1948 applies, the authority must so inform them, advise them of their rights and make a decision as to their need for services, as required by s.4 of the Disabled Persons' (Services, Consultation and Representation) Act 1986' (DH 1990, para 3.30).

DISCUSSION
Decision About CSDPA Services: Part of Community Care Assessment

It is perhaps unclear from the legislation whether there are two separate assessments: one for community care (under s.47(1) of the 1990 Act), and one under 47(2) for CSDPA services. Certainly, practice guidance (SSI/SWSG(PG) 1991; SSI/SWSG(MG) 1991) does not suggest that there are separate assessments; the guidance is clearly written on the assumption that assessment for CSDPA services is a part of the community care assessment system generally.

It is also worth pointing out, in the light of the 'needs-led' assessment urged by community care guidance, that the Act talks about a decision about what CSDPA 'services' are needed. It does not talk about 'needs' only. Thus, arguably, a pure 'needs-led' assessment (see p.142) of a disabled person, which does not mention services, would not conform to the wording of the legislation.

The local authority is under a duty to inform the person what is going on and what rights he or she has under the 1986 Act.

ANALYSIS OF THE DUTY UNDER SECTION 2 OF THE CSDPA 1970

The duty under s.2 is towards individuals and has been seen over the years as a 'strong' duty. This is one reason why the duty has featured so prominently in discussion about community care and why there is concern that authorities might incur excessive obligations under s.2.

Section 2 of the CSDPA 1970 states that if a local authority is 'satisfied' that a person needs certain services, and if it thinks that in order to meet those needs, it is 'necessary' for the authority to make arrangements, then the authority is under a duty ('shall') to make the arrangements.

This is a 'strong' duty inasmuch as it is a duty towards each individual. It has also long been understood to mean that once an authority has assessed a need, then it has a duty to meet the need. However, this is probably not quite accurate and the following paragraphs analyse the duty and the various qualifications which there are to it.

These qualifications have the effect of making the duty rather less than absolute – although in one sense, it is difficult to conceive of an absolute duty anyway, since there will almost inevitably be various conditions underlying any duty.

The duty can be analysed in terms of:

(1) the defining of 'need' by authorities according to the resources they have available;

(2) the meaning of 'making arrangements' for provision (as opposed to direct provision by the authority);

(3) when an authority becomes 'satisfied' that people's assessed needs can only be met by the authority and it then becomes 'necessary' for the authority to meet those needs (this is not the same as meeting assessed needs automatically);

(4) whether an authority can plead lack of resources for not meeting an individual's assessed needs.

EXTRACTS
Legislation: s.2 of the CSDPA is reproduced in full on page 44.

DISCUSSION
Need
The CSDPA preceded the NHS and Community Care Act 1990 by 20 years. Neither the legislation itself nor guidance on it outlined the elaborate assessment framework introduced by the 1990 Act. What it did do was to lay down a basic duty to ensure that assessed individual need is met. Barbara Castle emphasised in 1975: 'I repeat that, once a local authority accepts that need exists in respect of one of the services listed in s.2, it is incumbent on it, I am advised, to make arrangements to meet that need' (H35 1975).

Circular guidance states quite clearly that if local authorities are 'satisfied that an individual is in need...they are to make arrangements which are appropriate to his or her case' (DHSS 12/70,para 7).

In 1984 the Prime Minister attempted to explain that whilst there certainly was a statutory duty to meet need at one level, there was actually discretion at another level:

'I seem to remember that in that Act there is a good deal of discretion as to how it is applied. It is not absolutely mandatory. Any questions arising from the case...would not be for me but would a matter for the courts to decide' (H36 1984).

This answer caused confusion and had to be explained at a later date:

'Where a local authority is satisfied of an individual disabled person's need for one of the services listed in s.2 of the Act, it has a duty to make arrangements to meet that need. In that sense this part of the Act is certainly mandatory. However, it is for the local authority itself to assess need and to determine how it should best be met. To that extent there is also an element of discretion. You can rest assured that it was not my intention in any way to question the statutory duties imposed by the Act on local authorities, nor to indicate any change in the advice given by successive Ministers for the Disabled on this point' (H37 1985)

Determining Need in Line with Resources

Thus the duty is not 'absolute'. Elasticity of the term 'need' has long been recognised. Twenty-four years ago, Circular guidance (DHSS 12/70) suggested how local authorities could avoid the apparently unlawful position of not meeting needs once they had been assessed: 'Criteria of need are matters for the authorities to determine in the light of resources' (para 7). In principle, successful application of this advice, would preclude the situation arising where an authority has insufficient resources to meet assessed individual needs.

Barbara Castle explained in 1975

'Of course "need" is an imprecise concept and local authorities have discretion in determining that need. Parliament did not attempt to define that precisely, so that there is and must be an area of discretion of which local authorities will take advantage in dealing with the conflict between what they desire to do and the resources they have available' (H38 1975).

In similar vein, a Parliamentary ombudsman investigation in the 1970s remarked that legal advice to the DHSS at the time was that whilst lack of resources might be no excuse for failing to meet assessed individual need, nevertheless 'a local authority could exercise some discretion in fixing the standard by which the need is to be determined' (PCA C.12/K 1975–1976).

Community care guidance makes the distinction between 'need' and 'preferences' (see above). Similar distinctions have long been made in connection with the CSDPA 1970. For example, a Parliamentary ombudsman investigation noted in passing that a council was justifying non-provision of a telephone aid for a disabled person on the grounds that it was 'desirable', but not essential according to their assessment criteria (PCA C656/87, 1987–1988).

Furthermore, the term 'satisfied' in such legislation is usually considered to be a subjective term – ie it is for the authority to decide whether it is satisfied, rather than for the courts to say whether the authority should have been satisfied (see Chapter 6).

Balancing Legislative Purpose and Resources

Though Circular guidance (DHSS 12/70) urges the control of 'criteria of need', it also states of the CSDPA:

'Its underlying purposes are to draw attention to the problems, varying with age and incapacity, of people who are handicapped by chronic sickness and disablement; to express concern that these problems should be more widely known and studied and to urge that when priorities are settled, full weight is given to finding solutions. While recognising the effect of constraints on resources, the Government are confident that local authorities will have these purposes in mind' (DHSS 12/70, para 3).

'Making Arrangements' for Provision of Services

Section 2 is governed by the phrase 'make arrangements' for the services described in the section. This phrase qualifies the term 'provision'. Therefore, it is arguable that an authority would be fulfilling its duty to meet an assessed need if it enabled, in some way, the need to be met. This could be, for example, through voluntary organisation provision and payment for the service; or even telling a person that they could buy a reaching stick from a local pharmacy. However, in this last example, the duty would probably not be discharged if the person could not afford the stick or could not obtain it for some other reason: because the assessed need would endure.

In the context of home adaptations, where people are unable to meet their contributions (assessed by the housing department) to disabled facilities grants, social services might fulfil its 'continuing duty' by offering, for example, an interest free loan (DoE 10/90,para 17). This does not equate with direct, outright provision.

The Audit Commission (1993) has suggested about community care in general that 'providing services is not the only way of meeting needs' and that advice, guidance, information, counselling and sympathy are all components of assessment as a service in its own right. Providing these is one way of discharging local authority duties and 'this sort of advice could become an important way of meeting needs further down the needs pyramid, broadening the base (and the appeal) of local authority activities with services provided only in exceptional circumstances' (p.5).

The local ombudsman has on a number of occasions referred to views that local authorities' duty to 'make arrangements' is not 'necessarily to make provision themselves' (CLAE 90/C/2203,p.2). A Borough Solicitor is reported as stating that the duty to make arrangements can be discharged 'by the Council carrying out the work, or by the Council assisting the disabled person to apply for grants and advising him or her of the adaptations necessary to secure greater safety, comfort or convenience' (CLAE 89/C/1114,p.4).

In another local ombudsman case, the complainant had wanted a word processor, a video tape selector and a mobile telephone. The assessing officer gave information about grants available from the Education Department and subsequently financed the software, though not the word processor machine itself. The officer did not know about the video selector and did not identify this as a need. The request for the telephone was recorded to be unnecessary, since the person already had access to a telephone. The local ombudsman found that the advice and assistance given were reasonable (CLAE 91/C/0565 & 92/C/1400), though they involved a minimum of direct provision.

Investigating an application for home adaptations, the local ombudsman noted that 'the Chronically Sick and Disabled Persons At 1970 does not place a statutory obligation on the council to make a financial contribution. Indeed, I do not doubt, that in the prudent management of a limited budget the Council would wish to assess the claimants' resources' (CLAE 90/B/1676,p.19).

A Parliamentary ombudsman (PCA C.799/81 1981–1982) investigation noted (in passing) that a local authority which had ceased to provide financial assistance for holidays, nevertheless claimed to be still fulfilling its duty under s.2. It 'had considered the option of continuing the provision of the service of the Red Cross as hitherto but recouping the full charge from the individuals concerned...'. This would be another way of 'making arrangements' – in this case through a third party.

In 'making arrangements', a local authority had assessed a person for an outdoor electric wheelchair. The local ombudsman investigation, whilst not necessarily accepting that the local authority had no duty to provide an outdoor electric wheelchair, found in any case a failure even to help (ie. make adequate arrangements for) the person concerned to seek the necessary charitable funding (CLAE 91/C/0565).

Distinction Between a Person's Needs and the Necessity to Meet Those Needs

The wording of the legislation appears to mean that once an individual's needs have been assessed, the local authority then has to decide whether in order to meet those needs it is necessary for the authority to make arrangements. This would seem to mean that the duty to make arrangements is not triggered simply by assessment of need, but by a further decision-making stage. For example, there might be a number of ways in which the needs could be met, some of which might *not* require the local authority to make arrangements.

Pleading Lack of Resources When Not Meeting Individual, Assessed Needs

There has long been a view that once an individual's need under s.2 has been assessed, lack of resources would not be a defence for not meeting that need. However, this view is not based on any court cases and it is not impossible that the courts might be reluctant to rule against authorities simply because they lack resources (see p.156).

CSDPA s.2 SERVICES AS 'COMMUNITY CARE SERVICES': THE EVIDENCE

CSDPA (s.2) services are not defined explicitly in s.46 of the NHSCCA 1990 as 'community care services', but there is very strong evidence that they are in fact community care services because they are an extension of s.29 of the National Assistance Act 1948 (which is covered explicitly by the definition of 'community care services').

However, the wording of the NHS and Community Care Act 1990 does not make it clear how an assessment for CSDPA services (under s.47(2) of the 1990 Act) relates to a general community care assessment under s.47(1).

In any event, CSDPA services are central to the stated aims and objectives of community care. This is because the services available under s.2 of the CSDPA are precisely those services which enable people to remain in their own homes: and this is the preferred aim of community care policy.

(1) CSDPA (section 2) is Incorporated into the National Assistance Act 1948,s.29 – on the Face of the Legislation

First, services under Part III (including s.29) of the National Assistance Act 1948 are defined as community care services.

Second, s.2 of the CSDPA states quite clearly that 'where a local authority having functions under s.29 of the National Assistance Act 1948...it shall be the duty...to make those arrangements in exercise of their functions under the said s.29'.

(2) Interpretation of the Courts

The Court of Appeal in 1978 was in no doubt about the status of s.2 of the CSDPA. In the *Wyatt v Hillingdon LBC 1978* case, the judge at first instance had held that 's.1 and 2 were incorporated into s.29 of the National Assistance Act 1948'.

Lord Justice Lane upheld this, finding that 'the importance of that s.[2], particularly the last words of it, is to indicate that in the end it is s.29 and the other relevant sections of the National Assistance Act 1948 which are the governing factors in this sort of situation'. Eveleigh LJ, having quoted the last words of s.2 then said: 'It is upon s.29 therefore, that the activities of the local authority are based'.

Indeed, the use of s.36 (of the National Assistance Act) default powers in *Wyatt v Hillingdon* for complaint about s.2 (CSDPA) duties would not have been possible unless s.2 was part of s.29, for the default powers applied only to failure to discharge functions under Part 3 of the 1948 Act.

(3) Direction on Community Care Services: Reference to Section 2 Services

A direction stating that local authorities must publish in their community case plans details of proposals to purchase non-residential community care services from the independent sector, includes holidays under s.2 of the CSDPA as a community care service (Community Care Plans (Independent Sector Non-Residential Care) Direction 1994: attached to LAC(94)12).

(4) Statement by the Secretary of State for Health: CSDPA Section Covered by Definition of Community Care Services

During the passing of the NHS and Community Care Bill, an unsuccessful amendment proposed to extend the definition of community care services to other legislation, including the CSDPA 1970. In reply, Virginia Bottomley explained that the CSDPA 'relates to local authority functions under s.29 of the National Assistance Act 1948, and it is therefore already covered by the definition of community care services in the Bill' (H93 1990).

(5) Community Care Special Transitional Grant

One of the conditions attached to this grant is that it can be spent only on community care services as defined by s.46 of the NHS and Community Care Act 1990 (LASSL(94)1,annex C).

If the CSDPA 1970 is not to be regarded as such a community care service, then none of this grant can be spent on assisting (via CSDPA services) people to stay in their own homes instead of in residential care. (This would seem to make no sense, given that the government is encouraging the independent sector to provide more domiciliary services; and that s.2 services under the CSDPA are all about those types of service.)

(6) Circular and Other Guidance

Circular guidance (LAC(93)10, appendix 4) has described s.29 as 'extended by s.2 of the Chronically Sick and Disabled Persons Act 1970'.

An advice note from the Social Services Inspectorate also states clearly that local authorities have the power to make charges for services provided under s.2 of the CSDPA 1970. This is because although s.17 of the Health and Social Services and Social Security Act (HASSASSA) 1983 does not mention the CSDPA, it does list s.29 of the NAA 1948. The advice note explains that s.2 services 'are arranged by local authorities in exercise of their functions under s.29' (SSI 1994b,p.1).

(7) Practical Considerations: Home Support Services: Main Aim of Community Care

Policy guidance states that the first preference when constructing community care packages should be: 'support for the user in his or her own home including day and domiciliary care, respite care, the provision of disability equipment and adaptations to accommodation as necessary' (DH 1990, para 3.24). The services listed in s.2 of the CSDPA 1970 are precisely those services which enable people to remain in their own homes. The CSDPA would thus appear central to community care aims and objectives. As the Earl of Longford stated in 1970, during the passage of the CSDPA, the purpose of s.2 was to ensure 'that the disabled should, wherever possible, be enabled to earn their own living, and in any case to live in their own homes' (H92 1970). It would be extremely odd if the services most relevant to community care aims and objectives were actually deemed not to be community care services.

(8) Objection That if Section 2 of the CSDPA is Part of Section 29 of the NAA 1948, Then Section 47(2) of the NHSCCA 1990 is Redundant or 'Otiose'

S.47(2) of the NHSCCA 1990 states that if a local authority is making a community care assessment and the person appears to be disabled, then the authority has also to decide what services mentioned in s.4 of the Disabled Persons (SCR) Act 1986 the person requires. The services mentioned are those available under s.2 of the CSDPA 1970.

It might be argued that if the CSDPA (s.2) is simply part of s.29 of the NAA 1948, then s.2 services will already be assessed for under s.47(1) of the NHSCCA 1990 (which covers assessment of needs for 'community care services'). In this case s.47(2) would be unnecessary.

This argument is not decisive and can be countered:

(1) The draftsman might be employing broadly the legal principle of 'ex abundanti cautelo' (excess of caution), and be making it quite clear that s.2 services are to be considered in community care assessments;

(2) If the draftsman had not done this, the place of s.4 of the DP(SCR) 1986 in community care assessment might have remained unclear. For example, without such clarification, it might have seemed that half way through a community care assessment under s.47(1) of the NHSCCA 1990, assessment

would have been interrupted. The person being assessed might then have had to request, under s.4 of the 1986 Act, an assessment for CSDPA services – and possibly a separate assessment would then have been needed. Yet practice guidance (SSI/SWSG (PG) 1991) appears to assume that assessment of CSDPA services is part of community care – not a separate operation.

CHAPTER 12

UNCERTAIN AREAS OF RESPONSIBILITY FOR SERVICES

KEY ISSUES

The community care system contains deep-rooted uncertainties about the responsibilities of authorities for particular services. This is because relatively few specific services are mentioned in legislation; and even where they are mentioned, they are often not well-defined. In addition, people's needs do not always fit neatly into statutory service categories, and even less so when their condition fluctuates from week to week and month to month. Even where a service is to some extent defined in legislation, there can still be uncertainty about how to apply the definition. For example, in social security law the courts have had to rule on what 'assistance with bodily functions', part of the definition of 'personal care', really means.

Services occupying these 'grey' areas of uncertain responsibility might include, for example, disability equipment, incontinence laundry, washing, dressing, bathing, lifting, mobility rehabilitation, respite care. Practice guidance explains that these can all be viewed as either health care or as social care.

The existence of these grey areas can lead to both overlaps and gaps in services provided by local authorities and by health authorities. For service users, the result can be that they remain uncertain about who provides what. This uncertainty is sometimes shared by practitioners, which means that even they, as service providers, cannot always advise people about the 'system' and refer them effectively to other parts of it. It is acknowledged that this situation has contributed to the fragmented services sometimes received by both elderly and younger disabled people (16–64 years old).

This is probably why community care legislation places duties on local authorities to consult with other agencies. Policy and practice guidance also stress the importance of collaboration between agencies, so that service users receive a 'seamless' service. Indeed, the need for collaboration has long been recognised; for example, the NHS Act 1977 places duties on health and social services authorities to co-operate.

One of the difficulties in allocating responsibilities between statutory agencies is that some responsibilities are interchangeable (eg. a person might need a 'social services bath' from a personal care assistant, or a 'health service bath' from a district nurse. Yet in some cases the personal care assistant is probably carrying out 'nursing' (health care) tasks; whilst sometimes the nurse is probably only performing 'personal care' (social care) tasks.)

To confuse matters more, the needs of a person might alter from week to week: he or she might need more, and therefore nursing, help one week; but less (and therefore only personal care) the next. In such circumstances, the distinction between nursing and social care breaks down. Similarly, as described in the next chapter, grasping the distinction between the need for long-term NHS care and for private nursing home care can be difficult.

The fact that the distinction breaks down is probably inevitable and not necessarily a problem. Indeed, at best, such 'grey' areas mean that authorities can deliver services flexibly. However, at worst, they afford excuses to authorities to 'pass the buck' when resources are scarce. Although passing the buck might benefit the agency which jettisons an unwanted and expensive service, it does of course tend to increase pressure on other agencies, whether statutory or voluntary. Service provision for individuals can be delayed, and where, for example, health care is re-defined as social care, what was a free (health) service might suddenly become subject to means-testing and charges by social services.

These areas of uncertain responsibility, coupled with lack of resources, can pose substantial problems when local authorities and health authorities try to plan their services. Even where a local agreement is reached, there is always a danger that one authority might unilaterally withdraw from the agreement at a future date.

For these same reasons, service users and their representatives or advisers may find it difficult to know where and how to get particular services. However, one possible 'silver lining' to all this uncertainty is that if one authority does not provide a service, then another might be able to.

Chapter 6 matches services with legislation and demonstrates how a number of services are available under different legislation and from different agencies.

'SEAMLESS' SERVICES

The NHS and Community Care Act 1990 places duties on local social services departments both to consult with other agencies about community care plans and to invite health and housing authorities to participate in individual community care assessments where appropriate. Both policy and practice guidance refer to the importance of a 'seamless' service, to avoid the service fragmentation of the past.

EXTRACTS

Legislation: the NHSCCA 1990 imposes statutory duties relating to inter-agency working: both at policy and planning level (see Chapter 19) and at individual assessment level (see p.101). It does not mention 'seamless' services, nor any equivalent concept.

Policy guidance (DH 1990) states the importance of a 'seamless' service (para 2.3) and collaboration between agencies (para 3.32).

Policy guidance states about agreements and plans between different agencies:

> 'At an early stage they should draw up joint resource inventories and analyses of need which enable them to reach agreement on the key issues of 'who does what', for whom, when, at what cost and who pays' (DH 1990, para 2.11).

Practice guidance states emphatically that 'providing a **seamless service** to users and carers, is one of the fundamental objectives of the NHS and Community Care Act 1990'. Agreements between agencies should include statements about the responsibilities of each agency. It goes on to list not only health and housing authorities in general amongst collaborating agencies, but specifically: general practitioners, community nurses, therapists; as well as employment, leisure, criminal justice, independent sector and advocacy services (SSI/SWSG(MG) 1991,pp.81–99).

DISCUSSION

Fragmentation of Some Service Provision in the Past

Fragmented service provision has long been recognised as a problem. For example, community care practice guidance states: 'In 1986, the Audit Commission report "Making a reality of community care" showed that, while there had been some progress in developing co-operation between community care agencies, much remained to be done. Services were still experienced by users as fragmented, uncoordinated and wasteful in their use of resources' (SSI/SWSG 1991(MG),p.81). In 1992, the Audit Commission (1992,p.2) emphasised again the obstacles of agencies' different priorities, organisational styles and cultures, leading to 'uncomplimentary opinions of each other and a reluctance to work cooperatively'. Strained relations, misunderstandings and even hostility can be the result (SSI/NHSE 1994d,p.25). In 1991, the National Association of Health Authorities and Trusts concluded that the range of services needed by disabled people led to formidable organisational problems, and that the overall fragmentation of such services led predictably to gaps and overlaps (NAHAT 1991,p.125).

A National Audit Office (1992) report found some 'gaps and duplication in the services provided for physically disabled people due to intrinsic difficulties in distinguishing between health and social care arrangements in individual cases' (p.2).

Early reporting on community care, points out that the 'old problems' of divided responsibilities could threaten the new system (SSI/NHSME 1994b,p.27); and that there is 'limited evidence' of funding tensions including, for example, disputes over bathing (SSI 1993h,p.8).

Demarcation of Responsibilities

Community care practice guidance (SSI/SWSG(MG) 1991) states that to achieve clear agreements, a 'considerable amount of negotiation may be required' (p.84). The guidance declines to 'define a rigid demarcation between health and social care; the interface between the two is for local discussion and agreement'. It warns against 'sterile debates or rigid demarcation' (p.85).

The Social Services Select Committee (1990,p.xiv) quoted one uncomfortable view (Wistow 1989) of what creates demarcation: 'One can predict incentives for groups and agencies to identify their territory more or less narrowly. Indeed to some extent what we identify as health or social care needs tend to reflect the level of resources particular occupational groupings think they can gain or defend'.

Perverse Incentives

Audit Commission evidence to the Health Committee (1993,vol.1,p.xvii) pointed out that even if the boundaries of health and social care could be agreed in principle, 'funding arrangements between authorities do not always match those agreements'. One reason for this is the existence of 'perverse incentives'.

For example, since April 1993, nursing services for residential and nursing home care are paid for by social services. But nursing services for people in their own homes are provided by the health service – and legislation prohibits social services from paying for this. Thus 'there is disincentive for the health authorities to see people placed in the community' (vol.2,p.7) – since of course health authorities are prohibited by law from charging for home nursing services (see Chapter 18).

Budget Restrictions at Local Level

Even where agreements between authorities are reached, sudden and unexpected unilateral budget cuts can cause unilateral withdrawal from an agreement. Hence the warning of Circular guidance (EL(93)18) against 'unilateral withdrawal' of services.

Pooling of Resources

Pooling of authorities' resources to the extent that 'the origin of that money in terms of its respective authorities is virtually lost' can begin to overcome some of the problems. The money can be used to meet immediate individual needs: debate about whether it was health or social need can take place later. Joint 'contingency' funds are another possibility (Henwood 1994,p.30).

However, even given local 'joint working and shared values', it has been recognised 'that if finances are very, very difficult there might be a temptation for the various parties to retreat, as it were, into their financial corners' (NAHAT evidence to the Health Committee 1993,vol.2,p.60). For example, attempts have been made over the years to rationalise disability equipment provision by creating joint health and social services stores. Such stores are regarded as generally representing good practice, but they do not necessarily overcome all the problems. One local policy document 'recognised that the variation in budget levels, which remain clearly distinct from each other at agency level will tend to limit joint store philosophy' (Mandelstam 1993,p.59).

Even where there is every incentive genuinely to pool resources and 'joint commission' services, awkward questions might arise including the legal status of the money and the danger of entering into ultra vires agreements (Health Committee 1993,vol.1,p.xxxviii–xxxix). For example:

> 'How much should each authority put in the pool? Who is to be held accountable for it? What is the role of democratically elected councillors – is the money being removed from democratic control? What are the limits of legality of such schemes? Local authorities cannot purchase health care – but can pooled budgets be used to purchase health care? How are disputes to be resolved?' (Health Committee 1993,vol.2,p.2).

It seems that joint commissioning has to date been confined mainly to specialist fields such as learning disabilities (SSI 1993h,p.8). However, Circular guidance (HSG(92)43 and LAC(92)17) explains and encourages the use of joint finance schemes between health and social services, whereby health authorities have the power (NHS Act 1977,s.28A) to make payments to local authorities for provision of social services: especially, for example, for people who leave long-stay hospitals. (In fact, s.28A gives health authorities powers to make payments to social services, education and housing authorities for purchasing respectively social services, education for disabled people and housing).

Difficulties of Resolution

There are undoubtedly genuine difficulties in the way of achieving a 'seamless' service, and universal definitions may be inadequate in terms of detail and flexibility. The National Association of Health Authorities and Trusts put it to the Health Committee (1993,vol.2,p.60) that the problem is 'not going to be resolved by diktat'. Yet an alternative such as 'commonsense agreement' at local level risks disparity of practice between localities (1993,vol.1,p.xvii).

In the light of the potential difficulties of dividing responsibilities consistently and effectively, the Health Committee (1993,vol.1,p.xviii) has emphasised the importance of establishing 'a clear and publicly promulgated system of arbitration'.

EXAMPLES OF 'GREY' AREAS OF RESPONSIBILITY

A number of community care services fall into 'grey areas', where responsibility can 'go either way' between agencies (SSI/SWSG 1991(PG),p.86) depending on local arrangements. Practice guidance gives a number of examples of services which occupy this grey area.

EXTRACTS

Legislation makes no mention of uncertain areas of responsibility; nor of how demarcation lines should be drawn up.

Practice guidance contains 'indicative advice' on the 'division between health and social care'. Significantly, many of the items listed fall into the category of being 'either' health or social care. For example, disability equipment, incontinence laundry, washing, dressing, bathing, lifting, mobility rehabilitation, medicine application, learning disability behavioural management, mental health promotion and rehabilitation, drug/alcohol misuse counselling and HIV/AIDS rehabilitation (SSI/SWSG(MG) 1991,p.86).

DISCUSSION

Health or Social Care?

The above advice in practice guidance was based on a study published by the National Association of Health Authorities and Trusts (NAHAT 1991), which also included a 'swathe of "grey area"'(p.14). The introduction noted that in the

> 'widest sense, health and social care are difficult to differentiate. The nurse who enters the client's home to treat a leg ulcer is performing health care; but by her or his personal contact with the client, is also conducting an important social function. Equally, many aspects of social care, (if not all) such as house and personal cleanliness, poverty (possibly because of non claiming of benefits), or social life (reduction of stress) have important health or ill health sequelae' (p.5).

Thin Dividing Line Between Alternative Solutions

A passage in Joint Circular guidance illustrates how a range of solutions might exist for similar problems. Depending on the choice of solution, different services, authorities and financial arrangements might be involved. The dividing line between solutions might be fine; the consequences, considerable.

In practice, inevitably, finance is a consideration. For example, a commode in a person's sitting room is a lot cheaper to provide than a stairlift or a groundfloor bathroom extension or conversion – although the cost in erosion of dignity and social life is another matter.

For example, in the passage from Circular guidance quoted immediately below, solutions and agencies might be:

- nursing home care (social services with health authority consent);
- residential care (social services);
- domiciliary support (social services or health service);

- major adaptations (social services assessment; housing authority provision, using one grant system);
- minor adaptations (housing authority, using another grant system; or social services).

The passage reads:

'Social services authorities and housing authorities should construct an individual's care plan with the objective of preserving or restoring non-institutional living as far as possible, and of securing the most appropriate and cost-effective package of care, housing and other services which meets the person's future needs.

'For some people the most appropriate package of care will be in a nursing or residential home, but in many cases this will be achieved by bringing in domiciliary support and making any necessary adaptations to the individual's existing home. The balance between these two should be considered carefully.

'For example, where expensive or disruptive adaptations or improvements are being considered it may be more cost-effective to provide domiciliary care and support together with more minor works. In other cases adaptations or improvements (eg. to help people bathe or cook by themselves) may reduce or obviate the need for domiciliary support' (DoE 10/92, para 16).

There are many other examples. For instance, in the past, two bed blocks for tilting a bed (for fluid drainage) might have been provided by the health service; but four blocks for raising the level height of the bed (for easier transfer to and from bed) by social services. In one locality, a bath seat might be supplied by social services for 'independence'; but by the health service for a 'medical' need (eg. for a person with psoriasis and arthritis). In another area, the health service might simply categorise bath seats (for whatever purpose) as 'daily living' items and simply not provide them at all. In the past, some social services and health authority agreements would see hospitals loaning a commode for up to six months for 'nursing' needs. After six months, the commode would, in theory at least, be taken back by the hospital and replaced by social services for longer term 'daily living' needs.

As already mentioned, bathing has fallen into the grey area between health and social care. An Age Concern (1994a,p.41) report gives examples:

- a person's mother with mental health problems and who is incontinent is deemed not to need a medical bath; and social services does not provide a bathing service: her son would have to find private help;
- a woman who has had a stroke cannot bath herself; she is sometimes incontinent, her husband is unable to help her but she is not considered to need a medical bath. As a result she cannot have a bath.

Division Between Residential and Nursing Care

Legislation defines the difference, for the purpose of registration and inspection, between residential home care and nursing home care.

In practice, the division is maintained with difficulty, since many people in residential care require more or less nursing care. This might be provided unofficially by staff in the residential home or officially by NHS community nursing services. At some point, a person might be deemed to need nursing home care, but this point can be difficult to identify, given people's fluctuating needs, the effect on a person of moving home, and the availability and cost of a suitable nursing home place (see eg. RCN 1992,p.11; NAHA 1984,p.20).

Residential care is defined as 'residential accommodation with both board and personal care for persons in need of personal care by reason of old age, disablement, past or present dependence on alcohol or drugs, or past or present mental disorder'. Personal care means 'care which includes assistance with bodily functions where such assistance is required' (Registered Homes Act 1984, ss.1,20).

The definition of nursing home includes 'any premises used, or intended to be used, for the reception of, and the provision of nursing for, persons suffering from any sickness, injury or infirmity' (Registered Homes Act 1984,s.21). The term 'nursing' is not defined.

'Personal care' is a term which the courts have taken responsibility for defining. For example, in a related field (attendance allowance) they have stated that 'bodily functions' is a 'restricted and precise [phrase]', narrower than, for example, 'bodily needs'; and that the phrase '"attention...in connection with his bodily functions"...connotes a high degree of physical intimacy between the person giving and the person receiving the attention'. This meant that assistance with cooking did not qualify for attendance allowance (*Woodling v Secretary of State for Social Services 1984*; and see *R v National Insurance Commissioner, ex p. Secretary of State for Social Services 1981*). The courts have also ruled that a blind person who needs assistance to walk in unfamiliar surroundings needs attention in connection with his or her bodily functions (*Mallinson v Secretary of State for Social Security 1994*).

The courts (*Harrison v Cornwall County Council 1991*) have also found that assistance with bodily functions is not a *necessary* component of residential care. In particular, the judges found the words 'where such assistance is required' decisive, because they implied that such assistance would not always be necessary; and residential care included emotional and psychiatric as well as physical care.

Social Service Provision of Health Services

Certain provisions of the National Assistance Act 1948 appear to limit what local authorities can provide. It seems that these provisions can be interpreted in two ways: narrow and broad. If interpreted narrowly, the excluding provisions merely state that a *local authority* cannot provide under the National Assistance Act 1948 what *it* can provide under the NHS Act 1977.

However, a broader interpretation prohibits *local authorities* from providing what can be provided by *health authorities* under the NHS Act 1977. The broader interpretation carries with it wide ramifications. It would generally preclude social services departments from purchasing/providing health, including nursing, care in either residential or non-residential settings.

The relevant sections of the 1948 Act are s.21(7), 21(8), s.29(6); and in the Health Service and Public Health Act 1968, s.45. Whatever the correct interpretation of this legislation, it is not quite clear anyway what the effect would be, given the existence of 'grey' areas of responsibility as described in this chapter. For example, some of the legislation states that social services departments cannot provide what is 'required' to be provided under the NHS Act 1977. But how could sense be made of this legislation when there are both 'health' and 'social' baths; occupational therapists working in both health and social services; commodes supplied by the health service and social services for ostensibly different purposes (health or daily living). In addition, given that the NHS Act 1977 is vague and mentions scarcely any specific services (see Chapter 16), it would be very difficult to state exactly what is 'required' to be provided under that Act.

Occasionally, the local ombudsman has had to deal with this sort of question. For example, one investigation considered the provision of electric wheelchairs for outdoor use. In the past, the health service has as a general rule not provided wheelchairs of this type (see Mandelstam 1993,chapter 6) – although Scotland is now an exception to this rule. The ombudsman commented that she 'was reluctant to view the County Council as having no responsibility for this under s.2 of the Chronically Sick and Disabled Persons Act' (CLAE 91/C/0565, p.18).

EFFECT ON SERVICE USERS OF UNCLEAR RESPONSIBILITIES

Uncertain divisions between different agencies can cause confusion amongst service users as to what is available and from where. It can also cause delay in provision of services, whilst the authorities concerned try and reach an agreement. Even if there are clear divisions, service users might suffer unless there is flexibility and close working between different agencies.

EXTRACTS

Legislation says nothing about avoiding delay in services caused by a dispute between different types of agency (eg. between social services and health).

Policy guidance states that: 'Care should be taken that individuals are not repeatedly referred from one agency to another' (DH 1990, para 3.34).

Circular guidance also adverts to the issue:

> 'provision of proper care should not be delayed pending resolution of a dispute over responsibilities…recourse to formal dispute arrangements should be regarded as a rare and serious event. The aim should be to ensure that disputes are resolved at the lowest possible level' (EL(93)18/CI(93)12, para 17).

DISCUSSION

Effect on Users

It has been pointed out by, and to, the (former) Social Services Select Committee, that from 'the point of view of the person who is receiving it, there should not be health care and social care, but simply care'. As one witness put it: 'the distinction between health and social care is one which makes sense at the Treasury and the upper reaches of the Government but to the clients, to the customers, to the people we serve, it is a meaningless distinction' (IHSM: Social Services Committee 1990,p.xi).

Evidence given by the National Carers' Association to the Health Committee (1993,vol.1,p.xvi) makes the same point: 'your normal community care user or carer does not know or care who provides the services; it is the quality of the service which is important to them'.

People in need might be unsure about whom to contact for particular community services. This uncertainty may well be explicable if there is confusion between the statutory services themselves: for example, between community nursing services and local authority domiciliary services as to who should provide bathing, getting-up, and going-to-bed services (NAO 1992,p.24).

A recent study on hospital discharge (Henwood 1994,p.36) reported health authorities' statements that because of difficulties in clear demarcation of responsibilities, 'individual decisions would have to be made to deal with problems as they arose, but that the nature of such decisions might be idiosyncratic and inequitable'.

A recent study by the King's Fund Centre and the Nuffield Institute (1994a) identified the following specific concerns about the health and social care boundary:

- changing responsibilities and the impact on users in terms of charges and the appropriateness of care;
- unacceptability of home care staff giving intimate personal care;
- inequity between users receiving free NHS services and those receiving similar care from social services for which they have to pay;
- the question of how well home care staff are alert to changes in people's conditions;
- lack of coordination and continuity between agencies (Henwood 1994a,p.15).

Dispute and Delay

An example given to the Health Committee (1993) involved

> 'a young woman, a teenager, with multiple handicaps. The health authority are saying…that this person has very great care needs, but does not have medical needs and therefore it is the social services' responsibility; the social services are saying this person needs round the clock nursing care. For 14 months this child has been in an assessment bed, blocking it for everybody else because neither side will say it is their responsibility' (vol.2,p.39).

Another case cited by the National Carers' Association further illustrates the point. A woman had a district nurse coming in to bath her husband who had Parkinson's Disease. When the nurse ceased to come in, social services provided a care attendant who was, however, instructed not to carry out 'any intimate personal tasks'. The problem was resolved only because the care attendant ignored the instruction (vol.2,p.168).

Inequity

It has been pointed out that the local, piecemeal approach to resource allocation 'almost certainly exacerbates inequalities in access to health and social care'. This is because 'there is no guarantee that an area which is deficient in resources in one sector is compensated by more resources for complementary services in another'. Thus local priorities might not reflect local needs (Judge, Mays 1994).

CHAPTER 13

CONTINUING (LONG-TERM) NHS CARE

KEY ISSUES

(N.B. This chapter was mostly written before draft guidance was issued by the Department of Health in August 1994. Because this guidance is only in draft; because the effect of it anyway is probably unpredictable; and because it cannot be understood without an appreciation of what has gone before, we have left most of the chapter intact. A summary of the draft guidance is given immediately below, and reference made to it at appropriate points in the chapter.)

Draft Guidance

At the time of writing this book, draft Department of Health guidance (NHSE 1994) has attempted to clarify the issue of continuing NHS care. It states that most NHS patients who require continuing care in nursing homes will not be paid for by the NHS: they will be means-tested by social services. However, people with 'complex or multiple health care needs' who require 'continuing and specialist medical or nursing supervision' should remain the responsibility of the health service. The draft guidance also states that people who do not qualify for NHS care do not ultimately have a right to remain in hospital – this is a departure from previous guidance which had appeared to state the opposite.

Whether this draft guidance clarifies matters for individual service users and their families is open to question – although it does tend to confirm the wide discretion of health authorities. First, it remains for local health authorities to determine their own criteria of eligibility of need for continuing NHS care. This invites considerable local variations in policy and practice, as well as disputes about what terms such as 'complex or multiple health care needs' really mean. Second, as the guidance also makes clear, any NHS responsibilities are subject to 'available resources'. Thus, authorities can alter their criteria from time to time, and even in the case of failing to provide for individuals who apparently meet the criteria, authorities could probably successfully argue (legally) a lack of resources. Third, the model of care which the guidance puts forward is one that has probably more or less existed in practice for some time (see eg. Timmins 1994a); and the Secretary of State of Health has herself pointed out (Bottomley 1994) that no 'set of guidelines is likely to make less sensitive the dividing line' between health and social care. Fourth, it has been suggested that if the guidance implies that people can be discharged against their wishes into care where they have to pay the fees, then such guidance might be unenforceable if it undermines a basic principle of the law of contract (namely, that a contract is an agreement entered into voluntarily by both parties) (Clements 1994a).

Nevertheless, the guidance does apparently support a recent decision of the health service ombudsman to the effect that a health authority could not have a rigid policy which systematically denied NHS continuing care to people in severe need. This decision might be based in part on the legal principle that authorities should not fetter their discretion (see p.81) and in part on the legal duty to provide 'comprehensive' services under the NHS Act 1977 (Clements 1994a).

Uncertainty of Provision

The previous chapter has explained the existence of uncertain and 'grey' areas of statutory responsibility for services – when it is not clear which authority is going to provide which service.

A major example of such uncertainty, central to community care policy, concerns people's rights to NHS beds, especially in relation to long-term care. There has been uncertainty for health authorities about how far, legally and politically, they can 'wash their hands' of people who need such continuing care. This uncertainty affects their ability to plan and make priorities, and can cause legal anxieties. For patients and their families, there is uncertainty about whether the health service will provide the care free of charge; or whether they will have to pay for it themselves in private nursing homes.

The problem of responsibility for continuing care is most likely to affect elderly people, but might also affect other people, such as those with head injuries, severe learning disabilities or with requirements for convalescent or terminal care (Henwood 1994a,p.15).

The 1989 community care White Paper stated that health authorities would have duties to provide long-term, continuing care for people who need it. Yet despite these apparently clear statements, long-term care remains a politically, financially and practically difficult problem (see eg. Laing 1993).

Current Circular guidance and other government advice has left open a number of uncertainties. For example, it has been unclear how far health authorities can use their discretion to make priorities and simply not provide long-term care to some people even if those people have 'clinical needs'. Circular guidance (from 1989) has stated that people should not be placed, against their wishes, in residential or nursing homes where they will have to pay their own fees. In addition, the guidance has stated that before any decisions are made, patients and their relatives should be given written details about the fees of nursing homes. But the legal effect of the guidance is uncertain and in any case there is a question about what 'against somebody's wishes' really means. For example, if hospital staff give the impression that patients have no choice but to enter residential or nursing homes, then patients might be 'willing' in one sense – but only because they have been deprived of information.

If the priority of individual patients is determined by the 'clinical judgement' of doctors, then it can sometimes become difficult to distinguish clinical decision-making from decisions made on the basis of available resources. Unclear also is the distinction between a need for 'NHS nursing care' and (non-NHS) 'private nursing care' – if there is such a distinction.

The health service ombudsman, investigating a number of cases, has considered these points and sought advice from the Department of Health. Even this advice has been only of limited help since it has declared basically that there is a duty which, however, does not apply in all cases, because authorities can always take resources into account (at both policy level and in individual cases). It therefore has given individual patients and their relatives little to rely on.

The chapter compares, in particular, five decisions of the health service ombudsman which concern the provision of NHS beds. These are instructive practical examples of how disputes arise and how difficult it can be to solve them. One recent decision concerned a health authority's refusal to provide care for a severely disabled, brain-damaged patient. The upholding of the complaint limited the health authority's discretion not to provide continuing care for some people. It is this decision of the ombudsman which has ostensibly led to the issuing of draft guidance by the Department of Health (see above for summary).

Because of the confusion which has characterised this most important area of provision, substantial extracts from the White Paper, policy guidance, Circular guidance, and Department of Health advice are included immediately below. For the sake of greater clarity, each extract is numbered. The extracts will repay reading by both authorities and service users, since their vagueness and apparent inconsistency supply both sides of the 'argument' with ample material.

EXTRACTS

(1) Legislation (NHS Act 1977,s.3) places general duties on health authorities to provide hospital and other accommodation, medical and nursing services, after-care services etc. (see Chapter 16). It is on these basic duties that hospital discharge decisions and arrangements are founded, although hospital discharge is not actually mentioned.

(2) The community care White Paper (Secretaries of State 1989) states:

(enabling people to stay in their own homes) the 'aim of health authorities should be to ensure that community health services are available to enable people to live in their own homes for as long as possible';

(health service duties to provide longterm care) however, there:

> 'will always be some people who cannot be supported in their own homes. Where such people require continuous care for reasons of ill-health, it will remain the responsibility of health authorities to provide for this. Examples here might include mentally ill people who require specialised residential health provision; as, indeed, may some people with mental or physical handicaps. Some frail elderly people may require continuous health care, traditionally provided in long-stay hospital wards... Health authorities will need to ensure that their plans allow for the provision of continuous residential health care for those highly dependent people who need them, but that people should not be placed in this type of care unnecessarily. Whether this requires an increase or a reduction in the level of continuous health provided through the NHS will depend very much on local circumstances...' (paras 4.19–4.21).

(3) Policy guidance, listing what the objectives of individual care should be in order of preference, places last 'long-stay care in hospital' (DH 1990,para 3.24).

(4) Policy guidance states about leaving hospital:

> **(agreement about discharge arrangements)** 'Subject always to consumer choice, patients should not leave hospital until the supply of at least essential community care services have been *agreed* with them, their carers and all the authorities concerned' (*our.* DH 1990, para 3.44).

(5) A booklet accompanying Circular guidance (DH 1989,para A2, with HC(89)5) about hospital discharge states clearly in a key passage that procedures should provide for:

> **(communication in writing about fees)** 'Where a person moves from hospital to a private nursing home, it should be made quite clear to him/her in writing before the transfer whether or not the health authority will pay the fees, under a contractual arrangement...'

> **(patient's choice not pay private residential and nursing home fees)** 'No NHS patient should be placed in a private nursing or residential care home against his/her wishes if it means that he/she or a relative will be personally responsible for the home's charges' (DH 1989,para A2).

(6) Department of Health memorandum to the Health Committee of the House of Commons. In 1991, the government, giving evidence to a House of Commons Health Committee (DSS/DH 1991), confirmed that: 'Health authorities have a responsibility to provide nursing care for those who cannot or do not wish to pay for it. Department of Health guidance is clear that people should not be discharged into private nursing homes when they have no wish to pay' (Memorandum 1991).

(In July 1992, the government reiterated in Parliament: 'nobody should be discharged into a private sector establishment against his or her will, unless the full costs are to be met from public funds. If a contribution is required, the agreement of the individual will be needed' (H99 1992).)

(7) A letter from the Minister of State for Social Security and the Disabled quoted by the health service ombudsman states:

> **(clinical, not financial, decision to discharge)** 'Decisions about the discharge of people from hospital are for the consultant in charge of the patient's care to make and must be made on clinical grounds. Financial considerations should not enter into the decision.'

> **(NHS bears cost wherever care provided)** 'Where it is decided that a patient requires continuing in-patient medical or nursing care, it falls to the NHS to supply it at no cost to the patient. The on-going care can be provided either by the patient remaining in an NHS hospital bed or for example by transfer to a private nursing home under contractual arrangements, with the NHS meeting the full cost and retaining the ultimate responsibility for the patient's care.'

> **(discretionary 'level' of care)** 'It is of course for individual health authorities to decide the level of contractual arrangements. In making such decisions a variety of factors is to be taken into account; cost is an important factor but it is not the overriding consideration.'

> **(inability to pay for nursing home fees)** 'In the last analysis, where a person in a home can no longer meet his fees but still requires nursing home or residential home care it will fall to the NHS or local authority as appropriate to provide that care if it is not otherwise available to the person.' (quoted in HSC W.194/89–90)

(8) Communication from Chief Executive of the NHS Management Executive. The health service ombudsman obtained further guidance from the NHS Management Executive. Basically, it confirms that there are difficulties and that whilst there is a duty to meet the clinical needs of people, that duty is qualified by the amount of resources available.

> **(problems)** 'There are, undoubtedly, real problems in the area which you are examining but it is difficult to be prescriptive about particular local circumstances. The position set out in the [Minister's] letter [see immediately above] is quite correct...'

> **(professional judgement about NHS care)** 'If in a doctor's professional judgement a patient needs NHS care, then there is a duty upon the health service to provide it without charge (except for items where there is a specific power of charging)...'

> **(three care options)** 'this can be done by providing community nursing care to the patient's own home, by providing in-patient care or by a contractual arrangement with an independent sector home (ie paid in full by the health authority)...'

(discretionary level of service) 'The level of service provided overall is a matter for individual health authorities in the light of local circumstances and priorities'. (quoted in HSC W.194/89–90)

Further detail provided by the NHSME to the health service ombudsman is as follows:

(no general duty even if a person is in need) 'there is no general duty on a health authority to provide inpatient medical or nursing care to every person who needs it. Legal precedents have established that the Secretary of State's duty under Section 3 of the [NHS] Act is qualified by an understanding that he should do so "within the resources available"';

(clinical priority) 'in any particular case the provision of such care may be deferred so that cases may be dealt with, in order of clinical priority, within the resources available';

(non-provision of in-patient care to somebody in need) 'consideration of clinical priority may mean that a particular patient may never be provided with in-patient nursing care';

(three options open to a health authority)

- **(direct NHS care)** 'to provide an NHS in-patient bed in the hospital or other suitable NHS premises (if beds were available)';
- **(NHS care elsewhere)** 'to purchase a bed for their patient in a private hospital or home (if resources extended to this category of patient)';
- **(no NHS care)** 'to advise…that their resources did not extend to [either of the above two options] and the alternatives were that [the person] should be cared for at home, with some NHS services provided by the DHA or GP and such social services as could be provided by the Local Authority; [or] that [the person] should apply for a place privately in a private nursing home to which the NHS could not contribute.' (quoted in HSC W.194/89–90)

DISCUSSION
Basic Legislative Duties
Legislation places duties on the Secretary of State for Health (delegated to health authorities) to provide, amongst other things, hospital or other accommodation, medical and nursing services, care for persons who are ill and after-care for people who have been ill. All these duties are general duties to be provided to the extent that they are 'necessary to meet all reasonable requirements'. The duty to provide care and after-care is qualified also by the phrase 'as he considers are appropriate as part of the health service' (NHS Act 1977 s.3).

The question remains about the circumstances in which these general duties oblige health authorities to provide long-term care. In addition to the above guidance and advice already quoted, the government continues to make statements about longterm care. For example, in March 1994 the government stated that 'patients who require specialist medical and nursing supervision will continue to be the responsibility of the NHS. This means the NHS will continue to be responsible for providing assessment and rehabilitation facilities, and for retaining long-stay facilities for those whose medical needs or patterns of behaviour would be difficult to manage in a community-based setting' (H42 1994). Or, more simply, 'the provision of continuing care for those who need it for reasons of ill health remains the responsibility of the national health service' (H43 1994). These statements, apparently straightforward, in fact fail to address the complexities which have arisen and are, by omission, a little disingenuous.

This is because the broad statement that there are general duties to provide services is of little use to individual patients and their relatives when they find, locally, that those duties are qualified by 'lack of resources' – because of a local policy to divert resources to other services. In fact, the draft guidance (NHSE 1994) issued by the Department of Health seems to assume as a matter of course that NHS responsibilities in general are subject to 'available resources'.

Health Service Ombudsman Investigations: Five Examples Compared

The following paragraphs summarise five investigations of the health service ombudsman

Example 1: Clinical Medical Emergency: Failure to Provide Service not Justified

In one case, the health service ombudsman concluded that the health authority had a duty to provide care for a person with an emergency medical condition. In fact the case was not about long-term care, but did concern provision of an NHS bed for a person who had medical needs.

A person, deemed by doctors to be in need of emergency medical need, could not be found an NHS bed in either of the two local hospitals. Instead she was admitted to a private nursing home for which she had to pay. The ombudsman's opinion was that

'a health authority has a duty to provide accommodation when a patient from one of their districts needs admission to hospital immediately as an emergency. The Authority's failure to provide a hospital bed for the mother when she required one in a medical emergency amounted to a failure in a service which they had a duty to provide; I must therefore criticise them for this' (HSC W.111/75–76).

The ombudsman reached this conclusion despite the fact that the authority was aware of the problem and was faced with a large population of elderly people who were 'blocking beds' – which meant that the number of beds available for medical emergencies had been reduced. In addition, there were staff shortages. An alternative solution of increasing the number of NHS beds by increased contracting with private nursing homes had not been adopted because it was deemed lower priority than other needs for resources within the authority.

Therefore, in this case, the ombudsman effectively limited the discretion of health authorities not to provide NHS care to people in need under s.3 of the NHS Act 1977.

Examples 2 and 3: Non-Provision of NHS Care Justified by Lower Priority in the Light of Resources

More recently and in contrast to the above case, the health service ombudsman investigated two cases in which he seemed to accept that a patient's clinical priority could be determined at least in part by the availability of resources at the particular time in question.

He investigated the case of a person denied admission to hospital for eight months after his GP had requested he be admitted because his wife felt she could no longer manage caring for him. He was suffering from a chronic, debilitating condition. The ombudsman did not uphold the complaint. The consultant concerned had assessed that the person did not need frequent medical intervention and so did not need '24-hour hospital care'.

The ombudsman stated that 'where demand exceeds available resources there may be some whose clinical priority is such that their needs cannot be met under the NHS. I find that the decision by the DHA about the allocation of resources for the care of the chronic sick was a discretionary matter, and I cannot question such a decision unless I find evidence of maladministration in the way in which the decision was made...'. This decision was reached despite the ombudsman's statement that health authorities 'have a duty to provide some level of care for persons such as the complainant's husband, who are judged to need long-term nursing care' (HSC W.599/89–90).

In another case of non-admission to an NHS bed for a person with cerebral atrophy, the ombudsman found that health authorities 'have a duty to provide some level of care for persons such as the father, who are judged to need long-term nursing care. However, where – as in this case – demand exceeds available resources there may be some whose clinical priority is such that their needs cannot be met under the NHS'. Crucially, it was a decision made by a consultant which determined the lower priority and it was a decision made 'in the exercise of clinical judgement', even though the 'need for long-term nursing care had been established'. The ombudsman thus accepted the clinical decision not to provide an NHS bed (HSC W.194/89–90).

Both these cases indicate that so long as clinical judgement has determined a person's priority, then failure to provide a service can be justified if there is simply not enough money to provide the service – even if a person has a clinical need. It should be noted, however, that both these cases were about people who were trying to gain access to NHS beds, rather than trying to remain in them.

Examples 4 and 5: failure to Provide Nursing Care: Not Justified

Two further recent cases have ended in findings against health authorities, and it is not totally clear how they differ essentially from the two previous cases.

In the first case, a woman with severe head injuries had been in a neuro-surgical unit. A decision was made to discharge her to a private nursing home where she would have to pay the fees. The health authority's position was that they

'had finite resources and had to have regard to their responsibility for all patients and to consider what category of care was most appropriate for the particular needs of a patient who was recovering from head injuries...not all such patients were, under the provisions of the Act, the responsibility of the DHA...the complainant's mother's needs [were] primarily for social care with clinical support...the Act did not...impose a responsibility upon health authorities for all head-injured people who no longer required in-patient medical care.'

However, the ombudsman stated, given the severe incapacity of the person and the consultant's view that 'she is likely to need sustained nursing care for the rest of her life', that it 'seems to me incontrovertible, therefore, in the light of the level of continuing care the complainant's mother will require and the chief executive's advice [see above], that the DHA had a duty to continue to provide the care...required at no cost to her or her family' (HSC 478/89–90).

In the second case, well-publicised at the beginning of 1994 (the 'Leeds case'), the health service ombudsman investigated the way in which a health authority had exercised its discretion to set priorities. It had decided not to provide directly, or pay for elsewhere (eg. a nursing home), continuing care for people with neurological conditions: the health authority neuro-surgical contract did not refer to institutional care at all.

The person discharged was doubly incontinent, could not eat or drink without assistance, could not communicate, had a kidney tumour, had cataracts in both eyes and had occasional epileptic fits. There was no dispute that when he was discharged he did not need active medical treatment but did need 'substantial nursing care'. The health authority defended its position with reference to resources, priorities and national policy (which was being followed by other health authorities).

The ombudsman found a failure in service. He cites s.3 of the NHS Act 1977 at the beginning of the report, including s.3(1)(e) which refers to 'after-care'. His findings read: 'This patient was a highly dependent patient in hospital under a contract made with the Infirmary by Leeds Health Authority; and yet, when he no longer needed care in an acute ward but manifestly still needed what the National Health Service is there to provide, they regarded themselves as having no scope for continuing to discharge their responsibilities to him because their policy was to make no provision for continuing care. The policy also had the effect of excluding an option whereby he might have the cost of his continuing care met by the NHS. In my opinion the failure to make available long-term care within the NHS for this patient was unreasonable and constitutes a failure in the service provided by the Health Authority. I uphold the complaint'.

The ombudsman recommended that the health authority reimburse nursing home costs already incurred by the man's wife and meet future costs; and also that it should 'review their provision of services for the likes of this man in view of the apparent gap in service available for this particular group of patients' (HSC E.62/93–94).

Rationale of the Ombudsman Investigations

The rationale of the above five cases is not absolutely clear and there appears to be some inconsistency in the decisions that were made. Two of the five accepted a health authority's discretion not to provide NHS care. What might distinguish these cases from the others, as an Age Concern (1991,p.5) document points out, is that neither of the people concerned were in hospital. The rationale might therefore be that the health authority has a duty to provide continuing care for people already receiving inpatient care.

Nevertheless, if this is the rationale of the decisions, it is not immediately evident why this should necessarily be so. First, people not in hospital might still be under NHS care and receiving, for example, district nurse and GP services. It is not clear why, if the person's needs deteriorate, he or she should *in principle* be in a worse position than somebody already in hospital, especially given the policy of care in the community (ie. in people's homes). Second, this rationale would anyway not explain the first investigation summarised above, which concerned a person not in hospital and yet which was decided against the health authority.

Another suggestion has been that although there is strong Court of Appeal authority (*R v Secretary of State v Hincks 1979*) for health authority discretion in making priorities within a particular service, it might not be authority for total non-provision of a particular service (Dimond 1994). This would be the distinction between whether a service is provided at all, and what level it is provided at.

However, this distinction itself raises the question of what 'non-provision' of a service really means. For example, it could mean non-provision of a particular service (eg. continuing care) to *some individuals;* a policy of non-provision to *one group* of people (eg. those with neurological conditions) but provision to another group (eg. elderly people); or non-provision of a particular service to *all* (eg. no continuing care whatsoever). It is only in the last case that it is certain that a service is not being provided altogether.

The ombudsman's ruling in the Leeds case has worried health authorities and the government because of the financial implications (see eg. Timmins 1994) – and led to the issuing of draft guidance (NHSE 1994, see head of chapter).

Meaning of 'Nursing Care'

There are other conceptual difficulties. For example, an Age Concern (1991) submission to a House of Commons Select Committee suggests that a distinction was being made between 'continuous NHS nursing care' and 'continuous nursing care'. The submission suggested there was no substance to such a distinction, since 'on the face of it' nursing care is simply a health matter and the province of the NHS whether in an acute unit or elsewhere (for example, NHS nursing homes) (p.8).

The new draft guidance (see head of chapter) has not really cleared this problem up. It does make the distinction between ordinary nursing home care and NHS care ('continuing and specialist medical or nursing supervision'). However, such NHS care will be only for people with 'complex or multiple health care needs'; the definition of such needs will be for health authorities to define; and access to such care will be governed by local (and thus variable) criteria of eligibility. It would therefore seem quite clear that disputes are likely to arise about eligibility (see eg. Timmins 1994a).

Meaning of 'Clinical Judgement'

Age Concern (1991) has also questioned exactly what the term 'clinical judgement' means, since it can apparently be an exercise in resource management:

> 'Is it solely clinical judgement when a patient is judged as having a need for continuous nursing care, but when the consultant is prevented from offering suitable care because the health authority does not have this provision, and has a policy not to make such provision? This could arguably be seen as a matter of health authority policy, and not *solely* a matter of clinical judgement. In effect, this appears to be a way of saying, "If the services are not available, there cannot be a clinical need". This could be seen as a distortion of the concept of clinical judgement' (p.6).

In fact, clinical judgements need not be distorted. So long as such judgements acknowledge people's need for care, they do not lose their integrity by going on to assess priority. However, clinical judgements might lose their integrity where there is conflation of the concepts of 'clinical need' and 'priority for NHS care'. An example, would be where therapists working in elderly care hospital wards, under increasing workloads, set priorities for their patients which they would not have set a year a two ago. They might have a dilemma of whether to write in patients' notes that *rehabilitation is needed but that it cannot be supplied*; or whether to collapse this two-stage judgement into one and write only that *no rehabilitation is needed* (personal communication: senior hospital therapist, 1994). It is arguable that in the latter case, integrity of judgement becomes invisible.

Even if clinical judgements do not lose their integrity in the face of hard decisions about priorities, what might be lost is equity within the health service. However, this is not the fault of the staff making the clinical judgements, nor does it mean that individual judgements are based on inappropriate considerations. Thus, one person might be given an NHS bed one month, but another person with similar needs fail to get one the next month because there is no bed available – and other people are judged to be of higher clinical priority. In related vein, it has been reported (Henwood 1994,p.36) that the distinction between people who pay privately for nursing care and those who remain NHS patients is not necessarily based on differences in clinical need. Instead, the distinction might come about because those who remain NHS patients, together with relatives, have become aware of their 'rights' to NHS services and so have refused to pay for nursing home care.

Extent of Health Authorities' Duties to Provide Care

Despite the Department of Health draft guidance (NHSE 1994) summarised at the head of this chapter, NHS duties, whether informed by the old or the new guidance, are still generally subject to resources both at policy and individual level. In the light of the draft guidance, the position would appear to be that authorities cannot adopt rigid policies which deny continuing care to people with complex and specialist needs. However, even a policy to provide care for such people would appear, in individual cases, to be subject to available resources.

The advice given to the health service ombudsman (extract 8 above) contains two apparently contradictory statements:

(1) 'If in a doctor's professional judgement a patient needs NHS care, then there is a duty upon the health service to provide it without charge';

(2) 'There is no general duty on a health authority to provide inpatient medical or nursing care to every person who needs it. Legal precedents have established that the Secretary of State's duty under Section 3 of the [NHS] Act is qualified by an understanding that he should do so "within the resources available".'

However, there is not in fact a contradiction. First, both statements refer to a general duty, which is not the same as a duty towards every individual (see p.61). Second, there is in fact a difference between saying that a person has a *clinical need* and that a person has a *clinical need for which this health authority is going to provide NHS care*. The second need does not necessarily follow from the first, since the second need is only determined after priorities have been taken into account.

The health service ombudsman has tried to explain this. He states in his annual report (for 1990–1991) that 'finite resources and other priorities can limit the help that is provided' (HSC 1991,p.5). In a recent investigation (W.256/92–93), he puts it another way, stating that he does 'not dissent from the view of the Department [of Health] that health authorities do not have an inalienable duty to provide hospital care for a person who is judged not to need it'. However, even this statement by the ombudsman seems to illustrate the confusion, because the Department of Health's view is not just that there is no duty to provide care for somebody who *does not* need it; but also that there is no absolute duty to provide care even for somebody who *does* need it.

The ombudsman goes on to state in his annual report for 1993–1994, that whilst this 'inalienable duty' might not exist for authorities, nevertheless: 'That is not the same as maintaining that they can reasonably choose not to provide full-time continuing nursing care under the NHS in every case where acute care in hospital is no longer needed' (HSC 1994,p.5). The ombudsman appears to be sounding a warning to health authorities not to adopt rigid policies (see p.81) which exclude, as a matter of course, the provision of continuing nursing care to all people who might need it.

Legal Effect of Department of Health Circular Guidance

The draft guidance (head of chapter) implies that if people refuse to leave NHS care, then authorities are not obliged to continue to care for them if other patients have greater needs. This is a marked change from previous guidance; in effect it makes clear that ultimately patients and their family cannot exercise a veto on discharge from hospital.

The booklet accompanying the 1989 Circular guidance states that: 'No NHS patient should be placed in a private nursing or residential care home against his/her wishes if it means that he/she or a relative will be personally responsible for the home's charges' (see extract 5 above).

This is a very important statement, since were it binding on health authorities and were patients and their relatives informed about it, it could effectively obstruct on a large scale health authority policies to reduce provision of continuing care.

Circular guidance is thought generally not to place legal duties on authorities (see p.71). Nevertheless, the health service ombudsman has stated that it does. For example: 'that is not to say that the Health Authority were entitled…to consider what is said in circular HC(89)5 as merely guidelines which they were free not to implement'. This was in rejection of the view of a deputy manager which was that 'the advice in that circular was no more than guidelines and that, while the Health Authority would do their best to follow them, the booklet…used 'should' and not 'must', when referring to not transferring a patient who was unwilling to move and be responsible for the home's charges' (HSC W.256/92–93).

However, even if the 1989 Circular guidance does impose obligations on authorities, the problem is that nobody is quite sure what the obligations are. The ombudsman has conceded that the guidance is 'capable of different interpretations' and is obscured by an 'unfortunate lack of clarity' (HSC 1994,p.5). He seems to accept that it is also subject to the fact that authorities do not have an 'inalienable duty' to provide for everybody (see above section).

The ombudsman does refer to previous Department of Health advice to a health authority about whether this guidance gives 'relatives or carers the power of veto'. The advice is summarised as follows, though it sheds little light on the problem: 'in all cases hospitals were expected to discuss discharge arrangements with the patient or his/her relatives or carers; that if the patient's relatives or carers were not happy with the proposed arrangements (particularly when they were expected to meet any costs) they should be expected to put forward alternatives; that health authorities were expected to do what was reasonable, which did not include keeping in hospital patients about whom the clinical judgement was that they did not need hospital care; and that only where there had been a Secretary of State's direction were health authorities legally bound by the Department's advice' (HSC W.256/92–93).

Pressure on Patients and Relatives

Despite the above ('old') 1989 guidance stating that people cannot be forced to leave hospital and enter a private nursing home, there is concern that some people, unaware of their rights, have been subjected to pressure.

This concern was expressed to the House of Commons Health Committee (1993,vol.1,p.xiv) by the Alzheimer's Disease Society:

'It is quite clear that the relatives – and I am quite sure the older people themselves – are not aware of their rights and are not being made aware of their right to insist on staying where they are or continuing to receive an NHS funded bed, and they are often being very vigorously encouraged to seek a placement in an independent nursing home'.

If a bed is blocked

'the pressure from managers and doctors to get that person into a nursing home is immense and the person's wishes may also be blocked. They may go into a home which is too far from their family or on the wrong bus route' (1993,vol.2,p.15).

The health service ombudsman notes in his latest annual report that in his experience the Department of Health guidance 'is not adequately known or observed. In some instances patients or their relatives have simply not been properly told about the financial implications of discharge to a private nursing home' (HSC 1994,p.5).

Giving People Written Information About Fees

If there is lack of clarity about whether the old Circular guidance means that patients and relatives can exercise a veto on discharge, the guidance is clearer about giving people information in writing about fees which they will have to pay.

The new draft guidance (NHSE 1994) also states that patients and their families 'should be fully informed' about discharge, assessment and care options. The health service ombudsman accepts that this imposes obligations on health authorities and will make findings against them if they do not do what the guidance says (see below).

The old guidance (see extract 5 above) states that: 'Where a person moves from hospital to a private nursing home, it should be made quite clear to him/her in writing before the transfer whether or not the health authority will pay the fees, under a contractual arrangement...'.

The health service ombudsman is prepared to make findings against health authorities which do not follow this guidance. In one case (see immediately below), he found that the deprivation of this information, together with other pressure, amounted to duress. In another case, a woman who had a fall and fractured her leg was discharged to a private residential home where she stayed for about a month and faced a bill of over £900. The ombudsman found that she had not been given information by the hospital about the fees and that therefore the NHS Trust 'did not carry out their responsibilities to the woman under the terms of the circular' (HSC W.524/92–93).

Duress

In the Leeds case, the health service ombudsman made a finding of duress, despite the fact that the wife of a brain-damaged person had apparently accepted the decision about discharge:

> 'Since it was made clear that continuing occupation of an acute bed was not clinically appropriate, the complainant was left in the difficult position of choosing between refusing to accept his discharge or meeting the [private nursing] home's charges. None of the hospital staff was aware of – nor did Infirmary policy apparently provide for – the requirement in the guidance [see above] to set out in writing, before discharge to a nursing home, who would pay the fees. I criticise this significant omission. The complainant was not given that information. I therefore regard her as having placed under duress through that failure to inform her of all the relevant considerations...'

> 'Although she acquiesced in the need for her to pay the nursing home fees, in my opinion that was inequitable in the circumstances. I recommend that Leeds Health Authority remind their providers of the need to follow the Department of Health's guidance on discharge procedures' (HSC E.62/93–94).

Local Policy Documents and Standards

Whatever the legal effect of the Circular guidance (extract 5), or the draft guidance (when it is finalised) health authorities/hospitals might have their own local policies and standards. Failure to adhere to such local standards might result in a finding of maladministration by the health service ombudsman. For example, in one case where a woman was discharged to a nursing home without being advised about the fees she would have to pay, the ombudsman found that the staff did not 'adhere fully to what was required of them under the local policy standard'. The standard had been signed by the sister in charge of the relevant department and concerned consultation about, and recording of, arrangements for discharge (HSC W.524/92–93).

CHAPTER 14

PROVISION OF SERVICES IN RESIDENTIAL AND NURSING HOMES

KEY ISSUES

The provision of health (and other) services to residents of residential and nursing homes is complicated. This is because services are affected by a number of uncertainties. For example, neither legislation nor guidance, both imprecise, clarifies in detail who should be providing what and who should be paying for it. Residents of homes can fall into different categories, depending on how they are being financially supported, and thus be covered to some extent by different legislation and guidance. Residents of homes are also an obvious target for being deemed by health authorities 'low priority' (when compared with people living in their own homes).

As a result, provision in homes of health services is thought to vary widely from home to home and from area to area. The consequence is that residents and their relatives are unlikely to know what to expect either in theory or in practice; health authorities appear to have almost unlimited discretion about what services to provide and at what level.

Registered Homes Tribunals sometimes deal with cases about the facilities and services which have to be provided in homes by home owners. A number of these Tribunal cases are summarised in this chapter. These give insight into the issues and disputes which can arise in residential and nursing homes – and into the factors to be taken into account when solutions are sought. The decisions of the tribunals sometimes demonstrate also the number of different factors which have to be taken into account when judging whether services are adequate. Thus, these decisions are not necessarily predictable and often seem to depend on the particular facts and circumstances of each case – even when these facts and circumstances appear, superficially at least, to be similar.

NHS SERVICES IN RESIDENTIAL HOMES

The NHS Act 1977 places general duties on health authorities to provide health services to the population (see p.256). There is nothing in the Act which excludes people in residential care from receiving these services. In principle therefore, health authorities should provide services to people in residential homes on the same basis as to people in their own homes.

Where health care in residential homes *is* required, it is to be provided by the health service: Circular guidance states that social services contracts for residential care should not include items which the health service has responsibility for providing. However, in practice, it has been long recognised that there is considerable variation in the level and types of health services provided to people in residential homes, who are sometimes in danger of being regarded as 'low priority'.

EXTRACTS

Legislation (NHS Act 1977, s.3) places general duties on the Secretary of State to provide medical and nursing services to the population. There is nothing to suggest that people in residential care should be excluded.

Circular guidance (HSG(92)50) states:

(community health services) 'It will continue to be the responsibility of the NHS to provide where necessary community health services to residents of LA and independent residential care homes on the same basis as to people in their own homes. These services include the provision of district nursing and other specialist nursing services (eg. incontinence advice) as well as provision, where necessary, of incontinence and nursing aids, physiotherapy, speech and language therapy and chiropody. Where such services are provided they must be free of charge to people in independent sector residential care homes as well as to residents of local authority Part III homes' (Annex,para 2).

Guidance endorsed by the Department of Health. In 1984, the Centre for Policy on Ageing published 'Home Life'. Circular guidance explained that the Secretaries of State 'endorsed it as a guide to good practice'. Local authorities were 'asked to regard the code in the same light as general guidance that is issued from time to time' under s.7 of the Local Authority Social Services Act 1970 (LAC(84)15,para 6) (see p.67).

Since then, Home Life continues to be referred to by government, for example, as a reason for not introducing proposals to ensure residents' security of tenure or to ensure written contracts between residents and homes: since Home Life, the 'established code of practice', already advocates procedures covering such concerns (H53 1992).

The Registered Homes Tribunal also frequently refers to Home Life when assessing facilities and services in residential care homes.

Memorandum of guidance (1977). In 1977 the DHSS (as it was then) issued a detailed memorandum of guidance about health care arrangements in local authority residential homes for elderly people.

DISCUSSION
Same Rights to Health Services for People in Residential Homes as for People in Their Own Homes?
The statement in the guidance (HSG(92)50) that people in residential homes have the same rights to provision as people in their own homes is not necessarily helpful in a practical way. This is because community health services both for people in their own homes and for those in residential homes are subject to local priorities and resource allocation. People in residential homes might often be regarded as lower priority because less at risk, since they are not living alone.

For example, one health service ombudsman investigation (HSC W.360/77–78) found that although there was no local policy to withhold community nursing services from people in private residential homes, nevertheless they 'would normally be considered a lower priority than...a patient in his own home'. A letter written by the area nursing officer and referred to in the report is instructive about the fears within some health authorities (even though the letter was found subsequently to be erroneous). It stated that given over-demand, 'to extend the service to private homes would be creating a "precedent service" they had no means of supporting'. The investigation accepted that 'assessment of priorities has to be made'.

Variation in Practice of Health Services to People in Residential Homes
An SSI (1988) report, (issued with HN(89)7 and PL/CNO(89)3) on health care in local authority residential homes, found that the specific guidance set out in the 1977 memorandum (see above) had been patchily implemented. The extent of implementation 'varied from home to home, even between individual homes within the same local authority'. Therapy and nursing services were amongst those services in need of improvement.

More recent (and long awaited) Circular guidance (HSG(92)50: see above) has tried to clarify the position. It is very brief guidance, does not go into detail as did the 1977 guidance, nor does it mention that guidance. There is evidence that provision of health care in residential homes continues to vary from home to home.

For example, one SSI report on community care implementation found that both health and local authorities were implementing both the letter and spirit of the guidance very variably. For example, incontinence services might be funded in a very limited way and might or might not be included in the contract price paid by local authorities. Similarly, paramedical services might be limited, absent altogether or charged privately to residents; and there was no clear understanding of what entitlement to such services was. Meanwhile, health authorities were claiming that they had not been given the additional funding they needed (SSI 1993h,p.13; see also SSI 1994,p.25; SSI/NHSME 1994,p.21).

Daily Living Equipment

Although residential homes have a duty to provide adaptations and facilities to make the home suitable for disabled people, residents might also require particular items for their personal use. Circular guidance (LAC(86)6) explains that local social services authorities are not precluded 'from supplying individual aids such as walking frames and dressing aids to residents in private and voluntary homes provided such items are supplied individually for their personal use and on the same basis as for other people living in the community' (para 11).

SERVICES AND FACILITIES PROVIDED BY RESIDENTIAL CARE HOMES

Adequate services and facilities in residential homes are demanded by legislation. Residential care home owners/managers in the independent sector are subject to the Registered Homes Act 1984 and associated regulations. This legislation states that the owner must be a fit person, the premises be fit, and certain services and facilities provided. Residential homes are both registered and inspected by local authorities. Appeals go to Registered Homes Tribunals which have interpreted some of the requirements placed on homes.

Though carrying no direct statutory force, a code of practice called 'Home Life' has been firmly endorsed by the Department of Health and is regularly referred to by Registered Homes Tribunals. (At the time of writing, the need for a review of 'Home Life' is being considered (H3,1994.)

The following selection of Tribunal cases is instructive in giving insight into the issues and disputes which can arise in residential homes – and into the factors to be taken into account when solutions are sought. The decisions of the tribunals sometimes demonstrate also the number of different factors which have to be taken into account when judging whether services are adequate. Thus, these decisions are not necessarily predictable and seem to depend on the particular facts and circumstances of each case – even when these facts and circumstances appear, superficially at least, to be similar.

EXTRACTS

Legislation states that:

> **(independent sector homes: fitness of person, premises; provision of services and facilities)** An applicant for registration can be refused by the local authority if he or she (or anyone else concerned in the running of the home) 'is not a fit person'. He or she might also be refused if the premises are not fit to be

used because of 'their situation, construction, state of repair, accommodation, staffing, or equipment'. Similarly, an application may be refused because 'the way in which it is intended to carry on the home is such as not to provide services or facilities reasonably required' (Registered Homes Act 1984,s.9).

(independent sector homes: services and facilities) Regulations (SI 1984/1345, r.10 made under the Registered Homes Act 1984) a number of services and facilities must be provided,

'having regard to the size of the home and the number, age, sex and condition of residents.' The list includes:

- employment of enough suitably qualified and competent staff, 'adequate for the well being of residents';
- reasonable accommodation and space;
- adequate and suitable furniture, bedding, curtains and where necessary equipment and screens;
- adequate washing facilities and lavatories;
- making of adaptations and providing facilities necessary for physically disabled people;
- adequate light, heating and ventilation;
- keeping of all parts of the home in good repair, clean and reasonably decorated;
- adequate fire and accident precautions;
- sufficient and suitable kitchen and eating equipment;
- 'suitable, varied and properly prepared wholesome and nutritious food in adequate quantities'
- satisfactory hygiene in the home;
- regular laundry service and provision for residents to do their own laundry so far as 'reasonable and practicable in the circumstances';
- arrangements for residents to see GPs and dentists;
- arrangements concerning handling, keeping, recording, disposal of drugs;
- arrangements for residents' training, occupation, recreation;
- safe place for residents' valuables to be kept;
- connection of the home to a public telephone service, and so far as 'reasonable and practicable in the circumstances, make arrangements for residents to communicate with others in private by post or telephone'.

DISCUSSION (SUMMARIES OF REGISTERED HOMES TRIBUNAL CASES: CASE NUMBER GIVEN)

Situation of the premises

A residential home situated in a village was found unsuitable on the basis of its situation: because the residents 'would be unduly restricted in their independence and ability to move freely outside the house'. This was mainly because of the 'unlevel nature of the site' and poor access to the shop and Post Office (RHT 5).

However, in another case, the Tribunal found in favour of a home despite a number of apparent disadvantages: for example, the area around the home was too small to allow active recreation; the parking facilities could on occasion prove inadequate; and the steepness of the hill posed some risk to unaccompanied wheelchair users. Against these however, was the fact that there was nearby a large public car park, a bus route, an area of grassland. The home's own vehicle was available for use and had a parking space alongside the home. Perhaps the home might take care in the future not to accept, as far as possible, wheelchair users (RHT 83).

Where residents would not be able to maintain independence and become part of the community because of the home's distance from amenities and inadequate transport facilities, the Tribunal found the home not suitable. The fact that many of the residents might not want to go out 'fails to appreciate a fundamental characteristic of independence': namely independence of choice. This was to be measured not in 'quantitative terms, that is, how many residents of care homes can go out, but in qualitative terms, that is, are they able to enjoy and be part of the local community if they wish to?'. The Tribunal referred to 'Home Life' which states that the location and surrounding environment need to be 'suited to the stated aims of the establishment, and at the same time provide a setting which enables the home to blend into the neighbourhood. The accessibility of local facilities, community health services and public transport should be considered fully prior to registration' (RHT 145).

Management of Residents and Quality of Life

An authoritarian approach by a home owner included insistence on set times for getting up and going to bed, on doing exercises before breakfast, and on compelling people to eat and drink against their will. The owner lost her appeal against being deemed an unfit person (RHT 9).

One example which resulted in loss of registration included regimentation (meal-times), staff distancing themselves from residents, little stimulation, lino in bedrooms (indicating acceptance, instead of prevention, of incontinence), no regular opportunities to go out to the shops, no concern about residents' individuality, autonomy and control of their own finances (RHT 15).

A system to be avoided in residential homes is 'warehousing': 'keeping the residents clean, warm and fed and sitting them in front of the TV'. In this particular case, this was not present in its worst form. However, good care practice 'does not require a home to be run like an over hearty holiday camp but it does require that residents be treated as individuals and helped to follow their individual interests'. The Tribunal was left 'with the impression of a good hospital geriatric ward but not a good residential home' (RHT 147). In one case, under a heading of 'management of residents', a number of observations were made which contributed to the home losing its appeal. They included regimentation, lack of privacy, no screening, overcrowding, few personal possessions, no telephone for residents able to use one, and restraint (eg, being bound with a cord) (RHT 23).

In another case, there was an 'unacceptable degree of regimentation of residents who were not allowed in their bedrooms during the daytime unless they were sick, were subjected to rigid dressing, undressing, toileting and meal time routines and had little autonomy or opportunity to live as individuals' (RHT 69).

It is 'faulty running' of a home where a resident 'was not toileted with sufficient regularity, leading to incontinence problems, the removal of her underwear, catheterisation and an entirely unnecessary dispute about who should do her personal laundry'. Similarly, the tying of residents to commodes was 'destructive of...comfort and dignity' (RHT 53).

In another case, the dignity of residents was not respected: for example, two ladies were accorded no privacy at bath-time; another 'enfeebled old lady' was left on the lavatory for many hours (RHT 58).

The installation of electronic listening devices, ostensibly to monitor one member of staff, was used, on the balance of probabilities, to record resident and staff conversations. The Tribunal found that 'use of equipment of this nature is regarded as being a very serious breach of the right to privacy of staff and residents' (RHT 195).

Sufficient Qualified and Competent Staff (SI 1984/1345,r.10)

The Registered Homes Tribunals frequently investigate this matter. However, as the regulations state, what is adequate depends on the size of the home and the number and type of residents. As a result, there are many variables involved and this book cannot cover the decisions in sufficient depth. However, relevant factors include night cover, the effectiveness and organisation of rota systems, competence etc.

Reasonable Accommodation and Space (SI 1984/1345,r.10)

The guidance 'Home Life' states that single rooms are normally preferable, and that if more than two people share a room then there must be special reasons. However, depending on (perhaps exceptional) circumstances a three-bedded room might be acceptable. However, this does not mean that the Tribunals enforce the guidance to the letter – for example, where a 'Council's decision [against the home] was taken on the matter of principle alone without as full a consideration of all the circumstances as there might have been. This is not a case, in our view, for the rigid application of a rule of thumb'. The home won its appeal (RHT 10).

In another similar case, the tribunal found that the council had not acted with sufficient 'circumspection and flexibility' when demanding a reduction in the number of residents in a home with three-bedded rooms. The tribunal found that two of the three-bedded rooms could continue to be so used (RHT 16).

On the other hand, for example, a three-bedded room with shared wardrobe, beds close together, one armchair and a commode and no screening failed to provide privacy and dignity. The home lost its appeal (RHT 12). Where three-bedded rooms were used by two permanent residents and periodically by a third short-term (respite care) resident, the tribunal found that despite the general high standards of care this practice was potentially disruptive to the residents. The home was given about six months to phase out the three-bedded rooms (RHT 25).

Where a home appealed against the phasing out of three-bedded room within five years, the Tribunal found in favour of the local authority which 'has both the right and the duty to seek to implement those standards set out in the Code of Practice, standards which strive to attain "the good rather than…the acceptable". The dignity of residents must be preserved and maintained. Fundamental to dignity is the right to privacy and true privacy may only be attained in single rooms'. For example, in one of the rooms 'privacy for one resident was invaded each time the other residents entered to reach their own beds. Attempts had been made to use cupboards as room dividers but the essential lack of privacy remained, the only effect achieved being a tiny claustrophobic area with poor lighting' (RHT 71).

The following observations were generally accepted by the Tribunal as evidence of inadequate efforts to provide suitable accommodation: lack of privacy, absence of personal space, three beds in a room with 18" gaps between them, passageway passing through a bedroom, and no lift, which meant that residents were marooned (RHT 23).

Home Life states that though single rooms are preferable, there are a number of factors to consider when determining the ratio of double to single rooms in a home. For example, standard of care provided, size and nature of rooms, degree of privacy provided in them, and the amount of other public space provided for residents. In finding in favour of a home's appeal against a reduction of the number of double rooms, the Tribunal took into account size, attractiveness (which would be spoiled by division), difficulty of division, and the generous provision of public space for residents (RHT 52).

In another case the Tribunal outlined the difficulties facing a local authority: if

'a registration authority formulate rigid guidelines, particularly concerning matters such as occupancy and space, it must nevertheless take account of the totality of each situation presented and be ready to apply them flexibly in an appropriate case. Such an approach was visualised in paragraph 9 of Local Authority Circular (86)6 by the statement: "Decisions on the size and occupancy of bedrooms will need to take account not only of the design and construction of the premises but also of the levels of dependency of prospective residents and their likely needs for privacy and care". We appreciate the conflicting considerations often faced by a registration authority; on the one hand it is expected positively and confidently to apply its policies without suspicion of weakness or favouritism, but on the other hand it has to do so in a sensible way that takes account of the circumstances of each individual case, and therefore may appear to be discriminatory' (RHT 99).

This approach illustrates the tension for public authorities in applying policies consistently without 'fettering their discretion' (see p.81).

Where a home was appealing against the decision restricting it to 11 single and 3 double rooms, instead of 10 single rooms and 4 double rooms, the Tribunal found for the home – and against the local authority. The Tribunal acknowledged that the question of double rooms most obviously revolved around privacy and the provision of a 'homely, non-institutional atmosphere'. However, other factors relevant to residents' welfare might include 'the character of an attractive building; the danger of a proprietor being tempted or even obliged to reduce the benefits available to residents in order to survive financially; the maintenance of such good relations and mutual respect between the proprietor and the registration authority and its officers that they can work in partnership for the benefit of residents; and no doubt a number of other factors that may be relevant in particular cases'. The local authority, having adopted a policy of a certain ration of single to double rooms 'must not slavishly apply that ratio in every case' (RHT 56).

In another instance, the Tribunal stated that in the case of the particular home '(and for the avoidance of doubt we make it clear that we are not laying down any principles of general application), it would not be inappropriate to have two double rooms in order to accommodate residents who wanted to share (eg. sisters, spouses, very old friends), or were prepared to share...'. This decision was based on the fact that the criteria for shared rooms 'should first and foremost be the choice of the residents themselves'; and despite the fact that 'even a most respectable and responsible home owner, financially motivated to keep all available beds filled, could unintentionally or even deliberately persuade an elderly person to agree to share, in circumstances where the resident's consent was not entirely voluntary' (RHT 106).

However, where a home opposed limitations to the number of residents permitted and made a 'head-on attack' against single rooms, stating that its philosophy was that 'sharing improves human morale', the Tribunal had no difficulty referring to 'Home Life' and finding against the home. It stated that 'a single room is a very valuable asset in a residential care home because it gives a resident that private territory and opportunity for privacy which is so necessary for most people' (RHT 57).

The Tribunal considered in one case two narrow, single rooms which both fell below the minimum size prescribed by the local authority. Both residents were happy in the rooms. One, which the Tribunal approved (though not unanimously) contained all the furniture recommended in 'Home Life' but looked like the inside of a caravan because it was fitted so closely. The other room was disapproved of unanimously: it was not suitable for occupation by an elderly resident. For example, there was no room for a bedside table; and there were great difficulties in transferring a resident from wheelchair to bed (RHT 112).

Kitchen/Dining Area

A kitchen area used for staff should not be available to residents as well and it was 'not desirable to have dining accommodation for the residents in the kitchen area where food had been prepared and cooked' (RHT 19).

Sufficient Number of Baths, Water Closets etc

Unacceptable is a home where there was no ground floor bathroom and the male toilet facilities consisted only of urinals (RHT 46).

Adequate and Suitable Furniture

Where residents had to keep their clothes in lockers outside the bedrooms, but there was space in the bedrooms for wardrobes, the tribunal dismissed the home's appeal and stated that wardrobes should be installed in all the bedrooms. Thus residents would be enabled to 'at least have some say in what they wear, even though some may not be capable of exercising a rational choice' (RHT 30).

Adaptations and Provision of Facilities Necessary for Physically Disabled People

A home lost its appeal for a number of reasons including the small size and lack of facilities in the bathrooms (eg. no handles on bath or on wall); a staircase was too narrow to enable two people to assist anybody who needed assistance; it would be difficult for residents using a zimmer frame or wheelchair to use a WC without leaving the door open (RHT 36). A lack of free-standing baths and extra handgrips or handrails to help infirm residents was not acceptable (RHT 46).

The lack of a lift in a home with ambulant residents might not be fatal to registration, but in the particular circumstances the lack of a lift contributed 'to the restricted and depressing life offered to the residents' (RHT 53).

A home wished to bring its basement into use as a dining area. The Tribunal considered whether the staircase was suitable. It found that the staircase could not be safely used. This was because it was narrow and steep, made narrower by the existence of a handrail. Without a chair lift 'the problem of getting an old and or infirm person up and down the staircase is self evident. Twelve residents would use the staircase twice a day in order to take lunch and tea'. Yet a chair lift would have caused other problems. For example, the door at the top of stairs would have to remain off its hinges: yet a condition of registration was that the door remain locked. Further, the chair lift would have had to travel some way along the ground floor in order for people to get on and off. This would have caused congestion. The home lost its appeal (RHT 90).

An unsuitable staircase might be a principal reason for refusal of registration. The Tribunal concurred with the decision of the local authority, pointing out that the staircase 'is steep and the treads are too narrow even for a reasonably agile person to use without care. It is difficult to come down safely without turning one's feet at an angle to the stair and exercising some caution. The obstruction of the entrance to [the] lounge by the protrusion of [1.5] steps makes access to that room, both from the stairway and the hall difficult and hazardous for elderly and infirm persons' (RHT 104).

Food
Though not in itself sufficient grounds to cancel registration, the cooking of food in one home and transporting of it to another was stated by the Tribunal to be 'undesirable practice' (RHT 208).

Adequate Heating
A county council's guidelines, interpreting the regulations, stated that 'a full central heating system which maintains adequate heating levels to all parts of the home must be provided'. The temperature should have been 68' F in living accommodation and bedrooms during the day; and in all night-time accommodation at night. Inspectors had found lower temperatures and other witnesses stated that they often felt cold. It seemed that the heating system was deliberately programmed and sometimes switched off in order, probably, to save money. This was one of the grounds on which registration had been cancelled and the Tribunal found that the proprietors indeed failed in their duty under regulation 10(1)(f) (RHT 58).

Adequate Fire and Accident Precautions
Locks on front doors preventing the escape of residents in case of fire were found not acceptable and had remained without being remedied for nearly nine years (RHT 15).

In one case, a home's application to increase its number of residents was rejected for a number of reasons. These included failure to carry out requirements covering regular tests to (and certificates for) the electrical system, emergency lighting, fire alarm system, gas installation, audibility of alarm, and lift. In addition there was failure to fire-proof basement ceilings, to link the emergency lighting and alarm systems, to provide window guards, to propose how hot water should be regulated, to renew the heating system and to provide a lavatory for food-handlers (RHT 217).

Hygiene
Unacceptable was a sluice consisting of a large kitchen sink situated adjacent to a vestibule with a potato peeler and a deep freeze; and where the same room contained washing machines and a tumble drier (RHT 46). Amongst a number of shortcomings posing a risk to the health and/or welfare of residents in one home was the fact that clothes, bed linen and the clothing of incontinent residents were not laundered separately. As a result all clothing smelled of urine (RHT 129).

Arrangements Concerning Handling, Keeping, Recording, Disposal of Drugs

Observations leading to a home losing its appeal included, for example, non-existent or inadequate medical records, incomplete medical cards, tablet bottles re-used so date on the bottle was incorrect, tablets/medicines not corresponding to record cards, bottles inadequately labelled or unreadable, out of date eyedrops not disposed of (RHT 23).

NHS SERVICES PROVIDED IN NURSING HOMES

Legislation places general duties on health authorities to provide health services to the population. There is apparently nothing in the legislation to exclude people in nursing homes from receiving these services. However, Department of Health guidance has stated that basic nursing services to individual residents should be provided by the nursing home and not by the NHS. Nevertheless, the position both in theory and practice seems to have long been complicated, and to remain so even after the April 1993 changes which introduced community care.

In summary, it is difficult to state, beyond a few specific services and a few generalities, who provides what for whom and who is going to pay for it in any particular situation.

EXTRACTS

Legislation (NHS Act 1977, s.3) places general duties on the Secretary of State to provide medical and nursing services to the population. There is nothing to suggest that people in nursing homes should be excluded.

Circular guidance (HSG(92)50) states that:

(statutory services responsibilities for service provision in private nursing homes for people placed by social services) 'When…a local authority [social services] places a person in a nursing home after a joint HA/LA assessment, the local authority is responsible for purchasing services to meet the general nursing care needs of that person, including the cost of incontinence services (eg. laundry) and those incontinence and nursing supplies which are not available on NHS prescription. Health authorities will be responsible for purchasing, within the resources available and in line with their priorities, physiotherapy, chiropody and speech and language and therapy, with the appropriate equipment, and the provision of specialist nursing advice, eg incontinence advice and stoma care, for those people placed in nursing homes by local authorities with the consent of the DHA…'

(resources and priorities) 'The extent to which community health services can be provided is a matter for health authorities' judgement taking account of the resources available and competing priorities. In securing such services, health authorities will also need to consider the medium to long term resource implications given that the number of people placed in nursing homes by local authorities will increase in future years. Changes in overall levels of provision should be discussed first with the local authority concerned' (Annex, paras 3,10).

Guidance commended by the Department of Health In 1984, the National Association of Health Authorities (1984) produced a handbook on the registration and inspection of nursing homes. It, and the supplement (NAHA 1988), recommends what facilities and services would represent good practice. Commended by the DHSS (HC(84)21), it has been widely used by health authorities, and to an unknown extent by nursing homes.

The Registered Homes Tribunals make reference to the guidelines when investigating cases.

DISCUSSION
Four Classes of Resident
There are four main classes of private nursing home resident to consider. Those who entered a home before April 1993 and are paid for by social security; those who entered after April 1993 and are paid for by social services; those who are placed and paid for by a health authority; and those who pay for themselves.

General Practitioners and Referral to Other Services
For all residents, home owners have a duty to make adequate arrangements for residents to see their GPs. Thus, through GP referral, any resident has access to other health services. If a resident then goes, for example, to a hospital as an inpatient or outpatient, he or she would receive these services 'as normal'.

Basic Nursing and Incontinence Services
Such services should, according to guidance, normally be provided to individual residents by the home and paid for by the home (where they are not available on NHS prescription through the GP). The cost to the home of these services should therefore be included in the home's fees, whether paid by social security, by social services, by a health authority (which has placed a person in a home as an NHS patient), or by people paying for themselves.

Circular guidance (HSG(92)50), applying to people placed by social services in nursing homes since April 1993, states clearly that social services are responsible for contracting for these services.

For people paid for by social security or paying for themselves, Tim Yeo answered in 1992: 'Our guidance to health authorities is that support services such as...incontinence materials fall within the care that nursing homes could reasonably be expected to provide for their patients. Health authorities may provide support services to nursing home patients at their discretion' (H54 1992). This answer conforms to 1974 Circular guidance (HC(74)16) which states that health authorities 'should not therefore provide' home nursing aids and equipment...and laundry services for incontinent people 'direct to patients in nursing homes'.

(Under s.7 of the Medicines Act 1988, health authorities can supply nursing homes with incontinence (or other nursing materials) generally (but not to individuals) for an element of profit (H94 1991).)

In practice, for example, provision of incontinence materials in nursing homes are likely to vary from home to home, both in quality and in how the materials have been paid for. It seems that some homes have provided a better service within their fees than others; sometimes residents and relatives have to pay extra. It might not be a question of whether, for example, incontinence pads are provided at all; but whether the appropriate types are provided and in sufficient quantities.

Whether or not social services' new responsibility for paying the fees (and specifying contracts for services) will alter the position is unclear. The responsibility still lies practically, as it has done in the past, with the nursing home to provide adequate services within the fees, and much would seem to depend on what the contracts specify and how they are enforced.

Scottish Circular Guidance

Scottish guidance seems to be inconsistent with the English guidance (even though deriving from very similar legislation: the NHS (Scotland) Act 1978). Scottish guidance states explicitly that private nursing home patients are entitled to community nursing and therapy services if prescribed/ recommended by their general practitioners (NHS 1989(GEN)39; SHHD/DGM (1991)67). This is clearly not what English guidance envisages. Nor does the Scottish guidance abound with cautionary phrases about discretion, resources and priorities. It states simply that if a GP treats his or her NHS patient in a nursing home and recommends a community nursing or therapy service, that patient is entitled to the recommended service.

Paramedical Services

Circular guidance (HSG(92)50) states that, for people placed in homes by local authorities with health authorities' consent, health authorities are responsible for purchasing services such as physiotherapy and chiropody. However, this is to be done 'within the resources available and in line with their priorities'. Furthermore, the guidance warns about the future resource implications of providing community nursing services to increasing numbers of nursing home residents. This guidance therefore leaves a very broad discretion to health authorities and does nothing to indicate what level of service either should, or is likely to, be provided.

For people paid for in nursing homes by social security, or paying for themselves, previous guidance is of little help. It does state that chiropody services can be provided to people in private nursing homes by health authorities (see Circular HC(78)16 which corrects, four years later, Circular HC(74)16, para 6). Guidance is otherwise silent about therapy services, but Tim Yeo answered in 1992: 'Our guidance to health authorities is that support services such as physiotherapy…fall within the care that nursing homes could reasonably be expected to provide for their patients. Health authorities may provide support services to nursing home patients at their discretion' (H55 1992).

People in private nursing homes are likely to be accorded a low priority by health authorities and, in the past, some (and probably many) health authorities have as a matter of policy not provided services to individuals in private nursing homes. It becomes a matter of chance whether people receive NHS therapy services (eg. Chartered Society of Physiotherapy 1993,p.2). A study (Collyer 1989) of chiropody services to private nursing homes in London found a variable picture which included the following possibilities:

(1) the health service provided services to all residents;

(2) the health service provided services to some residents;

(3) the health service provided services to no residents;

(4) DSS-supported residents had their treatment provided by the home within the fees paid, whereas private residents paid in full (p.5).

Indeed, in 1989, Kenneth Clarke confirmed the variable picture: 'In my experience, people who are living in private residential and nursing homes are not deprived of all rights to NHS ancillary care, but I agree that the practice varies widely from place to place' (H56 1989).

(In fact this statement is itself a little unclear because it uses the word 'ancillary' which in the Registered Homes Act is differentiated from 'professional'. One would not normally class NHS professionals providing services to nursing homes as 'ancillary' workers.)

From the point of view of what private nursing homes provide within their basic services, there are different possibilities in practice. Some homes might provide such services within the fee; in others, people or their relatives have to pay extra for such services. For example, a home could provide no physiotherapy services within its fees. Or the home could provide within its fees general physiotherapy classes (such as an exercise class once a week for interested residents); but any individual physiotherapy would have to be paid for separately by residents or their relatives. Or, third, the home might include physiotherapy for individual residents as part of the service it provides within the fees.

SERVICES AND FACILITIES PROVIDED BY NURSING HOMES

Private nursing home owners are subject to the Registered Homes Act 1984 and associated regulations which together state that the owner must be a fit person, the premises be fit, and certain services and facilities be provided.

Under the 1984 Act, homes are both registered and inspected by health authorities. Appeals go to Registered Homes Tribunals which have interpreted some of the requirements placed on homes. The following summaries are a selection of Tribunal cases, relating to the provision of services and facilities.

The cases are instructive in giving insight into the issues and disputes which can arise in nursing homes – and into the factors to be taken into account when solutions are sought. The decisions of the tribunals sometimes demonstrate also the number of different factors which have to be taken into account when judging whether services are adequate. Thus, these decisions are not necessarily predictable and seem to depend on the particular facts and circumstances of each case – even when these facts and circumstances appear, superficially at least, to be similar.

(The interpretation which a home owner places on the legislation affects how much additional health service support is needed – or how much extra residents or their relatives have to pay if they need certain health services. Regulations state that the home must provide adequate professional staff, medical and nursing equipment. This legislative requirement appears to cover a diversity of practice: for example, whether or not homes provide, within the fees, incontinence pads to the right quantity and quality is thought to vary from home to home. However, the decisions of the Registered Homes Tribunals seem not to have considered this aspect of provision to any extent).

EXTRACTS
Legislation (provision by nursing home) states that:

(fitness of person, premises) An applicant for registration can be refused by the local authority if he or she (or anyone else employed in the home) 'is not a fit person (whether by reason of age or otherwise)'. He or she might also be refused if the premises are not fit to be used because of 'their situation, construction, state of repair, accommodation, staffing, or equipment' (Registered Homes Act 1984,s.25).

(services and facilities) Under regulations (SI 1984/1578, r.12) a number of services and facilities must be provided, 'having regard to the size of the home and the number, age, sex and condition of the patients'. The list includes:

- 'adequate professional, technical, ancillary and other staff';
- 'adequate accommodation' for each patient;
- 'adequate furniture, bedding, curtains and where necessary adequate screens and floor covering';
- 'adequate medical, surgical and nursing equipment and...treatment facilities';
- 'adequate wash basins and baths supplying hot and cold water and adequate water closets and sluicing facilities';
- 'adequate light, heating and ventilation';
- keeping of all parts of the home in good repair, clean and reasonably decorated;
- adequate fire and accident precautions;
- adequate food, kitchen and eating equipment, food preparation and storage facilities;
- adequate laundry facilities;

- adequate arrangements for disposal of used medical and nursing materials;
- adequate arrangements for patients to see GPs and dentists;
- adequate arrangements concerning handling, keeping, recording, disposal of drugs;
- adequate arrangements to prevent infection;
- adequate arrangements for residents' training, occupation, recreation;
- adequate facilities to receive visitors in private;
- connect the home to a public telephone service.

DISCUSSION (SUMMARIES OF REGISTERED HOMES TRIBUNAL CASES: NUMBER OF EACH CASE IS GIVEN)

Adequate Qualified and Competent Staff (SI 1984/1578,r.12)

The Registered Homes Tribunals frequently investigate this matter. However, as the regulations state, what is adequate depends on the size of the home and the number, age, sex and condition of the residents. As a result, there are many variables involved and this book cannot cover the decisions in sufficient depth. Because of the variables involved, the NAHA (1985) guidelines do not list staffing ratios but do list a number of factors to be taken into account (pp.25,65–66).

Arrangement of Residents

A home lost its appeal, given that there was, for example, insufficient understanding of mentally handicapped people, shouting, threats, excessive obsession with routine and hygiene leading to over-regimentation, and set and rigid ideas (RHT 45).

Another appeal was lost for reasons including the fact that the home was 'permeated by the stench of urine, the general attitude was of poor care, residents were wearing unlaundered or dirty clothing and some residents were apparently wearing no clothing below the waist other than a blanket. An honest, accurate and damning indictment' (RHT 34).

Lifts

Where, given their average age, residents have difficulty negotiating steep and narrow stairs between floors, then although 'some of the residents were satisfied to remain in their own area…the provision of a lift might enable some residents to lead a fuller life, and association with others'. The Tribunal implied that this would have been desirable although did not explicitly refer to this when finding against the home owner (RHT 8). In another case where the home lost its appeal, the absence of a lift meant that top-floor residents were 'virtually isolated there indefinitely' (RHT 29).

Accommodation/Privacy

A tribunal found that the local health authority's approach to approving only exceptionally rooms with more than two beds was based on 'Home Life' which applied to residential homes (but not nursing homes). This was the wrong approach. Instead the authority should have considered 'all the facts and circumstances' in deciding whether proper facilities were provided in the relevant bedrooms. The tribunal found the accommodation satisfactory (RHT 27).

In one case a health authority opposing use of a double room was insisting on 100 square feet per person. This was both greater than NAHA's guidelines which suggested 86 square feet, and apparently more stringent than most other authorities' requirements. The Tribunal stated that even the lower figure should not be taken as an absolute minimum, since the Tribunal was inclined to agree with the opinion 'that a purpose-built room may be regarded as having the same special attribute as a less well-designed room up to 30 sq. ft. larger simply by reason that the doors and windows and other fittings are sensibly positioned'. Thus the particular room in question, though not conforming even to the NAHA guidelines had a 'special attribute' that is quite sufficient in all the circumstances' (RHT 61).

Use of a four-bedded room was accepted by the Tribunal in the particular circumstances of one case. The Tribunal was satisfied that the room was not used in connection with maximum occupancy in (and therefore maximum income from) the home. It was used as a nursing station for seriously ill patients and was more in the nature of a hospice ward than a sick bay. The Tribunal inspected the room and found it attractive and of a light and tranquil atmosphere which would not be distressing to patients. Patients, relatives and sometimes the patients' doctors would be consulted before a move into this room (RHT 207).

Second-Floor Accommodation

A tribunal did not agree with the local health authority that only exceptionally could second floor accommodation be provided. NAHA guidelines did not state this and none of the residents on the second floor had substantial difficulty using the stairs. The Tribunal had 'regard to the lack of disapproval in NAHA guidelines, to the fact that we were referred to no other authority which had adopted a similar approach to that of the respondent, to the lack of any expert evidence of any detrimental effect on patients generally from occupying second floor accommodation'; and it took into account the views of its own expert members.

The authority needed to 'look with great care at the use of such accommodation to ensure that there were adequate means for patients to move between floors, that the fire safety precautions were adequate and that patients could be properly cared for on a second floor'. For example, the stairway was not ideal because it was rather narrow and the chair lift did not reach the last few steps. However, 'the evidence was that the patients with rooms on the second floor were all ambulant and had not experienced any substantial difficulty in negotiating the stairway'. There were always staff to attend to people when using the stairs and chair lift and there was no evidence that the care of the patients was affected adversely through being on the second floor. However, the Tribunal did order that a condition of registration should be that only ambulant patients occupy the second floor (RHT 27).

In another case the Tribunal ruled that the second floor could only be occupied by people who were ambulant, and not dependent on wheelchairs or walking aids, and not mentally confused. The staircase between the first and second floors needed handrails on both sides. There was a lift but the stairs needed to be useable in case of failure of the lift; and there was evidence that some people would not use the lift anyway (RHT 60).

Day/Dining Space

Where a health authority refused registration of an additional bed because of the day/dining space involved, the tribunal noted a lack of clarity arising from NAHA's guidelines which talked about space per ambulant patient, not space per bed. For example, the fact that somebody was not ambulant did not mean they could not use the day/dining space. In this specific case, the tribunal allowed the home's appeal, but noted that different considerations would apply in other cases (RHT 28).

A Tribunal found in favour of a home which was proposing to use a particular room as a communal sitting room, despite the fact that it failed to conform in size to either NAHA's or the health authority's guidelines. The Tribunal felt that 'a separate dining room, and 25 sq. ft. of space in a communal room for each of the patients, is not necessary – and even the lack of a separate staff room we regard as unimportant in all the circumstances. We do not doubt that nowadays the number of ambulant patients is seen to be decreasing so that a requirement that "one or more sitting rooms must be provided to give 25 sq ft of space for all patients" within the home would appear to merit some reconsideration' (RHT 61).

However, in another case a Tribunal held that the lounge should be big enough to accommodate all the residents whether or not all of them used it: for example, in the future, a greater proportion of the residents might be ambulant. In addition, if one took into account a main and busy thoroughfare through the dayspace (dining room and lounge), the amount of space fell below the NAHA guidelines (RHT 124). Similarly, where a home had day space 'barely appropriate' for 14 patients, the Tribunal was not prepared to consider an increase in the number of patients. It was 'no answer to say that many of the patients are/will be bedridden and will not choose to use the day room'. Indeed, there was no lift, 'and so patients would have to be mobile, or be carried, to negotiate the stairs to reach the day room, and they would not be inclined to do this (or to ask nurses to assist them downstairs) if they are aware that the room is already overcrowded. So it is no answer that the room is not used by all'. The Tribunal was prepared to accept that day space could be 'scattered';

but in the particular case, the suggested areas of entrance hall and upstairs landing were not appropriate for reasons such as obstruction, hazard of being near the top of a staircase and so on (RHT 175).

In one home, the space required for bed sitting rooms was achieved by the use of folding beds. The Tribunal noted the weighty objections in principle against their use but approved them in the particular case, whilst emphasising that they were not setting a precedent. Reasons for their acceptability in the particular circumstances were that it was easy for a nurse to move a chair a foot or two in order to fold or unfold the bed; the beds could be lowered in a matter of seconds; nearly all the patients would anyway have to call a nurse for assistance whether moving from a chair to any type of bed, folding or not; the beds were easily height adjustable; though ripple mattresses could not be used with them, sheep skins were satisfactory for pressure sore prevention; the rooms were made more pleasant to sit in with the beds folded away (RHT 75).

Kitchen, Food and Eating Facilities

A Tribunal found a number of below-standard features of nursing home kitchen, including damp, flaking paintwork, cracked and uneven floor looking dirty, lack of crockery storage space, rusty refrigerator and old-looking freezer. In addition, dry food was being stored near damp ground and near domestic cleaning materials (RHT 124).

Heating

A Tribunal found a proprietor an unfit person because, despite warnings that the home was too cold, he maintained it at a 'totally unacceptable temperature', knew that the boiler was old and unreliable and should be repaired or replaced. Secondary, compensatory, heating was not provided. Patients were bathed in unacceptably cool water which was not only uncomfortable for the patients but could have increased risk of hypothermia. Sometimes the temperature during the day was verging on an unacceptable condition of work for staff; and at night there was no heating (RHT 187).

Where heating and lighting to a home is put at risk because of failure of the home to discharge its financial responsibilities (eg. to the electricity and gas boards), the home is seriously failing to maintain standards of care. Patients are put seriously at risk thereby (RHT 138).

Washing Facilities and Lavatories

A health authority's apparent reliance on 'Home Life' (applying to residential homes) for the proportion of lavatories to residents (1 to 4) was not reasonable. For example, where residents were dependent upon staff assistance to get to the lavatory, a high proportion of lavatories would be superfluous. There would be enough staff to justify the proportion. The home's appeal was allowed (RHT 27).

Laundry Facilities (SI 1984/1578,r.12)

It is unacceptable for sluices (for soiled linen) to be in close proximity to laundry facilities because of the danger of cross-infection. The home lost its appeal (RHT 8). In another case where the home also lost its appeal the tribunal noted as serious the absence of proper sluicing facilities on either floor in a home where heavily dependent patients and soiled linen had to be dealt with (RHT 29).

A sluice in a bathroom/lavatory with a paper towel dispenser over it was not acceptable. There is a danger of cross-infection if a sluice is situated in a bathroom or lavatory; it should not be made of ceramic; it should not be sited and provided with paper towels so as to invite people to wash their hands in it (RHT 75).

CHAPTER 15

DISCHARGE FROM HOSPITAL

KEY ISSUES

People's needs when leaving hospital can be complicated, involving physical ability, mental ability and attitude, social and environmental factors – and so on. There are sometimes many arrangements to make. Whether or not optimum arrangements are eventually achieved would appear sometimes to depend on chance, since there are many variable factors which influence the outcome of discharge. This makes the discharge process unpredictable and yet one more potential 'uncertainty' in the community care process.

Legislation, with the exception of the Mental Health Act 1983, is silent about hospital discharge. Yet hospital discharge is a crucial element of community care, involving decisions about where, how and with whom people are going to live. Against a background of evidence that practices could be improved, Department of Health guidance continues to emphasise the importance of good hospital discharge practice.

Guidance essentially seeks to ensure that people do not leave hospital before adequate arrangements have been made for them, and before those arrangements have been understood and agreed by patients and their carers. Hospital consultants have ultimate responsibility for discharging people and the guidance states that any delegation of that responsibility must be clearly understood. Department of Health communications continue to reflect concern about the inadequacy of hospital discharge practices.

The health service ombudsman regularly investigates cases concerning hospital discharge. Some of the issues which he has investigated include inadequate consultation, decisions based on inadequacy of information, and failure to follow Department of Health guidance. The ombudsman cannot by law question 'clinical' judgements, but can investigate widely the circumstances and foundations on which such judgements are made. At times this seems to blur the line between clinical and non-clinical decisions.

The basis for hospital discharge procedures for mentally ill people are three-fold:

(1) the statutory duty to provide after-care services under the Mental Health Act 1983;

(2) the (non-statutory) Care Programme Approach described and advocated in guidance;

(3) the general community care assessment and care management system described in this book.

In practice, there appears to be some uncertainty about how these three approaches interlock.

HOSPITAL DISCHARGE GENERALLY

While there is little legislation on hospital discharge, policy and Circular guidance is considerable. In general, this states that continuity of health and social care should be ensured. It covers assessment of need, and responsibility for discharge, as well as planning for support services, and family and carer involvement. However, good practice in these areas has been found to be more prevalent in specialist elderly care than in general medical or acute units, and there is considerable disparity in eligibility criteria from place to place.

EXTRACTS

Legislation, with the exception of the Mental Health Act 1983 (s.117), does not refer to hospital discharge or leaving hospital.

Community care policy guidance states that hospital discharge practices should ensure continuity of health and social care for people; and that people should not have to leave hospital until suitable arrangements have been agreed with them and their carers:

> **(continuity of health and social care):** 'health authorities, in conjunction with local authorities, are responsible for designating staff to develop, implement and monitor individual discharge plans. To ensure the continuity of health and social care the local authority and NHS staff working in the community and GPs should be given adequate notice of discharge to enable them to assess and provide for any community care needs, especially where residential or nursing home care may be a possible choice. Local housing authorities may also need to be involved' (para 3.42).

> **(decision-making: social services responsibilities):** 'Health authorities should bear in mind that responsibility for assessing and meeting needs for community social services (including nursing home care where the user is expected to contribute to the cost) rests with the SSDs. Subject to any arrangements agreed between authorities, local authorities should not be expected to endorse decisions about an individual's care needs, or ways of meeting them, taken by health authorities in advance of a recognised community care assessment' (para 3.43).

> **(consumer choice):** 'Subject always to consumer choice, patients should not leave hospital until the supply of at least essential community care services has been

agreed with them, their carers and all the authorities concerned. Patients who have lost their homes should not be expected to leave hospital until suitable accommodation has been arranged. In such cases early liaison with the local housing authority is essential' (para 3.44).

Circular guidance. The principle of securing adequate and timely assessment before hospital discharge is not new. Circular guidance of 1989 (HC(89)5), itself replacing a Circular of 25 years earlier (HM(63)24), 'emphasises the importance of ensuring that, before patients are discharged from hospital, proper arrangements are made for their return home and for any continuing care which may be necessary'.

The circular, together with an accompanying booklet, delivers its message in firm language and includes a number of detailed points:

- **(consultants' responsibility for discharge):** 'Only a consultant (or a principal in general practice responsible for GP beds) can accept medical responsibility for patients admitted to NHS units. No patient may be discharged from hospital without the authority of the doctor holding responsibility for that patient. This authority may be delegated only by the doctor concerned, but where this is the case, the extent of that delegation must be clearly understood';

- **(arrangement of community services before discharge):** 'Patients should not be discharged until the doctors concerned have agreed and management is satisfied that everything reasonably practicable has been done to organise the care the patient will need in the community...';

- **(early planning for discharge):** 'For non-emergency cases where it is known that support will be required on discharge, planning should start before admission. For emergency cases it should start as soon as possible after admission...';

- **(user and carer involvement and agreement):** 'the patient, and if appropriate, the family or carer(s) must be at the centre of the planning process. It will help to reduce any anxiety which patients may feel if they fully understand and agree with the arrangements planned, are given as much time as possible to adjust to what is proposed and are told who will be informed of their return or transfer...';

(the related local authority Circular (LAC(89)7 states perhaps more strongly: 'Local authorities must ensure that the patient and, if appropriate, his or her family or carer are always at the centre of their planning for discharge. Patients should be fully consulted and should agree and understand the arrangements that are being made').

- **(key worker):** 'responsibility for checking that the necessary action has been taken before a patient leaves the hospital should be given to one member of staff caring for that patient';

- **(checklist):** 'The member of staff should have a check-list of what should have been done. If the completed check-list is filed in the patient's notes it will provide a permanent record of action taken before discharge...'.

- **(residential/nursing home placement):** 'No NHS patient should be placed in a private nursing or residential care home against his/her wishes if it means that he/she or a relative will be personally responsible for the home's charges' (accompanying booklet: DH 1989,para A2).

Circular guidance, five years later, continues to express concern about hospital discharge. Agreements between health and social services authorities have been a precondition for receipt by social services of the community care special transitional grant (see eg. LASSL (93)16); and anyway 'health authorities should be clear that their hospital providers have explicit and comprehensive procedures to ensure that there are no organisational delays to prevent patients being discharged from hospital when they are ready to go home' (EL(94)8,paras 1,4).

In 1994, continuing concern has led to a 'hospital discharge workbook' being issued by the Department of Health (1994) to promote good practice. It does not affect previous Circular guidance.

The Patient's Charter (standard number 9) states that before people are discharged from hospital, arrangements will be made for their continuing health and social care needs.

Consultation document on proposed community care charters includes reference to hospital discharge standards which should ensure that:
- nobody is discharged unless it is clinically appropriate;
- nobody is discharged unless appropriate arrangements are in place and those arrangements can begin straightaway after discharge;
- patients and their families and friends will be fully informed and involved in decisions; be given time to make decisions; and told how to challenge them (DH 1994c).

DISCUSSION
Past practice
A recent King's Fund report refers to the 'consistency of research findings, stretching back over at least twenty years, which document the breakdown of routine discharge procedures'. It exposes a number of tensions 'between professional groups, between health and local authorities and between national guidance and local possibilities' (Marks 1994,p.6).

On the whole, it seems that good practice is more likely to be found in specialist elderly care units than in general medical or acute units (Henwood 1994,p.14). Even where there is good practice, the arrangements described by the Circular guidance (HC(89)5/LAC(89)7) might not always be achieved (SSI 1992,p.1). The Audit Commission (1992) noted that discharge procedures 'are often poorly organised' with 'frequent delays in arranging transport and take-home medicines as well as longer delays because of the need to organise domiciliary support. Discharges are sometimes also delayed because residential or nursing home places cannot be easily be found' (p.1).

A recent 'snapshot' of the community care reforms, based on a 'vertical cross-section of stakeholders in a range of localities', found a number of difficulties over hospital discharge. These included conflicts between staff over assessments, poorly understood eligibility criteria, lengthy procedures, discharge of people to nursing homes who would have previously remained in hospital beds (and who then die very soon afterwards), decision-making responsibilities – and so on (Henwood 1994a,p.17).

An unsuccessful amendment to the NHS and Community Care Bill sought to make mandatory the assessment of people leaving hospital, the specifying of services needed and the appointment of a person to ensure that people's assessed needs are met. The government objected to the amendment as a 'blunt instrument', the aims of which could be better achieved by a mixture of legislation and guidance (H40 1990). Fixed times for assessment procedures could 'very often become a maximum amount of time and create inflexibility'. Instead, what should happen is that 'assessment will take as long as is necessary' (H41 1990).

Differing Local Social Services Departments' Criteria of Eligibility

A single hospital, attempting to arrange discharges efficiently, consistently and equitably, might be faced with the considerable difficulty of having people from 'four counties, each of which is going to have its own different and separate criteria of eligibility for assessment and service provision' (Age Concern evidence to: Health Committee 1993, vol.2,p.168).

An SSI/NHSME (1994b,p.28) study found that ward staff might be confused 'by a variety of documentation, different eligibility criteria and delays in decision making and subsequent discharge. In one hospital there were three hospital teams from different Local Authorities, each with different systems and procedures!'.

Delay in Discharge and Premature Discharge

The delay in provision of services can delay discharge: for example, equipment and home adaptations can cause such delay. An SSI/NHSME (1994b,p.25) study on community care implementation found that even the need for simple items of equipment such as commodes could delay discharge for several days; special beds might be delivered only once a week; and assessment by community OTs could take several months. Equipment budgets were under increasing pressure, which in turn increased the likelihood of demarcation disputes. It is possible that such delays can affect even people who are dying: for example, a person who has been assessed so that she can go home to die might be unable to do so, or is delayed in doing so, because the relevant community health unit cannot supply the special (pressure relief) mattress which is required (Personal communication: senior hospital therapist, 1994).

Alternatively, people are sometimes discharged too soon. For example, a University of Edinburgh research report has found that people might not be prepared physically or psychologically if they are informed about the discharge at short notice; might not cope well (eg, they might be unable to leave the house, be in pain or have bladder and bowel problems); and sometimes not receive services for the first two weeks after discharge (Worth 1994).

HEALTH SERVICE OMBUDSMAN INVESTIGATIONS

The health service ombudsman regularly investigates complaints about hospital discharge. The ombudsman cannot investigate clinical judgement (HSC 1993,p.5) but can investigate the surrounding circumstances and the basis on which clinical decisions are made (see p.375). For example, he considers inadequate consultation, inadequacy of information forming the basis of judgements, and failure to follow Department of Health guidance. The ability to investigate such elements of decision-making appears to give the ombudsman a wide discretion which appears sometimes to blur the distinction between 'clinical' and 'administrative' decision-making.

EXTRACTS (NOT RELEVANT IN THIS SECTION)

DISCUSSION

Consultation and Adequate Arrangements

The health service ombudsman will not uphold a complaint simply because genuine misunderstandings arise. A carer's mistaken belief is not enough: for example, where she believed that her mother would not be discharged but given a rehabilitation bed whilst she (the carer) was unable (following an operation) to cope. However, where, in the same case, the carer first knew about the discharge through a telephone call telling her that her mother was already on her way home, there had clearly been a breakdown in communication. No hospital 'key worker' had been identified. The ombudsman also found more broadly that discharge policy and procedures were not fully operational and unknown to some staff. The complaint was upheld, and the health authority set about reinforcing its policy (HSC W.254/88–89).

The health service ombudsman can comment extensively on inadequate arrangements, including for example, failure to warn the GP, incorrect information being passed to community nursing and social services, deficiencies in filling in nursing discharge forms (including lack of signatures and omissions of content) (HSC W.421/88–89).

Another health service ombudsman (HSC W.40/84–85) investigation into hospital discharge of a woman with Huntingdon's Chorea found fault with a consultant who had 'made his proposal to send the patient home before he had consulted sufficiently with the social services department and voluntary organisations to ascertain whether they were in a position to provide the cover and assistance the patient required. I am in no doubt that the assurances which the consultant gave the complainant were faulty and I uphold this complaint'. The community organisations in question could not in fact deliver what the consultant had stated would be possible.

In another case a hospital consultant had assured a woman's husband that if his wife was discharged from hospital, both home adaptations and home care would be available from social services or voluntary agencies. The health service ombudsman found in fact that the consultant had not consulted others suffi-ciently 'to ascertain whether they were in a position to provide the cover and assistance the patient required' (HSC W.113/84–85).

The health service ombudsman might accept that discharge is a clinical decision which he cannot challenge, but nevertheless find fault with surround-ing factors. For example, in one case the decision was made 'solely in conse-quence of the exercise of…clinical judgement and therefore I may not question it. But having reached that clinical decision the HA and their staff had a duty to satisfy themselves that the environment in which she would be placed was suitable in the light of her prevailing medical condition and particularly her physical limitations'. This they did not do.

> 'I consider that in several respects the HA failed in that duty. The [house officer] wanted an [occupational therapist] to review the patient's condition but failed to ask an OT do so. All the medical and ward nursing staff considered that the patient required substantial support from the social services department but none, it appears to me, had an accurate understanding of the extent of the support which was planned. Furthermore their actions implied that once the [social worker] had been alerted to their intention to discharge her, the patient's welfare was not their concern unless readmission to hospital became necessary'.

> 'I regard this as a dangerous misconception. The hospital staff had a duty to *ensure* that the implementation of their decision to discharge the patient would result in her being placed in an environment which they knew to be satisfactory; in my opinion it is not sufficient for them to *hope* that the outcome would be satisfactory and to offer re-admission to hospital should it prove not to be. For these reasons I consider that the administrative arrangements for the patient's discharges were unsatisfactory…' (HSC W.420/83–84).

This statement describing the duty of hospital staff goes a lot further than anything to be found in legislation and is expressed a great deal more firmly than anything in guidance. Therefore, it is possible that what the ombudsman is referring to amounts to what he considers to be a general 'duty of care' (see p.84) which hospital staff owe towards patients.

Inadequate information, or Failure to Take into Account Relevant Information

The health service ombudsman may look for evidence that a person was discharged in order to make a bed available, but failing to find it may then 'have no reason to doubt that the decision was taken solely in consequence of the exercise of doctors' clinical judgement which accordingly I may not question'. In the same case, similarly the 'nursing staff on the ward exercised their professional judgement in determining what domiciliary care a discharged patient required and I have no reason to doubt that the first sister's decision was made on that basis'.

However, in this investigation, the ombudsman did criticise the nurse's decision because she failed to take account of all 'relevant factors'. This was because the decision was based on the pattern of the person's previous admissions for chemotherapy and overnight stays. But this particular admission had been under different circumstances which had not been recorded in the nursing notes. So discharge decisions were made without full and up-to-date information (HSC W.286/86–87).

The above case is instructive. Pressure to clear beds is a fact of life for most hospitals, and sometimes hurried discharges are not in patients' best interests. However, where such decisions are made, it is not too surprising when investigation of surrounding factors and circumstances reveals shortcomings in such decisions. It was such shortcomings which the ombudsman seems to have identified in this particular investigation.

Similarly, another investigation (HSC W.24 and W.56/84–85) criticised health service staff for not arranging the necessary district nursing support for a discharged 68-year-old woman. The criticism arose because although a district nurse visit had been arranged, the arrangement had been made before the person's condition deteriorated. By the time of discharge, she was suffering severe abdominal pain, had been scalded and had fallen on the morning of discharge. The discharge arrangements had not taken account of the changed circumstances.

In another case, a woman had complained that she was unable to cope with the twice-daily bathing needs of her husband who had been discharged from hospital. The health service ombudsman found that he could not question the surgeon's clinical decision about discharge. However, he did find that inadequate 'consideration was given to the consequences and in particular to the domestic circumstances'. The clinicians had overlooked 'vital' information from the GP that the woman could not cope. Misunderstandings between the sister concerned about the discharge and the registrar 'cast considerable doubt on the effectiveness of the registrar's communications'. There was little evidence of a multi-disciplinary approach to the discharge (as recommended by the guidance accompanying HC(89)5), and no system of recording discharge arrangements on patient records. The complaint was upheld (HSC SW.82/86–87).

The health service ombudsman (HSC W.24 and W.56/84–85) might criticise a decision made on the basis of 'insufficient thought'. For example, a 68-year-old woman was discharged to her home without, according to the complainant, the necessary equipment including wheelchair, commode or toilet seat extension, and oxygen equipment. The ombudsman could not question the clinical decision of the consultant that the oxygen equipment was in fact not needed. But the ombudsman found that the need for a commode had been assessed at least a week earlier, even before her condition had deteriorated. Thus,

'arrangements should have been made for both a commode and a toilet seat extension to be available when the patient was discharged. The failure to do so indicates that insufficient thought was given to the immediate problems the patient and her husband were likely to face on her discharge and accordingly I uphold this aspect of the complaint.'

HOSPITAL DISCHARGE (MENTAL DISORDER AND MENTAL ILLNESS)

The basis for service delivery to mentally disordered people discharged from hospital seems to fall primarily into three main categories. First, health authorities and social services have a legal duty to individuals with a mental disorder who have been detained in hospital to provide after-care services under section 117 of the Mental Health Act 1983. This duty has been characterised judicially as a strong duty towards individuals and to be distinguished from more 'general' duties to provide after-care under the NHS Act 1977.

Second, the 'Care Programme Approach' (CPA) has been described and advocated by guidance. The CPA approach to after-care applies to people with a mental illness (including dementia) who are referred to the specialist psychiatric services. Subsequent guidance has suggested that the CPA should apply where relevant to the after-care of all mentally disordered patients.

Third, the general community care assessment and care management system applies.

In practice, there seems to be uncertainty about how the three different systems mesh. In addition, following public concern about the plight of some mentally ill people, guidance requires health authorities to keep supervision registers of people who are liable to be a violent risk to themselves or to other people.

EXTRACTS
Legislation (Mental Health 1983, s.117) states that for people who have been admitted compulsorily to hospital under s.3, 37 or 47/48 of the Mental Health Act 1983:

(after-care): 'It shall be the duty of the District Health Authority and of the local social services authority to provide, in co-operation with voluntary agencies, after-care services for any person to whom this section applies until such time as the District Health Authority and the local social services authority are satisfied that the person concerned is no longer in need of such services'.

Code of practice (made under s.118 of the Mental Health Act 1983) states that in establishing a care plan for after-care, a number of professionals should be involved in the discussion. These are the person's 'responsible medical officer', a hospital nurse involved in caring for the person, a social worker specialising in mental health work, the person's GP, a community psychiatric nurse, a voluntary organisation representative (where appropriate and available), the person (if he wishes) or a nominated relative or other representative.

The issues to be considered should be:

- 'the **patient's own wishes** and needs';
- 'the **views of any relevant relative, friend or supporter** of the patient';
- 'the need for **agreement** with an appropriate representative at the **receiving health authority** if it is to be different from that of the discharging authority';
- 'the possible **involvement of other agencies,** eg. probation, voluntary organisations';
- 'the establishing of a **care plan,** based on proper assessment and clearly identified needs, in which the following issues must be considered and planned so far as resources permit: day care arrangements, appropriate accommodation, out-patient treatment, counselling, personal support, assistance in welfare rights, assistance in managing finances, and, if necessary, in claiming benefits';
- 'the appointment of a key worker from either of the statutory agencies to monitor the care plan's implementation, liaise and co-ordinate where necessary and report to the senior officer in their agency any problems that arise which cannot be resolved through normal discussion'.
- 'the identification of any unmet need'.

In addition, a timescale for implementation should be agreed; people with specific responsibilities should be identified; changes to the plan must be fully discussed; the plan should be recorded in writing; the plan should be regularly reviewed – this is the responsibility of the key worker. Responsibility for ensuring the whole procedure is followed lies with the 'senior officer' responsible for s.117 in the key worker's agency (DH,WO 1993, pp.107–108: our emphasis).

Circular guidance (HC(90)23/LASSL(90)11):

(care programme approach) requires the health service 'to implement the care programme approach...for people with a mental illness, including dementia, whatever its cause, referred to the specialist psychiatric services...'

(social services) 'asks social services authorities to collaborate with health authorities in introducing this approach and, as resources allow, to continue to expand social care services to patients being treated in the community'

(resources) 'Health authorities are expected to meet any health service costs arising from the introduction of more systematic *procedures* from existing resources. Introducing the care programme approach places no new requirements to provide *services* on either health or social services authorities... Health authorities will judge what resources they make available for such services. Social services authorities will make similar decisions but will have available specially targeted resources through the new specific grant'

The guidance (Annex) outlines the main components of this approach. It 'builds on the general circular on hospital discharge HC(89)5' (see p.242). The approach is to 'ensure that in future patients treated in the community receive the health and social care they need'. Key elements involved are:

- 'systematic arrangements for **assessing the health care** needs of patients who could, potentially, be treated in the community, and for regularly reviewing the health care needs of those being treatment [sic] in the community';
- 'systematic arrangements, agreed with appropriate social services authorities, for assessing and regularly reviewing what **social care** such patients need to give them the opportunity of benefitting from treatment in the community';
- 'effective systems for ensuring that agreed health, and where necessary, social care **services are provided** to those patients who can be treated in the community' (our emphasis).

Circular guidance (supervision registers) (HSG(94)5) 'requires' from October 1994 that all mental health care provider units set up supervision registers to identify and provide information about patients who are or are liable to seriously neglect themselves, commit suicide or commit serious, violent acts.

Circular guidance (care programme approach: further guidance) (HSG(94)27) sets out good practice, based on the Care Programme Approach for health authorities. It suggests that the CPA is sometimes relevant not just to mentally ill people but also to some other people with personality disorders and some people with learning disabilities. The Circular gives guidance on risk assessments, and generally emphasises the importance of clear and explicit contracts which should lead at least to a mental health information system (including supervision register), adequately trained staff and suitable management and supervision for them, suicide audits, and agreed procedures in case of murder or assault by a patient.

DISCUSSION

Continuing Duty Under Section 117 to Individuals

In the case of R v Ealing District Health Authority, ex p. Fox 1992, the judge interpreted s.117 of the Mental Health Act as placing a strong duty (to individuals) on health and social services authorities. He stated that

'the duty is not only a general duty but a specific duty owed to the applicant to provide him with aftercare services until such time as the district health authority and local social services authority are satisfied that he is no longer in need of such services... I consider a proper interpretation of this section to be that it is a continuing duty in respect of any patient who may be discharged and falls within section 117, although the duty to any particular patient is only triggered at the moment of discharge.'

The *Encyclopaedia of Social Services and Child Care Law* points out that s.117 does not, as has sometimes been suggested, simply duplicate s.3 of the NHS Act 1977 'because while the 1977 Act directs local authorities and health authorities to provide for the after-care of the generality of mentally disordered persons, this section places a duty on local authorities and District Health Authorities to consider the after-care needs of each individual to whom the section applies' (vol.3, E1-285).

Similarly, the duty placed by s.117 on social services departments is a stronger duty (towards individuals) than their general duty (towards people in general) to provide after-care for mentally disordered people under the NHS Act 1977 (Directions made under schedule 8).

Nevertheless, for people who do not qualify for after-care under s.117 of the 1983 Act, the more general duties to provide after-care under s.3 and Schedule 8 of the NHS Act 1977 remain relevant. It should also be noted that although the judge emphasised the strength of the duty under s.117 of the 1983 Act, he also seemed deliberately to avoid considering the situation where authorities plead lack of resources for non-performance of duty (see p.154).

Concern over Discharge and After-Care

Concern over people with mental health problems leaving hospital remains. Unimplemented is s.7 of the DP(SCR)A 1986, which imposes statutory obligations on both health and social services authorities. The obligations would be to secure assessments of needs of people who have been in hospital for six months or more – before they leave hospital.

Government has produced a code of practice under the Mental Health Act 1983,s.118 and urged that all staff involved in services under the Act use it (HSG(93)45; LAC(93)19). It includes a chapter on 'after care' including hospital discharge (DH,WO 1993,pp.106–110). There is nevertheless a view that legal obligation is required to make good practice a reality (see eg. Social Services Committee 1990, pp xii–xiii).

There appears to be some confusion in practice over the relationship between the Care Programme Approach, general community care assessment/care planning, and after-care provision under s.117 of the Mental Health Act 1983 (SSI 1993,p.10; SSI/NHSME 1994c,pp.37–49; North *et al* 1993,p.101).

Some well-publicised cases have raised concern about the effectiveness of discharge and community care procedures for at least some mentally disordered people. For example, the report into the killing of Jonathan Zito by Christopher Clunis found a 'catalogue of failure and missed opportunity' on the part of a number of people and agencies. It expressed its concern that 'doctors, nurses and social workers who are primarily responsible for providing this aftercare may not fully understand that the principles underlying s.117 and Care Programme Approach are the same'. Of s.117, the report stated: 'We consider that this is a vital provision to ensure effective care in the community. Its impact should not be diminished by any other provisions for care in the community' (Ritchie 1994,pp.105–111).

In April 1994, the House of Commons Health Committee delivered a report finding that mental health care services across the country were highly uneven. Problems include a lack of coordination between agencies, lack of resources (eg. in inner city areas), and lack of information about both people with mental health needs and about services (Health Committee 1994,vol.1, pp.xix–xxx). Other reports have noted similar concerns (eg. Mental Health Foundation 1994; Audit Commission 1994).

CHAPTER 16

HEALTH SERVICE ASSESSMENT AND PROVISION

KEY ISSUES

The provision of health services introduces considerable additional uncertainty into the system of community care. This is so for a number of reasons. Health services, though recognised by guidance as in practice essential to care in the community, are nevertheless not defined as 'community care services'. Instead, they are provided under different legislation, and health authorities do not even have a duty to participate in the pivotal process of the community care system – assessment.

As far as types and levels of health services are concerned, health service legislation is even more vague and imprecise than community care legislation. The duties are mostly of the weaker 'general' type (towards the population) rather than of the stronger variety (towards individuals), and few specific health services are mentioned. Health authorities appear to have great discretion to make priorities, allocate resources and regulate levels of services – and sometimes even to determine the existence of some services. The courts, and often the health service ombudsman, have confirmed this wide discretion. Therefore, it seems that, most of the time, health authorities have little to fear legally unless their policies are illegal or extremely unreasonable. Bad publicity and public opinion might be a greater threat.

Such discretion means that service users can not lay claim to services as of right and that services can vary greatly from one authority to another. Once again, the services which people receive can depend not solely on their needs, but on where they live.

HEALTH SERVICE CONSENT TO SOCIAL SERVICES PLACEMENT OF PEOPLE IN NURSING HOMES

Community care legislation states that social services cannot normally place people in nursing homes without the consent of the health authority. If the need is urgent they can make the placement but must still then seek the health authority's consent.

EXTRACTS

Legislation states:

> **(consent of health authority except in case of urgency):** that except in case of urgency (see below), social services cannot place somebody in a nursing home without the consent of the relevant health authority (NAA 1948 s.26).

Social services can make arrangements for nursing home care without health authority consent in case of urgency. However, 'as soon as practicable after any such temporary arrangements have been made, the authority shall seek the consent' of the DHA (NAA 1948, s.26(1C) as inserted by NHSCCA 1990 s.42).

DISCUSSION

Placement in Nursing Home by the Health Authority

During the passing of the NHS and Community Care Bill, the government stated that if health authorities were to place people in nursing homes directly, without seeking the consent of the social services, then the latter would be under no obligation to pay for the placement – at least until it had carried out an assessment of its own and agreed that nursing care was required. Of course health authorities are themselves free to place, and pay for, people in nursing homes (H44 1990).

INVITATION TO HEALTH AUTHORITIES TO ASSIST IN COMMUNITY CARE ASSESSMENTS

The NHS and Community Care Act states that if a local authority is assessing a person for community care services who might need health or housing services, then it must notify the health or housing authority (or both) and invite them to assist in the assessment. The duty is imposed on the local authority, but not on the health authority – which therefore, apparently, is not legally obliged to accept the invitation and to give the assistance. Even if it does accept, the invitation is only to assist as is 'reasonable in the circumstances'.

EXTRACTS

Legislation states:

> **(community care assessment):** 'If at any time during the assessment of the needs of any person under subsection (1)(a) above, it appears to a local authority':

(need for health services): '(a) that there may be a need for the provision to that person by such District Health Authority as may be determined in accordance with regulations of any services under the National Health Service Act 1977...'

(notification): 'the local authority shall notify that District Health Authority...'

(invitation to assist): 'and invite them to assist, to such extent as is reasonable in the circumstances, in the making of the assessment; and, in making their decision as to the provision of services needed for the person in question, the local authority shall take into account any services which are likely to be made available for him by that District Health Authority or local housing authority' (NHSCCA 1990, s.47(3)).

COMMUNITY CARE ASSESSMENT: INVOLVEMENT OF HEALTH SERVICE STAFF

There are a wide range of health services particularly relevant to community care.

EXTRACTS

Legislation states that when a local authority is assessing a person for community care services and it thinks there is a need for health or housing services, then it must notify health or housing (or both) and invite them to assist in the assessment (see above).

Legislation (regulations) concerning general practitioners' terms of service state that general practitioners are obliged to offer an annual consultation (including a home visit) to patients on their list who are at least 75 years old (SI 1992/635, Schedule 2, para 16). The GP has to assess and record a number of matters including:

- sensory functions;
- mobility;
- physical condition including incontinence;
- social environment;
- use of medicines.

Policy guidance (on community care) refers frequently to various health service practitioners: for example to community nursing services and the 'possibilities for supporting users with nursing care needs through community nursing services whether in their own homes, or in residential care homes, or in sheltered or very sheltered housing' (DH 1990, para 3.37).

Of general practitioners, it 'is expected that, as a matter of good practice, GPs will wish to make a full contribution to assessment. It is part of the GP's terms of service to give advice to enable patients to avail themselves of services provided by a local authority' (DH 1990, para 3.47).

Practice guidance refers to the potentially important roles of practice nurses, district nurses, health care assistants, occupational therapy, physiotherapy, speech therapy, psychology, chiropody, and therapists for both hearing and visual impairment (SSI/SWSG 1991 (MG), pp.87–89).

DISCUSSION

General Practitioners

The terms of service summarised above are particularly relevant to community care since elderly people and particularly those who are least 75 years old are the 'biggest users of community care services' (Leedham, Wistow 1992,p.10).

There has long been evidence that many doctors, including general practitioners, are not as well informed about rehabilitation and disability as they might be. It has been observed that 'GPs tend to base their assessments on the medical model, rather than the social/educational model. This is largely a reflection of their training and their work priorities. Furthermore, their assessments tend to be service-led rather than needs-led'. This makes it likely that GPs will generally play a supportive, rather than a lead role, in community care assessments (Leedham, Wistow 1992,p.15).

There are also considerations of confidentiality (p.10). The BMA considers that it would be improper for GPs to carry out community care assessments for their own patients and where GPs do contribute to community care assessments, they should not assessing eligibility for services (Health Select Committee 1993, vol.2, pp.71,190).

Other Services

There are a number of particular health service specialisms particularly relevant to community care. Medical specialisms include, for example, neurology, rehabilitation, elderly care, rheumatology, urology, otology, ophthalmology, ear-nose-throat (ENT), orthopaedics, diabetes, specialist psychiatric services. Nursing specialisms include, for example, stoma care, continence care, community nursing, health visiting, practice nurses (based in GP surgeries). Therapy specialisms include occupational therapy, physiotherapy, speech and language therapy, hearing therapy. Chiropody too is an important 'paramedical' service.

The level, organisation and, in some cases, the existence of these services varies from place to place.

GENERAL HEALTH SERVICE DUTIES

Health authorities' statutory duties remain basically unchanged by community care legislation. This means that the provision of many health services relevant to community care is governed by general duties placed on the Secretary of State (and delegated to health authorities) to provide a comprehensive health service, and to provide services and facilities so far as 'necessary to meet all reasonable requirements'. The NHS Act 1977 applies this broad duty to the provision of hospital and other accommodation, medical, nursing, dental, ambulance, prevention of illness, care of ill people and after-care services. The Act does not mention particular medical or nursing specialisms, nor therapy services which in principle are so important for community care and enabling people to remain in their own homes.

These health service duties are towards the population generally and so are 'weaker' duties – compared with the stronger duties towards individuals to be found in some of the social services legislation (see p.61). Accordingly, health authorities appear to have very broad discretion to make priorities and allocate resources locally. Such is this discretion, that the general 'duty' to provide services under s.3 of the NHS Act 1977 is sometimes seen, in respect of any particular service, to be almost a 'power' only. Specific services tend to vary in level from authority to authority; and particular services might not exist at all in some places.

The law courts appear to have confirmed this broad discretion as has, in general, the health service ombudsman. It would seem that so long as health authority policies are not illegal, excessively unreasonable or unfair, then neither the courts nor the ombudsman will challenge them. The assumption seems to be that those priorities will be based broadly on 'clinical' priorities, and neither the courts nor ombudsman will substitute an opinion (about clinical precedence) for that of a health authority. There are many examples of how this broad discretion is exercised and the context can range from hole-in-the-heart operations, to means-testing for chiropody, to hearing aid provision.

Therefore, just as in the case of social services, local policies and practices can vary significantly and be subject to the operation of the same unpredictable elements of priorities, resource allocation, and definitions of what constitutes 'need'. Nevertheless, the extent of the discretion appears to have been questioned in the first half of 1994 in the context of NHS continuing care. A health service ombudsman investigation found unacceptable a health authority's policy which denied as a matter of course continuing nursing care to patients with neurological conditions. This is explained elsewhere (see p.212), although its wider significance is (at the time of writing) unclear.

However, in general, it does seem that health authorities have more to fear from bad publicity and public opinion (eg. about age discrimination), than from the law courts. For service users, this picture of health service provision suggests that, far more than is perhaps usually realised, patients do not receive services as of legal right.

EXTRACTS
Legislation (NHS Act 1977) states that:

> **(duty as is considered necessary to meet all reasonable requirements)** 'It is the Secretary of State's duty to provide throughout England and Wales, to such extent as he considers necessary to meet all reasonable requirements' a number of services including:

- medical, dental, nursing services (s.3(1)(c));
- 'hospital accommodation'; 'other accommodation for the purpose of any service provided' under the Act' (s.3(1)(a-b);
- 'such facilities for the prevention of illness, the care of persons suffering from illness and the after-care of persons who have suffered from illness as he considers are appropriate as part of the health service' (s.3(1)(e)).

(comprehensive health service): Section 1 of the NHS Act 1977 places on the Secretary of State 'a duty to continue the promotion in England and Wales of a comprehensive health service designed to secure improvement (a) in the physical and mental health of the people of those countries, and (b) in the prevention of, diagnosis and treatment of illness, and for that purpose to provide or secure the effective provision of services in accordance with this Act'.

Legislation (regulations: SI 1991/554) made under the NHS Act 1977:

(delegation of functions): delegates the Secretary of State's functions to health authorities.

Community care policy guidance states: 'The statutory responsibilities of health authorities to meet health care needs are unchanged...' (DH 1990, para 3.36).

DISCUSSION
Discretion as to Particular Services and Levels of Service
The NHS Act 1977 (s.3) does not list specific services which 'must' be provided. 'Medical' and 'nursing' services are referred to, but these are very broad terms covering in principle a range of services and specialisms. Therapy and other paramedical services (chiropody), so important for community care, are not mentioned at all.

Services provided under s.3 only have to be provided if they are 'necessary to meet all reasonable requirements'. This appears to mean that health authorities can set priorities and allocate resources locally, thus exercising wide discretion in deciding levels of service and sometimes even the very existence of particular services.

The effect of this discretion appears to be that although services as a whole are covered by the general duties to provide health services, the level (or even provision at all) of any one service is not mandatory, so long as its level (or even non-provision) is justifiable in terms of local priorities and resources.

This wide discretion of health authorities has been confirmed by strong (Court of Appeal) judicial authority: for example, the discretion to set priorities which result in people with serious medical needs waiting considerable periods.

In one such case, Lord Denning went so far as to imply additional words into s.3 of the NHS Act 1977, to the effect that the duty to provide services was inevitably subject to resources. He stated that it seemed to him inevitable that the following had to be implied: ie provision of services 'to such extent as he considers necessary to meet all reasonable requirements *such as can be provided within the resources available* (our italics indicate Lord Denning's 'extra' words). (*R v Secretary of State, ex p. Hincks 1979*).

The implication of all this is, according to one writer (Brazier 1992) at least, an 'absence of any right to health care'. Indeed,

'it has the effect of encouraging overstretched health authorities to withdraw services if resources are stretched rather than to struggle on doing their best. For while patients have no right to demand care, once a patient is admitted to a clinic or hospital a duty of care to him arises. If, owing to lack of resources, he suffers some injury resulting from lack of care, he may have a right to compensation from the authority. It will often be "legally safer" to close an underfunded casualty unit rather than seek to keep going with weary overworked staff' (p.23).

Limits to Health Authority Discretion

In the first part of 1994, however, the health service ombudsman effectively challenged the limits to health authorities' discretion, at least in the context of long-term continuing NHS care. At the time of writing, widespread uncertainty about the wider implications of the decision continues (see Chapter 13).

The question of whether the NHS discriminates against older people has also arisen (eg. Hunt 1994; *Therapy Weekly* 1994,p.1; *Therapy Weekly* 1994a,p.1). In response to a Parliamentary question about safeguards against such discrimination by 'refusal to provide, or withdrawal of treatment', the government replied: 'It is the duty of all health authorities to ensure that people of all ages have access to acute care and that specialist care is available to those who suffer with chronic conditions due to the aging process' (H1 1994). This answer appears only to re-state the general duty to provide health services and does not spell out the implications for individuals of local priorities and rationing.

The Royal College of Physicians summarises the biological and financial considerations concerning older people's access to acute services: 'it is difficult to set any age (whether 65,75 or 82 years) as a cut-off point for defining services on biological grounds, though local circumstances and resource constraints may provide a rationale for such an arrangement' (RCP 1994,p.5).

Likewise, Age Concern England has pointed out that if priorities are based on clinical needs, then priorities which are not so based violate the Patient's Charter which states that every citizen has a right to receive health care on the basis of clinical need. For example, there is evidence that coronary care units operate age-related admissions and thrombolysis treatment (reducing blood clots) policies – yet it is also argued that there is no scientific evidence which supports the logic of such an approach. If this is so, then people are being denied treatment not on the basis of their clinical needs but on the accident of their age (Whelan 1993).

However, this sort of problem is generally one of policy and is likely to be solved – or not solved – according to the climate of professional, political and public opinion, rather than by the law courts or the ombudsman.

'Blanket' Criteria of Eligibility

A related issue is whether health authorities can 'prioritise' services by laying down 'blanket' policies which exclude, wholesale, certain groups of people whether by age or by some other criterion.

At one extreme, the alternative to priorities is to assess clinically every individual who might need a service, and only then decide whether in fact that individual commands a sufficiently high priority. This extreme alternative would seem effectively to preclude the creation by policy of priority groups, and scarcely seems practical, given limited time and resources within the health service.

The answer probably is that health authorities need, practically, to make priorities. However, if challenged by excluded individuals, the authorities would have at least to consider and make individual decisions. Not to do so might invite legal problems, since authorities are not supposed to 'fetter their discretion' by following policies slavishly (see p.81).

In fact, blanket criteria and priority groups have been a relatively uncontroversial fact of life for years. For example, health authorities have long targeted chiropody services at four priority groups of people, and, in some authorities, only these groups of people are likely to receive services. Such a policy reflects government guidance given as long ago as 1974 which stated that: 'In general treatment should continue to be restricted to the existing priority groups' (HRC(74(33). The policy has been relatively uncontroversial because, in general, the priority groups do in fact cover those people most in need (see p.268).

Even at the National Health Service's inception, it was recognised that there would be temporary exceptions to 'comprehensiveness' of service: 'A full dental service for the whole population, for instance, including regular conservative treatment, is unquestionably a proper aim in any whole health service and must be so regarded. But there are not at present, and will not be for some years, enough dentists in the country to provide it. Until the supply can be increased, attention will have to be concentrated on priority needs' (Ministry of Health, Department of Health for Scotland 1944,p.9).

Equity in the Health Service

An even broader question to be asked is to what extent health authorities' increasing local exercise of discretion threatens the principle of an equitable, national health service (see eg. Whitehead 1994;); and whether such a tendency might run counter to the very principles of the health service (Whitehead 1994a). Certainly, one of the purposes behind the creation of the health service was to remedy the uneven distribution of, and access to, health services which existed before the war (Ministry of Health, Department of Health for Scotland 1944, pp.6–7).

Yet, it has been pointed out that the

'central issue is the lack of coordination of the different funding arrangements both within and across health and social services. For example, funds for hospital and community health services, general practitioners, prescribed drugs, and personal social services are determined largely in isolation from one another. The scope for agencies to abdicate responsibility and for inequities to flourish is much greater than is commonly supposed' (Judge Mays 1994).

It has also been suggested that since the boundary between health and social care is becoming more blurred, questions of equity (an explicit 'guiding principle' of health care legislation in the NHS Act 1946, but not of social care legislation in the National Assistance Act 1948) are increasingly spilling over into the area of social care (Challis, Henwood 1994).

The question of equity is important but not one easily tackled in individual remedies. For example, the courts might refer to the importance of questions about levels of resources and facilities in the health service – but state that such questions are for Parliament and not the courts (*In re Walker's Application 1987*). Even the health service ombudsman, who has explored, further than the courts, the limits of health authority discretion, has explained that he cannot 'conduct a more general review into variations in the level of service provided by different health authorities within the NHS' (W.707/85–86).

(The government *has* confirmed both in Parliament (H2, 1994) and in Circular guidance (EL(94)19 that for urgent needs, there should be common hospital waiting lists, so that people's priority does not depend on the state of GPs' budgets.)

Levels of Rationing

There appear to be different levels of policy-making and priority-setting. National and publicised (see eg. DH guidance on priorities, EL(94)55) planned priorities might be one thing; but 'lower level', sometimes ill-considered and arbitrary decisions might be another. Authorities and service users should be aware that the latter might be more susceptible to challenge (see below).

The National Association of Health Authorities and Trusts has examined health authority priority setting at a 'high' planning level, reviewing stated priorities and allocation of resources to particular services or groups of people. Even at this level, it seems that statements about explicit rationing are often avoided. Instead, one finds implicit rationing, that is 'the limitations on the availability of, and access to, services implied by the existing distribution of resources' (Redmayne, Klein,Day 1993,p.3). However, this level of analysis does not necessarily uncover the rationing which sometimes takes place at 'lower levels' in the system and although such studies might report on health authorities' publicly declared rationing policies (eg. concerning tattoo-removal or infertility treatment), there is less focus on the less formal, but longstanding rationing of some of the less 'glamorous' services – such as provision of incontinence materials or chiropody (see also *Which?* 1994).

At a lower level, a middle manager might realise that a particular budget is running out and almost in panic decide to reduce or withdraw suddenly the provision of incontinence pads to people in residential homes. Such decisions might be challengeable, since they might be regarded by public law courts as 'unfair' because they disappoint the 'reasonable expectations' of people receiving, and relying on, a particular service (see p.79). It might also be claimed that there is a general 'duty of care' which the providing authority owes to patients: sudden termination might lay it open to a charge of negligence if physical harm were to be caused (see p.84). In one instance, a health authority in 1992 retreated from its plans simply to cease providing incontinence people in residential homes with incontinence pads. Instead it agreed to reassess all the residents involved individually before making a decision (Wyatt 1992).

Indeed, a Department of Health Circular warns authorities, when changing or withdrawing the supply of incontinence aids, not to do so until an 'assured alternative' is in place and not to expose vulnerable people to anxiety (EL(91)28).

There is, for example, yet another level of priority-setting or rationing, less visible than the above two levels. An example might be a hospital therapy department which has lost staff and faces increased workloads. There might come a point where senior, but still practising, therapists are under such pressure that they have to devise a means of reducing the demands on their time. Part of their strategy might be a formal policy: for example, to take only specific referrals from other hospital staff and therefore no longer see all patients on their wards. But another possible reaction might be to decide, informally almost, to alter their 'clinical' judgements so as not to provide rehabilitation for patients who, previously, would have received it. The therapists might write that a person does need rehabilitation, but that it cannot be provided; or they can write that the person simply does not need rehabilitation. Either way there is 'rationing'; but in the latter case, it has become indistinguishable from financial decision-making and the integrity of the recorded clinical decision has become questionable.

EXAMPLES OF LOCAL DISCRETION, PRIORITIES, WAITING TIMES

The following are examples of how health authorities might exercise discretion to set priorities and allocate resources, and of how this discretion affects patients. Although each example concerns a particular service, the principle at issue in each case can be taken generally to apply to any service, since generally speaking all services are covered by the same duties in legislation. The health service ombudsman investigations confirm the wide discretion of health authorities to determine local priorities.

There is a general assumption that health authority priorities are based on clinical priorities and neither the courts nor the health ombudsman are in the business of substituting their judgement for that of a health authority. The courts might only interfere, in judicial review, if a policy was illegal, procedurally defective or excessively unreasonable. (Judicial review is explained elsewhere in this book). Thus, health authorities appear free to allocate resources as they wish – and in one case, the health service ombudsman accepted the health authority's use of means-testing to determine who should receive chiropody services. Thus, the fact that, generally, local priorities might not in reality reflect local clinical needs, but rather reflect widespread (and therefore normal) haphazard funding arrangements, would not generally be the concern of the courts.

EXTRACTS
Legislation is silent about priorities and waiting times.

DISCUSSION
Waiting Times (Hole-in-the-Heart Operation)
The Court of Appeal (*In re Walker's Application 1987*) ruled on a case brought against a health authority for postponing an operation five times because of the lack of suitably trained nurses and accompanying facilities. The postponements were related also to the treatment of other more urgent cases. The court found no evidence of illegality, procedural defect or unreasonableness amounting to irrationality. The court suggested that the case was not an attack on the health authority but a general criticism of the health service and of those who provided the facilities. These questions were of enormous public interest and concern but they were questions to be dealt with outside the courts. The judge firmly stated that the courts did not have a role in such cases: it should not even contemplate making an order in such circumstances.

The Court of Appeal upheld this decision, declining to interfere and substitute its own judgement for that of those responsible for the allocation of resources. It would only interfere if there had been a failure to allocate funds in a way which was 'unreasonable' or if public-law duties were breached. Even then the court would exercise a judicial discretion and take account of all the circumstances of the case. Thus the court would be reluctant to intervene.

In a similar case (*R v Central Birmingham Health Authority, ex p. Collier 1988*) concerning a baby with a heart condition, the court came to a similar conclusion. The court found that there was no evidence that the authority had allocated its resources unlawfully or unreasonably.

Waiting Time (Orthopaedic Services)
A court case which eventually went to the Court of Appeal was about a number of people who had waited for treatment for periods longer than 'medically advisable'. The delay occurred because of a shortage of treatment facilities

which was due partly to a decision not to build a new block on the grounds of cost. The applicants claimed that the Secretary of State, regional health authority and area health authority had all breached their statutory duties under both s.1 and s.3 of the NHS Act 1977. S.1 is about the duty to promote a comprehensive health service; s.3 includes provision of accommodation, facilities and services (see p.257).

The judge stated 'that it was not the court's function to direct Parliament what funds to make available to the health service and how to allocate them'. The Secretary of State's duty under s.3 to provide services 'to such extent as he considers necessary', gave him a discretion as to the disposition of financial resources. The court could only interfere if the Secretary of State acted so as to frustrate the policy of the Act, or as no reasonable Minister could have acted. The Court of Appeal upheld the decision, finding that resource limits had to be read into statutory duties to provide services (*R v Secretary of State for Social Services, ex p. Hincks 1979*).

A health service ombudsman investigation (HSC W.224/78–79) of a wait for a knee operation accepted that 'the backlog of patients for orthopaedic surgery was outside the control of the Authority and they were unable to give a reliable estimate of when the complainant could expect to have her operation'. The authority was waiting for the opening of an upgraded operating theatre and was also short of anaesthetists.

The priority accorded to the complainant was a clinical decision which the ombudsman could not question. However, a letter (quoted by the ombudsman) from the Minister of State for Health illustrates how concepts such as 'need' and 'priority' are 'elastic' in such circumstances: 'Priority is given to the most urgent cases but there is now a high proportion of patients on the waiting lists who must be regarded as urgent from the point of view of the degree of pain and disability they are suffering'. Therefore, not everybody with urgent needs would also be given priority.

Allocation of Resources and Rationing (Infertility Treatment)

In October 1994, the High Court denied permission to a 37-year-old woman to challenge a health authority's decision to deny her infertility treatment because of her age. She claimed that the authority had acted illegally, improperly and irrationally (see Chapter 7).

The judge ruled that the authority was entitled legally to employ the criterion of age when faced with budgetary restrictions; and was not obliged to provide the service on demand 'regardless of the financial and other concerns of the authority'. The authority had acted on medical advice that in-vitro fertility treatment was generally less effective for women over the age of 35; the judge said that it was not for the courts to impose the appropriate cut-off point (*R v Sheffield Health Authority, ex p. Seale 1994*).

Waiting Time (Hearing Aids)

The health service ombudsman (W.371/83–84) investigated a very long delay (18 months) in provision of a hearing aid. He concluded that the delay was not caused by 'administrative failures' (which are within the ombudsman's jurisdiction). Instead it was caused

> 'as a direct result of insufficient resources being available. But the allocation of resources within the HA was, and continues to be, a matter to be decided by them, and I have found no evidence of maladministration which would entitle me to criticise the respective priorities given by the HA to the competing demands for competing finance'.

Waiting Times (Wheelchairs)

The wheelchair service has been criticised for delays in provision for many years, from the McColl (1986) report which resulted in devolution of the service to health authorities, right up to the present, for example, the Committee of Public Accounts (1993,p.10).

Level of Provision (Incontinence Services)

Parliamentary replies on the provision of incontinence materials have stressed the powers of health authorities to make priorities locally. For example:

> 'We have received a number of representations about the supply of incontinence pads to private nursing and residential homes. The free provision of incontinence pads does not extend to people living in private nursing homes; the same legislation provides that district health authorities may provide incontinence materials and other nursing aids to people in their own homes and at their discretion to residents of local authority residential homes. The extent to which this discretion is exercised varies from place to place and information about these decisions is not held centrally'. (H45 1990)

One specific example quoted in 1990 was of a health authority's consultation document, proposing to withdraw 'free incontinence aids' from 400–500 people living in independent sector residential homes, though still continuing to advise home owners and sell supplies to them at cost price (H46 1990).

Concern about inadequate provision and rationing of incontinence materials continues (eg. Hinchcliffe 1994). Indeed, the Department of Health itself has acknowledged over a period that there have been 'wide variations in the level of services to people with incontinence' (H48 1991). For example, four years previously, the restriction of services in some areas had led to considerable concern about the situation and a request had been made by the Department to health authorities for information about their practices (D(87)45).

Such has been the growing level of public concern that the Department of Health felt moved to issue the following guidance to health authorities: 'In particular, should any changes be proposed, it is obviously important that vulnerable patients or clients should not be exposed to anxiety, and that where for example a change in the supply of incontinence aids is proposed, there should be an assured alternative in place before action is put in train' (EL(91)28).

Baroness Masham of Ilton attempted, unsuccessfully, to amend the NHS and Community Care Bill passing through Parliament: 'In carrying out its primary functions a District Health Authority shall provide a district wide incontinence service and shall identify a continence advisor and a consultant to take a special interest in incontinence'. The government in reply reaffirmed health authorities' discretion: 'in this as in other areas of health care provision district health authorities should be left free to determine the pattern and level of service in their districts in the light of local needs and circumstances' (H47 1990).

Baroness Masham has explained the problems of incontinence to the House of Lords:

> 'The general public who are healthy and well have no idea that at such a basic level people who are incontinent are having many problems. They are having to buy pads or have them rationed or cut off. The mother of a spastic daughter who cannot speak and is doubly incontinent, living in a Cheshire Home, was told that she would have to pay for her daughter's incontinence pads as the Cheshire Home has nursing home status. The mother has to choose between supplying her daughter with pads or giving her a holiday. She cannot afford to do both. Other people have been told that they cannot have the pads which are the most suitable for them. If this goes on there will be an increase in pressure sores and all sorts of problems costing the health service millions of pounds. In addition to this, there are difficulties for carers who may find dealing with other people's urine and faeces none too pleasant. If people do not have adequate pads, life will become unbearable' (H52 1990).

Administrative Decisions (Pressure Sore Treatment)

The health service ombudsman has investigated a certain number of cases involving incidence of pressure sores. The ombudsman cannot question clinical decisions about methods of treatment and care, but can challenge administrative arrangements for that treatment and care. For example, the lack of foresight in travel (hospital discharge) arrangements to protect adequately 'those with pressure sores or recently healed sores' (HSC SW.28/84–85).

Pressure sores can develop quickly, for example, within a couple of hours, and may be the result of vulnerable skin tissue developing over a longer period beforehand. Thus, it may not be easy to decide when or where lack of care, if any, contributed to a sore. However, where nursing records and care plan documents are incomplete, thus making such a judgement impossible, the ombudsman might uphold a complaint anyway (HSC W.547/92–93).

Level of Provision (Community Nursing Services)

Like other health services, the level of community nursing service provision is also governed by health authorities' discretion. The advent of community care is almost certainly increasing the demands on community nursing services (eg. SSI 1993j,p.13; SSI 1993k,p.18). Even before April 1993, there was evidence that community nursing services might be inadequate to meet the needs of, for example, physically disabled people aged 16–64 (SSI 1988a,p.14); or, for example, might be unable for various reasons to deliver effective equipment services (Ross,F 1992,p.92).

One health service ombudsman investigation (SW.28/84–85) into the quantity (as opposed to the quality) of home nursing care for a 91-year-old woman following hospital discharge, accepted the community nurse's policy. This was that 'requests for her patients were assessed against the needs of other patients and the resources available and priorities were determined. These decisions stemmed from the exercise of professional judgement which I may not question'.

Referral/Funding (Communication/Speech Equipment)

Local priorities and resource allocation can affect the funding of equipment. So, for example, Circular guidance (HN(84)12, para 5) suggests that when people with communication difficulties are assessed at communication aids centres: 'referrals should be routed to a consultant associated with the Centre concerned by the patient's consultant…when a patient is referred to a Centre the health authority of the referring consultant will be expected to provide the aids that may be recommended by the Centre. It will be the responsibility of the patient's own consultant to prescribe such aids…'

Despite this guidance, the provision of communication aids remains confused. Practices vary widely, with provision (where it takes place) unpredictably spread between the health service, social services and the voluntary sector. Sometimes in the past, special assessment centres have preferred not to see people unless funding for equipment required was guaranteed (Mandelstam 1993, Chapter 13).

Level of Service (Speech and Language Therapy Services)

The discretion invested in health authorities leads to some caution in Parliamentary answers to questions about the obligations health authorities have to provide speech therapy services. For example, the Secretary of State for Health has replied: 'It is the responsibility of health authorities to assess the health needs of their local population and to obtain appropriate services for them, including speech and language therapy services. We encourage the NHS to deploy qualified speech and language therapists as effectively and efficiently as possible…' (H49 1991). This type of statement appears to leave all to local discretion and prohibits neither a low level of service provision, nor possibly even non-provision.

The health service ombudsman (W.783/85–86) investigated alleged delayed and intermittent speech therapy provided by a health authority to a two-and-a-half-year-old child with severe communication difficulties. The ombudsman accepted the health authority's position. This was that, although the speech therapy service was understaffed and underfunded by national and regional norms, the health authority was well aware of, and concerned about, the situation. The 'HA have to balance the needs of the STS against other services and I am aware, from other investigations, of the problems health authorities face in deciding between competing demands. The HA is vested with the discretion to decide how to allocate its resources...and the legislation which governs my work does not permit me to question such a decision unless I find evidence of maladministration in the way it was reached'.

Limited Resources (Hearing Aids)

Beyond a standard range of hearing aids, local health service discretion has affected the provision (or non-provision) of, for example, commercial hearing aids, health service batteries or maintenance for privately purchased hearing aids. In one case of non-provision of a commercial hearing aid and of batteries for a commercial aid, the Parliamentary ombudsman investigated – and accepted – the Welsh Office's explanation. This was that 'the resources available for the extension of Health Services are limited, and the case for development in each field of care and treatment has to be weighed carefully with other pressing demands' (PCA 5/915/78, 1978– 1979).

Another Parliamentary ombudsman investigation about non-provision of NHS batteries for a privately bought hearing aid concluded that non-provision was justified 'because there are no powers in the NHS Acts to do this' (PCA 5/325/77, 1977–1978). In fact, it does seem that, in practice, NHS treatment, at local discretion, does sometimes include provision of NHS batteries for private hearing aids.

Priorities and Means-Testing (Chiropody Services)

Chiropody services have long been subject to considerable demand and to explicit priorities sanctioned by central government (HRC(74)33 para 11). The inadequacy and variability of services has likewise been acknowledged by government (HRC(74)33,para 11; HC(77)9, para 1). The priority groups have been four: elderly people, disabled people, expectant mothers, school children.

Investigating the use of local health services discretion to make priorities, the health service ombudsman (HSC W68/77–78) investigated the use of a means test to make those priorities. He found the authority vindicated and quoted a DHSS letter to the authority:

'We know that many [authorities] do not have the manpower or other resources to provide a satisfactory service for even the elderly and have therefore decided to introduce their own criteria for determining priority amongst this and other groups...decisions as to level of provision rest with individual [authorities] and if your [authority] considers that a "means" type test is the best way of determining priority amongst those seeking treatment that is entirely a matter for the authority...'.

Administrative Decision-Making on Priorities (Crutches Provision)

A health service ombudsman (HSC WW.3/79–80) investigation into refusal to provide crutches to a person leaving hospital found that the decision was not a clinical one, made by a medical doctor, but administrative and made by a technician. The technician had varied the policy on provision of crutches according to stock levels. Thus, 'he sometimes had to refuse crutches to patients for whom they ought to have been provided and would have been, had stock levels permitted'.

The ombudsman's view was that 'it was unreasonable to have withheld crutches from the complainant for any reason other than a medical one'.

Fluctuating Clinical Need (Contact Lenses)

A health authority can respond to fluctuating demands for services by altering its priorities. This in turn can affect the priority afforded to any particular individual seeking a service.

The health service ombudsman (W.707/85–86) investigated a case where a person was assessed as having a clinical need for contact lenses at one hospital; assessed as not having a clinical need for them at a second hospital; and finally, whether or not he had a clinical need, was denied treatment at a third hospital which on account of limited resources would take no new contact lens patients anyway.

The ombudsman explained that although he could investigate individual health authorities, he had no power to 'conduct a more general review into variations in the level of service provided by different health authorities within the NHS'. Similarly, he had no jurisdiction to question the clinical assessment made by the second hospital.

The third hospital had decided to provide only ophthalmic services which could not be obtained elsewhere through the 'general ophthalmic services'. This decision arose from a review of services, and the HSC found no maladministration in the reaching of the decision.

Rehabilitation: People with Physical or Sensory Disabilities

Although rehabilitation services are vital to disabled people, their availability varies across the country depending on local priorities. This leads to the lack of a clear picture of what is available and to gaps and shortages in services (eg. NAO 1992,p.3; Committee of Public Accounts 1993,p.xi; Beardshaw 1988).

There is concern that despite increased emphasis in principle on rehabilitation services, wide disparities in levels of services are found. For example, physiotherapists are key rehabilitation workers, yet comparing two adjacent London health authorities there might be (relative to the local population) nearly three to four times as many physiotherapists in one authority as in the other (Public Accounts Committee 1993,p.11).

The NHS Management Executive's view of such variation has been that it might be due to differing local needs and arrangements and that it would not set national targets, even broad ones (Public Accounts Committee 1993,p.12). Continuing concern has been expressed, for example, about the shortage of units for brain-injured people (eg. Edwards 1990; Public Accounts Committee 1993,p.viii).

Circular guidance on people with physical or sensory disabilities notes that it is giving 'advice, guidance and an initial checklist on some of the main issues which authorities should consider when developing services for people with physical or sensory disabilities'. It notes the main policies set out in a 1981 document and that even where progress had been made it was uncoordinated (HN(88)26), para 2).

A Parliamentary reply has stated about rehabilitation services that health authorities 'fund rehabilitation services out of their general allocations and existing guidance sets out the range of services we would typically expect to see'. Though mentioned in an appendix of the Green Paper on the Health of the Nation, rehabilitation did not survive as a 'key area' into the White Paper because of 'insufficient knowledge about appropriate performance targets' (H51 1992).

In answer to a question about the need for the active rehabilitation of people before going home from hospital, the government has replied that a 'wide range of rehabilitation facilities exists within the national health service and local social services authorities. Decisions about rehabilitation services are for the professional judgement of those concerned with the individual case' (H50 1993).

NATURE OF PARTICULAR HEALTH SERVICES

S.3 of the NHS Act 1977 mentions no services other than medical, nursing, dental and ambulance. For example, it does not list specific services or specialisms which fall under 'medical' and 'nursing' services; and fails to mention altogether therapy and other paramedical services – which in principle do not fall under 'medical' or 'nursing' services. Possibly, paramedical services fall under the category of services which are for the prevention of illness, the care of people who are ill and the after-care of people who have been ill.

From time to time, however, government does issue guidance of various types to health authorities about desirable developments in particular services. The following are but a few examples of such guidance relevant to community care.

EXTRACTS
Physical or sensory disabilities
Circular guidance about people with physical or sensory disabilities (HN(88)26) states that authorities should 'consider': '*effective assessment and referral systems*, co-ordination and collaboration both within and between health authorities; and with outside agencies, statutory and voluntary'.

It goes on to draw attention to various needs of different groups of disabled people including:

- the *rehabilitation needs* of people with brain injury, stroke, progressive neurological diseases, spinal injury, epilepsy;
- *disability equipment*: need to ensure adequacy of service;
- *disabled young people* moving from child to adult health services: need for appropriate planning;
- *treatment of disabled people* for conditions unconnected with their disability: need for staff awareness;
- *personal relationships, sexuality and family planning*: need for advice and guidance;
- *availability of therapy services* to people in the community;
- *low vision aid service* for blind and partially-sighted people: need for access (travelling) particularly for elderly people;
- *hearing aid* centres, audiological rehabilitation services, and psychiatric services for deaf people;
- *people who are both deaf and blind*: need to bear in mind dual disability;
- *the need for district wide continence services*, including continence adviser, identified consultant and physiotherapist, adequate supply of incontinence aids and reasonable access to a urodynamic clinic;
- *physically, sensorily and multiply disabled people who also have learning difficulties* (mental handicap);
- *counselling* for people with chronic, fatal conditions. (our italics).

Continence services
Circular guidance (EL(91)28 reinforces the message contained in the guidance summarised immediately above (HN(88)26 about the provision of district-wide continence services. It was pointed out that a 'properly based incontinence service will bring both better quality and less expensive services. There is evidence that many people using expensive incontinence aids could, with the appropriate treatment and support, regain continence'.

The Department of Health is aware of the need for better continence services and is developing ways of promoting better practice (see eg. Sanderson 1991; Public Accounts Committee 1993,p.38).

Pressure Sores

Circular guidance (EL(94)3) points to the 'largely avoidable' but high prevalence of pressure sores: and their costs in terms of treatment and litigation. Previous circular guidance (EL(93)54) encourages local authorities to reduce prevalence by 5% per annum. The Department of Health guidance document, 'Pressure Sores – a key quality indicator' (DH 1994a) has been 'commended' to health service managers.

People with Learning Disabilities

Circular guidance (HSG(92)42) makes clear that people with learning disabilities (mental handicap) have the same rights of access to NHS services as everyone else, although they might need assistance to use services. Health service contracts should refer specifically to provision for such people and if necessary to special provision where needs cannot be met through the normal range of health services.

The guidance goes on to list examples of special provision which might be needed, including alternative dental services, specialist mental health provision, 'long term residential care in a health setting', and 'transitional responsibility for people in mental handicap hospitals'. It states that full use should be made of 'arrangements for joint finance, dowry payments and the powers available under section 28A of the NHS Act 1977' (Annex A).

Mentally Ill People

The White Paper, 'Health of the Nation', identified mental illness as one of the five main 'targets'. A 'key area handbook' (SSI 1993o), issued to health authorities and social services and 'illustrative rather than prescriptive' (CI(93)7), highlights a number of 'themes for management action'. These include cooperation between agencies at various levels; systematic approach to assessments; consultation; implementation of the Care Programme Approach; mental health information systems; targeting on different groups of people a balance of prevention, treatment, rehabilitation, continuing care (SSI 1993o,p.14).

Blind or Partially-Sighted People

Circular guidance, referring to the certification and assessment arrangements (involving hospitals and social services) carries recommendations (quoted from a DH working group report) including:

- effective management responsibility within social services;
- individual people should be assigned a specified member of staff (preferably at 'first line' management level);
- a full time worker to give advice and reassurance should be assigned to eye hospitals or large ophthalmic out-patients departments where there sufficient numbers of patients to justify such a full-time worker;

- people certified as blind or partially sighted should be contacted quickly to discuss their needs for services and to make a comprehensive assessment;
- the first priority of local agencies should be co-ordination at system and case levels (HN(90)5).

People with Haemophilia

Circular guidance (HSG(93)30) 'reminds NHS purchasers of the considerations they will need to take into account in order to secure continuity of access to comprehensive treatment and care' for people with haemophilia. Considerations are listed:

- 'variability and severity of the haemophilic condition';
- 'complexity of the condition which may require a diverse and complex range of services. Given the nature of the condition, the amount of treatment required by individual patients will be unpredictable';
- 'expertise in treatment of haemophilia patients is not uniformly available across the country';
- 'the need for ease of access of blood products to support home treatment programmes';
- 'the prevalence of HIV, which is a significant problem in this group of patients, and the need for treatment and counselling for HIV infected haemophilia patients';
- sophisticated treatment to be available through the planning and contracting processes.

CHAPTER 17

HOUSING SERVICES

KEY ISSUES

Housing would seem, according to common sense, to be a very important part of community care, since the preferred aim of community care is to enable people to remain in their own homes. If the home is not suitable, or cannot be made suitable, this will not be possible. However, housing services are not defined formally as 'community care services' and housing authorities do not even have a duty to accept local authorities' invitations to participate in community care assessments. Once again, here is one more piece of the community care jigsaw which does not quite seem to fit. In addition, some particular housing services, such as home adaptation provision, can be very complicated to understand and so represent another potentially uncertain and unpredictable part of community care.

HOUSING AND COMMUNITY CARE

While legislation is silent on the subject of housing in community care, it is covered by Circular guidance.

Legislation (NHSCCA 1990,s.46) does not define housing services as 'community care services'.

Joint Circular guidance (DoE 10/92) states: 'Adequate housing has a major role to play in community care and is often the key to independent living' (para 1). The Circular goes on to discuss a number of areas of work in which housing authorities might be involved in relation to community care. These include:

- community care planning;
- community care assessments;
- local housing strategies (within the Housing Investment Programme), involving cooperation with housing associations, and considering, for example, the closure of longstay hospitals and the 're-provision of services on a comprehensive local basis', and special needs housing;

- provision for homeless people;
- home adaptations.

DISCUSSION

Housing and Community Care

There is a view that the importance of housing in community care has been inadequately reflected in the main community care legislation and guidance. Now it is perhaps being recognised – for example, as a 'key' task in 1993 Circular guidance, and it is featured in the joint Circular of 1992 (immediately above) (see Francis 1994; Arnold *et al* 1994). Housing is seen by some as even the foundation of community care (see eg. Arnold *et al* 1993).

A pressing need for the development of housing and support services, for example, for severely disabled people aged 16–64 years, was suggested by a 1988 report by the Prince of Wales Advisory Group on Disability (Fiedler 1988,p.69).

INVITATION TO HOUSING AUTHORITIES TO ASSIST IN COMMUNITY CARE ASSESSMENTS

The NHS and Community Care Act states that when social services is assessing a person for community care services and it thinks there is a need for housing services, then it must notify the local housing authority and invite it to assist in the assessment. The duty is imposed on social services, not on housing authorities, which therefore appear not legally obliged to give assistance. Even if the invitation is accepted, the assistance requested is whatever is 'reasonable in the circumstances'.

The duty does not apply where the local authority is both a social services and a housing authority: ie, metropolitan authorities. This is presumably because the legislation assumes that different departments within one local authority anyway consult each other and work closely.

EXTRACTS

Legislation states:

(community care assessment): 'If at any time during the assessment of the needs of any person under subsection (1)(a) above, it appears to a local authority':

(health service): 'that there may be a need for the provision to him of any services which fall within the functions of a local housing authority (within the meaning of the Housing Act 1985) which is not the local authority carrying out the assessment'

(notification): 'the local authority shall notify that...local housing authority...'

(invitation): 'and invite them to assist, to such extent as is reasonable in the circumstances, in the making of the assessment; and, in making their decision as the provision of services needed for the person in question, the local authority shall take into account any services which are likely to be made available for him by that…local housing authority' (NHSCCA 1990, s.47(3)).

HOMELESSNESS: VULNERABLE PEOPLE

Housing authorities have a duty to an individual who is homeless (or threatened with homelessness), who has priority needs and has not made him- or herself homeless intentionally. The duty is to 'secure' that accommodation is available for that person (Housing Act 1985, ss.65(2),66(2),(68(2)).

People in priority groups include those who are 'vulnerable as a result of old age, mental illness or handicap or physical disability or other special reason, or with whom such a person resides or might reasonably be expected to reside' (Housing Act 1985, s.59(1)).

Coverage of homelessness legislation and court cases is beyond the scope of this book – although the courts have been very active in this area of law, judicial review has been used extensively and breach of statutory duty (for failure to offer accommodation to people in priority need) has been established (*Cocks v Thanet 1982*: see eg. *Homeless persons: Arden's guide to the Housing Act 1985, Part III* (Hunter, McGrath 1992)).

HOUSING FOR CHRONICALLY SICK AND DISABLED PEOPLE: GENERAL DUTY

Housing authorities have a general duty to consider the needs of disabled people when they are considering future provision of housing in their area.

Legislation states that:

'A local housing authority in discharging their duty under section 8 of the Housing Act 1985 to consider housing conditions in their district and the needs of their district with respect to the provision of further housing accommodation shall have regard to the special needs of chronically sick or disabled persons' (CSDPA 1970, s.3).

HOME ADAPTATIONS

Both policy guidance and Circular guidance recognise that home adaptations are important to community care policies. Home adaptations are of many types and include, for example, facilities such as handrails and fixed support frames, ramps, special bath or shower units, raised plug sockets, automatic garage doors, emergency call systems, accessible rooms, downstairs extensions, widened doorways.

Home adaptations can be provided through a number of different channels, including housing authorities' general powers and duties towards their own housing stock; disabled facilities grants (DFGs); minor works assistance (MWA: for elderly people receiving benefits); and through social services departments.

Even where the housing authority is likely to provide the adaptation, the social services department often carries out the assessment. In the case of an application for a disabled facilities grant, a housing authority has a duty to consult the social services department. Where the social services department assesses a need for a home adaptation but a housing authority does not provide (adequate) assistance, and the need cannot be met in any other way, then a continuing duty remains on the social services department to make arrangements to ensure that the need is met.

Home adaptations can be lengthy, complicated and disruptive, and sometimes be made worse through poor practice by social services and housing authorities. As a result, delay in home adaptations features prominently in local ombudsman investigations and findings of maladministration. (A number of summaries of ombudsman investigations are included in this chapter.)

EXTRACTS

Legislation: see the following sections.

Community care policy guidance includes 'adaptations' as one of the means of achieving the prime objective of community care: 'support for the user in his or her own home' (DH 1990, para 3.24).

Circular guidance (DoE 10/92) states:

(adaptations, improvements, repairs): 'Housing needs may include adaptations, repairs or improvements to allow people to stay in their existing home. In most cases this package of services will be based on a person's existing home, but in some cases it may mean alternative accommodation...

Referral procedures will need to be developed and agreed locally. Both housing and social services authorities should adopt joint arrangements to deal with assessments and should consider the need to nominate particular officers to be responsible for listing and agreeing the possible housing options' (paras 9–10).

(assessment, resources, needs and entitlements); 'Both community care planning and individual assessment and care management must take account of all the costs involved, including housing and other accommodation costs, and of the resources available to the various parties, and of the other claims on such resources. In no case should the resources of any authority be committed without the agreement of that authority. The ideal solution for an individual or group of individuals, based on a systematic assessment of needs, may not be achievable either immediately or in the near future, but it should inform the planning process. Community care in itself creates no new category of entitlement to housing, and housing needs which are identified by community care planning and individual assessments should be considered alongside existing processes and local priorities' (para 15).

HOUSING AUTHORITY GENERAL POWERS TOWARD THEIR OWN STOCK HOME ADAPTATIONS

Housing authorities have powers under Part 2 of the Housing Act 1985 to 'alter, enlarge, repair or improve', as well as to 'fit, furnish and supply a house provided by them under this Part with all requisite furniture, fittings and conveniences' (ss. 9–10).

Using these powers, housing authorities can carry out work directly at no cost to tenants – and therefore by-pass the disabled facilities grant scheme (see below).

DISABLED FACILITIES GRANTS (DFGs) FOR HOME ADAPTATIONS

Disabled facilities grants are part of the renovation grant system introduced by the Local Government and Housing Act 1989. Housing authorities have a duty to approve applications by disabled people for grants for home adaptations, if certain conditions are met. Social services must be consulted by the housing authority. If the housing authority accepts that the adaptation is needed for certain daily living (mainly access) purposes prescribed in legislation, then it must approve the application. If the adaptation is needed for other purposes (prescribed as accommodation, welfare or employment), the housing authority has the power, but not duty, to approve the application. The grants are known as 'disabled facilities grants'.

After approval of an application, the amount of the grant is determined by a means-test and it can vary from 0% to 100% (up to £20,000) of the total cost of the adaptation. Thus approval of an application does not automatically trigger financial assistance.

EXTRACTS

Legislation (Local Government and Housing Act 1989, s.114) states that:

(duty to consult social services) In considering an application for a grant, the housing authority 'shall consult the welfare authority' (social services) about the necessity and appropriateness of the proposed works.

(adaptations must be necessary and appropriate) Housing authorities cannot approve applications for disabled facilities grants unless they are satisfied that 'the relevant works are necessary and appropriate to meet the needs of the disabled occupant'.

(adaptations must be reasonably and practically executable) Housing authorities also have to be satisfied that 'it is reasonable and practicable to carry out the relevant works, having regard to the age and condition of the dwelling or building'.

(purposes of adaptation) Applications must then be approved if the following purposes have been assessed as needed:

- facilitating access to: the dwelling; principal family room; room used or useable for sleeping; room with lavatory, bath, basin or shower;
- facilitating preparation and cooking of food;
- improving or providing heating system;
- facilitating use of sources of power (light, heat);
- facilitating access and movement around dwelling by disabled person in order to care for another person (LGHA 1989,s.114).

(duties to approve an application) Assuming the above conditions are met, the housing authority must approve the application.

(means-test) However, an approved application is not tantamount to carrying out the works: a statutory means-test has to be applied to determine the amount of grant. As a result of the means-test, contributions can range from 0% to the full cost of the adaptation (up to a ceiling of £20,000) (S 1994/648).

(disability) The person for whose benefit the work is to be carried out must be disabled in the sense defined by s.29 of the National Assistance 1948 (LGHA 1989, s.114).

(approval of application: timescale) 'A local housing authority shall, by notice in writing, notify an applicant for a grant as soon as reasonably practicable, and, in any event, not later than six months after the date of the application concerned, whether the application is approved or refused' (LGHA 1989,s.116).

DISCUSSION
Adaptations Which are 'Necessary and Appropriate'
Joint Circular guidance explains these terms at some length (DoE 10/90). They entail some of the following considerations:

- whether the proposed adaptation is needed to implement a care plan and enable the applicant to remain at home;
- non-imposition of strict definitional boundaries on 'necessity and appropriateness';
- differentiation by authorities between what is needed and what is desirable;
- impact on family and carer;
- whether terminally ill people will live to benefit from the adaptations (paras 36–39).

The guidance suggests how well-balanced decisions can be made, weighing up user needs and wishes against available resources:

'This may require sensitive handling in particular where the disabled person has fixed ideas about his adaptation needs with which the welfare authority cannot concur, though wherever possible authorities will no doubt wish try to accommodate their clients' wishes. This may be important when determining the level of independence which can be expected as a result of the adaptations. Adaptations enabling a severely disabled person to live independently may be very expensive, and a more modest scheme of adaptations coupled with care services might be an acceptable alternative. By contrast, where the only alternative to major adaptation is for the disabled person to live in long-term institutional care, the welfare authority may consider the adaptation scheme to be a more appropriate solution to that person's needs' (para 42).

Adaptations Which are 'Reasonable and Practicable'

Circular guidance (DoE 10/90) explains that consideration of 'reasonable and practicable' factors by housing authorities needs to take account of age of the property, condition of the property (paras 45–47) as well as other miscellaneous factors (para 48).

Decision-Making Responsibilities

The legislation states that: 'a local housing authority shall approve an application for a disabled facilities grant if the relevant works are for any one or more of the following purposes...' (LGHA 1989, s.114).

Circular guidance (DoE 10/90) makes it quite clear that the final decision to approve an application is for the housing authority. This applies when considering both the above tests: 'necessary and appropriate'; and 'reasonable and practicable'.

Deciding about necessity and appropriateness requires consulting social services. The guidance explains

'Whilst the housing authority must consult the welfare authority as to whether the proposed works are "necessary and appropriate", it is for the housing authority to decide what action to take on the basis of that advice, and it follows that they may not necessarily follow the recommendations of the welfare authority in any particular case. In practice this should be a rare occurrence but there may be exceptional circumstances where the housing authority are unable to approve a mandatory or discretionary grant...'(para 23).

A housing authority could choose not to follow a social services recommendation to approve an application because of other requirements of the legislation. For example, refusal of the application might be because of the inability of the applicant to show 'requisite interest in the dwelling'; to provide a certificate of future occupation; or to show that the home (eg. mobile) can be classed as a 'dwelling' (para 58).

Whilst the housing authority has the 'final say', it needs to follow acceptable procedures. For example, the local ombudsman has found maladministration where the housing authority decided not to proceed with the adaptation recommended by social services without having obtained all the relevant facts from social services and without notifying the applicants (CLAE 92/C/2753).

Council Tenants' Eligibility for Disabled Facilities Grants

Notwithstanding Circular guidance that it is 'open to Council tenants them-selves to initiate adaptation works to their homes by applying for disabled facilities grants' (DoE 10/90,para 21), some councils apparently deny this option to their tenants.

A local ombudsman has stated in one case that he was 'not persuaded that subsidy arrangements should exclude Council tenants from the benefits of DFGs' (CLAE 91/A/2523,p.10). Another investigation was concerned that 'three years after the relevant legislation came into force, the City Council seems unsure as to whether its tenants can apply for a Disabled Facilities Grant' (CLAE 92/C/2753).

Test of Resources (Means-Testing)

Regulations (SI 1994/648) set out how means testing is to be carried out. The test operates a sliding scale and means that an applicant might be eligible for the whole of the cost (up to the limit: see below) of the adaptation, for some of the cost, or for none of it. In outline the test of resources:

* resembles the housing benefit test;
* assesses income not just of the applicant but other household members who are 'relevant persons';
* includes a number of premiums calculated to assist particular groups of people;
* disregards altogether some types of income (listed in detail), including an applicant's income support (though other household members, not on income support, might be assessed);
* disregards savings up to a certain amount.

Despite the complexity of the means-testing system, the local ombudsman has found maladministration, when an authority failed to give 'sufficiently clear' information to a grant applicant. He misunderstood the costs involved and incurred unexpected debts – for a lavatory and shower for the his wife who had Huntington's Chorea (see eg. CLAE 92/C/0579,p.10). The giving of incorrect advice to a woman that she was too young (under 60 years old) to qualify for a renovation grant also amounted to maladministration (CLAE 92/C/3402,p.9).

Limit to Grant

The limit which a local authority can pay for a disabled facilities (and general renovation) grant is £20,000 in England and £24,000 in Wales. This sum is less than the previous limit of £50,000 (SI 1993/553 as amended by SI 1993/2711). Concern has been expressed by government at what is perceived to be a 'demand-led' system of provision – and a consultation document has suggested various options including reducing the maximum amount of grant still further. In this connection it also suggested another option which would remove the mandatory nature of grants – so that authorities would no longer have a duty to provide grants if certain conditions are met, but could provide them if they wished (see DoE 1993a).

Timing of Means-Test and Information

There are sometimes inevitable difficulties about applying the means-test. Initial, informal assessment might precede the formal financial assessment. If the two assessments are inconsistent, applicants might have expectations dashed. In one such case, the local ombudsman found no maladministration where an initial assessment was incorrect. This was because the formal assessment followed the informal assessment quickly and there was no evidence that the applicants were substantially misled when they first applied for assistance (CLAE 92/C/0298,p.8).

JOINT SOCIAL SERVICES AND HOUSING AUTHORITY RESPONSIBILITY FOR HOME ADAPTATIONS

As explained above, there are a number of different ways in which home adaptations can be provided. On the one hand the Chronically Sick and Disabled Persons Act 1970, s.2 refers to a social services duty of 'arranging for the carrying out of works of adaptation' in the home. On the other hand, there are at least three different ways in which a housing authority could carry out home adaptations.

In the past, housing authorities and social services have therefore divided up responsibilities. Social services has carried out assessments for many adaptations and provided 'minor adaptations' (non-structural, portable), whilst more major, expensive and permanent adaptations have been arranged by housing authorities (see DoE 10/90, para 19; Mandelstam 1993, Chapter 3).

Sometimes, however, if social services has assessed a need for an adaptation and for some reason the housing authority does not provide what is required – and the person cannot afford to pay for it and cannot obtain it in any other way – then a 'continuing duty' rests on social services to ensure that the need is met.

Delay in the provision of home adaptations features prominently in local ombudsman investigations, and, in any case, even in the absence of maladministration, major adaptation work can be a long and disruptive process.

Split Responsibilities for Assessment and Provision

Owing to two sets of legislation, both social services and housing authorities have responsibilities in relation to home adaptations. For many years the joint circular DoE 59/78 (now obsolete) was a crucial document for many occupational therapists in social services, and for housing and environmental health officers. As does its successor, DoE 10/90 (though less exhaustively), the 1978 circular suggested basically that major structural adaptations fall to housing authorities. Minor, non-structural adaptations should fall to social services – although some adaptations might now be eligible for minor works assistance from the housing authority. The 1978 guidance provided extensive lists of examples of major and minor adaptations. This was useful because it helped authorities reach local agreement on who should provide what, and it meant that there was likely to be at least some conformity from area to area.

Continuing Duty on Social Services

Social services departments assess for most adaptations, whether major or minor. This means that where housing authorities do not implement the recommendation of the social services, the individual involved has a continuing assessed need which social services has to consider.

Circular guidance explains that such a continuing duty might arise: 'where the needs as assessed by the welfare authority exceed the scope for provision by the housing authority under s.114(3) of the 1989 Act and where that authority decline to use their discretionary powers under section 114(4)'. A Parliamentary answer from the Department of Environment confirmed that in such circumstances, social services has 'responsibilities under the 1970 Act to provide financial assistance in cases where a disabled person will otherwise face hardship in meeting their share of the cost of adaptations' (H73 1992).

The Circular guidance explains that:

'Such a responsibility might arise when, for instance, the welfare authority considers there is need related to the individual's social needs that demands a greater level of provision than is required for the disability alone, and where the housing authority chooses not to exercise its discretionary powers. This may occur, for example, where the size of a bedroom for a disabled child is required to be greater than is necessary for sleeping, because it needs to fulfil the role of bed/sitting room to provide more independent social space' (DoE 10/90, paras 15–16).

Two Means-Tests and 'Topping Up' by Social Services

The Circular guidance goes on to state that social services might also have a continuing duty where the housing authority is contributing to the adaptation, but not sufficiently (as a result of means test). This is a difficult question, because if social services then provide extra assistance, it means in effect that two means tests are being applied, each reaching different conclusions. Where an authority is unified (as a metropolitan borough), these two means tests are even applied within the same authority.

Circular guidance tries to explain:

'the welfare authority may find they have a continuing duty to provide assistance...where a disabled person asks the welfare authority for financial assistance...with that part of an adaptation which he is expected to finance himself in the light of the test of resources for the disabled facilities grant.'

The guidance goes on to explain that the contribution asked from social services could even be the total cost of the adaptation (if the housing authority has provided nothing by way of grant). It then states, perhaps less than clearly, that on the one hand social services 'should not try to make their own separate assessment of what a grant applicant is expected to pay; but they might consider whether, in their opinion, the meeting of those costs would cause hardship'. This does seem to imply in substance two different means tests: the difference between 'assessment' and 'consider' remains obscure.

The guidance suggests that social services could make a loan repayable with or without interest. Exceptionally, social services could waive repayment, for example, where an applicant is caring for a disabled person on behalf of social services and the adaptation is needed because of the caring; or where 'such unreasonable hardship would be suffered by the disabled person or the applicant as a result of the contribution repayments, that the application for grant is likely to be withdrawn, and the welfare authority required to purchase residential care facilities which they consider are not in the best interests of the disabled person' (DoE 10/90,para 18).

The local ombudsman has investigated a number of cases which include reference to such a continuing duty resting on social services. For example, maladministration was found, where having identified a need for a downstairs extension, social services failed to act for 20 months – after the housing authority had offered a grant which the applicant family could not accept because it entailed a contribution which the family could clearly not afford. The 'Council appear to have ignored the fact that their statutory responsibility to provide assistance did not come to an end with the offer of a grant [by the housing authority]' (CLAE 91/C/1972,p.11).

In another case of maladministration, social services did 'not seem to have a system for responding to the situation where the City Council [housing authority] declines to act on its recommendation' (CLAE 92/C/2753,p.12). The local ombudsman has also stated that where a housing authority home adaptation scheme 'is not immediately able to provide the necessary funding, the Council must meet the costs of making provision under the terms of the Chronically Sick and Disabled Persons Act by other means in its capacity as Social Services Authority' (CLAE 89/C/1114,p.17).

Similarly, the local ombudsman found maladministration where a council took two years to agree to provide an interest free loan as part of its 'continuing duty', following the inability of a person to meet the contribution which had been assessed by the housing authority (CLAE 92/C/0298). Again, the ombudsman has doubted a council's initial view (later reversed) that once it had assessed the need for a disabled facilities grant, it had done its duty under s.2 of the CSDPA. What it failed to do in this particular case was then to establish whether the applicants could actually afford their contribution to the adaptations themselves, and if not, possibly offer an interest free loan (CLAE 92/C/2376).

LIMITED RESOURCES

Renovation grants (including disabled facilities grants) are mandatory: that is, once certain conditions are satisfied, housing authorities must approve grant applications - and depending on people's means, give financial assistance. In order to avoid incurring obligations which they cannot meet, housing authorities might, for example, limit publicity about the grants, give people enquiry forms rather than application forms (thus prolonging the whole process) or maintain long waiting lists once the annual budget is spent (Heywood 1994,p.75). This might be in addition to restricting discretionary grants (eg. minor works assistance and the discretionary element of the disabled facilities grant scheme: see above).

One of the local ombudsmen has recognised the difficulty which authorities face and explains in the 1994 annual report that she has 'not been critical of councils which have, in effect, introduced a rationing system for limiting the number of applications they approve provided that the system has been designed fairly and operates fairly, and provided that the council concerned has done what can reasonably be expected to secure the resources needed to meet its responsibilities in this area' (CLAE 1994,p.24).

WAITING TIMES FOR HOME ADAPTATIONS (LOCAL OMBUDSMAN INVESTIGATIONS: EXAMPLES)

Long waiting times seem to characterise the provision of home adaptations. Part of the reason for this is that the home adaptation process simply is complex, involving as it can, for example, social services, the housing department, planning department, means-tests, builders, architects and considerable disruption for service users and carers.

However, it does seem that delay is also caused by a range of other factors such as lack of coordination between departments and agencies, and lack of money. The delay can precede assessment (see p.124). The following section deals with delay following assessment and gives a range of examples from local ombudsman investigations.

Home Adaptations Process: Complexity

It is true that the arrangement of home adaptations can be a complex process involving, for example, social services, the housing department, planning department, means-tests, builders, architects and considerable disruption for service users and carers.

Thus, an 18-month wait for major adaptations following assessment, including design and construction taking a year, has been deemed by the local ombudsman not to be 'unreasonable delay' (CLAE 91/A/3466,p.12).

The ombudsman has not criticised a council for failing to predict construction, foundation and drainage problems; nor the council's inability to get work finished quicker by a contractor. This was because to have terminated the contractor's contract would ultimately have led to further delays; and a fixed term contract had not been obtained in the first place because of the council rules about obtaining other tenders which in this case could probably not have been obtained; and therefore the architect could do no more than 'cajole' the contractor (CLAE 90/C/2438,pp.12–14).

The local ombudsman has not found maladministration where delay is caused by disagreement between the client and staff; by the seeking of advice from a doctor; by the client indicating, without good cause, that she needed no further help because she was unhappy at delays; and where it was not the council's responsibility that the client had bought a home which was in such a condition as to make modification difficult (CLAE 91/C/1254,pp.8–9).

Statutory Timescale for Formalising Application

The local ombudsman can find maladministration where the statutory timescale (six months: see above) for approving an application is not complied with – and has commented that local authorities 'should not use any form of enquiry system as a means to delay unreasonably a formal application and thus postpone the start of the six-month decision period' (CLAE 91/A/3602,p.23).

Such a finding is consistent with Department of Environment guidance which states that authorities 'should not, however, use any form of enquiry system as a means to delay unreasonably a formal application and thus postpone the start of the six month decision period which runs from the receipt of a valid application' (DoE 12/90, para 15).

However, by contrast, the local ombudsman has been prepared more recently to sympathise 'with the approach adopted by some councils of using the preliminary screening of applications for improvement grants to slow down the number of enquiries that proceed to formal application'. This in itself might not be maladministration; but, in such circumstances, the ombudsman might still find maladministration 'in the way in which the Council had determined the level of financial and staffing resources to carry out its responsibilities in this area' (CLAE 92/C/1381).

Administrative Deficiencies

A 19-month period between application and final assessment was maladministration, including as it did insufficient record keeping, possible lost papers and the applicant's consequent uncertainty throughout the period about what was going on (CLAE 91/C/2376,p.12).

A considerable lapse of time caused by obtaining medical opinion, drawing up plans and getting planning permission might be reasonable in the eyes of the local ombudsman. However, once all this was done, further delay in approving and submitting plans was maladministration; as was inadequate monitoring by the council of a contractor whose defects caused further delay (CLAE 90/C/2413,p.12)

The fact that a complex system requires considerable communication and cooperation between different departments and agencies does not mean that the local ombudsman will overlook administrative deficiencies. For example, problems of correspondence in a large organisation did not make it 'right that a Council should rely on a service user to follow up delays caused by non-arrival of internal mail. It should not be beyond the capability of the Council to devise a system of keeping track of applications such as this' (CLAE 91/C/0121,p.7). Where attempts by senior officers to discuss delay with their opposite numbers in social services failed, 'officers in both departments should have taken responsibility to ensure such discussions took place'. Not to do so was maladministration (CLAE 91/A/3911, p.19).

Inadequate co-ordination between departments leading to delay in the meeting of assessed needs for equipment or adaptations is not acceptable; the council should 'exercise proper management to ensure that no unreasonable delays occur before those needs are met' (CLAE 89/C/1114,p.17).

In another case, the local ombudsman found a scheme to alter a bathroom 'characterised by a complete breakdown of communications between departments. Once it became clear that there had been confusion over the extent of the scheme...it should have been a matter of days to rectify the situation. Instead, a further 16 months passed before a fresh order was raised...'. This was maladministration (CLAE 91/C/3811,p.13).

The local ombudsman has found maladministration where an eight-month delay between the approval and the placing of an order for an adaptation was regarded as not unusual and with 'apparent equanimity' by the council (CLAE 91/C/3811). A lack of 'effective liaison' between social services and housing authority, resulting in delay for adaptations, has been found to be maladministration (CLAE 91/A/1481,p.16). A wait of seven and a half months between receipt of instructions from social services and the housing department's sending of a preliminary form to the applicants was maladministration (CLAE 92/C/0298,p.8).

Similarly, the 'process of establishing what needs were to be met, the drawing up of plans, the obtaining of grant aid, and the granting of planning permission involved three different departments of the Council (and two separate sections of one of those departments). If such a process is to work properly, then different parts of the Council must work together more effectively than happened in this case. The failure of officers to co-ordinate their activities led to the submission and processing of an unacceptable planning application and consequent delay. The Council's failure to co-ordinate their activities was maladministration' (CLAE 91/C/1972,p.11).

Notifying Service Users About Delay

Whether or not delay itself is reasonable, failure to notify people about what is going on might be found by the local ombudsman to be maladministration. For example, a Borough Council's 'failure to notify [the applicant] formally of the decision to delay the work and then its failure to notify him formally of its schedule for carrying out the work...was maladministration'. Similarly, in the same case, the failure to notify the applicant about the fluctuations in the authority's views of what the applicant's needs really were was maladministration (CLAE 91/C/0565,pp.16– 17).

Conflicting Policy and Practice

For example, one ombudsman investigation found a policy of raising an order (for a stairlift) within 7 working days of an assessment visit; but in practice, this did not happen for 22 months. This was maladministration (CLAE 91/A/1481).

Delay Caused by Financial Pressure

Even where need has been formally identified, financial pressures can cause inordinate delays. Thus, one ombudsman investigation found that the housing authority imposed a moratorium on expenditure having discovered half way through the financial year that finance was 'tighter than anticipated'. The need for a stairlift identified by social services therefore remained unacted upon for a long period. Social services in turn did not act (as it might have, given the continuing duty on it to meet needs for adaptations if housing authorities fail to meet the need (see p.283)) on the grounds that the housing department had not made a final decision one way or the other. The ombudsman found maladministration which had caused a two-year wait CLAE 91/A/1481).

A delay of 11 months in sending a form once adaptations had been agreed to, because financial restrictions meant there was little chance of the work being done, amounted to maladministration (CLAE 91/C/1970,p.8).

Transfer of Accommodation

Under the Housing Act 1985, s.8(1) housing departments have a duty to consider housing conditions in their area and to pay special regard to the needs of disabled people (CSDPA 1970,s.3). A disabled person might applied for a transfer on medical grounds, but have to wait because of a shortage of suitable housing, and according to the local policy of dealing with such applications. The local ombudsman, in such a case, has not found maladministration in the delay (CLAE 91/C/1970).

MINOR WORKS ASSISTANCE FOR HOME ADAPTATIONS

Housing authorities have discretion to provide minor works assistance to certain groups of people. It is available to people who (or whose spouses) are receiving at least one of a number of benefits.

Because minor works assistance is discretionary, its availability varies around the country. Where it is available, the local authority often operates the scheme through housing improvement agencies. The scheme is designed to be quick and easy to use compared to the renovation (including the disabled facilities) grant system.

EXTRACTS

Legislation states that a local housing authority 'may give assistance':

- **(staying put)** 'to an elderly owner or tenant of a dwelling for the carrying out of works of repair, improvement or adaptation';
- **(elderly resident adaptation)** 'for the carrying out of works to adapt a dwelling to enable an elderly person who is not an owner or tenant of the dwelling but who is or proposes to be resident in the dwelling to be cared for';
- **(thermal insulation)** provision or improvement;
- **('patch and mend')** works of repair (must be in a Clearance Area) (Local Government and Housing Act 1989,s.131; see also DoE 4/90, paras 14–20).

Circular guidance (DoE 4/90) explains that:

> **(community care)** 'Regarding the elderly, the Secretary of State wishes authorities to give careful consideration in particular to the role minor works assistance should play (along with the disabled facilities grant and major renovation grant)' (para 6).

> **(speed and simplicity)** 'The statutory and advisory framework aims to facilitate the maximum simplicity, speed and flexibility in delivery which can be realistically achieved, without risk to quality. Where minor work is all that is needed, minor works assistance should therefore be able to achieve better overall value for money than major renovation grant'.

DISCUSSION

Conditions of Receiving Assistance

Applicants (or their spouses or the people they live with as a spouse) must be receiving housing benefit, council tax benefit, income support or family credit (SI 1990/388 as amended; see also DoE 4/90).

The assistance can be in the form of a grant or materials. It is available to owner occupiers and private tenants, but not to public sector tenants. The assistance is limited to a certain amount (currently £1080) per application and a maximum value of £3240 in three years where a person makes more than one application (see LGHA 1989,s.131; SI 1990/388 as amended). In addition, 'staying put' or 'elderly resident' assistance is available only for people aged 60 years or over.

Prevalence of Minor Works Assistance

Minor works assistance is employed variably by local authorities in England. In 1992, 13 authorities still provided none, whilst 23 provided it on a limited scale. All authorities in Wales provide the assistance. It is thought that there is no clear relationship between the variable levels of provision and the potential need for it – in terms of pensioner households (Macintosh, Leather 1993,p.6).

The assistance is often operated on behalf of housing authorities by home improvement agencies, an arrangement which Circular guidance seems to encourage (DoE 4/90,para 7); since such agencies can be effective coordinators (eg. Macintosh, Leather, McCafferty 1993).

WARDEN AND WELFARE SERVICES

Housing authorities provide a number of categories of sheltered housing, known as Part 1, Part 2 and Part 2.5.

Part 1 can be described as ordinary council housing stock in which elderly people live and which is managed in the ordinary way. Part 2 is sheltered housing which is 'warden-assisted'. Part 2.5 housing is sheltered housing, warden-assisted, with additional support provided by social services staff. (Part 3 housing refers to residential accommodation provided or arranged by social services departments.)

Traditionally, within Part 2 housing, wardens have provided a range of welfare services, including counselling, cleaning and laundry, organising activities, liaising with health and social services staff about tenants' health needs, errand running, personal care and so on. Recent legislation has both clarified and to some extent limited this provision of welfare services by prohibiting some welfare services from being charged to the Housing Revenue Account.

Community Alarm Systems

For council tenants, community alarm systems fall within the category 'welfare services' covered immediately above. In addition, housing authorities sometimes operate community alarm schemes for people in private, as opposed to public, sector property.

EXTRACTS

Legislation states that:

> **(meals and laundry for public sector tenants)** 'A local housing authority may provide in connection with the provision of housing accommodation by them under this Part…facilities for obtaining meals and refreshments, and…facilities for doing laundry and laundry services' (Housing Act 1985,s.11);

> **(welfare services generally for public sector tenants)** 'A local housing authority may provide in connection with the provision of housing accommodation by them (whether or not under this Part) such welfare services, that is to say, services for providing the welfare of the persons for whom the accommodation

is so provided, as accord with the needs of those persons... In this section "welfare services" does not include the repair, maintenance, supervision or management of houses or other property' (Housing Act 1985,s.11A);

(meals and recreation for elderly people) 'A district council shall have power to make such arrangements as they may from time to time determine for providing meals and recreation for old people in their own homes or elsewhere and amy employ as their agent for the purpose of this paragraph any voluntary organisation whose activities consist in or include the provision of meals or recreation for old people...' (HASSASSA 1983, schedule 9, Part 2, para 1).

(charges) 'The authority may make reasonable charges' for welfare services, for meals and refreshments, and for laundry facilities/services provided under the Housing Act 1985 (ss.11–11A); and for meals and recreation arranged for old people under the HASSASSA 1983 (s.17).

DISCUSSION

Welfare Services Provided by Wardens

In 1993 a Department of Environment consultation paper (DoE 1993a) identified a number of services:

- 'counselling, monitoring and support in connection with tenants' well being and health, and their personal needs other than those directly related to housing issues' (normally covered by wardens and met through the Housing Revenue Account);
- 'monitoring and alarm schemes, in place to reflect increased personal dependency/frailty of tenants';
- 'cleaning tenants' rooms and windows and their laundry services, reflecting their reduced ability to do so themselves';
- 'organising social/leisure activities and functions';
- 'liaising with medical/social services staff/GPs about tenants' health needs';
- 'providing and supervising restaurants/meals and ancillary services thereto';
- 'counselling and liaising with relatives';
- 'running regular errands because tenants are unable to do themselves';
- 'administering first aid';
- 'responding to out of hours calls by tenants';
- 'helping tenants into and out of bed';
- 'toileting, dressing, feeding, bathing/shaving tenants';
- 'administering tenants' medication';
- 'nursing care'.

Funding of Welfare Services

Before the explicit recognition of welfare service provision in 1993 (when s.11A, above, was inserted into the Housing Act 1985), welfare services were provided under Part 2 of the 1985 Act on the assumption that they were part of the landlord function of local housing authorities. It seems that they were also charged to the Housing Revenue Account – again this was before explicit statement in the legislation that this could be done (see below).

However, in 1992 the Court of Appeal, in a case (*R v London Borough of Ealing, ex p. Jennifer Lewis 1992*) involving a tenant who opposed rent increases, had ruled that welfare services did not come within the description of 'management of houses or other property' and could not thus be covered by the HRA. So in order to clarify the situation, legislation was passed giving housing authorities formal powers to provide welfare services under the Housing Act 1985 and to charge them to the Housing Revenue Account (Housing Act 1985, Part 2, s.11A; Local Government and Housing Act 1989, schedule 4, Part 3, para 3A: both inserted by the Leasehold Reform, Housing and Urban Development Act 1993: see ss.126–128).

Nevertheless, at the same time, the amending legislation, clarifying the powers to provide welfare services, also gave the Secretary of State powers to repeal the amendments. Secondary legislation (SI 1994/42) duly followed and excluded certain welfare services from being charged to the HRA. This does not seem to mean that housing authorities cannot provide them but that they must be charged to the 'general fund' and not the HRA, thus presumably discouraging their provision. The *excluded* welfare services are:

- assistance with personal mobility;
- assistance at meal times;
- assistance with personal appearance or hygiene;
- administration of medication;
- nursing care.

Community Alarm Systems

Community alarm systems can be provided by housing authorities to council tenants as welfare services under section 11A of the Housing Act 1985.

In practice, housing authorities also provide such systems to non-council tenants. The power to do this lies in s.137 of the Local Government Act 1972. Under s.11A(4) of the 1985 Act, the exercise of this power is not prevented, which it otherwise would be, by use of the powers under s.11A of the 1985 Act. Section 137 gives housing authorities powers to 'incur expenditure which in their opinion is in the interests of, and will bring direct benefit to, their area or any part of it or all or some of its inhabitants'.

However, the basis on which this section authorises provision is a little unclear. This is because it seems that charges might not be permissible under the section – whereas in practice housing authorities generally do charge when providing community alarm systems in non-council accommodation.

CHAPTER 18

CHARGES FOR SERVICES

KEY ISSUES

This chapter covers charges made by social services and health authorities.

Charges can in practice serve as a rationing device for authorities to use. Ample uncertainty exists because of different classes of resident in residential and nursing homes; variable charging practices amongst local authorities; periodic confusion about health service powers to make charges; and the re-defining of free (health) care as (social) care which can be charged for.

SOCIAL SERVICES CHARGES: RESIDENTIAL AND NURSING HOME CARE

The system of charging for residential and nursing home care is complicated, is itself divided into 'old' and 'new', and contains many exceptions. Other sources cover these in detail (eg. the Child Poverty Action Group's *National Welfare Benefits Handbook* (1994–95 edition), or the *Disability Rights Handbook* (1994–95 edition) by the Disability Alliance (1994)). Age Concern England produces a series of factsheets and briefing papers explaining the system and some of the complexities. The Department of Health produces a regularly updated, looseleaf manual called the *Charging for residential accommodation guide* available free of charge from: Health Publications Unit, No. 2 Site, Manchester Road, Heywood, Lancashire OL10 2PZ.

EXTRACTS

Legislation: reference is made to legislation in the following discussion.

DISCUSSION

Classes of Resident

There are different 'classes' of resident in residential and nursing care.

(1) There are people who were living in a home before April 1st 1993 and were supported (either wholly or partly) by the social security system (Department of Social Security). These people have 'preserved rights' and continue to be supported by social security. Legislation prevents social services providing accommodation for such people (National Assistance Act 1948, s.26A(1)).

(2) There are people who have entered a home after 31st March 1993 and require at least some public support. They come under the new system, in which social services assesses people's needs and finances and arranges accommodation and financial support as appropriate.

(3) There are people who are placed (whether before or after March 31st 1993) contractually in nursing homes by the health service. These retain the status of NHS patients and their care is paid for by the health service. They are not entitled to 'higher rates' (for residential accommodation) of income support.

(4) A fourth category exists apparently because of a legal loophole. From April 1st, the community care system was intended to terminate the system of social security support for people in residential and nursing homes (except for those with 'preserved rights'). However, it appears that people might still be able to enter a home supported by social security, and therefore 'by-pass' the new system of social services assessment and placement. For example, a single person over 65 might be able to claim income support, higher pension premium, residential care allowance, attendance allowance and severe disability premium (Wistow, Henwood 1994).

(5) There are people who themselves pay the whole costs of their residential or nursing care from their own resources. This group has in effect nothing to do with either the old or new systems of publicly supported residential care – unless or until their money runs out.

The 'Old' System: Social Security and 'Preserved Rights'

The old social security based system applies still to those with preserved rights because they were already resident in a home before April 1st 1993. Higher rates of income support are provided up to certain maximum amounts, depending on the type of care involved, ranging, for example, from £185 per week for elderly people in residential care to £315 for physically disabled people in nursing homes. The amount of social security support, up to the maximum level, depends on a means-test of income and capital.

Social services departments are generally prohibited from assisting people with 'preserved rights' (NAA 1948,26A). However, there are exceptions to the prohibition. For example, social services departments can 'top up' payments for people under 60 (women) or 65 (men) and occasionally for people over those ages. Topping up covers any shortfall between the amount of social security support and the home fee (see LAC(93)6; SI 1992/2977).

The 'New' System: Social Services Department Duty to Make Charges

Social services has a duty to charge people it places in residential or nursing homes (NAA 1948,s.22).

Standard Rate/Usual Cost

The local authority must set a standard rate to charge people – up to which it will pay for people who cannot afford the charge (NAA 1948,ss.22,26). The rate should represent the full cost to the local authority of providing the accommodation. This is not as simple as it sounds.

Costs will vary depending on the type of care involved and the locality. This factor is relevant, for example, 'where an authority might judge the need to move to another part of the country to be an integral part of an individual's assessed needs (eg. to be near a relative) and therefore one of the factors to be considered in determining what the authority would usually expect to pay' (LAC(92)27).

However, Circular guidance states that authorities should not 'set an arbitrary ceiling on the amount they are willing to contribute towards residential care and require third parties to routinely make up the difference. If challenged an authority would need to be able to demonstrate that its usual cost was sufficient to allow it to provide people with the level of service they could reasonably expect did the possibility of contributions not exist' (LAC(92)27, para 10).

There is concern that in practice this discretion can lead to 'widely varying levels of contributions from relatives' (Health Committee 1993,vol.1,p.xxiv). An SSI report (1993h, Summary) seemed to find evidence that some authorities were setting too low a 'usual cost', so that most placements in those areas were achieved only by third party contributions: for example, extra payment by relatives.

Standard Rate/Usual Cost and Choice of Home

A 1993 High Court case (*R Avon County Council ex p. M 1993*) illustrated the difference between a person's 'preference' and 'need' for a particular home. A local authority had denied that the wish of a person with Down's Syndrome to go into a particular home was a need, characterising it instead as a mere preference. On this ground it claimed that the cost involved was more than the 'usual cost' and so refused to meet it. The court upheld the finding of the local authority's complaints procedure review panel which found that the person's 'entrenched position' (in being determined to go to the particular home) was part of his psychological needs. This meant that the wish to go to the home was not a mere preference but a need – which the authority was obliged to meet.

Price Increases

Circular guidance explains that a home's fees and the local authority's usual amount of contribution might change. But they might not change at the same rate. Thus, authorities should tell residents and third parties 'that there cannot be a guarantee that any increases in the accommodation's fees will automatically be shared evenly between the authority and the third party should the particular accommodation's fees rise more quickly than the costs the authority would usually expect to pay for similar people' (LAC(92)27,para 11.8).

Comparison with DSS Supported Residents

There is some concern that discrepancies are arising between residents supported by DSS (ie, those in accommodation before April 1993) and those supported by local authorities. For example, if the local authority sets its contribution level higher than that of the DSS, homes in the area might raise their fees to the higher level (Age Concern 1994,p.8). This leaves DSS-supported residents and their relatives with a shortfall to make up – or possibly face eviction. If local authorities then act to help, people have to move to another home – they cannot receive local authority assistance in the home in which they have been living up to that point (Age Concern England 1993,pp.22–23; Age Concern 1994,p.9).

Means-Test

The local authority has a duty to carry out a means test of people's income and capital. The test is similar to the assessment for income support, though with some differences. One of these is that the person's home should be ignored as capital if it is still occupied by the person's partner or by a relative who is either 60 years old or over or is incapacitated (SI 1992/2977, Schedule 4,para 2; see CRAG, s.7, para 7.003).

For residents who are 'less dependent', local authorities can choose to vary the means-test and disregard more of a person's resources than usual. A person is less dependent if he or she lives in private or voluntary sector accommodation which does not have to be registered under the Registered Homes Act 1984; or lives in local authority accommodation which does not provide board (SI 1992/2977,r.2).

Personal Expenses Allowance (PEA)

The means-test must be calculated to allow a person to retain a personal expenses allowance each week (NAA 1948,s.22). This is currently set at £13.10 per week (SI 1994/826) although local authorities have power to alter the amount: guidance has suggested that the amount could be increased for, for example, residents who are being encouraged to live more independently (LAC(92)19,para 9). It is 'intended to enable residents to have money to spend as they wish, for example, on stationery, personal toiletries, treats and small presents for friends and relatives' (CRAG(3),para 5.001). An item such as 'personal toiletries' should not include basic toiletries, since a home should be providing basic items within the agreed fees. Nevertheless, there is concern that people's PEA can be eroded by 'extras' charged by the home (eg. physiotherapy or incontinence pads provided for people in nursing homes, or private laundry charges). In principle, people could be protected from such extra healthcare costs by local authority contracts with nursing and residential homes (Age Concern 1994,p.7). In practice, such protection would clearly depend on the clarity and detail of contracts and their supervision.

Circular guidance states that in the Department of Health's view, the PEA cannot be used to contribute to fees which are not wholly covered by the local authority's contribution. It states that the

> 'National Assistance Act requires authorities to leave all residents with their PEA. Authorities may not therefore take these amounts into account even for "more expensive accommodation" and they should not enter into agreements which involve the use of PEA' (LAC(94)1, para 13).

In practice there is some concern that homes routinely charge residents a little more than the local authority's contribution: the PEA being used to bridge the gap (Age Concern England 1993,p.19).

Local Authority Responsibilities

Circular guidance states that local authorities are responsible for the full cost of accommodation. This includes the situation where the accommodation is more expensive than usual and a third party makes up the extra cost. Thus the authority 'must contract to pay the accommodation's fees in full'.

This liability remains, even where an agreement has been made (under NAA 1948,s.26(3A)) for the extra costs to be paid direct by the resident to the provider of the accommodation – and where the resident or third party then defaults on payment.

The guidance states also that local authorities 'should assure themselves' that third parties will be able to keep up payments, which should represent the difference between the actual cost of the accommodation and what the authority would normally pay. The calculation should be on gross costs (LAC(92)27, paras 11.1–11.7).

Recovery of Money Owing and 'Deprivation of Assets'

If a resident fails to pay, then under HASSASSA 1983,s.21 a local authority can recover from any third party 'any assets which have been transferred by the resident, at less than their value, to a third party whilst the resident is in the residential accommodation, or within the previous six months, with the intention of avoiding or reducing the charge for accommodation' (LAC(92)19, para 21).

The local authority can also place a charge on any land in which the resident has a beneficial interest (HASSASSA 1983,s.22); and if the resident dies owing money, the authority can 'charge interest at a reasonable rate on the outstanding amount which is owed to the authority and charged on the property until the debt is paid' (HASSASSA 1983,s.24) (details explained in: LAC(92)19).

Temporary to Permanent Residential Status

The local ombudsman has investigated a case where the local authority belatedly informed the husband of an elderly resident of a local authority home that her status had changed from temporary to permanent resident. This change meant that the authority would take into account the value of the person's own home when calculating her contribution to the residential home fees. The authority took out a claim against the estate of the resident, who had subsequently died.

The ombudsman found maladministration, pointing out that had the son been informed earlier, he would have acted to sell his mother's house earlier, and so avoided a loss of interest on the money which would have been obtained. The ombudsman suggested that the local authority 'should also issue clear guidelines to staff about the criteria for deciding when such changes in status occur and how clients and/or their relatives should be informed of any such changes. They should also consider preparing information sheets about this and the charging procedure generally which can be given to clients and relatives before such charges first become due' (CLAE 91/C/0774,p.10).

Short-Term Breaks (Respite Care) in Residential Homes

Short breaks (up to eight weeks) in hospital, residential or nursing homes, are known as respite care. Such care is often to give carers a rest, and can be charged for by social services.

If the normal full rate is charged, this can be a very considerable burden on families. However, the local authority has a discretion not to apply the normal statutory means-test but to charge less (NAA 1948,s.22(5A)). As a result, it seems that some authorities do not conduct a means test and instead charge a much lower flat weekly rate (Balloch 1993,p.6). The result can be enormous variation: for example, an Age Concern Scotland survey of Scottish local authorities found charges ranging from £43.45 to £322.00 per week (Thomas 1994,p.18).

SOCIAL SERVICES CHARGES: NON-RESIDENTIAL SERVICES

Social services departments have powers, but not duties, to make charges for non-residential care services. That is, legally, they can charge if they want but they don't have to. Community care guidance encourages local authorities to charge, and this is what local authorities appear to be doing increasingly. Policy guidance makes clear that assessment itself cannot be charged for. Guidance states also that financial assessment should take place separately from assessment of need. A charge can only be made if it is 'reasonably practicable' for the person to pay.

The legal principle of fairness (see Chapter 7) might apply particularly to the imposition of charges. The local ombudsman has explored in detail some of the requirements of fairness including appeal procedures; and the courts too might display a greater than average sympathy for users in this area of community care.

EXTRACTS

Legislation states that local authorities 'may recover such charge (if any) for it as they consider reasonable' (HASSASSA 1983,s.17). The legislation goes on to state that if a person:

(means test and reasonable ability to pay) 'satisfies the authority providing the service that his means are insufficient for it to be reasonably practicable for him to pay for the service the amount which he would otherwise be obliged to pay for it, the authority shall not require him to pay more for it than it appears to them that it is reasonably practicable for him to pay.'

(recovery of charges) 'Any charge under this section may, without prejudice to any other method of recovery, be recovered as a civil debt.'

The community care White Paper states:

'If a user represents that they cannot afford to pay the charge the local authority are statutorily required to reduce the charge to such amount (if any) as appears reasonable to them. The Government proposes to preserve these arrangements, which will apply equally to services provided through other agencies. This provision permits charging for home help, home care, meals provision and day care services' (Secretaries of State 1989,p.29).

Policy guidance states:

(encouragement to charge) 'It is expected that local authorities will institute arrangements so that users of services of all types pay what they can reasonably afford towards their costs' (DH 1990, p.29).

Circular guidance states:

(encouragement to make charges) 'The Government's view, confirmed in the Community Care White Paper "Caring for People" of 1989 and in the subsequent policy guidance, has consistently been that users who can pay for such services should be expected to do so taking account of their ability to pay. The White Paper and Policy Guidance also make it clear that ability to pay should not influence decisions on the services to be provided, and the assessment of financial means should therefore follow the care assessment.'

(accountability to local and national taxpayers) 'Authorities are locally accountable for making sensible and constructive use of the discretionary powers they have, in order to prevent avoidable burdens falling on council and national taxpayers. Authorities are reminded that the standard spending assessment formula for domiciliary care for elderly people does not take account of the level of income from charges actually received by each authority. This means that any authority which recovers less revenue than its discretionary powers allow is placing an extra burden on the local population or is foregoing resources which could be used to the benefit of the service' (LAC(94)1, paras 17–18).

DISCUSSION

Services Covered by the Power to Charge

This power to charge affects services under:

- section 29 of the National Assistance Act 1948 (welfare arrangements for disabled people);
- section 45 of the Health Services and Public Health Act 1968 (welfare of old people);
- Schedule 8 of the NHS Act 1977 (prevention of illness and care and after-care and home help and laundry facilities);
- Schedule 9 (Part 2,para 1) of the HASSASSA 1983 (meals and recreation for old people provided by district councils) (HASSASSA 1983,s.17(2)).

Charges for services under s.2 of the CSDPA (range of services for disabled people) can be made since such services 'are arranged by local authorities in exercise of their functions under s.29 of the 1948 Act' (SSI 1994b,p.1)).

Thus, of the services defined as community care services by s.46 NHSCCA 1990, only services (for after-care) under s.117 of the Mental Health Act 1983 are not covered by this power to make charges (SSI 1994b,p.2).

Discretion to Make Charges

The Circular guidance (see above extract) does not state that authorities *have* to make charges, since the legislation does not place a duty on authorities to do so. However, the guidance possibly carries a veiled threat by referring to the accountability of local authorities to local taxpayers. This is almost certainly referring to the possibility that the law courts might find that authorities have a 'fiduciary duty' to taxpayers – much as the courts found, 13 years ago, that the GLC had such a duty when planning its transport policy. A fiduciary duty is basically a duty of faith to use people's money wisely.

Equally, however, such a duty in this context is not the same as a duty to maximise income; it is not a general revenue-raising provision (see Cooper 1992 commenting on *R v Manchester City Council, ex p. Donald King 1991*, a case about street-trading licences).

Basis for Means Test: Full Cost of Providing Service

An SSI (1994b,p.3) 'advice note' states that local authorities have discretion to decide what a 'reasonable' charge is. However, it is 'the Government's view, in setting charges (whether flat rate or on a scale) authorities should take account both of the full cost of providing the service and within that of what recipients can reasonably be expected to pay'. It suggests that capital, managerial and other overheads directly connected with provision can be taken into account, but not costs associated with the purchasing function or operation of the charges scheme.

The legislation (see above) refers to what it is 'reasonably practicable' for a person to pay. As a study by the Association of Metropolitan Authorities points out, it is precisely in 'deciding what charges are "reasonable" that the unresolved political problem rests' (Balloch 1994,p.25).

Flexibility of Charging Bands

The SSI (1994b,p.3) advice note states that initially 'authorities should perhaps consider the likely range of financial circumstances and ability to pay of the generality of users of the service as a group, although they will always have to be able to allow for exceptions to be made in individual circumstances'.

Timing of Financial Assessment

Policy guidance states: 'But the provision of services, whether or not the local authority is under a statutory duty to make provision, should not be related to the ability of the user or their families to meet the costs, and delegated budgeting systems should take this into account. The assessment of financial means should, therefore, follow the assessment of need and decisions about service provision' (DH 1990,para 3.31).

The SSI advice note states that information about charges should be given to people 'at the same time that they are given written information about the care assessment process and the available services'. This is so that people will not commit themselves to particular care plans without knowing what they might have to pay (SSI 1994b,p.9)

Nevertheless, concern exists that some local authority assessment forms are designed to combine care need and financial assessment, so that the duty to assess could in effect become also 'a power to ration services at the point of assessment according to the means of the person' (Age Concern England evidence to: Health Service Committee 1993,vol.2,p.142). Equally, a drawback of separating the two types of assessment is that people's expectations can be raised unrealistically.

There is also concern that where financial assessment is prolonged after service provision has commenced, actual charges calculated subsequently might exceed the estimated figures – particularly for non-residential services. There is related concern about the general quality of the financial advice and the possible need therefore for local authorities to utilise specialist financial assessors (SSI/NHSME 1994a,p.26).

At the other extreme it has been reported (Age Concern 1993,p.18) that some authorities are simply refusing to assess people or arrange accommodation for them where they have a property but insufficient income to pay for care.

Assessment of Family Carers or Spouses

SSI advice states that local authorities are legally empowered to charge only service users and should therefore be assessing only those people's ability to pay. This means that family members should not be required to pay charges unless they are managing the resources of service users; nor should family members' own resources be taken into account (SSI 1994b,p.6).

An Age Concern England (1993,p.18) report found that some authorities were financially assessing the means of spouses and telling spouses that they should sell their homes in order to pay for care. For example, a solicitor was quoted:

> 'Families are being given advice as to how they should raise the money for paying for their relative in residential or nursing care. They are being told to seek Bank loans or to take out second mortgages on their house. This of course is contrary to the legislation and indeed is a direct breach of the Financial Services Act.'

Having a Policy on Means-Testing

The local ombudsman has found maladministration where a local authority has failed to have:

- 'a properly recorded policy on financial assistance';
- 'a statement of the criteria for the basis of assessing financial resources and need';
- 'advice and explanation of this together with information on what information must be submitted' for the assessment.

In this particular case, part of the problem arose because the local authority refused to disregard charitable pledges which the applicants had received for adaptations for their daughter who had cerebral palsy. The applicants claimed that such assessment was inconsistent with the purpose of the pledges designed to bridge the shortfall between the authority's contribution and the actual cost of the works. The ombudsman did not fault the authority for wanting to practice 'prudent' budget management, but for the absence of a policy and criteria for such practice and lack of advice and explanation (CLAE 90/B/1676,p.20).

Services Which Should not be Charged for

Local authorities provide some services for which government has stated that it would not be appropriate to charge. These include social work support, occupational therapy, advice and assessment of client needs (Secretaries of State 1989,p.29). Practice guidance states that local authorities 'cannot charge for care management and assessment' (SSI/SWSG(PG) 1991,p.64); and other SSI (1994b) advice that they 'are not empowered to charge for providing advice about the availability of services or for assessment, including assessments of community care needs' (p.2).

Taking Account of the Extra Costs Associated with Disability

SSI (1994b) advice states that authorities should 'have regard' not only to the income of service users but also to their overall financial circumstances. This means that they should take account in particular of additional expenditure 'incurred because of the user's disabilty or frailty' (p.7).

This reiterates the gist of long-standing Circular guidance on charges made for services under the Chronically Sick and Disabled Persons Act:

'wherever clients of an authority are required to make a payment for a service or facility (or are entitled to claim a rebate from their expenditure) and the authority in exercising its discretion in such matters takes account of the cash resources and requirements of such a person, authorities are invited to take into consideration any claim by a chronically sick and disabled person that he does, by reason of disability, incur abnormal expenditure and to make sure that clients know this and that they will do so. This is not to imply any diminution of the statutory powers of discretion of authorities to determine charges or waive them...' (DHSS 12/70,para 40).

This sort of advice was clearly formulated to discourage authorities from imposing excessive charges. On the other hand the SSI (1994b,p.5) advice note recommends against automatic exemption from charges for people on benefits. This is because there should not be 'automatic exemption' from charges simply because people receive benefits such as income support, attendance allowance, invalidity benefit, housing benefit, severe disablement allowance, disability living allowance, disabilty working allowance or payments from the Social Fund. Instead, authorities should assess the level of any charges in relation to individual financial circumstances.

(In 1983, two unsuccessful CSDP amendment bills in the Houses of Commons (Robert Wareing) and Lords (Earl of Longford) respectively attempted to make mandatory the disregarding of attendance and mobility attendance when assessing for charges – except where the services provided were in connection with attendance or mobility needs).

Charges for Home Help

During the passing (Committee stage) of the NHS and Community Care Bill in the House of Lords, the government resisted the disregarding of attendance allowance in general but did concede that it 'should not be taken into account for home help services' since attendance allowance was not intended for domestic help.

However, the government stated that if the 'home help' included personal care, then attendance allowance could be taken into account quite appropriately (H74 1990). This statement followed discussion of an old 1971 Circular (DHSS 53/71) which had stated explicitly that local authorities should disregard attendance allowance when assessing charges for home help. However, there is evidence that in practice now ordinary home help services are decreasing and instead personal care is being provided (eg. Age Concern Scotland 1994,p.21) – for which attendance allowance or the care component of disability living allowance *can* be taken into account by the local authority.

Current anxieties over local authorities' methods of means testing have been reported by the House of Commons Health Committee (1993,vol.1,p.xxiii). For example, some local authorities have apparently not been disregarding benefits such as attendance allowance or disability living allowance which are not 'income-maintenance benefits'. One case cited to the Committee (from Community Care journal) involved a woman 'being charged £20.00 per month for a home-help who provided two hours service, a sum she was expected to pay from her Attendance Allowance. However she used her Attendance Allowance to pay for an orthopaedic bed and chair, a bed-settee for nights when she cannot get up the stairs to bed and a motorised scooter to get to the nearest village' (vol.2,p.156).

The AMA (Balloch 1993) surveyed charges for 'cleaning and domestic services' and found the following pattern. First, people ineligible for disability living allowance (DLA) or attendance allowance (AA) would pay a flat rate charge. Anybody on income support or disability working allowance would pay a lower rate or nothing; those with savings of over £8000 would pay a higher rate. Second, those eligible for DLA or AA would be charged a proportion (eg. 50%) of their benefits. Third, charges for existing users would be introduced incrementally – new users would pay the assessed charge straightaway. Fourth, because users receiving income support or housing benefit might be exempted from charges, only 20–30% of people assessed for home care services actually pay anything (pp.4–5).

People who Refuse to Pay

There is nothing in legislation to suggest that authorities can withdraw, or refuse to provide, services solely on the grounds that a person will not pay for services. It might be unlawful to do so. Instead, the legislation empowers authorities to recover charges as a civil debt.

Introduction of Charging Systems

The introduction of charging systems can be a complicated process. This has been explored by the local ombudsman. For example, in one investigation (discontinued because the authority took steps to remedy inadequacies), the ombudsman covered the following points:

(1) payment procedures were revised so that people did not have to pay postage charges in making their payments (instead they could pay via Girobank at post offices, and they were sent pre-paid envelopes)

(2) not all people had been informed that the authority had the discretion to reduce or waive charges;

(3) no appeals procedure had been provided;

(4) the authority confirmed its commitment to leaflets, forms and letters about charges needed to be available in different languages;

(5) the authority stated it did not 'withdraw the service from any client as a result of the charging policy, or of a client's refusal to pay'

(6) the authority went to some lengths (including checking of records, advertisements in the local press) to identify people who might have suffered from the way in which charging was introduced – and to invite them to have a reassessment (CLAE 91/A/3782).

Features of An Appeals System

In another case, also concerning home help, the local ombudsman investigated and reported in detail on a system of appeals against charges which had been imposed on everybody (including those getting Income Support) receiving home help. The report concluded that the arrangements made fell short of the basic standards of an appeals system.

(The high standards which the ombudsman seems to require for an appeals procedure might be administratively impossible to achieve within reasonable time and expense. This is because an adequate level of fairness and personal attention for hundreds or perhaps thousands of people would be unattainable. For example, in this case, the appeal board sometimes considered 200 or more appeals in one sitting – and consequently did not give reasons in individual cases.)

The ombudsman summarised the features of a good appeals system. It should be:

(1) based on 'clearly thought out and relevant criteria';

(2) accurate and sufficient information should be available to those adjudicating in an appeal so that they can reach a proper decision in line with the criteria;

(3) people appealing should be aware of any rights to challenge the outcome of the appeal;

(4) clear reasons should be given for the outcome of the appeal so that an appellant can judge whether to persist (CLAE 90/A/2675,pp.31–32).

The ombudsman went on to explain particular shortcomings:

- *reasonably practicable payment*: the failure to give careful thought as to how much someone on Income Support 'could reasonably be expected to pay' seemed to be a failure to follow section 17 HASSASSA: namely finding out what charge is reasonably practicable for the person to pay;

- *arbitrary financial threshold*: the threshold (of £10 expenses greater than income), which determined the success or failure of appeals against the charges, was found to be 'quite arbitrary'. The council was unable to justify the figure and the ombudsman had 'no confidence' that this criterion had been 'well thought out';

- *use of irrelevant criteria:* in addition to financial assessments, 'social reports' (about degree of risk consequent upon withdrawal of service) were considered by the appeals committee when considering possible reduction of the charges. The ombudsman found that there were apparently no written criteria used: rather decisions were left to the discretion of members of the committee. The ombudsman found that 'the "at risk" criteria introduced a consideration of need which does not seem to me to have been relevant to the task hand. The clients who had appealed against the charges had all been assessed as needing the service under the terms of the 1977 Act. It was quite inappropriate for the Appeals Group to consider the question of need when deciding on ability to meet the charge, because it introduced factors which had nothing to do with a client's ability to pay' (p.33);
- *variable quality of information on which appeals were decided:* the information available to the committee in the 'social reports' was of variable quality, could be incomplete and inaccurate. This meant there was a risk of some people having an unfair advantage in the appeals proceedings (pp.33–34);
- *lack of information about re-appealing:* people were not informed that they could re-appeal (p.34);
- *inconsistent appeal outcomes:* the appeals seemed to be determined inconsistently. The earlier sets of appeals resulted in a greater proportion of charges being waived or reduced than did later appeals. There seemed no reason for this, other than that at the earlier stage there were fewer appeals being considered (p.34);
- *no reasons for decisions:* the appeals committee gave no reasons for its decisions: 'Had Members used clear and objective criteria which were more closely related to clients' ability to pay, as referred to in the 1983 Act, it would have been much easier to provide a client with a clear reason for the decision, which the client could have challenged if this appeared to be based on accurate information' (p.35).

Local Patterns of Charging

Local authorities have been encouraged to charge for services and there is evidence that this is now happening, and at higher rates (see eg. Thomas 1994,p.22; Balloch 1993; AMA,LGIU 1992; AMA,LGIU 1991; Age Concern 1992).

Evidence to the Health Committee (1993) has highlighted 'disparity in charging policies between local authorities' and also the possible ulterior purposes of setting charges. For example, payments for home care might range between the full economic cost of the service (eg. £27.00 for three hours), a token payment and no payment at all. Concern was also expressed that charges for services are sometimes used as rationing devices (vol.1,p.xxiii).

Different services might be subject to different charging patterns. For example, the AMA (1993) survey found, for cleaning and domestic services, a move away from no charging and flat rate charges to means testing. On the other hand, meals on wheels were generally charged at a flat rate, sometimes with different price bands for frozen and freshly cooked food.

Day care services appeared not to be charged for, but in fact the costs were sometimes hidden in the cost of the meal at the day centre. Some authorities waive the charges for some people (eg. people with learning disabilities), but raise them for others (eg. people from a different authority or people with physical disabilities). Transport appears not to be widely charged for.

Some authorities are beginning to charge not for specific services but for packages of care. One authority doing so included day centre charges so as to remove the inequity of people at home paying for services but those at a day centres not doing so (Balloch 1993,pp.7–10).

Effect of More Widespread Charging Practices

There is some concern about the effect of increased prevalence and level of charges. For example, The Alzheimer's Disease Society has adverted to the practice of

> 'charging for home care which goes against the preventative nature of community care by discouraging users in the early stages where a small amount of home help, cleaning help, shopping help, would enable them to go on staying at home. Those pensioners on low incomes faced with a home care of £6 an hour will just say: "I can't afford that, that is such a chunk out of my pension I'll do without it", and the likelihood is they will need health care sooner rather than later if that is the case' (vol.2,p.178).

An Age Concern Greater London (Collyer 1992) report, based on older people's own views, found that general home help services were being reduced 'in favour of intensive personal care support for a relatively small number of highly dependent older people, in order to delay or prevent the need for residential or nursing home care'. This meant that many other people were being deprived of, or were receiving inadequate, home help. The introduction of charges for this home help meant that 'older people on limited income who cannot afford these charges are forced to give up the service or use it less frequently' (pp.ii–iii).

An example quoted by another Age Concern (1993,p.16) report involved a rise of over 200% for assistance with the daily needs of an 82-year-old disabled and housebound woman: from £9.50 per week to £28.45 (later reduced on appeal).

Reimbursement by Local Authority of Money Paid

Normally it might be assumed that a local authority will not reimburse money which a person has spent on a service or facilities on their own account. There might be exceptions. For example, the local ombudsman investigated a case where an applicant had installed a downstairs WC for his disabled wife and then requested reimbursement from social services. Conflicting reasons were given by social services staff and Members about why reimbursement could not be made. These were that it was against policy to make retrospective payments; or that reimbursement was possible if the work was the same as the Council would have recommended. In the event the adaptation was not what the Council would have recommended. Nevertheless, the ombudsman recommended that the applicant be reimbursed because of unreasonable delay by the Council in giving advice about the adaptation (CLAE 88/C/0814,pp.15–16).

FAIRNESS AND CHARGING BY SOCIAL SERVICES DEPARTMENTS

The legal concept of fairness is explained elsewhere in this book (Chapter 7). It is possible that charging might attract more than the average amount of sympathy from judges and that the standard of fairness required of authorities might be relatively high. The local ombudsman has already suggested high standards in this area (see above) – and it is possible that the courts might refer to such standards at least as a guide.

Some aspects of fairness are covered in the SSI (1994b) advice note on charges. For example, the need to give people information about charges generally and about how to complain about charging decisions. People should also usually be given an indication in writing about what charges they will have to pay. It is suggested also that when changes to the charging system are being considered, existing users should be consulted.

Concern has been reported that inappropriate or incorrect advice is sometimes given by local authority staff to service users – sometimes over major matters such as the selling of people's homes (Age Concern 1994a,p.25). Such inappropriate advice could be regarded in a serious light by the local ombudsman or even by the courts.

HEALTH CARE OR SOCIAL CARE: IMPLICATIONS FOR CHARGES

There is some concern about services which lie on the 'boundary' between health and social care. It seems that some 'health' services are being re-defined as 'social' care. Previously provided free by the health service, they might now be charged for if provided through social services (eg. respite care, baths or long-term continuing care).

Examples of Transition of Health Care into Social Care

Blurred boundaries between health and social care have been covered in other sections of this book: for example, the boundary between continuing NHS care (free of charge) and private nursing home care (means-tested); and the 'grey area' of a range of home care services including, for example, washing, dressing, equipment, laundry and so on.

Because health services are generally free of charge, there are significant financial implications for service providers and users, depending on how services are defined. For example, respite care previously provided free by the health service, might now have to be payed for by users and their relatives if provided in residential or nursing homes. This can impose a severe financial burden on users and their families. They have to seek care elsewhere, either paying privately or through social services on a means-tested basis (Alzheimer's Disease Society 1993,p.9; see also SSI/NHSME 1994,p.27).

From another point of view, health authorities might perceive an imbalance insofar as they cannot charge for services but social services can. This might 'impose an additional and unscheduled burden on the health authority' (RCN; Spastics Society 1992,para 8.1) and provide an incentive for health authorities not to provide some services.

The Health Committee (1993) reported concerns that due to the community care changes, a number of health services provided hitherto free of charge are in fact being redefined as 'social care' services for which charges may be made. There is a view that 'a fundamental right of the individual to free health care from the NHS is being eroded with little public awareness of the implications of the new policies' (Age Concern evidence, vol.2,p.144). For example, if a person who has had a stroke is cared for at home by services purchased by a GP, then those services will be free. If provided by social services, the person could be liable to contributions (vol.2,p.74).

Another specific example is when a service such as bathing, delivered free by a nurse, is re-defined as social care. There might be 'substitution of an inexperienced home carer for a nurse to bathe her mother, who had frequently collapsed and needed medication during the bathing process. The older woman was charged at the £5.88 hourly rate for a 20-minute bath, which had formerly been provided free by the National Health Service'. Such redefinitions can result in people being unable to pay and services consequently being withdrawn (Age Concern and Carers' National Association evidence: vol.2,pp.143, 156).

Apart from the inequity which can arise when one person is charged and another is not for a similar service, a legal complexity which arises is the charging for services which are arranged jointly by social services and health authorities (Balloch 1994,p.25); since the latter cannot legally make such charges.

Distinction Between Hospital and Nursing Home Care

On the other hand, there are limits to such re-definitions of health care as social care. For example, in August 1993, the Court of Appeal (*White and Others v Chief Adjudication Officer and Another 1993*) made a ruling affecting the funding of people leaving longstay hospitals. A health authority had contracted with a dual registered (nursing/residential) home for the home to accommodate former long-stay hospital patients. The assumption was that the former patients, now residents, could claim income support which would be paid to the nursing home in addition to the health authority's contribution.

However, the Court of Appeal ruled that the home fell under the definition of 'hospital or similar institution' (NHS Act 1977,s.128). This meant that the residents were ineligible for income support. Even if nursing was not the dominant purpose of the home, it could still be defined as a hospital or similar institution, since it had agreed to maintain nurses amongst its permanent and resident staff. If the nursing requirement had been minimal then the home might not have been a hospital.

The point this case seems to illustrate is that either people are NHS patients or they are not (in this context). If they are, then the health authority has to pay all their residential costs; if they are not, then the authority does not have the power to pay any part of their residential costs.

The Department of Health issued advice in 1990 to health authorities and NHS Trusts (EL(90)MB/45). The advice is still valid. This is to the effect that if patients are being discharged to homes where they can claim higher rates of income support, then authorities can only make contractual payments to such homes under the Health Service and Public Health Act 1968 (s.64) and the NHS Act 1977 (s.28A). These sections limit such payments to voluntary organisations. Alternatively, if payments are made under s.23 of the 1977 Act, then the residents are deemed to be patients, cannot be charged and cannot claim the higher rates of income support.

HEALTH SERVICE CHARGES

Health services, unless otherwise specified, are by default free of charge.

Legislation does specify certain charges, for example, for equipment and drugs prescribed by general practitioners; dental services and appliances; spectacles and contact lenses; certain items such as wigs, abdominal or spinal supports and surgical brassieres. There are distinctions to be made depending on the status of a patient: for example, inpatient, outpatient, private patient. There are also exemptions from, or reductions in, payment depending on factors such as the age, condition and financial status of patients. Nevertheless, despite this relatively clear position, misunderstandings and illegal charges do sometimes occur. Confusion periodically breaks out about this, whether amongst MPs in Parliament, health authority managers and staff, or service users and their advisers.

Although health authorities do not have the wide powers to charge that social services do, health authorities do apparently – and ironically – have a wide discretion not to provide services at all. For example, though a health authority cannot charge for incontinence pads, it can choose not to supply, or at least to ration, them: for example, in the case of people who are 'in need' but are not defined as a priority.

EXTRACTS

Legislation states that health services:

'shall be free of charge except so far as the making and recovery of charges is expressly provided for by or under any enactment, whenever passed' (NHS Act s.1(2)).

Circular guidance issued in 1991, stated:

'Section 1 of the NHS Act 1977 requires that NHS services provided under the Act to NHS patients must be free of charge, except where the making and recovery of charges is expressly provided for by legislation. Later legislation, including the NHS and Community Care Act 1990, does not alter this position. Nor does it enable partial charges to be made to health service patients... Health service managers should ensure that the statutory requirements are observed at all times. Before any charges are made the legality of the position must be established' (EL(91)129).

Circular guidance states that:

'services and equipment must not be charged for except where the legislation expressly indicates that a charge should be made. In all other cases, where an authority (taking account of resources, needs and clinical priorities locally) decides that a piece of equipment should be provided as part of NHS treatment, it should be provided free of charge. This applies whether the equipment is supplied on a permanent basis or on loan. It is also the responsibility of the health authority to check and maintain NHS equipment where necessary, and this should also be free' (EL(92)20).

DISCUSSION

Health Services Free by Default

Health services are free by default: ie, unless otherwise specified. Legislation does provide for the making of regulations to charge for drugs and appliances (NHS Act 1977,s.77) and for non-UK residents (NHS Act 1977,s.121). But otherwise, the health service has no broad discretion, in contrast to social services, to make charges for a wide range of services.

Illegal Charges

The law about NHS charges might seem to be clear, but in practice confusion sometimes affects managers, staff and patients alike.

In 1992, it was reported that one NHS Trust had been charging people a £10 fee towards the provision of surgical footwear. This was illegal, and it seemed clear from the report that the Trust's financial controller had simply been unaware of the law; and that up to 500 people and £10,000 might have been involved (*Therapy Weekly* 1992).

Specifically, a Health Service Commissioner investigation found that a health authority had tried to make ultra vires (illegal) charges for chiropody appliances (orthoses) supplied to a 13-year-old girl. The attempted justification by the health authority of local financial constraints was not valid, since such constraints could not permit either a health authority or NHS Trust to breach their statutory duties. Furthermore, Circular guidance (HC(89)24) had made clear that services, new or existing, should be planned within resources. Thus, the health authority could at its discretion decide to continue or discontinue altogether the bio-mechanics service; what they could not do was make ultra vires charges for it. There were possibly 20 patients involved in such charging: the health authority was urged to investigate all 20 (HSC/W.226/91–92).

Clinical and Non-Clinical Need

All health service provision is based on clinical need. If a person is not assessed as having a clinical need, there is no duty to make provision. Conversely, however, clinical need does not necessarily mean that provision will be made. Sometimes, the application of priorities by a health authority means that a person, though 'in need', is deemed to be 'low priority' and could be denied a service.

Items Which Can Be Charged For

Items which can be charged for include:

- GP-prescribed drugs and appliances as well as some other items prescribed at a hospital: surgical/abdominal supports, wigs and surgical brassieres (SI 1989/419 as amended, made under the NHS Act 1977);
- spectacles, contact lenses (SI 1989/396 as amended, made under the NHS Act 1977);
- dental appliances (SI 1989/394 as amended, made under the NHS Act 1977).

Exemptions from Charges

Depending on factors such as age, disability, illness or financial status, people might be exempt from some or all payment for the above-mentioned equipment which can be charged for under the NHS Act 1977 (SI 1989/419; SI 1989/396; SI 1989/394; SI 1988/SSI – all as amended).

Repair/Replacement Charges

If there is a defect in an appliance 'as supplied', then NHS patients cannot be charged for replacement or repair (NHS Act 1977, schedule 12, para 1). If, however, the need for repair or replacement is due to an act or omission of the patient, then a charge can be made (NHS Act 1977,s.82).

Health Service Power to Charge Where There Is No Clinical Need?

In the past, some health authorities seem to have assumed that where there is no clinical need, charges might be made in some cases even though not expressly authorised by legislation.

Some years ago, for example, the health service ombudsman found that a hospital occupational therapy department was justified in charging for a pick-up stick. The person's social services department, whose responsibility it really was, would eventually have provided one free, but the patient didn't want to wait; so the hospital OT charged a small amount (HSC W.340/80–81).

In similar circumstances, it seems that many hospital therapy departments have in the past provided non-clinically needed equipment on a not-for-profit basis. The advice given by the Department of Health is that such activities are probably not legal. Ways around the problem might be for a hospital shop to stock the equipment which the therapist recommends. In this way money is not actually passing into hospital therapy departments. Department of Health correspondence stated: 'We see no objection to the purchase of equipment being regarded as an option for some people. This could be through retail outlets or voluntary organisations and there would be clear advantages if some of these could be located on NHS premises. The only objection is to the NHS selling equipment' (DH 1992a).

This advice was given in the sensitive aftermath of Parliamentary debate about charges in the NHS for items such as nebulisers. As a result hospital occupational therapy departments have had to reconsider their practices, although enforcement of the law might not benefit people in the particular context of therapy departments. This is because, for example, patients might have to, or prefer to, buy items in hospital for a number of reasons including their failure anyway to meet social services criteria; desire for new equipment rather than secondhand equipment (eg. raised toilet seats); or better quality equipment (eg. padded rather than a hard bathboard) (North West Thames Regional Occupational Advisory Group 1993).

In fact it is arguable that under s.7 of the Health and Medicines Act 1988 (about income generation), hospital occupational therapy departments actually do have the power to sell equipment. This would be on the condition that the equipment is being sold not to meet clinical needs, but to meet 'social' needs. Some support for this point of view might be gathered from Department of Health guidance on income generation. It explains how free hospital transport must be given to people with 'medical' needs – but not necessarily to people with 'social' needs only. For example, 'patients who, in the opinion of a clinician, do not have a medical need for transport but who have no suitable public transport and no recourse to private transport of their own or assistance from a relative or friend (ie the need is a 'social' rather than a medical one) may under s.7 be charged for provision of transport' (DH 1989a,para 45).

The Department of Health's advice (above) to refer people instead to retail outlets or a charity shop on hospital premises seems a sensible solution. However, such a solution carries with it also the danger of abuse. For example, in principle what is to stop a health authority defining 'need' or priority so high, or providing such unattractive (and cheaper) items, for example, ortho-paedic footwear – that users no longer qualify or wish for NHS provision and are then referred to a shop on the hospital premises (see eg. Tomkin 1991)?

Non-Provision of Services: Asking People to Buy Their Own Services or Equipment

The health service does not have the power to charge for services or equipment (except those specified by legislation). However, ironically, it does have the power not to provide services or equipment at all either on the grounds that there is no clinical need, or that the person is in need, but it is a low priority need which cannot be met.

A Circular (EL(92)20) issued to health authorities in March 1992 explained:

'Where authorities do not provide equipment, a consultant may advise a patient that such equipment could be used on an optional basis if the patient wishes. In such cases, the health authority has no responsibility for supplying or maintaining the equipment, and the patient should make their own arrangements to obtain it… Any patients who have erroneously been required to pay for equipment which should have been provided free should be appropriately recompensed' (paras 3–4).

There is sometimes confusion, as shown by 1991 exchanges in the House of Commons over NHS charges and in particular the provision of nebulisers (oxygen breathing equipment) and incontinence pads. The Secretary of State for Health made it quite clear that 'NHS patients cannot be charged and will not be charged' (H75 1991). Accusations had been made that some health authorities had been charging patients for equipment. If true, then the health authorities would have been breaking the law. However, if they had simply said to patients that they (the authorities) could not provide the equipment and the patients should buy it themselves, then the authorities would have been acting legally (if following a rational policy and local clinical priorities). There was considerable confusion at the time as to what had in fact occurred in individual instances. (A bill was introduced at the time by Rhodri Morgan to 'clarify the law': the NHS (Supply of Medical Equipment) Bill 1991. It did not progress).

The health service ombudsman has investigated a case where the complain-ant had bought a transcutaneous nerve stimulator (TNS) for the relief of pain and wanted reimbursement from the hospital. The ombudsman accepted the hospital's explanation that normally it could not loan its own stock of TNS machines on a semi-permanent basis because of demand and a finite budget. It seemed however that a long term loan might have been possible from elsewhere. It transpired that the hospital had not explained that there was a loan scheme at all, and the ombudsman found fault with this lack of information provision to the complainant. One of the hospital staff also explained that there was a point at which people 'had to look after themselves', since if they attended the hospital indefinitely, the system would grind to a halt (HSC W.263/83–84).

Another example might be where a terminally ill person in hospital has been assessed to return home for a few weeks in order to die. On the point of discharge, it transpires that the relevant community health unit cannot supply the special mattress required. Discharge is delayed for a week or two – until the family is able to hire the mattress privately at about £60 per week (Personal communication: senior therapist, 1994).

In/Out Patient Status

NHS inpatients receive all services and equipment needed for their treatment free of charge (NHS Act 1977, schedule 12; see HSG(94)12, Annex A, para 15). This is the case, whether they are inpatients on NHS premises or on other premises (though still paid for by the NHS), for example, a nursing home. Circular guidance has stated the importance of ensuring that patients on other premises are not persuaded to pay for extra services they do not need; and that there is 'no disparity between the clinical care and services provided to NHS patients and the hospital or nursing home's own private patients' (HC(81)1,annex,para 6).

Transfer from Private to NHS Treatment

This area of service provision sometimes confuses. Prior to DHSS guidance in 1986, confusion arose over the procedures for such transfer and specifically over whether patients had to go through the usual NHS admission procedures, 'all over again' when transferring from private to NHS treatment (eg. HSC W.194/78–79).

DHSS (1986) guidance confirms that though a person is free to change between private and NHS treatment, there are conditions. Dual status is not possible 'for the treatment of one condition during a single visit to a health service hospital' (para 22). However, a private inpatient could change status if, for example, after admission for a minor condition, 'a different, more serious complaint' is found (para 23). However, if a person does change status, then there must be 'an assessment of the patient's clinical priority for treatment as a NHS patient' so that he or she gains 'no advantage over other NHS patients' (paras 24–25).

Private Treatment Because of Anxiety Over Waiting

The health service ombudsman has explained that sometimes 'patients write to me alleging that they have had to pay for private care out of anxiety after a long time on a NHS waiting list' (HSC 1990,p.8).

One such case (W.533/87–88) occurred where a consultant persuaded a man awaiting an urgent operation to go to a private clinic. In fact the man would have been transferred to the appropriate NHS hospital on the same day had he not moved into private care. The consultant had not found this out, and the man and his family did not know this. The family was reimbursed by the health authority.

Private Patient Charges in NHS Hospitals

Misunderstandings sometimes arise over payment of private patient charges. Guidance states that (under the NHS Act 1977, ss.65–66) patients should give written undertakings to pay the charges prior to treatment. This applies both to private in- and outpatients. They must be warned also that if they stay longer than anticipated, then the charges will be higher than estimated; and that treatment which continues after April 1st in any year might be subject to a higher rate of charges from that date (DHSS 1986, paras 50–54).

Equipment provided as part of the treatment should be covered by the fixed daily charge which has been agreed to: 'supplementary charges must not be made for implants, aids and appliances, even if an appliance has been fitted after discharge, provided they have been prescribed for somebody while he was a private resident patient as part of the treatment for the medical condition for which he was admitted' (DHSS 1986, paras 83–84).

Home Dialysis Patients

Circular guidance since 1974 has established that the health service is responsible for costs of electricity, telephone and heating all needed for the home dialysis (HSC(IS)11). Further guidance has been issued to cover the metering of domestic water supplies: the health service is responsible for the costs of the water used for the dialysis (HSG(93)48).

Oxygen Equipment

For longer term use, oxygen cylinders are prescribed by general practitioners and attract a standard prescription charge. Oxygen concentrators, prescribed for people who need oxygen for long periods of the day, are prescribed in England mainly by general practitioners (and in Scotland by hospital respiratory consultants). There are no prescription charges for oxygen concentrators (see eg. HSG(92)10).

HOUSING AUTHORITY CHARGES: DISABLED FACILITIES GRANTS

This is dealt with in the previous chapter.

HOUSING AUTHORITY CHARGES: WELFARE SERVICES

Housing authorities can make 'reasonable' charges for welfare services provided under s.11A of the Housing Act 1985 and for meals and recreation for old people provided under Schedule 9 of the HASSASSA 1983 (see s.17).

CHAPTER 19

PLANNING FOR COMMUNITY CARE

KEY ISSUES

Planning features prominently in community care legislation and guidance. Perhaps the pivotal element in planning, as outlined by this guidance, is assessment of the local needs of the population. On this assessment rests the ability of authorities to plan, within budget, services for those people who most need them – and to set criteria of eligibility. However, it is this very pivotal element which is so uncertain, because authorities seem generally not to have (at present anyway) high quality information about local needs. On one view, this fact alone could undermine the possibility of a 'rational' and equitable community care system.

Challenges about Consultation

Health and housing authorities could legally challenge social services departments' failure to consult, since legislation states that those authorities must be consulted locally. However, although legislation and Directions state that voluntary organisations and independent sector providers must also be consulted, this legislation does not of course determine locally exactly which organisations the local authority consults.

The general right to consultation, which is part of the legal principle of fairness (see Chapter 7), might apply if an authority has promised a particular organisation that it would consult it – or if in the past it had always consulted that organisation. The organisation would then have a 'legitimate expectation' of being consulted. A right to be consulted might also apply if an organisation was of such stature and significance locally, that it would be totally unreasonable (see Chapter 7) for an authority not to consult with the organisation.

Although the Department of Health has issued guidance about the nature of consultation, the courts sometimes impose their own standards about what consultation should consist of – and could do this in the context of consultation about community care plans.

Challenges to An Authority's Published Plan

Legislation does not state what a community care plan should contain and it is probably unlikely that a person's expectations (based on guidance rather than legislation) about a local plan would be recognised by the courts. The person might be able to complain through the local authority complaints procedure and it is possible that the local ombudsman might find maladministration if the authority failed to provide information in a reasonable range of other languages and media. However, the courts are unlikely to uphold such claims, having stated that 'where an English statute says information is to be provided, that information need only be provided in English' (*R v Governors of Small Heath School, ex p. Birmingham City Council 1989; R v Birmingham City Council, ex p. Kaur 1990*). A complaint by a voluntary organisation that the people it represented were being inadequately provided for because they were not mentioned in the local plan might be received unsympathetically by the courts since, they might say, lack of information does not necessarily mean absence of provision of services.

PREPARATION, PUBLICATION AND CONTENT OF COMMUNITY CARE PLANS

Local authorities have a duty to prepare and publish community care plans. They must publish either modifications or new plans at least every year. Legislation does not specify what information these plans must contain, but policy guidance states what they 'should' contain. The guidance lists a number of headings including assessment (including assessment of the needs of the local population), services, consumer choice, quality, resources, consultation, publishing information.

EXTRACTS
Legislation states:

'Each local authority…shall…prepare and publish a plan for the provision of community care services in their area;…shall keep the plan prepared by them…and any further plans prepared by them under this section under review; and…shall, at such intervals as the Secretary of State may direct, prepare and publish modifications to the current plan, or if the case requires, a new plan' (NHSCCA 1990,s.46(1)).

Directions state that local authorities:

'shall…prepare and publish modifications to the current plan, or if the case requires, a new plan at intervals of not more than one year' (Community Care Plans Directions 1991; attached to LAC(91)6).

Community care policy guidance states: 'In their plans SSDs should identify:

(assessment)

- the care needs of the local population taking into account factors such as age distribution, problems associated with living in inner city areas or rural areas, special needs of ethnic minority communities, the number of homeless or transient people likely to require care;
- how the care needs of individuals approaching them for assistance will be assessed;
- how service needs identified following the introduction of systematic assessment will be incorporated into the planning process.

(services)

- the client groups for whom they intend to arrange services...;
- how priorities for arranging services are determined;
- how they intend to offer practical help, such as respite care, to carers;
- how they intend to develop domiciliary services.

(quality)

- the steps they are taking to ensure quality in providing and purchasing services...;
- how they intend to monitor the quality of services they have purchased or provided;
- the setting-up and role of inspection units...;
- the setting-up and role complaints procedures...'

(consumer choice)

- how they intend to increase consumer choice;
- how they intend to stimulate the development of a mixed economy of care.

(resources)

- the resource implications, both financial and human of planned future developments;
- how they intend to improve the cost effectiveness of services;
- their personnel and training strategy for meeting both short and longer term developments.

(consultation)

- how they intend to consult on plans with DHAs, FHSAs, housing authorities, voluntary organisations representing service users, voluntary organisations representing carers, voluntary housing agencies and other bodies providing or community care services (as required by s.46(2) of the Act).

(publishing information)

- what arrangements they intend to make to inform service users and their carers about services...;

- how and when they intend to publish CCPs in the following year' (DH 1990 para 2.25).

DISCUSSION
Content of Plans in Practice
The list is considerable. Some items are probably easier to specify than others. For example, details of future resourcing for community care might be difficult to spell out if there is uncertainty about the level of central funding (Hardy 1993,p.47).

The informativeness of plans can vary. For example, in listing services, a well-structured plan might include a range of services for misusers of alcohol and drugs as well as plans for new services. On the other hand, many plans might not list services for these people at all or do so only vaguely, using words such as 'prevention', 'rehabilitation', 'support' with no further detail (O'Brien,Wurr 1993,pp.1,25).

(It has been pointed out that independent living for disabled people depends on many circumstances outside of 'community care services', such as appropriate housing, personal safety and accessible transport and buildings. Planning should take account of these (Bewley,Glendinning 1994,p.36). This suggestion broaches the 'social model' of disability and the desirability of community care plans' including broader issues.)

PUBLISHING INFORMATION ABOUT ARRANGEMENTS FOR PROVISION OF NON-RESIDENTIAL CARE SERVICES BY THE INDEPENDENT SECTOR

Local authorities have a duty, under a Direction, to publish details about their proposals for purchasing non-residential services from independent sector providers.

Directions (delegated legislation) state:
'Each local authority shall include in the plan which they prepare and publish for the provision of community care services in their area details of such proposals as they may have for making arrangements to purchase non-residential services from independent sector providers of such services as part of the local authority's overall provision for community care services in their area.'

Independent sector providers are defined to exclude employees of local authorities and organisations owned, controlled or managed by one or more local authorities. Non-residential services exclude:
- residential accommodation provided under the National Assistance Act 1948 (s.21 and 26);
- hostel arrangements (National Assistance Act 1948, s.29);
- holiday arrangements (under CSDPA 1970,s.2 and s.21/schedule 8 of the NHS Act 1977);
- after-care accommodation arrangements (Mental Health Act 1983,s.117)

(Community Care Plans (Independent) Sector Non-Residential Care Direction 1994: with LAC(94)12; made under the LASSA 1970,s.7A).

PUBLISHING INFORMATION ABOUT THE FORM OF CONSULTATION

Local authorities have a duty under a Direction to publish in their community plans details about *how* they propose to consult. Circular guidance goes on to state that the aim is to make consultation open and effective, and that it is helpful to clarify consultation method and timetable at an early stage.

EXTRACTS

Directions (delegated legislation) state:

'Each local authority shall include in the plan which they prepare and publish for the provision of community care services in their area pursuant to section of the National Health Service and Community Care Act 1990...details of how they propose to consult those specified in...s.46(2) of the 1990 Act, and...article 2 of these directions' (Community Care Consultation Directions 1993, made under the LASSA 1970,s.7A and the NHSCCA 1990, s.46(2)(f); attached to LAC(93)4).

Circular guidance (LAC(93)4) states that:

(statement of intention) 'authorities must state in the community care plan how they intend to consult in the next round of planning all those they are required to consult under s.46 of the NHSCC Act 1990 and under the first Direction' (para 16).

(openness and effectiveness of consultation) 'This is a separate and different requirement from that to consult representatives of independent sector providers. The aim is to make the consultation process more open and effective by ensuring that all those involved are aware of what the process will be...' (para 17).

(early and advance discussion) 'Statements in plans should be concerned mainly with authorities' intentions and the processes which authorities will adopt. It is good practice to make clear at an early stage to those who will be consulted the timetable and method of consultation. There is also considerable advantage in discussing the method of consultation in advance with relevant representatives. Many authorities already have effective consultation processes with many of the groups covered by the Act. But some will need to make improvements in the light of experience. The Direction is intended to ensure that good practice becomes standard policy and that in every case the consultation process is as open and effective as possible' (para 19).

Practice. A survey (Hardy 1993,p.4) of community care plans found that whilst some authorities were publishing details of the form of consultation, others were apparently failing to comply with the Direction.

PLANNING FOR PARTICULAR GROUPS OF PEOPLE

Legislation is silent about which specific groups of people should be covered by community care plans. Policy guidance, though declaring a non-prescriptive approach, nevertheless names some groups of people to whose needs 'balanced consideration' should be given. It then names some other groups of people, for whom services 'should' be included in plans.

EXTRACTS

Legislation is silent about which groups of people should be specifically covered by community care plans.

Policy guidance states that the Department of Health

'does not wish to be prescriptive about how these are categorised but groupings should show evidence of a balanced consideration of the needs of such groups as dependent elderly people, those with disabilities whether of a learning, physical or sensory nature and those whose needs for social care may be intermittent such as those affected by HIV/AIDS or women suffering domestic violence. Plans should include services for people with multiple and low incidence disabilities and will be required to include services for mentally ill people (including those with dementia), and those who misuse drugs and/or alcohol' (DH 1990, para 2.25).

Circular guidance (LAC(92)15) on social care for people with learning disabilities provides detailed 'guidance' which local authorities 'should take account of…when preparing their community care plans…'.

DISCUSSION

Planning for Services for Specific Groups of People

Concern has been expressed that certain groups of people are at risk of being treated, inappropriately, as low priority. For example, during the Committee stage of the NHS and Community Care Bill in the House of Lords, eventually unsuccessful amendments proposed more specific duties in relation to community care plans. One such amendment concerned people with low incidence disabilities. The government (Baroness Blatch) argued that even without the amendment, community care plans anyway would have to be 'comprehensive of the totality of need which the local authority has to address and the totality of the service provision it aims to provide within the resources available to it' (H4,1990). In fact the substance of this amendment eventually did find its way into policy guidance (see above).

Similarly, an amendment requiring plans to consider 'the religious persuasion, racial origin and cultural and linguistic background' of communities was not adopted. The government stated 'that the need to take account of these factors will be stressed in our guidance, which can be reinforced by directions' (H5,1990).

More recently, Alfred Morris suggested placing duties on social services 'to draw up a specific policy for meeting the needs of young people and adults with multiple disabilities, under the responsibility of a named officer, and to include this within community care plans'. Tim Yeo replied that plans were expected 'to set out how the authority intends to meet the needs of the whole of its population, including disabled people' (H6,1993).

Practice

A survey of community care plans (Hardy 1993) analysed 'client group' coverage: 96% of plans dealt specifically with elderly people, people with mental health problems, people with learning disabilities, physically and sensorily impaired people. Other groups were less well covered, ranging from drugs/alcohol misusers (80%) to travellers (4%).

One of the reasons for attempts to amend community care legislation and policy is the recognition that in the past certain groups of people have been accorded inappropriately low priority. For example, SSI (1991g) inspected services for people with multiple impairment in Gloucestershire following the death of a person with such impairment. Two years after her death, none of the agencies (social services, health authority, voluntary agency) had 'published policies, procedural statements and practice guides in relation to disabled people' (p.2). Another recent report suggests that minority ethnic communities might neither be contributing enough to planning, nor receiving services appropriate for disabled people. Local authorities needed better knowledge of the local population and the particular needs of disabled people from these communities (SSI/NHSME 1994,p.24).

Policy documents and plans alone might not anyway ensure services of quality for particular groups of people. For example, even when an SSI (1988b) inspection of services for people with a visual impairment did find relevant policy documents, they were inadequate (and many authorities anyway had no such documents). It found that such documents might take 'only a partial view of a department's responsibility for people with a visual handicap' (p.13). Conversely, absence of, for example, rural issues from a community care plan doesn't necessarily mean the local authority isn't effectively planning for those issues (Gould 1994,p.95).

More recently a report (SSI/NHSME 1994) on the implementation of community care similarly found that despite some good practice, services for people with sensory impairment were ill-defined, had generally low priority, and were poorly funded (pp.25–26). Even where community care plans were of a good standard, there might be both lack of a 'shared vision' of services and of a 'clearly defined corporate policy' (p.3). Action plans for mental health might exist but fail to be underpinned by a 'framework of principles specific to mental health' (SSI/NHSME 1994c,p.23). The National Council for Voluntary Organisations has found that despite some good practice, 'community care planning for rural areas has been of no more than marginal concern for the majority of authorities' (Gould 1994,p.95).

A survey of coverage by community care plans of services for alcohol and drugs misusers suggests further complications beyond simple presence or absence of such services in plans. For example, it suggests that because of the low status given to such services by many authorities, their coverage in some plans is of low quality. This can occur, for example, when such services are absorbed into sections of the plan dealing with mental distress or HIV/AIDS (O'Brien,Wurr 1993,p.1).

CONSULTATION ABOUT COMMUNITY CARE PLANS

Legislation places duties on local authorities to consult with health authorities, housing authorities and voluntary organisations when preparing community care plans. These duties have been augmented by Directions about consultation with the 'independent' (private and voluntary) sectors (see below).

Non co-terminous boundaries between different authorities can sometimes pose considerable difficulties for consultation.

EXTRACTS

Legislation states that a local authority must consult:

(health authorities) '(a) any District Health Authority the whole or any part of whose locality lies within the area of the local authority;

(b) any Family Health Services Authority the whole or any part of whose locality lies within the area of the local authority;'

(housing authorities) '(c) in so far as any proposed plan, review or modifications of a plan may affect or be affected by the provision or availability of housing and the local authority is not itself a local housing authority, within the meaning of the Housing Act 1985, every such local housing authority whose area is within the area of the local authority;'

(voluntary organisations: community care services) '(d) such voluntary organisations as appear to the authority to represent the interests of persons who use or are likely to use any community care services within the area of the authority or the interests of private carers who, within that area, provide care to persons, for whom, in the exercise of their social services functions, the local authority have a power or duty to provide a service.'

(voluntary organisations: housing) '(e) such voluntary housing agencies and other bodies as appear to the local authority to provide housing or community care services in their area; and'

(other persons) '(f) such other persons as the Secretary of State may direct' (NHSCCA 1990,s.46(2)).

DISCUSSION
Joint Planning
Joint planning between statutory services has been urged for many years. It is not a new theme introduced by the NHSCCA 1990. For example, the NHS Act 1977,s.22 states that 'health authorities and local authorities shall co-operate with one another in order to secure and advance the health and welfare of the people of England and Wales'.

1971 Circular guidance about services for elderly people reads similarly to recent guidance:

> 'In practical terms the ability to provide a wide range of services in the domiciliary field will require the closest cooperation between those who are responsible for the various elements that make up the community health and social services...no individual service or group of services can be considered in isolation and planning of overall improvements will require the fullest consultation and exchange of views and information between those closely concerned with services for the elderly...' (DHSS 19/71,para 7).

Consultation Across Boundaries
Community care policy guidance recognises that, though ideal, joint plans between agencies may not be possible, in the short-term at least, because 'in some areas problems exist (not least where authorities do not have co-terminous boundaries)' (DH 1990, para 2.3).

An extreme case might occur where, for example, one social services authority encompasses the whole or part of up to four health authorities and six housing authorities. These health and housing authorities could conceivably be operating varying policies and practices. Indeed, Department of Environment Circular guidance has encouraged the coordination of procedures where one social services authority area covers a number of housing authorities (DoE 10/90, para 25): so that one social services authority is not having to cope with different housing policies and practices within its area.

In addition, the Audit Commission (1992) has pointed out the general fragmentation of health services even within the boundary of one health authority. There are community units, acute hospital units, GPs, health authority purchasers, providers, family health services authorities, all of which might relate separately to social services (pp.49–50).

Even in areas where boundaries between social services and health have been roughly co-terminous, joint planning can be threatened by the merger of health authorities to form a single purchasing unit (SSI/NHSME 1994c,p.28). In addition, the uncertainties of the expected reorganisation of local government might contribute to 'planning blight' in many areas (ADSS 1994,p.1).

Circular guidance (EL(93)119) has acknowledged that the 'prospect of organisational change for both local and health authorities could tend, at least for a time, to create barriers to joint working. But internal and personal uncertainties must not be allowed to inhibit the development of a better service for users...' (para 9).

Consultation with Housing Departments

Paragraph 46(2) of the NHSCCA 1990 places a duty on social services to consult with the local housing authority, if the local authority is not itself a housing authority. This duty does not therefore apply to metropolitan boroughs which are unified authorities (unlike non-metropolitan authorities).

However, this does not mean that departments within the same authority should not collaborate. Circular guidance clarifies the point: 'where social services and housing authorities are part of a unified authority...discussions should take place between the respective departments' (DoE 10/92).

During the passing of the NHS and Community Care Bill, there was some confusion about this. The drafters of the Bill seem to have assumed, rightly or wrongly, that consultation takes place anyway between departments in unified authorities. Thus, an amendment referring to consultation in unified authorities failed because it was deemed 'defective and unacceptable as it requires a local authority which is a housing authority to consult itself' (H7,1990).

CONSULTATION: DUTIES TO CONSULT WITH THE INDEPENDENT SECTOR

Directions place specific duties on local authorities to consult with independent sector providers of community care services, including both voluntary and private sector organisations.

EXTRACTS

Directions (delegated legislation), issued with LAC(93)4 (under LASSA,s.7A and NHSCCA 1990, s.46), state that:

'2. Each local authority shall in carrying out any of their functions under section 46(1) of the National Health Service and Community Care Act 1990 (community care plans) consult any representative organisation (including any incorporated or unincorporated body of persons) which represents providers in the authority's area with whom the authority may arrange to provide community care services as defined in s.46 of the National Health Service and Community Care Act...where that organisation notifies the local authority in writing of their wish to be consulted in respect of the authority's community care plans'.

Circular guidance (LAC(93)4 issued with the above Directions states that the first direction is 'intended to ensure that there is full and proper consultation between local authorities and independent sector providers on community care plans'. Independent sector/providers includes private and voluntary providers of services.

The requirement is that 'authorities must consult with representatives of independent sector providers of community care services in the authority's area' (para 11). This includes 'representatives of day and domiciliary service providers as well as providers of residential and nursing home care' (para 12).

Identity of representatives. As to who the representatives are, the Circular guidance explains:

> **(services within area)** 'Authorities must consult any national, regional or local independent sector association or organisation which represents independent sector providers of community care services within the authority's area and from whom a written request has been received. This applies whether or not the authority proposes to contract with the providers represented by the organisation concerned'.

> **(nomination)** 'It will be for the providers to nominate and choose their own representatives and so themselves determine whether they are 'representatives'. Authorities should take steps to ensure that representatives know what they need to do to be put on the list of those to be consulted...'(para 13).

> **('out of area' consultation)** 'There is no legal requirement to consult representatives of providers from another local authority area. Authorities will need to decide whether they should do so... Authorities should expect to consult out-of-area providers with whom they do actually contract' (para 15).

Guidelines. A report (DH/KPMG 1992) containing guidelines on independent sector involvement in community care planning was published by the Department of Health in 1992.

CONSULTATION PROCEDURES

Circular guidance does not prescribe consultation procedures but does outline certain basic principles, some of which 'must' be adhered to. These include the seeking of views on proposals and not just final documents; as well as allowing reasonable time for responses.

Legislation is silent about detailed consultation procedures.

Circular guidance (LAC(93)4) emphasises that consultation should amount to more than a token exercise, whilst leaving the precise form of the consultation to local discretion:

> **(discretion)** 'The nature and style of consultation will be a matter for each authority to decide. The basic principles, however, are clear':

> **(proposals)** 'views must be invited on proposals, not the final document; those being consulted will not only need to be made aware of the proposals but be able to comment on proposed changes in service patterns;'

> **(reasonable time)** 'reasonable time must be allowed for those consulted to formulate and give their view; views must be taken into consideration;'

(meetings) 'it may be sufficient to hold meetings or, where appropriate, place community care plan proposals on the agenda of a regular forum but care needs to be taken that those who need to be consulted are properly informed' (para 23).

DISCUSSION

Consultation Procedures in Practice

A survey (for the Department of Health) of community care plans published in 1993 found that few plans mentioned consultation before the draft Plan stage (ie, at the 'preliminary pre-draft stage'). As to other points made in the guidance, the survey was unable to discover how those consulted influenced the plans or whether they were satisfied with either the consultation process or outcome (Wistow *et al* 1993, p.29).

A second survey drew a distinction between other agencies' being 'consulted' and actually being 'involved' in the planning process (Hardy 1993, p.3): ie, the difference between involvement at the 'pre-draft' or 'post-draft' stage (p.24). Plans lacking joint signatures might nevertheless be 'demonstrably joint documents' (Hardy 1993,p.31). Conversely, the term 'jointness' might describe community care plans which nevertheless 'remain dominated by social services issues' (SSI/NHSME 1994c,p.26).

Users and Carers

Legislation does not state that users and carers should be consulted, though it does state that voluntary organisations should be. Concern has been expressed that 'much still remains to be done to secure effective consultation with the voluntary sector and in particular to involve smaller organisations and organisations in rural areas and those representing black and ethnic minorities' (Health Committee 1993,vol.2,p.116: NCVO evidence). A report by Counsel and Care found that a small number of user and carer groups, representing elderly people, were influencing policy agendas – but many not were not doing so (Means, Lart 1994).

Consultation with Specific Groups

Legislation does not prescribe consultation with specific groups of people or their representatives.

An unsuccessful amendment to the NHS and Community Care Bill attempted to create duties to consult (and to create consultation procedures) with specific groups. These included users; carers; voluntary organisations providing community care services and representing the interests of users or providing advocacy services; and bodies representing the interests of ethnic minorities; housing associations.

Virginia Bottomley, resisting the amendment, explained that whilst the government wanted to 'ensure practical, effective community care plans, taking all aspects into account', it did not wish 'to write on the face of the Bill precise mechanisms for consultation and to state precisely which groups should be considered'. This was for fear of creating a 'straightjacket', rather than a framework, for community care plans. Instead, guidance would allow flexibility, innovation and diversity and would be reinforced by Social Services Inspectorate monitoring and if necessary by Secretary of State Directions (H8,1990).

There is evidence, from the first community care plans, that some groups are particularly likely to be excluded from community care planning: for example, ethnic minority groups, people with sensory impairments, people from rural communities, and people with learning difficulties (Bewley, Glendinning 1994,pp.25–26).

PUBLICATION OF COMMUNITY CARE PLANS

Policy guidance states that local authorities must publish community care plans annually and should make them available in understandable form to the local population. In order to ensure public access to plans, the guidance suggests that the plans could be made available in other languages and in tape and braille form.

Terms such as 'available', 'understandable', 'public access' can be rather vague when applied to information provision and are probably difficult to measure. It has been suggested that local authorities need to think about, amongst other things, accessibility in terms of how many documents make up the plan; what 'level' the plans are written at; whom they are aimed at; and for what purpose.

EXTRACTS

Policy guidance states:

> 'in future all LAs will be required to publish CCPs annually. All CCPs should in future be available to the local population, presented in a form which is readily understandable. Authorities may wish to consider producing straightforward summaries of detailed statistical and financial planning documents. In order to ensure public accessibility authorities may wish to make plans available in languages relevant to the local population, in braille and on tape' (DH 1990, para 2.18).

DISCUSSION

Different Languages and Media

Policy guidance follows the language of obligation ('should in future be available') with the language of discretion about the form of plans: 'may wish to make plans available in languages relevant to the local population, in braille and on tape'. However, one report of a survey of community care plans has commented that in 'a real sense, unless Plans are produced in such formats they remain unavailable to certain sections of the community' (Wistow 1993, p.8). Yet, the survey (of 22 community care plans in 1992) found little evidence of plans produced either in different languages or in media other than the written word (p.30).

A second survey found that a substantially greater proportion of plans were being produced in languages other than English: the proportion had risen from 18% to 32% (Hardy 1993, p.2). In 1993, some 24% of plans (compared with 18% a year earlier) were available in non-written forms (p.3).

Accessibility: Number, Level, Target, Purpose of Community Care Plans

Community care plans sometimes comprise one or more documents, each containing a different level of information. Thus, one county, a single social services authority divided into five social services area teams, might have five separate 'distinctively different' community care plans (Wistow 1993, p.5).

Again, a local authority might have a plan which summarises a number of other planning documents also publicly available. This means that a full understanding might depend on reading all the documents. Other variations might include three updates of the plan in a single year; one three year plan with annual updates; two multi-volume editions with separate documents for a specialist service (eg. mental health); two separate plans where the social services area covers two health authorities. On the one hand, a single document serving all purposes might be too ambitious; on the other, there is a question about the accessibility of information which itself has to be explained by other information (SSI/NHSME 1994c,p.21).

Jargon, technical language, layout and small print are additional hindrances to accessibility (SSI/NHSME 1994c, pp.20–21).

Plans might be aimed at the 'general public', all those who have a 'stake in community care', a 'wide audience' (from government down to users and carers), or a 'primary target' of major service providers in the area (Wistow et al 1993, pp.5,8–9). Authorities might have to consider that a community care plan may be fulfilling different purposes, for example, public information/accountability as opposed to business plan. It has been suggested that the purpose of community care plans needs to be reviewed and clarified (Wistow 1993, p.33; Hardy 1993, p.9).

MONITORING OF COMMUNITY CARE PLANS

Policy guidance states that the SSI would monitor plans for the year 1992–1993, and offer advice and guidance to local authorities whose plans were unlikely to meet key objectives. Further sanction exists if the Department of Health advised the Secretary of State to use her/his powers to issue directions to an individual authority under LASSA 1970, s.7A. (DH 1990,p.17).

ASSESSMENT OF THE NEEDS OF THE LOCAL POPULATION

The NHS and Community Care Act is silent about the assessment of population needs. However, policy guidance explains the importance of adequate assessment of local population needs if community care is to work. The Audit Commission makes the same point. This is because without adequate information about local needs, it becomes difficult if not impossible to plan and target, within budget, services for the people most in need, and to develop 'criteria of eligibility' which regulate who qualifies for services.

First reports on community care implementation suggest that, for a number of reasons, local authorities have inadequate information about local population needs. Without such information, a local authority might in principle be hard-pressed not only to conform with the aims of community care, but also to explain on what basis it has set priorities for – or rationed – service provision.

EXTRACTS

Legislation (NHSCCA 1990) is silent about the needs of the local population.

Policy guidance makes it clear that information 'will be required for assessing the care needs of the resident population, to inform purchasing and to verify that contracts are being met in terms of both quality and quantity. SSDs will need to identify their information requirements and ensure that, where information is not available, they plan for its future provision' (DH 1990,para 4.32).

DISCUSSION

Pivotal Role of Information about Local Needs

Identification of local level of needs is thought to be particularly important given the need to plan services within limited budgets. For example, the Audit Commission (1993) has commented on the lack of logic present where local authorities claim to have set eligibility criteria but not to have estimated local needs, since it is only upon knowledge of needs that eligibility criteria can sensibly be based (pp.4–5).

In addition to the requirements of policy guidance, good practice guidance on the assessment of population needs has also been issued (DH 1993). This discusses and illustrates a wide range of methods which can be used to build up information about the local population.

Reports about community care implementation confirm that local authorities continue to need more information about local needs and to have problems in obtaining it (eg. SSI/NHSME 1994g,p.6; SSI/NHSE 1994h,p.11). A 1993 survey of community care plans has also emphasised the continuing difficulties local authorities face in mapping local needs, despite increasing use of a range of information sources (Hardy 1994,p.40).

Problems of technology, information compatibility and confidentiality might exist, whilst some local authorities might focus on one group's needs at the expense of another's (eg. elderly people at the expense of younger adults with physical or sensory disabilities). Local authorities' knowledge of the needs of minority ethnic groups might be limited (DH 1994b,p.3).

IDENTIFICATION OF LOCAL NEEDS: DUTIES UNDER THE CHRONICALLY SICK AND DISABLED PERSONS ACT 1970 AND NATIONAL ASSISTANCE ACT 1948

There is no duty to identify local population needs in the NHS and Community Care Act 1990. This contrasts with s.1 of the Chronically Sick and Disabled Persons Act 1970 which does place duties on local authorities to identify the number of disabled people locally. Social services departments also have duties under s.29 of the National Assistance Act 1948 to keep registers of disabled people. One of the purposes of such registers is perceived to be planning. These duties are most significant to community care, since they are, generally, about enabling people to remain in their own homes and this is the preferred aim of community care as stated in policy guidance. In addition, many people in need of community care services are likely to be disabled under s.29.

EXTRACTS

Legislation, CSDPA, s.1(1) states:

> **(number of disabled people locally)** 'It shall be the duty of every local authority having functions under section 29 of the National Assistance Act 1948 to inform themselves of the number of persons to whom that section applies within their area and of the need for the making of the authority of arrangements under that section for such persons'.

Circular guidance (DHSS 45/71) issued in 1971 explained that:

> 'in order to ensure the proper planning of services, there is a clear need for accurate information about the scale and nature of local need to be gathered quickly... One way of obtaining this information would be through local sample surveys...' (para 11).

Circular guidance of the previous year (DHSS 12/70) had explained that authorities were required:

> 'to secure that they are adequately informed of the numbers and needs of substantially and permanently handicapped persons in order that they can formulate satisfactory plans for developing their services. The DHSS are considering what guidance can be given to authorities as to economical means of using social survey techniques for these purposes...' (para 5).

Legislation (National Assistance Act 1948) refers:

> **(registers of disabled people)** to the power of local authorities to maintain and compile 'classified registers' of disabled people (s.29(4)(g)) to whom arrangements for welfare services under s.29(1) apply.

Directions convert this power into a duty (Directions attached to LAC(93)10 (Append 2,para 2(2)):

> 'The Secretary of State hereby directs local authorities to make the arrangements referred to in s.29(4)(g) of the Act (compiling and maintaining registers) in relation to persons who are ordinarily resident in their area.'

DISCUSSION

Nature of Duty to Identify Local Needs

In response to a 1988 Parliamentary question about the number of local authorities which had established the 'number and needs of people with disabilities', Mr. Scott replied: 'Local authorities have a clear duty under s.1 of the Act to inform themselves of the number of disabled people requiring services; to make arrangements for meeting any needs identified; and to provide information about relevant services. It is for local authorities to ensure that they fulfil these statutory duties' (H9,1988)

At one stage, it was proposed that the original Chronically Sick and Disabled Persons Bill contain the words 'such steps as are reasonably practicable' to govern the duty created by s.1.The potentially vitiating effect of these words was recognised (see discussion: H10 1970, H11 1970) and they were eventually removed in order to strengthen the duty (H12 1970).

Nevertheless, local authorities still have discretion in how they carry out the duty, as government has explained: 'Local authorities have a clear duty...to inform themselves of the number of disabled people in their areas and of their need for services. It is for individual authorities to determine how to fulfil this statutory duty' (H13 1988).

The government has also stated that it is 'for local authorities to ensure that they fulfil these statutory duties' (H14 1988) and that the government has 'no power' to direct local authorities to implement the duty since the 'requirements to implement duties contained in s.1 are laid directly on local authorities by that section' (H15 1982).

Practice of Identification of Local Needs

It is not clear how authorities have carried out their duties under s.1.

For example, one local authority recently reported that since 1970, 'there has not been a systematic study of the numbers and needs of people with physical disabilities... This makes it very difficult to plan services which are responsive to need' (quoted in: Wistow *et al* 1993, p.17).

A Department of Health (SSI 1989) report on services for deaf–blind people found that funding for this group of people was stifled because of an absence of 'useful data'. This seemed due to ill-kept records of existing service users, together with the 'problems of defining the group, identifying all those who needed services and devising suitable ways to provide them' (p.15). The report concluded that 'many deaf–blind people themselves were probably not actually known' to local authorities (p.22). Local knowledge about, for example, the needs of disabled people from ethnic minority groups might be limited (SSI/NHSME 1994,p.4).

Surveying local levels of need and disability can be difficult. For example, there are different views and definitions of need, including the difference between the social and individual models of disability/need, as well as cultural and conceptual barriers which hinder information-gathering (Arnold *et al* 1993,pp.8–13). The major, national disability survey by the OPCS published in the late 1980s opted for a method of asking people about their functional disabilities rather than obtaining medical diagnosis (Martin 1988,p.9).

By 1981, the limitations of the practical usefulness of section 1 of the CSDPA were being exposed (Topliss,Gould 1981). For example, a report had found that 'in general the inquiries had added little other than confusion to the known picture of need'. Problems included defective survey methodologies and the problem of currency of the information. For example, within 18 months of one survey, nearly a quarter of the people found to be disabled had undergone significant changes of circumstance (pp.94–97).

CHAPTER 20

INFORMATION AND PUBLICITY

KEY ISSUES

The NHS and Community Care Act 1990 is silent about the provision of information about assessment and services – apart from duties to publicise community care plans and complaints procedures (see Chapters 19 and 23). However, the Chronically Sick and Disabled Persons Act 1970 does place duties on local authorities to provide information about welfare services for disabled people.

There are a number of uncertainties surrounding information provision: for example, taking the words of the policy guidance literally, it seems a very ambitious task to make information accessible to 'all' *potential* users. In addition, if information is designed, as guidance says it is, to empower people, then this might also be difficult to achieve since it does not follow necessarily that information provision empowers people. It might also be difficult to produce reliable and effective information if it is having to describe an unreliable and unpredictable system. For example, if local authorities cannot predict demand and need for services, and so leave criteria of eligibility vague so as to cover all eventualities, then any information about services will also be vague.

Challenging Information Provision

In general it will be difficult to challenge aspects of an authority's provision of information. On the basis of what guidance states an authority should be producing in the way of information, a person might be able to complain through the local authority complaints procedure. However, given that the guidance does not impose statutory duties, and that it can be difficult to measure exactly what benefits information confers on particular individuals, challenges through the courts about information provision might be unlikely to succeed. For example, information might give a 'chance' to people to decide whether they want or need services; a 'chance' to decide whether they will approach an authority; and a 'chance' that they will actually qualify and might eventually receive (an unknown type and quantity of service). Such benefits might be difficult for the courts to measure – especially in terms of any remedies.

It is possible that the local ombudsman might find maladministration in relation to information/publicity provision; for example, if the authority failed to provide information in a reasonable range of other languages and media. However, the courts are unlikely to uphold such claims, having stated that 'where an English statute says information is to be provided, that information need only be provided in English' (*R v Governors of Small Heath School, ex p. Birmingham City Council 1989; R v Birmingham City Council, ex p. Kaur 1990*).

Nevertheless, under section 1 of the CSDPA there is a clear legislative duty to give information to individual service users. Failure to provide this information might give clear grounds for challenge, although even this duty is qualified since it depends on the authority's *opinion* about what other relevant services are and on the authority *having particulars* of these other services.

Similarly, there is a duty in the NHS and Community Care Act which obliges local authorities to publicise their complaints procedures. However, it is a general duty (not towards individuals) and it is to be carried out in a way which each authority considers 'appropriate'. Except in extreme circumstances, possibly where it could be shown that an authority provided no publicity at all, it would probably be difficult to challenge an authority about how it performs this duty.

BASIC CONTENT OF INFORMATION

Policy guidance states that local authorities 'will need' to make accessible to all potential service users and carers a wide range of information.

EXTRACTS

Legislation (NHSCCA 1990) is silent about community care information provision (other than about community care plans and complaints procedures). But there is a duty under the CSDPA 1970 (see p.348).

Policy guidance states that:

> 'local authorities will need to have in place...published information accessible to all potential service users and carers, including those with any communication difficulty or difference in language or culture, setting out the types of community care services available, the criteria for provision of services, the assessment procedures to agree needs and ways of addressing them and the standards by which the care management system (including assessment) will be measured' (DH 1990,para 3.56).

Practice guidance and Circular guidance elaborates on this policy guidance (see eg. SSI/SWSG 1991(MG)pp.41–42; CI(92)34,para 6).

Effects of Increased Publicity

In the past, some local authorities have been concerned that publicity can create excessive demands on services. For example, a 1991 review by SSI and Social Information Systems reported contrasting effects of publicity. One local authority publicised its intensive community-based services. Within nine months the service was saturated and publicity withdrawn. In a second authority on the other hand, an area team advertised itself 'aggressively' through leaflets, videos in post offices and the local press. It was not overwhelmed with 'unrealistic or inappropriate demands' and it concluded that people 'self select' and do not approach social services except as a last resort (SSI/SIS 1991,p.20).

A study (KPMG 1993) for the Department of Health found that a majority of authorities had gaps in information provision on the following subjects: eligibility criteria, charging arrangements, standards and targets, meaningful information about who provides particular services, choice of care home (p.39).

PURPOSE AND FUNCTION OF COMMUNITY CARE INFORMATION

Guidance states that the purpose of providing information is to give people greater choice and enable greater participation in the assessment and planning of services.

Legislation (NHSCCA 1990) says nothing about the purpose and function of information.

Policy guidance states that local authorities:

'should publish readily accessible information about their care services...' so as to 'enable users and carers to exercise genuine choice and participate in the assessment of their care needs and in the making of the arrangements for meeting these needs' (DH 1990, para 3.18).

Practice guidance states that information is about:

'empowering users and carers, enabling them not only to make choices about the services they receive but also to be more in control of the process through which they gain access to services' (SSI/SWSG(PG) 1991,p.31).

Information and Choice

Effective information provision about community care might be a difficult task. A KPMG (1993) report of a study on community care information points out that 'an authority can provide good readable and accessible material and yet this can have very little beneficial impact on users and carers' (p.8); and 'the users and carers we spoke to were not more empowered as a result of information provision; the majority did not understand how the system has changed and what this means for them' (p.15).

The Policy Studies Institute, reporting in 1991 on information about residential care, comments that anyway information does not necessarily deliver choice for all: for example, for people who are not capable of choice, such as mentally ill people or people with learning difficulties (Roberts,S 1991, p.123).

Where service users do not receive information about assessments either before or during assessment visits (SSI 1994g,p.12), then clearly choice and 'user empowerment' are likely to be impaired.

Clarity of Information

SSI practice guidance emphasises the necessity for clarity, in its very title: 'Getting the message across'. Local authorities should: 'ensure that people have information that is straightforward, relevant, accurate and sufficient so that they can make informed choices' (SSI 1991,p.11). Thus, the question that practitioners should ask themselves is: 'does the information give the public a clear understanding of their entitlements to service provision?' (SSI/SWSG(PG) 1991,p.9,35).

The guidance stresses that jargon needs to be avoided and gives (SSI 1991,p.20) examples of words which it found were misunderstood by service users. These included (mistaken meaning in brackets):

- advocacy (was associated with going to court);
- agencies (second hand clothes shops);
- allocation process (being offered re-housing);
- common (cheap and nasty);
- criteria (unknown to most);
- eligibility (good marriage catch);
- equitable manner (unknown to most);
- format (for wiping feet at the front door);
- gender (unknown to most);
- maintain (confused with divorce maintenance settlements);
- networks (unknown to most);
- sensitive (tender and sore);
- voluntary agencies (people with no experience, volunteers).

In 1990, the National Consumer Council and the National Institute for Social Work (Berry 1990, p.5) reported about social services information that

'the terms used in many of the leaflets were not always helpful. Some describe roles unfamiliar to people from other cultures. Others, though clear to professionals, would be less comprehensible to the general public. "Foster carers", for example. What does the term "fostering" mean to someone of a non-British family and social background? Why are people described as "carers" rather than parents? Are home helps carers? Potential users can be embarrassed and put off if they find themselves asking for the wrong thing.'

Jargon remains a potential problem. The KPMG (1993) report suggests that brevity and jargon together make for poor information: for example, a leaflet 'which lists a range of agencies and telephone numbers with jargon filled statements identifying the services they provide' (pp.27–29).

Information can be unclear if inconsistent in content (Berry 1990, p.18), out-of-date or simply undated (Steele 1993,Pt.3, p.44).

INFORMATION: EXPECTATIONS AND ELIGIBILITY FOR SERVICE

Policy guidance encourages local authorities to publish information about sensitive issues, such as criteria of eligibility determining who gets a service and who does not. In the past, many local authorities have tended not to publish these criteria either at all or at least not in any detail. Even in the light of community care guidance to publish such information, the question of how much detail to publish remains.

EXTRACTS

Legislation is silent about the publication of eligibility criteria.

Policy guidance states that published information should include 'the authority's criteria for determining when services should be provided and the assessment procedures' (DH 1990, para 3.18).

Practice guidance states:

> **(increased demand for services)** 'Because information is seen as one of the most effective ways of empowering users and carers, agencies should give this aspect of their work a high priority. It is recognised that this will generate increased demand but it is preferable that services should be allocated on the basis of known need rather than being rationed on the basis of public ignorance. This does mean, however, that the information should frame realistic expectations in the minds of potential users and spell out the priorities which will govern the response they receive...'

> **(communication to the public)** 'The challenge of communicating to the public their eligibility for assistance in terms of needs rather than services should not be underestimated. It is the essential starting point for the implementation of a needs-led approach' (SSI/SWSG(MG) 1991, p.42).

Practice guidance also refers to the need to explain to people 'what your department can and cannot provide' (SSI 1991, p.10).

DISCUSSION

Publicising Eligibility Criteria

Eligibility (who can get services – and who can't) is a sensitive issue. The existence of clear information might result in rationing openly by need; its absence might result in rationing covertly by ignorance (see eg. Steele 1993, Pt.1,p.12).

Nevertheless, recent reports have found such information sometimes still lacking (eg. KPMG 1993,p.39; Berry 1990, p.18). A Policy Studies Institute report (Roberts 1991, p.123) on information about residential care commented that practitioners might, even under the new community care system, 'feel that no good purpose is served by informing a client about services for which that particular client would not be eligible' (p.124).

Sometimes it seems clear that criteria, published or not, simply do not exist. For example, a RADAR (1993) project on the CSDPA 1970 reports a request made in May 1992, assessed within a few days but finally turned down in August. Eligibility criteria for 1992/1993 were neither published nor otherwise known to the applicant or assessor (p.25). Similarly, a local ombudsman investigation, about provision of holidays for disabled people under the CSDPA 1970, found no criteria determining how the £800 budget was to be allocated: this the ombudsman seemed to include in her finding of maladministration (CLAE 91/C/0565 & 92/C/1400).

Level of Detail to Publish

Detailed statements of eligibility might create a 'straitjacket', preventing local authorities considering special individual needs, or taking account of resources during the year. Detailed statements might not be read by service users (Steele 1993,Pt.3,p.42).

On the other hand, broad statements might mean little. For example: 'MEDIUM NEED. For people whose assessed needs falls within High and Medium eligibility, although NOT qualifying because by law the council has discretion, we will seek to provide a level of service depending on whether we have sufficient money available (having regard to High Need)' (quoted in: RADAR 1993, p.8).

The KPMG (1993) study for the Department of Health acknowledged the dilemma of how much information to publish, and suggested as unwarranted the assumption that 'shorter is better'. However, restricted time and money might anyway curtail information production (p.29).

Despite the optimism of the practice guidance, there clearly seem to be continuing difficulties for local authorities. The KPMG (1993) report explained this:

- a leaflet might contain details of services available but omit reference to limited provision imposed by lack of resources;
- priorities and criteria of eligibility might not be explained;
- resource constraints sometimes deny services even to people who are supposedly eligible to receive those services;
- information about such non-provision even for eligible people is not made public;

- the potential therefore exists for publicity to general 'false expectations' about available services (p.33).

INFORMATION: DISSEMINATION AND ACCESSIBILITY

Policy guidance states that local authorities need to make information accessible to all potential users and carers, including people who might speak different languages or people who have sensory impairments and require their information in different media.

EXTRACTS

Legislation (NHSCCA 1990) is silent about the dissemination and accessibility of information.

Policy guidance states that:

'local authorities will need to have in place...published information accessible to all potential service users and carers including those with any communication difficulty or difference in language or culture' (DH 1990, para 3.56).

Practice guidance takes up the same theme:

(targeting) 'Above all, any information strategy should be targeted on those most likely to require the services, particularly those in need who do not tend to seek help' (SSI/SWSG(MG) 1991, p.42);

(reaching users and carers) 'It is the responsibility of the practitioner to ensure that this published information reaches potential users and carers who are considering seeking assistance' (SSI/SWSG 1991(PG),p.31).

Practice guidance states:

'This information should be **presented in a readily accessible form** that takes account of potential users who have:

- a language other than English;
- a different cultural background;
- a sensory impairment;
- a communication difficulty (illiteracy or learning disability).

Subject to the availability of resources and departmental priorities, **experimentation with media other than the written word,** for example, videos or audio cassettes should be encouraged' (SSI/SWSG(PG) 1991,p.32).

DISCUSSION

Information for Existing and for Potential Users

Taken literally, the statement in policy guidance about information being accessible to 'all potential users and carers' is over-ambitious, though much depends on how local authorities interpret the terms 'accessible' and 'all'. Reaching potential users might be an onerous task. Early reports on community care have suggested, for example, the 'marginal impact' of information (KPMG 1993,p.46) and that many carers had not received an assessment simply because they didn't know about assessments (Warner 1994,p.48). One local authority had produced a leaflet describing services, and distributed it to a range of people and public places: yet still many other people interviewed had not seen it and stocks were not available for continuous use by voluntary organisations (SSI 1994e,p.13). Similarly, authorities might produce information for people with HIV/AIDS, but it might not be accessible if not placed, for example, in commonly-used hospital clinics both within and without the local authorities' areas (SSI/NHSE 1994h,p.6).

People might not 'tend to seek help' for a variety of reasons including attitudes and unwillingness to seek information, low perception of needs because of reluctance to seek help, loneliness and depression, antipathy toward social services, language barriers, disability (physical, sensory, mental) and so on (eg. Tinker *et al* 1993,p.5; Steele 1993,Part 2,p.18). People might fear loss of service if they 'make a fuss' about getting information (KPMG 1993,p.11).

Conversely, it might be that actual service users are offered less information than potential users (Berry 1990, p.9).

Minority Ethnic Groups

In practice, it seems that the existence and quality of information for minority ethnic groups is likely to vary. A 1990 report by the NCC and NISW found that social services information in minority languages was less well designed than the equivalent information in English (Berry 1990, pp.11,18).

By 1993, the KPMG (1993) study for the Department of Health reported that 'information was generally available in a variety of media pertaining to the ethnic and disability mix of the population' (p.37). Yet an SSI (1993d) complaints procedure inspection report suggested, as a result of its findings, that local authorities should 'show adherence to the principles of the Race Relations Act 1976 and other equal opportunities legislation' (p.17). Another Department of Health monitoring exercise reported on 'a dearth of appropriate, user-friendly and culturally sensitive information about community care policies, procedures and service options' (DH 1994b,p.8).

Difficulties for local authorities include the fact that translation of written information can be expensive and create an expectation that enquiries be answered orally in a particular language (see eg. KPMG 1993,p.38; Steele 1993,Pt.3,p.39).

People with Sensory Impairment

The policy guidance (above) uses the language of obligation ('should' and 'will need to have') on the need to reach 'all potential users and carers'. The practice guidance suggests more tentatively that authorities might wish to experiment with other media. It is arguable that without such experimentation, information will in some areas simply not be available to 'all' potential users and carers.

There is evidence that past practice has not always been effective. An SSI (1989,p.15) report on services for people both deaf and blind was 'concerned to find so little information about services in suitable formats...such as in Braille, large print or on tape. They were thus deprived of information readily available to sighted and hearing people'.

An SSI (1990) inspection report found that despite the existence of procedures and systems for information, most social services departments failed to provide information in braille or large print (and information in other languages was scarce). The conclusion drawn was discouraging, although it was reported that social services departments were attempting to rectify the situation (pp.3,24–25).

A later report on services for people with multiple impairments found that the 'majority of users and carers interviewed considered that they were given insufficient information about available services. Very little information was available other than in standard print, in English' (SSI 1993a,p.15). The KPMG (1993) report for the Department of Health found the existence of information in braille or large print variable (p.37).

INFORMATION: STAFF

Community care practice guidance states that staff need to be well informed if they are to operate the system of community care and to provide appropriate information to others. There is evidence from the past, that social services and other statutory service staff have not always been well informed, nor been effective in providing information.

EXTRACTS

Legislation is silent about staff being well-informed.

Practice guidance states:

> **(where to find information)** 'The information strategy should also address the needs of staff. There is no substitute for an informed workforce able to relate information to needs and provide the right amount of information, in the right way, at the right time. It may not be feasible for all staff to be regularly updated but they should all know where they can obtain the information they need' (SSI/SWSG 1991 (MG), p.42).

> **(in-depth knowledge)** 'The priority requirement for assessment staff will be an in-depth understanding of the needs associated with particular user groups and a knowledge of the range of services and community resources available to meet those needs' (SSI/SWSG (MG)1991,p.45).

> **(staff at all levels)** 'Staff at all levels require this information if they are to give a good quality service to people' (SSI 1991,p.10).

> 'Reception staff must know the types of services available,how they are accessed and the likely response times for assessment' (SSI/SWSG(PG) 1991,p.37).

Circular guidance issued in March 1993 stated that health authority managers 'should satisfy themselves' that health service staff know about community care policy and objectives; and that staff, particularly medical and nursing, are told about local community care arrangements. It stated also that staff directly involved in community care should be fully briefed and appropriately trained, and that health service managers should work closely with local authorities in planning communications (EL(93)22).

DISCUSSION

Practice: Staff Knowledge

The practice guidance explains the importance of well-informed staff. There is some evidence from past studies suggesting that staff working in statutory services are sometimes ill-informed about the needs of, for example, disabled and elderly people. Sometimes staff might also be poor information providers, because they give inappropriate, selective or obsolete information; they do not see themselves as 'information providers'; they are ill-informed; or they simply withhold information (eg. Garden (Lothian Disability Information Project) 1990,p.33; Tinker *et al* 1993,p.5).

For example, an SSI inspection of services for people with multiple impairments found that specialist staff within social services departments might provide only limited (specialist) information to users and carers. This contributed to the 'pigeon-holing' of users and was part of a widespread 'serious lack of information and communication between workers in the same department'. This in turn contributed to a lack of multi-disciplinary contribution and to partial assessments carried out from a limited perspective (SSI 1993a,pp.17–18). It is reported also that local authority staff are ill-informed about community care legislation (RADAR 1994,p.32, SSI 1994,p.21).

Example: Disability Equipment

Equipment and home adaptation provision are key community care ingredients which are mentioned prominently in policy guidance (DH 1990,para 3.24), and which also exemplify some of the long-standing difficulties in providing information. In 1984, the Research Institute for Consumer Affairs, reporting on disability equipment information, found haphazard referrals between agencies, fragmented information and ignorance of where to find it. The Coopers and Lybrand report of 1988 (para 3.7), commissioned by the DHSS, made similar findings about disability information in relation to service providers, disabled people and carers.

A 1988 King's Fund report (Beardshaw 1988, pp.27–28) found equipment 'the single most confused area of service provision for disabled people'. It is difficult to disentangle a poor information system, from the system of provision which the information is meant to be about: if the system is confused, then perhaps confused information is inevitable. For example, the 'Health of the Nation' Green Paper (Secretary of State for Health 1991,pp.96–97) referred to the concerns about 'deficiencies in the provision of aids and appliances'; a Department of Health 'guidance' document reported that it 'was very difficult to find a good all-round service' (DH 1992,p.1); the National Institute for Social Work Research Unit reported non-provision of equipment and adaptations as a prominent problem for elderly people discharged from hospital (Neill,Williams 1992,p.141); a research study of district nurses reported a confused and inefficient system of equipment provision with a scarcity of relevant and helpful information (Ross, Campbell 1992,p.1). Nor is the problem recent: twenty years earlier, the British Medical Association (1968, pp.8,25,35) had found 'glaring defects' in equipment provision and such fragmented administration and split responsibilities that 'few people are aware of all that is available'. The Mair report (1972, p.25) found 'a majority of staff of the health service, including medical staff, have an inadequate knowledge of what aids can be supplied, where they can be obtained and what their limitations are'.

LOCAL AUTHORITY INFORMATION PROVISION ABOUT OTHER SERVICES

Community care policy and practice guidance state that information should be provided not just about community care services but about a range of other services as well.

(This is an important issue for users whose needs do not always fall neatly into one statutory service or another but into several. Comprehensive information about different services will thus benefit all concerned: service users, carers and their advisers, as well as providers of services. For example, voluntary organisations or lawyers would be giving poor advice if they were aware of only 'half' the picture. Similarly, service providers can scarcely plan services generally, or make individual care plans, if they are unaware of what services are available and where).

EXTRACTS

Legislation (NHSCCA 1990) is silent about providing information about other services. However, the CSDPA does place duties on local authorities.

Policy guidance states that information should be:

'compiled in consultation with health and housing authorities and other service providers. The information should cover residential care homes, nursing homes and other community care facilities' (DH 1990, para 3.18).

Practice guidance states that information should contain 'the types of services available from all sectors, setting out the range of needs for which they cater' (SSI/SWSG 1991 (MG),p.41).

DISCUSSION
Inaccessible Information

Previous legislation (CSDPA 1970, s.1: see p.348) has also stressed the need for information about other services. Yet this has not always been available. As a result, disabled people, for example, might not benefit from services and suffer difficulties or hardship (see eg. National Audit Office 1992,p.2).

INFORMATION ABOUT COMPLAINTS PROCEDURES

Local authorities have a duty to publicise their complaints procedure in a way 'they consider appropriate'. Thus, the basic duty, but not the way in which it is carried out, is stipulated.

EXTRACTS
Legislation states:

> 'Local authorities shall give such publicity to the procedure established pursuant to this section as they consider appropriate' (LASSA 1970, s.7B(4).

Policy guidance states that the requirement to publicise complaints 'might' be met by using:

> **(leaflets)** 'leaflets: These should explain the procedure in straightforward terms and should include a reference to the role of the Commissioner for Local Administration (the Ombudsman) and to the separate leaflet 'Complaint about the Council?'. The leaflet should give the name, address and telephone number of the designated officer or of the person responsible for oversight of the procedure, and of organisations to whom those individuals might turn for advice. It should be made widely available. Where necessary, authorities will need to make available versions of their leaflet in ethnic minority languages in braille.'

> **(notices)** 'notices. These should be displayed in the authority's offices. They should also be supplied – with leaflets – to agencies offering independent advice.'

> **(visual/oral presentations)** 'visual and oral presentations. Authorities may wish to discuss with voluntary organisations and other local groups how information about the complaints procedure should be made available to those with sensory handicaps, the housebound and those whose first language is not English or who do not speak English' (DH 1990, para 6.26).

DISCUSSION
Complaints Procedure Publication

An SSI (1993c) monitoring report found that 98 out of 108 local authorities had publicised their complaints procedures. Most had produced leaflets and a significant minority had used their local media as well as video tapes and cassettes for people with sensory impairments (p.29). The report does not comment on the effectiveness of the publicity.

An SSI (1993d) inspection of five local authorities reported in greater detail, finding that the authorities had produced 'high quality procedures manuals, guides for staff and posters and leaflets for service users'. Distribution was reported to be not yet wide enough, since 'the majority of housebound service users and children in foster care were unlikely to have seen a leaflet giving details of how they could complain'. There was no evidence that the authorities were monitoring the availability of the information to users (pp.18–19).

INFORMATION: HOSPITAL DISCHARGE AND RESIDENTIAL/NURSING CARE

Hospital discharge can be a crucial stage of the whole community care process, when sometimes complicated decisions have to be made about whether a person goes home or into some form of residential care.

EXTRACTS

Legislation is silent about providing information about hospital discharge.

Circular guidance (HC(89)5), itself referred to in policy guidance (DH 1990, p.31), refers to the need for provision for families of 'necessary information and reassurance about the care of the patient after discharge' (para 1).

Other guidance, accompanying Directions on choice of residential accommodation, states that information is needed for genuine choice. People should be 'given fair and balanced information' and have their rights explained. Authorities 'might consider' including such information in a leaflet (LAC(92)27, para 17).

DISCUSSION

Lack of Information

There is some evidence that the provision of social services information to people leaving hospital is not always as full as it could be.

For example, SSI inspection has found examples of good practice but that 'overall, information available to people in hospital was sketchy and relied on previous experience or word of mouth'. Over 66% of users and carers interviewed had not received 'any information either written or verbal describing what they could expect from [hospital social services], their priorities or how to gain access to services'. This jeopardised equitable access to services by patients – although the inspection overall found users well-satisfied with the services provided (SSI 1993f, p.10).

INFORMATION ABOUT WELFARE SERVICES: CSDPA 1970

Local authorities have a duty under the Chronically Sick and Disabled Persons Act 1970 to publish information about welfare (non-residential) services.

Given that many potential users of community care services are likely to be disabled, that the preferred aim of community care is to enable people to remain in their own homes, and that the CSDPA (s.2) is about home welfare services – this duty to provide information about welfare services would appear central to community care.

EXTRACTS

Legislation states:

> 'Every...local authority...shall cause to be published from time to time at such times and in such manner as they consider appropriate general information as to the services provided under arrangements made by the authority under the said s.29 [of the National Assistance Act 1948] which are for the time being available in their area' (CSDPA 1970, s.1(2)(b)).

Circular guidance (DHSS 45/71) explained what the nature of such publicity (under the CSDPA) might be:

> **(encouragement to people)** 'The authority's publicity must be designed to encourage handicapped people themselves to come forward and seek services and hence facilitate the gradual building up of comprehensive lists of people needing help. Authorities should try to ensure that their publicity reaches those most in need of help and encourage them to seek it. To achieve this there is a need for publicity of a variety of kinds from a wide range of sources'.

> **(media and methods)** 'Authorities will, for example, need the cooperation of local newspapers and radio stations in making their services known and in supplementing their own leaflets and printed guides. They will also have in mind the help voluntary agencies can give in publicising services. Some authorities already avail themselves of the arrangement whereby local offices of the DHSS will enclose publicity material of this kind with notices of the award of retirement pensions. General practitioners will also be able to help here particularly as local authority staff are increasingly working in association with practices... Chemists may also be able to assist...' (para 21).

CSDPA DUTY TO INFORM SERVICE USERS ABOUT OTHER SERVICES

Local authorities have a duty under the CSDPA 1970, s.1 to tell existing service users about other services which the authority thinks relevant and which it knows about. This is a strong duty which a local authority has towards individual people; it is not just a general duty.

EXTRACTS
Legislation states:

'Every local authority...

(b) shall ensure that any such person as aforesaid who uses any other service provided by the authority whether under any such arrangements or not is informed of any other of those services which in the opinion of the authority is relevant to his needs and of any service provided by any other authority or organisation which in the opinion of the authority is so relevant and of which particulars are in the authority's possession' (CSDPA 1970,s.1(2)(b) as amended by the DP(SCR)A 1986, s.9).

Directions made under the National Assistance 1948,s.29 state that local authorities have a duty to provide advice and support to disabled (including mentally disordered) people.

DISCUSSION
Identity of 'Other' Services
A 'relevant' service is left to the opinion of the authority, but Baroness Masham explained, supporting the passing of the Disabled Persons (SCR) Bill: 'The list of what may be included is endless, but would obviously include all the activities of voluntary organisations, transport schemes, leisure opportunities, and I hope also education and employment opportunities. Basic information on benefits should be included as well as all the personal services provided by the Council and the NHS' (H57 1986).

The CSDP Bill, in one of its forms, actually listed particular services and benefits about which people should be informed, including aids and appliances, domestic help and financial benefits. Further amendment was proposed to include 'information to cover all relevant aids and appliances available from the local authority or the National Health Service'. All these specific references failed to reach the statute book.

The further amendment was opposed by the government for a number of reasons. First, the government did not want to place duties on social services 'to provide public information in a meaningful manner about medical services'. Second, there were dangers in giving information to disabled people if it put them in a position to demand or at least request services, thus undermining the role of professional workers. Third, the amendment assumed that 'the respective authorities and medical staffs are insufficiently informed about each other's services to be fully helpful to patients or clients'. If this was the case, the situation should be looked into at a later date when the new social services departments were well-established (H16 1970).

HEALTH SERVICE PROVISION OF INFORMATION: PATIENTS' CHARTER AND HEALTH INFORMATION SERVICES; INFORMATION FOR DISABLED PEOPLE; GENERAL PRACTITIONERS

In connection with the Patients' Charter, health service guidance has been issued about what sort of information should be made available to service users and how they might gain access to it. The legal import of a 'right' under the Patient's Charter is probably unclear.

Circular guidance exists asking health authorities to consider information for disabled people; and general practitioners have a duty to give people advice about local authority services.

EXTRACTS

Legislation is silent about NHS provision of information in general.

Circular guidance states that the Patient's Charter is a 'key priority for the Health Service'. The guidance talks of rights and included in these rights is access to information. One of the 'rights' is: 'to be given detailed information on local health services, including quality standards and maximum waiting times' (HSG(92)4,Annex,p.1).

This should include provision of information leaflets about hospital and community health services; of a 'well-publicised' information contact point; of information about local services in the media, local meetings etc.; of information to community health councils and other local groups to disseminate (HSG(92)4, Annex,p.1). The guidance, aimed at DHAs and FHSAs, also applies to FHSAs (see eg. HSG(93)27,Annex 1,p.2).

Circular guidance (HSG(92)21) explains that the 'Patient's Charter requires regional health authorities to set up general information services for the public from 1 April 1992'. The purpose is to help people to:
- 'understand their own health and NHS services';
- 'express their health needs to health service staff';
- 'exercise their rights within the health service, particularly through a greater knowledge of the services available and the mechanisms for enforcing their rights';
- 'make informed choices about health care...' (Annex A,p.1).

  Access to this information should be through an O345 line (charging calls at a local rate), as well as through writing and drop-in centres. The information should include:

  'definitions of services generally available – eg what services a chiropodist would be expected to offer. Information centres will want to refer to the NHS A-Z distributed to regions in March' (Annex A,p.2).

DISCUSSION
Patient's Charter Rights to Information
It is not wholly clear what legal 'rights' are actually conferred on people through the Patient's Charter (see p.377). Nevertheless, the government have confirmed in the House of Commons that the 'patients charter gives patients a right to information on local health services' (H58 1994).

Patient's Charter and Hospital Waiting Time Information: Ombudsman Investigation
The health service ombudsman has investigated a health board's application of the Patient's Charter for Scotland. It stated that people needing knee replacements were to be given 'special attention' and offered guaranteed treatment times. But the local charter guaranteed only that people would not have to wait longer than 51 weeks for either admission or first consultation. The person complained that the health board communicated no treatment date, not even the 51 week limit. The ombudsman found that the local charter was inconsistent with the Charter for Scotland; and upheld the complaint because the person should at least have been told about the 51 weeks even if no more specific information was available (HSC SW.81/92–93).

Health Service Liaison with Other Information Providers
It is perhaps noteworthy that the guidance (HSG(92)21) on information services states that regional health information centres should liaise with other information providers. DHAs, FHSAs, CHCs, Citizens' Advice Bureaux, Benefits Agency offices are all mentioned. Social services departments are not. This would appear surprising given the emphasis in community care guidance on the need for inter-agency working and cooperation. Yet notably three of the essential reference books listed in the guidance are about disabled people, social services and voluntary agencies (Appendix 2,p.1).

Information for People with Physical or Sensory Disabilities
A 1988 health notice (HN(88)26) identified issues which the health service should consider. Amongst these was 'disabled persons' *needs for service information in a suitable form*. Examples include large print and braille texts, simplified texts for language handicapped people, ethnic minority language leaflets and interpreter services for people handicapped by a communication problem' (Annex A,para xi).

General Practitioners: Advice-Giving About Social Services
Regulations containing general practitioners' terms of service include reference to GPs' duty in: 'giving advice, as appropriate, to enable patients to avail themselves of services provided by a local social services authority' (SI 1992/635,Sched.2,para 12). This would seem to imply that GPs need a certain amount of information about a range of social services if they to be able to fulfil their obligations.

Part IV

Remedies

CHAPTER 21

SUMMARY OF REMEDIES

Part V of the book explains what remedies there are, when they can be used and how to use them. Remedies are categorised into non-legal and legal remedies, and range from informal dispute resolution to judicial review in the public law courts.

Informal Resolution of Disputes

Informal dispute resolution is, of course, the obvious and most desirable option. Nobody, either service users or service providers, wishes to go to the time, effort, expense and stress of entering into formal disputes, whether non-legal (such as the formal complaints procedure) or legal. In addition, service users and carers will usually wish to maintain good relations with their authorities – and be concerned that explicit and possible legal confrontation might jeopardise this. If service users (and their advisers) and service providers are both well-informed about what the law is, what powers and duties authorities have, and what rights users have, then there should be a greater chance of avoiding or at least defusing disputes informally and at the lowest level.

It is with the aim of informing both authorities and service users, so that they can argue informally from a position of strength, that this book has been written.

Formal Non-Legal Remedies

Nevertheless, the uncertainties in community care about the nature of people's needs, about authorities' duties and about people's rights, do provide fertile soil for disputes. Failing informal resolution, there are a number of 'non-legal' remedies. These include local authority complaints procedures (both formal and informal); the local ombudsman; and the Secretary of State's power to declare that an authority is 'in default' of its duty. On the side of the health service, there are the main hospital complaints procedure, the clinical complaints ('second opinion') procedure, the health service ombudsman and the Family Health Services Authority complaints system (for GPs, dentists, pharmacists etc.).

Legal Remedies

Legal remedies fall into two main types: private law and public law remedies. Most community care disputes will probably be public law (judicial review) issues; the private law remedies of breach of statutory duty (ie when an authority doesn't perform its legal duty) and negligence appear scarcely to be viable in the community care field (although negligence is well-established in the health care field).

Finding Out Information

Sometimes service users and their advisers need to gain access to information in order to assist their case. This might, for example, be personal information about the service user; general information about what happens to other service user; or information about an authority's policies.

NON-LEGAL REMEDIES

KEY ISSUES

This chapter deals with 'non-legal' remedies – that is remedies which do not involve the law courts. As explained in the introduction to this book, one of the purposes of the book is to provide people with information so disagreements and disputes might either be avoided or at least be dealt with informally. For example, the service manager who is well-informed is less likely to impose illegal charges or institute an 'unreasonable' policy. Conversely, the well-informed service user is able quickly and conclusively to point out the illegality or the blatant unreasonableness of a policy. In both cases, a formal dispute is less likely to arise.

For reasons of time, effort, stress and money all parties usually wish to avoid formal disputes, especially those which utilise formal legal remedies. Nevertheless, where disputes do proceed further, a number of remedies exist. They are very different in nature and it is not always clear in what circumstances some of them can best be used.

The following sections summarise and explain these remedies, and includes some observations on their relative advantages and disadvantages.

SOCIAL SERVICES COMPLAINTS PROCEDURES

Under the NHS and Community Care Act 1990, Regulations and Directions have been made which place duties on local authorities to establish and operate complaints procedures. The legislation states that the procedures are for complaints about any social services functions (not just community care services). A person (or a representative) can complain only if the person is a 'qualifying' individual – that is the local authority must, or could, provide (or secure the provision of) services for the person. The local authority must also be aware of the person's need, or possible need, for services.

The complaints procedure will probably be suitable for most grievances and, because of the statutory time limits which apply to formal com-

On the other hand, from an authority's point of view, it is useful to be able to refer to central government guidance stating clearly that authorities have the power to make local priorities. For example, this could be useful to an authority if a resident of a nursing home complains that he or she was not receiving (adequate) NHS physiotherapy.

Resolving disputes informally is normally the preferable option; neither service user nor authority wishes to go to the time, trouble, stress and expense of engaging in a dispute.

INFORMAL REMEDIES

An 'informal remedy' is here used to indicate a dispute which never even 'gets off the ground' because well-informed service users or their representatives challenge authorities decisions' effectively at the outset; or alternatively, because well-informed authorities know they are on firm legal ground and can demonstrate that also from the outset. In either case, the potential dispute might be defused. If all concerned are better-informed – and if authorities' obligations and users' rights are better understood – then at least a proportion of disputes might be avoided. Nevertheless, it could be argued that the uncertainties (see p.33) inherent in community care almost invite disputes.

An example of informal dispute resolution might concern a decision to discharge somebody from hospital without domestic arrangements planned and arranged, and without consultation with the patient and relatives. If patients or their representatives can refer to government Circular guidance on hospital discharge which covers these matters, then the hospital might think twice. Better still, having to hand copies of guidance or legislation can have a disconcerting effect on health authority and local authority staff and managers.

Such is the confusion about some aspects of community care legislation and guidance, that it might be possible to worry an authority even if, in fact, there were nothing legally dubious about what it was doing. The authority might change its mind about a decision either because of legal anxiety (even if ill-founded), concern about the costs of litigation or simply because it wished to avoid bad publicity. For example, even obtaining permission from a judge for a judicial review case to proceed might put pressure on an authority – without the case ever proceeding to a full and final court hearing.

Similarly, MPs and Local Councillors might take up constituents' cases not on compelling legal grounds but simply for benevolent or compassionate reasons. For example, it is not unknown for a councillor to approve priority criteria in committee one month, and the next month, to oppose them when one of the councillor's own constituents falls victim to the criteria.

plaints, it should not be too protracted once a complaint has been made formal. (There is scope for delay whilst the complaint remains informal, since the time limits do not apply to informal complaints.)

In addition, there is an appeal procedure within the complaints system involving review panels, which seem to have fairly wide powers to examine not only the procedure an authority has employed, but also factual decisions which it has reached. This means, in effect, that it has quite extensive 'jurisdiction'. The complaints procedure is not, however, suitable for people who are seeking financial compensation.

The complaints procedure consists of three main stages: *informal, formal* and *review*. Local authorities must try to solve the matter informally. If this is not possible, they must send or give the person an explanation of the procedure and ask the person to submit the complaint in writing. The local authority must then respond to the complaint within 28 days or alternatively explain why this is not possible – and then, in any case, respond within three months.

The local authority must send its decision in writing to the complainant, normally (if different) the person on whose behalf the complaint has been made, and anybody else the local authority thinks has sufficient interest.

If the complainant is not satisfied and he or she writes to this effect within 28 days to the local authority, then the local authority has to appoint a review panel (which must contain an independent person). The panel must meet within 28 days, and then within 24 hours send its written recommendations to the local authority, the complainant, the person on whose behalf the complaint has been made (if appropriate) and anybody else the local authority thinks has sufficient interest. The local authority must then decide what it is going to do and write to the same people as above within 28 days. (The panel must also make a written record of the reasons for its recommendations).

EXTRACTS

Legislation states:

> **(establishment of procedure)** 'the Secretary of State may by order require local authorities to establish a procedure whereby a person, or anyone acting on his behalf, may make representations (including complaints) in relation to the authority's discharge of, or failure to discharge, any of their functions under this Act, or any of the enactments referred to in s.2(2) [other social services functions] of this Act, in respect of that person...'

> **(eligibility of complainants)** 'In relation to a particular local authority, an individual is a qualifying individual...if (a) the authority have a power or a duty to provide, or to secure the provision of, a service for him; and (b) his need or possible need for such a service has (by whatever means) come to the attention of the authority'

> **(directions)** 'A local authority shall comply with any directions given by the Secretary of State as to the procedure to be adopted in considering representations

made...and as to the taking of such action as may be necessary in consequence of such representations...'

(publicity) 'Every local authority shall give such publicity to the procedure as established as they consider appropriate' (our square brackets: LASSA 1970,s.7B as inserted by NHSCCA 1990, s.50).

Regulations (SI 1990/2244) state that local authorities must establish a representation/complaints procedure.

Directions (made under LASSA 1970,s.5B(6)) include the following statements:

- **(coordination)** 'The local authority shall appoint one of their officers to assist the authority in the co-ordination of all aspects of their consideration of the representations';
- **(knowledge of procedures)** 'The local authority shall ensure that all members or officers involved in the handling of representations...are familiar with the procedures';
- **(INFORMAL stage)** 'Where a local authority receives representations from a complainant they shall attempt to resolve the matter informally';
- **(FORMAL stage)** 'IF the matter cannot be resolved to the satisfaction of the complainant, the local authority shall give or send to him an explanation of the procedure set out in these Directions and ask him to submit a written representation if he wishes to proceed';
- **(assistance and guidance)** 'The local authority shall offer assistance and guidance to the complainant on the use of this procedure, or give advice on where he may obtain it';
- **(28 day response)** 'The local authority shall consider the representations and formulate a response within 28 days of their receipt, or if this is not possible, explain to the complainant within that period why it is not possible and tell him when he can expect a response, which shall in any event be within 3 calendar months of receipt of the representations';
- **(withdrawal of complaint)** 'The representation may be withdrawn at any stage by the complainant...',
- **(notification in writing of result)** the local authority must notify in writing the 'result of their consideration' to the complainant; a person on whose behalf the representation was made unless the local authority thinks that the person would not understand it or would be distressed; anyone else it considers has sufficient interest;
- **(REVIEW STAGE)** 'If the complainant informs the authority in writing within 28 days of the date on which the notification...is sent to him that he is dissatisfied with that result and wishes the matter to be referred to a panel for review, the local authority shall appoint a panel (including any independent person) to consider the matter which the local authority shall refer to it';
- **(review panel meeting)** 'The panel shall meet within 28 days of the receipt of the complainant's request for review by the local authority to consider the

matter together with any oral or written submissions as the complainant or the local authority wish the panel to consider';

- **(review panel decision)** the panel 'shall decide on its recommendations and record them in writing within 24 hours of the end of the meeting' and 'send written copies of their recommendations' to the local authority, the complainant, (if appropriate) the person on whose behalf the complaint was made, and any other person the authority considers has sufficient interest;
- **(panel's reasons)** 'The panel shall record the reasons for their recommendations in writing';
- **(local authority's response)** 'The local authority shall consider what action they ought to take, and notify in writing the persons specified [immediately above] of the local authority's decision and of their reasons for taking that decision and of any action which they have taken or propose to take within 28 days of the date of the panel's recommendation'
- **(independent person)** '"independent person"…means a person who is neither a member nor an officer of that authority, nor, where the local authority have delegated any of its social services functions to any organisation, a person who is a member of or employed by that organisation, nor the spouse of any such person'.
  (Directions: Complaints Procedure Directions 1990: in DH 1990,appendix C; made under LASSA 1970, s.7B(3)).

Policy guidance states that complaints procedures should be 'uncomplicated, accessible to those who might wish to use them and understood by all members of staff' (DH 1990,para 6.14).

DISCUSSION
Access to Complaints Procedure

The complaints procedure is in principle accessible to a broad class of people, since complaints can be made about any social services functions by people who need, or have only a possible need, of services.

However, somebody denied a community care assessment altogether because the authority thinks that he or she is not someone it 'may' provide services for might not be eligible to use the procedure.

It was explained by Baroness Blatch for the government during the passing of the NHS and Community Care Bill that if the authority judges that a person 'is not a person for whom they may provide community care services' and, as a result, declines to carry out an assessment, then the procedure could not be used. Instead it would be 'a matter of law' to be decided by the court: a complaints procedure would not be appropriate. On a practical level, availability of the procedure to such people could pave the way for vexatious applicants' wasting of authorities' time. However, she also pointed out that people could instead resort to local councillors, members of the social service committee or in the case of maladministration to the local ombudsman (H76 1990).

No Formal Judicial Appeal Procedure

Policy guidance explains that where disagreement arises over service provision, the representation/complaints procedure is the channel for contesting the decision. There is no formal judicial procedure.

The guidance explains that a 'formal judicial appeal procedure would be foreign to such arrangements and it would not be appropriate to introduce one' (DH 1990,para 3.54). The Secretary of State for Health resisted an amendment for a system of appeals during the passage of the NHS and Community Care Bill. She referred to the remedy of the complaints procedures, though admitted that an appeals system would be potentially more effective than such procedures. However, such an appeals system would not be appropriate because it would 'not be helpful for local authorities to embark upon a cumbersome, bureaucratic system of appeals at this time, when they already have many new proposals on their agenda' (H77 1990).

Statutory Time Limits for Response

There is some evidence that authorities are struggling to meet the statutory response times, of 28 days, or failing this, three months. For example, an SSI (1993d,pp.36–37) inspection of complaints procedures, despite finding good practice in many other respects, also found that formal investigations were often taking longer than three months – and that 28 days was considered an almost impossible timescale for formal complaints. Informal complaints were solved more quickly, and despite a lack of conclusive information about this, the inspection concluded on the evidence that 15 days would be reasonable. (In fact, the time limits do not apply to informal complaints.) An SSI monitoring exercise made similar findings: good progress generally but problems with time scales (SSI 1993c,p30).

To avoid challenges and, for example, possible findings of maladministration by the local ombudsman, authorities should provide clear information about procedures at the informal stage. For service users, one way around possible delay is to ignore the informal stage and begin with the formal stage: policy guidance states that it is possible to do this (DH 1990, para 6.30).

One local ombudsman investigation found admirable aims in one complaints procedure – but serious flaws in practice. The maladministration found was based on a number of criticisms. The complaints coordinator apparently made no real attempt to analyse the contents of a letter of complaint. The council did not respond to the complaint within 28 days as the law demands – nor did it explain in writing to the complainant why it could not respond in 28 days. No 'substantive reply' to the complaint had been forthcoming from the council after 16 months. There was a question of whether the staff involved had sufficient training to 'distance themselves from the personal, and to identify the very real, issues' which the complainant was concerned about (CLAE 92/A/3725).

Giving of Reasons During the Complaints Procedure

The Directions state that the review panel must give reasons – but at the earlier stage of the procedure it is the 'result' which has to be communicated. This does not necessarily mean that reasons have to be communicated at those earlier stages.

In addition to what the Directions state about the giving of reasons by the review panel, the courts might also require that those reasons be intelligible, comprehensive and deal with the relevant issues. The intelligibility requirement would probably relate to the subjective understanding of complainants or of people representing them.

Independence of Person on Review Panel

The Directions (see above) state that local authority members and employees cannot be independent. However, it is possible that a court, applying the principle of fairness that a decision-maker must not be (or seem to be) biased, might hold that other people are not independent. For example, if the proposed independent person were an employee of the local health authority – which might be involved in joint assessments with the local authority – the court might rule that there is an appearance of bias.

Review Panel Procedures

In addition to what the Directions (above) say, policy guidance expands on review panel procedure. It states that people appointed should, if possible, have relevant experience of the subject matter of the complaint. The guidance stresses the need for informality and states that if a complainant is accompanied by somebody (who might also speak for them at the meeting) that person should not be a barrister or a solicitor acting in a professional capacity. The complainant or accompanying person should be given the opportunity to make an oral submission before the authority.

However, it is possible that the courts might say that sometimes professional representation is permissible if, for example, legal complexity is involved (Gordon 1993,p.53) – despite what the guidance says.

The local ombudsman included in a finding of maladministration, the observation that he found it 'hard to see how a solicitor employed by the Council could be seen as an "unbiased observer" and consider the way in which he joined at the outset in the in camera deliberations of the Panel to be unwise at the very least' (CLAE 92/C/1042).

Review Panel Recommendations

In a High Court case (*R v Avon County Council ex p. M 1993*) the judge found against a social services committee which refused to adopt a review panel's recommendations on the basis of representations made by the director of social services. The judge stated: 'It seems to me that anyone required by law to give reasons for reconsideration must show they have given submission sufficient weight'. Though the judge stated that he 'would be reluctant to hold that in no circumstances could the social services committee overrule the panel in their exercise of their legal right', nevertheless, it is thought that the case makes it difficult for a committee to do so in future (Cox 1993).

However, in a subsequent community case, the judge did not accept that the *Avon* case had established a hard and fast rule that authorities must accept, in full, review panel recommendations (*R v North Yorkshire CC, ex p. Hargreaves 1994*).

There appears to be some uncertainty about the role of the review panel. Some authorities' review panels do consider the actual merits of decisions, while others concentrate only on the correctness of complaints system procedures. An SSI inspection report comments that panels 'should be concerned primarily with considering whether the action or decision being complained about was appropriate and whether it is still appropriate. Considering only whether the procedures have been followed correctly seems not to accord with the intention of the DH guidance' (SSI 1993d,p.29).

Certainly in the *Avon* case, the review panel made a finding of fact that the person concerned had a 'need', against the local authority's view which was that the person was expressing a 'preference' but did not have a need. The court upheld the view of the review panel.

Recording of Complaints

Informal complaints do not necessarily have to be in writing. Because they are 'informal' and possibly because of definitional problems, informal complaints might be less than thoroughly recorded and monitored (eg. SSI 1994c, pp.17,41). For example, in one authority there was a policy of not recording complaints made in residential care or day care settings unless they were referred to the manager. The point of this was to avoid recording 'minor grumbles', but it appeared to contradict the authority's own procedural guidelines and reduced protection for vulnerable people (SSI 1994f,p.25).

However, formal complaints should be recorded and when they are not the local ombudsman has found maladministration; for example, when an authority could not produce documentary evidence that a complaint had been thoroughly investigated and had failed to send 'a full, written response' following the investigation. This finding of maladministration was made despite the 'enormous staffing problems' (caused by an industrial dispute) in the local authority's neighbourhood office at the time (CLAE 92/A/4104,p.16).

SECRETARY OF STATE DEFAULT POWERS

If a local authority fails, unreasonably, to carry out any of its social services duties, the Secretary of State can declare that the local authority is 'in default', and direct the local authority to perform its duty. Such a direction can be enforced by the High Court. The default powers have never been used, although the Department of Health does make informal enquiries. These can take a long time – and anyway have never led to a default order being made.

The courts have sometimes used the existence of the default powers in legislation to argue that Parliament did not intend private law rights to exist in addition to such powers; and that public law remedies (judicial review) would only be available if the default powers were not an adequate alternative remedy to judicial review.

Because neither these powers, nor their predecessors, have ever been used, they are of little obvious use to service users and thus authorities would appear to have little to fear from this remedy. It is possible that the Department of Health enquiries (about whether to use the default powers), though sometimes slow, might be instrumental in effecting some pressure on authorities 'behind the scenes'.

EXTRACTS
Legislation states:

(declaration of default) 'If the Secretary of State is satisfied that any local authority have failed, without reasonable excuse, to comply with any of their duties which are social services functions (other than a duty imposed by or under the Children Act 1989), he may make an order declaring that authority to be in default with respect to the duty in question.'

(directions) The order can 'contain such directions for the purpose of ensuring that the duty is complied with within such period as may be specified in the order as appear to the Secretary of State to be necessary.'

(High Court enforcement) The direction 'shall, on the application of the Secretary of State, be enforceable by mandamus.'

DISCUSSION
Background

These powers replace default powers formerly available under section 36 of the National Assistance Act 1948. Those powers were never used. Jack Ashley had observed in 1979 that the powers of the Secretary of State were so sweeping that they were unlikely to be used since he 'can only suspend the operation of the social services department of the local authority concerned'. Thus, were he to intervene, 'he may end up by running a large part of the country's social services'. Given the Secretary of State's reluctance therefore to use the default powers, 'the individual disabled person can be ignored with impunity by a reactionary local council...' (H79 1979).

Differences Between the Old and the New Default Powers

The new section, 7D (LASSA 1970), differs from the old s.36:

(1) s.7D does not refer explicitly to the ultimate sanction (if a local authority did not comply with a Secretary of State direction) in s.36 of the taking over by the Secretary of State of the functions of the local authority;

(2) s.7D covers all social services duties (excluding children's services); whereas s.36 only covered the National Assistance Act 1948. However, s.7D does only refer to duties – whereas s.36 referred to functions (ie powers and duties);

(3) a direction under s.7D can be enforced by the High Court: there was no similar provision in s.36.

Use of the New Default Powers (s.7D, LASSA 1970)

During the passing of the NHS and Community Care Bill, the Under-Secretary of State for Health explained that normally there would be various stages to pass before the default powers were used:

'It is likely that there would have been earlier stages before reaching the legislative procedure on default – that is, perhaps a social services inspectorate investigation, a specific direction or even an inquiry. I share my hon. Friend's concern about not wanting to prolong an abuse or error. I assure my hon. Friend that the Department of Health will act with all speed in cases brought to its attention of clear abuse or when the general principles of the Act or the general directions given by the Secretary of State are clearly not being complied with. We do not want years of delay…' (H80 1990).

Use of the Old Default Powers (s.36, NAA 1948)

The old default powers were never used, although the Department of Health made a number of enquiries. For example, between 1979 and 1985, the Department made 33 sets of enquiries but found no need to take default action (H81 1985).

The Government, asked in 1987 about the use of default powers (under section 36 of the NAA 1948), quoted Mr. Justice Simon Brown from the case of *R v DHSS and Others, ex p Bruce 1986*:

'So far as that Ministerial power is concerned it is, in my judgement, perfectly clear that the Minister could not properly intervene so as to declare the authority to be in default unless the authority had manifestly failed in the discharge of any of their functions in such a way that no reasonable Minister could take a different view: putting it a different way, had conducted themselves in a way which could only be regarded as a failure on the part of the authority to perform the duty' (H82 1987).

Although the new default powers differ from the old, this judicial statement is probably still a guide to use of the new default powers.

Time Taken to Consider Potential Default Cases

Asked in 1986 about how long it took to investigate potential default cases, the government replied that the average time was five months, while the shortest was four weeks and the longest 28 months (H83 1986).

Use of Other Remedies

Under the old default powers, the courts stated that the existence of those powers meant that people could not decide to pursue *private law* remedies but had to use the default remedy (*Wyatt v Hillingdon LBC 1978; Southwark LBC v Williams 1971*).

However, where a *public law* remedy is a possibility, the default powers might not always be regarded by the courts as a suitable alternative. For example, in one case the courts have stated that the issue (consultation with residents about closing a residential home) was more appropriate for the courts to deal with. This was because (a) it was not clear that the general duty to consult was a social services function which the default powers applied to; and (b) that the issue was a legal one in a developing field of law and therefore more appropriate for the courts (*R v Durham County Council, ex p. Curtis and Broxson 1992*). In another area of local authority law (in connection with licences), the courts have referred to the inability of a statutory appeals procedure to determine the issue at stake (*R v Leeds City Council, ex p. Hendry 1993*).

GENERAL AND SPECIFIC DIRECTIONS

The Secretary of State can make both specific and general directions. Section 7A of the LASSA 1970 states that 'every local authority shall exercise their social services functions in accordance with such directions as may be given to them under this section by the Secretary of State'. The Directions must be in writing and 'may be given to a particular authority, or to authorities of a particular class, or to authorities generally'.

The Notes on Clauses (DH,SHHD,WO 1989,p.68), accompanying the NHS and Community Care Bill, stated that: 'Generally, it is intended that this power be used infrequently and only to the extent necessary to safeguard the interests of users of services and their carers'.

The Under Secretary of State for Health explained during the passing of the NHS and Community Care Bill that 'the specific directions break new ground because the Secretary of State for Health does not have the specific power at the moment to make directions concerning a home, for example...'. He went on to explain further that specific directions 'would be used in relation to the balance of care provision. If a local authority falls down in its duty as a result of either dogma or sheer inefficiency and abuse, the Secretary of State would have the power to intervene'.

There was concern that government might use both general and specific directions to 'prejudice local authorities' activities in providing local authority residential accommodation'. But the government pointed out that directions 'cannot upset the purpose of primary legislation and therefore the principles...which call for mixed care for the elderly in local authority residential accommodation and, in the independent sector, voluntary and private accommodation' (H78 1990).

SECRETARY OF STATE INQUIRIES

Under s.7C of the LASSA 1970, the Secretary of State can 'cause an inquiry to be held in any case, where on representations made to him or otherwise, he considers it advisable to do so in connection with the exercise by any local authority of any of their social services functions' (other than children's services). The Local Government Act 1972 (s.250(2)–(5)) applies to such inquiries.

The Notes on Clauses (DH,SHHD,WO 1989,p.68) state that the clause enables 'the person appointed to hold an inquiry to compel the attendance of witness [sic] and to take evidence on oath and enable the Secretary of State to make orders as to the payment of costs'.

RELATIONSHIP BETWEEN GENERAL DIRECTIONS, INQUIRIES, SPECIFIC DIRECTIONS AND USE OF DEFAULT POWERS

The Under-Secretary of State for Health explained, during the passing of the NHS and Community Care Bill, the possible sequence of use of the powers under s.7A (general and specific directions), s.7C (inquiries) and s.7D (default powers) of the LASSA 1970. The sequence could be 'general directions [7A] provided, in the sense of drawing up care plans and assessment, perhaps an inquiry [7C] if there is a problem, perhaps a specific direction [7A] to correct the errors discovered in an inquiry, and then perhaps a default order [7D]...' (our square brackets). He added that the 'new powers would complete the circle. In the past, the Secretary of State may have known of abuse, but could not act. He had no powers to set up an inquiry, to issue specific directions or to go to the courts in cases of default' (H84 1990).

(The reference to inquiries in this last comment is slightly unclear, since there *was* reference to 'inquiry' specifically in the old s.36 of the National Assistance Act and generally in s.54).

LOCAL OMBUDSMAN

The following represents a brief summary of the function of the local ombudsman. Of particular significance for this book is that local ombudsman investigations explore areas of social services and housing authority service provision quite widely. For example, the local ombudsmen have considered the use of priorities, length of waiting lists and closure of waiting lists, consistent application of eligibility criteria, provision of adequate information, communication within and between local authority departments and so on. The Commission for Local Administration (the office of the local ombudsman) has published a useful guide containing 42 axioms of good administrative practice (CLAE 1993a).

The local ombudsmen appear to make thorough and – within their remit of investigating maladministration and injustice suffered – wide-ranging investigations. In common with judicial review by the courts, the local ombudsmen investigate the way in which authorities act and make decisions rather than what those decisions and actions are. However, they do seem to investigate flexibly and it has been suggested that they are able to base their investigations on 'equity' (ie. general fairness or 'natural' justice) rather than law – in a way which the courts are unable to do (see eg. Williams, Goriely 1994).

They can investigate in response not just to the complaint of an individual person, but also of an appropriate organisation: for example, a local advice agency might make representations on behalf of a number of people affected by a common problem. They can also call for and examine information about other service users in a similar situation to that of the complainant.

The ombudsmen can recommend financial compensation, and although authorities are not obliged to follow the recommendations, they are likely to incur bad publicity if they do not. Generally speaking, the findings and recommendations of the ombudsmen are respected and followed.

EXTRACTS

Legislation: reference to legislation is included in the discussion below.

DISCUSSION

Function of Ombudsman

The local government ombudsman (formally known as the Commissioner for Local Administration – in fact there is more than one ombudsman and at the time of writing one is a woman) function under the Local Government Act 1974 as amended by the Local Government and Housing Act 1989 (see CLAE 1990,p.59 for changes explained). The ombudsman can investigate maladministration in, amongst others, district, borough, city or county councils.

Maladministration

Maladministration is not defined in legislation and the ombudsmen have themselves interpreted the term. Examples include 'arbitrariness, bias or discrimination; neglect, delay, incompetence or failure to observe established policies or procedures; failure to give reasons for an adverse decision; and failure to consider issues properly' (Thomas 1994).

In principle maladministration alone is not generally for the courts to investigate because bad administration is not unlawful and likewise the ombudsman, in principle at least, does not investigate matters which could be referred to a court of law (see below) (see Fordham 1994,p.212 on: *R v IRC, ex parte National Federation of Self-Employed and Small Businesses Ltd 1982,* when Lord Scarman explained maladministration in relation both to the role of the Parliamentary ombudsman and of the courts).

The Commission of Local Administration (the ombudsman's office) has published a useful guide (CLAE 1993a) to good administrative practice containing 42 axioms. These include, for example, the following considerations:

- understanding by staff of relevant legislation and council policies;
- communication of policies to service users;
- adherence to, and consistent application of, policies;
- provision of adequate and accurate information;
- giving of proper consideration to the views of relevant parties; carrying out of sufficient investigation to establish relevant facts; seeking of appropriate advice;
- giving of reasons for adverse decisions;
- ensuring that decisions and actions are taken within a reasonable time;
- compiling and keeping adequate records;
- avoidance of misleading statements;
- give undertakings or promises carefully and discharge responsibilities which follow;
- etc.

Procedure

Before complaining to the ombudsman, the council must be given an opportunity to deal with the complaint – through a complaints procedure. If the complainant is not satisfied then he or she can contact the ombudsman in writing (CLAE 1993,p.3). The ombudsman is thus a last resort (Thomas 1994).

Jurisdiction

The ombudsman cannot investigate:

- **(time limit)** a matter which occurred more than twelve months before the complaint is made unless the ombudsman accepts that there is a good reason for this;
- **(alternative remedy)** a matter which has already been referred to a court, a tribunal or government minister, or could be referred (unless the ombudsman accepts that it would be unreasonable to expect the complainant to do this);
- **(general matter)** a matter which affects all or most of the inhabitants of a local authority's area: eg. a waste of public money;
- court proceedings;

- personnel matters;
- school and college internal affairs;
- some contractual or commercial matters (but can investigate land transactions) (CLAE 1993,p.4).

(However, the ombudsman often exercises discretion to investigate cases even where there is an alternative remedy. For example, if the remedy is judicial review the ombudsmen 'would not normally expect the ordinary citizen to go to the trouble and expense involved in relation to a possibly small benefit' (Thomas 1994).)

Types of Complainant

The complainant can be an individual or body (whether or not incorporated).

Outcome of Investigations

Very few complaints result in findings of maladministration. It seems that only 3–4% of complaints become formal; and only 3% of these result in findings of maladministration. However, of the 16% settled locally without formal reports being issued, many might concern maladministration about which reports probably would have been issued (Thomas 1994).

Remedies

Where maladministration has caused injustice, the ombudsmen can recommend unlimited financial compensation and any other lawful remedy. Local authorities are empowered to pay the recommended compensation. The principle behind a remedy is to put the complainant in the position he or she would have been in. If a council refuses to adopt the ombudsman's recommendations, even after a second report, it can be forced to publish the ombudsman's report in a newspaper at its own expense (Thomas 1994).

Unlike the Commissioner for Complaints in Northern Ireland, (under the Commissioner for Complaints Act (Northern Ireland) 1969 as amended), ombudsmen in England, Wales and Scotland do not have a power to refer cases on to a court of law. The power in Northern Ireland had by 1989 been exercised only 30 times in 20 years (Northern Ireland Commissioner for Complaints 1990,p.123).

LOCAL AUTHORITY MONITORING OFFICERS

A local monitoring officer has a duty to report on actual or possible contraventions of legislation by local authorities, including contraventions of codes of practice made under legislation. The duty is also to report on actual or possible maladministration or injustice caused by the authority. The monitoring officer might be a useful avenue of approach for service users and their advisers, when questioning local authority policies.

The actual wording is that the monitoring officer has a duty, 'if it at any time appears to him that any proposal, decision or omission...constitutes, has given rise to or is likely to or would give rise to...a contravention of any enactment of rule of law of any code of practice made or approved by or under any enactment; or...any such maladministration or injustice...'

The proposal, act or omission – and the actual contravention – might be by the authority; by any committee. sub-committee or officer of the authority; or by any joint committee on which the authority is represented (LGHA 1989,s.5).

COMMUNITY CARE CHARTER COMPLAINTS

At the time of writing, a consultation document (DH 1994c) has been issued about community care charters. It is proposed that local authorities produce such charters by April 1996. The status of charters is explained in Chapter 6; and the way in which charter complaints are generally handled below (p.377).

HEALTH SERVICE COMPLAINTS: OVERVIEW

There are four main avenues of complaint short of formal legal action:

(1) the main **hospital complaints procedure;**

(2) **clinical complaints procedure:** ie complaints about clinical judgement, excluded from the main hospital complaints system, are dealt with by a separate system, sometimes known as the 'second opinion' procedure;

(4) the **health service ombudsman,** who can investigate maladministration, failure in a service, and failure to provide a service which there is a duty to provide. The health service ombudsman cannot directly challenge clinical judgements but nevertheless can question closely related factors.

(4) the **Family Health Services Authority (FHSA) complaints procedure** relating to general practitioners, general dental practitioners, community pharmacists, ophthalmic opticians, ophthalmic medical practitioners.

A report (Wilson 1994) recommending changes to, and simplification of, the complaints system has been published in 1994. Legislation is in prospect. The report makes a number of observations. These include the fact that there are reservations about whether the main hospital complaints procedure offers independent investigation. There is confusion about a separate system of complaints for clinical matters, especially given that there may be no clear distinction between clinical and non-clinical complaints. The clinical complaints procedure can take years to complete. The report finds that the health service ombudsman is highly regarded, although there is concern about the length of investigations (pp.25–27).

(Under s.85 of the NHS Act 1977, the Secretary of State has the power to declare a health authority to be in default of its duty. The power has, to the best of the writers' knowledge, never been used).

HOSPITAL COMPLAINTS PROCEDURE

This procedure is for complaints other than those about clinical decisions.

EXTRACTS

Legislation (Hospital Complaints Procedure Act 1985) requires the Secretary of State to issue directions ensuring that arrangements are made for dealing with complaints and that those arrangements are publicised (s.1).

Directions (in HC(88)37) made under the Hospital Complaints Procedure Act 1985) place duties on health authorities:
- **(designation of officer)** an officer must be designated to deal with complaints;
- **(officer's responsibilities)** this officer must receive formal complaints and ensure that they are acted upon; and assist in dealing with complaints which are likely to be solved informally;
- the officer must investigate and report on the investigation of formal complaints to the complainant and anybody else involved in the complaint;
- **(limits to officer's responsibilities)** the officer's duties do not include responsibility for investigating complaints about:
    - the exercise of clinical judgement;
    - serious incidents resulting in harm to patients;
    - staff conduct which merits disciplinary proceedings;
    - incidents which might reasonably merit police investigation;
- **(informal resolution)** arrangements must exist for staff to try and deal informally with complaints, and if this is unsuccessful, to advise complainants about making formal complaints;
- **(formal complaints in writing)** arrangements must ensure that formal complaints are made in writing;
- **(time limits)** complaints should normally be made within three months of an incident, but there is discretion to waive this limit;
- **(prompt response)** responses to formal complaints should be prompt and should enable complainant and hospital staff to submit relevant information;
- **(monitoring of procedures)** health authorities must monitor complaints procedures and prepare quarterly reports;
- **(publicity)** the authority must ensure that patients, staff and community health councils are fully informed about the complaints procedure.

DISCUSSION

People with a Mental Disorder

The normal hospital complaints procedure is open to people with a mental disorder. In addition, detained patients can complain to the Mental Health Act Commission under sections 120 and 121 of the Mental Health Act 1983.

CLINICAL COMPLAINTS PROCEDURE

Complaints about the exercise of clinical judgements by hospital medical and dental staff are not covered by the main hospital complaints procedures (see above). Separate provisions exist in the clinical complaints procedure.

EXTRACTS
See discussions below.

DISCUSSION
Circular guidance (HC(81)5, Memorandum) describes a three stage procedure to be followed in response to complaints about clinical judgements. The *first stage* is when the consultant concerned investigates and makes a response to an oral or written complaint made to him or her, or other health authority staff. (If there is a possibility of legal action, the consultant should inform the relevant health authority administrator).

If the complainant remains dissatisfied, the *second stage* involves renewing the complaint in writing to either the consultant or to health authority administrators.

Where necessary, a *third stage* of independent professional review can be invoked, involving 'second opinions' by two independent consultants working in the relevant field. The third stage is not intended to be applied in cases where there is likely to be court action or formal action by the health authority.

HEALTH SERVICE OMBUDSMAN

The health service ombudsman can investigate injustice or hardship caused to a patient through failure in service; failure to provide a service which there is a duty to provide; maladministration. This gives the ombudsman reasonably broad powers of investigation. The ombudsman's investigations sometimes expose important legal and policy issues: for example, a number of recent cases have examined the provision of longterm, continuing care by health authorities.

However, the ombudsman cannot question clinical judgement, or investigate complaints about GPs, general dental practitioners and other 'general medical services' practitioners. Nor can the ombudsman normally, although he can decide otherwise, investigate incidents which happened more than a year ago, or cases where there are alternative remedies.

EXTRACTS
Legislation (Health Service Commissioners Act 1993) provides for the health service ombudsman to investigate complaints about the sustaining of 'injustice or hardship in consequence of':
- **failure in a service;**
- **failure to provide a service** for which there is a duty to provide;

- **maladministration** (in the absence of maladministration, the ombudsman has no power to question the merits of decisions taken within the discretion of the decision-maker) (s.3).

DISCUSSION
Standards of Patient Care
The ability to investigate the above matters means, as the ombudsman's annual report explains, that the ombudsman's jurisdiction 'extends beyond maladministration into areas directly concerned with standards and delivery of patient care' (HSC 1993,p.2).

Maladministration has been described by the ombudsman's office as including:
- not following proper procedures and rules;
- not following agreed policies;
- not having proper procedures;
- giving wrong information;
- not explaining the care being given to a patient;
- unsatisfactory investigation by an NHS authority of the original complaint and unjustified delays in replying to complaints (Health Service Ombudsman for England 1991).

Limits to Jurisdiction
The ombudsman cannot investigate a number of matters including where:
- there is or has been an **alternative remedy** available unless the ombudsman 'is satisfied that in the particular circumstances it is not reasonable to expect that person to resort or have resorted to it';
- there is or has been a **formal inquiry** under the NHS Act 1977,s.84;
- the complaint is about action 'taken solely in consequence of the exercise of clinical judgement' and concerned with the 'diagnosis of illness' or the 'care or treatment of a patient';
- the complaint is about 'general medical services' (eg. GPs, dentists, pharmacists) or a family health services authority's action concerning a formal complaint;
- staff/personnel matters;
- the complaint is made more than a year after the event/matters complained about – unless the ombudsman thinks it is reasonable still to accept the complaint (see: Health Service Commissioners Act 1993,s.4–9).

Types of Complainants
Complaints can be made by individuals or suitable body (whether or not incorporated) representing patients (HSCA 1993 s.8): for example, a Community Health Council or a Citizen's Advice Bureau.

Procedure

The complaint must be in writing and must first of all have been made to the relevant health service body, which must have been given a 'reasonable opportunity' to investigate and respond to the complaint (HSCA 1993, s.9).

Remedies

Legislation does not lay down formal remedies, although the health service ombudsman can make recommendations as to remedies. The ombudsman will send a report of the findings to the complainant and the health authority. If the complaint, or at least part of it, is upheld the report will also state whether the health authority has agreed to remedy the injustice or hardship. The health authority might, for example, apologise or agree to change its policies and procedures (Health Service Ombudsman for England 1991,p.5). Sometimes the health authority might pay financial compensation if as a result of its actions, costs have been incurred by a person or their family: for example, private nursing home fees.

POWER TO DECLARE A HEALTH AUTHORITY IN DEFAULT OF ITS DUTY

Under s.85 of the NHS Act 1977, the Secretary of State can declare health authorities or NHS Trusts to be in default of their duty. This would be where 'they have failed to carry out any functions conferred or imposed on them by or under this Act, or have in carrying out those functions failed to comply with any regulations or directions relating to those functions'.

It seems that the section has never been used – no default order has ever been issued.

PATIENT'S CHARTER

As explained elsewhere in this book (see p.74), the Patient's Charter creates certain rights and standards for NHS patients. If these are not adhered to, people can write to the Chief Executive of the hospital. The NHS Executive (part of the Department of Health) can also exert pressure on hospitals when charter rights and standards have not been breached.

However, in the last resort there appear not to be enforceable remedies within the charter scheme. (eg, the draft consultation document (DH 1994c) on community care charters states that when things 'go wrong', people will receive an explanation and apology; and that authorities will learn lessons. However, it states that people should also be given information about their legal rights to make complaints and about the local and health service ombudsman – suggesting that people might still have to use these other remedies).

On the one hand, the charter offers in principle a simple, direct and cheap route to obtaining apologies and redress from health authorities. On the other hand, it does not replace other remedies (such as the hospital complaints procedure or legal action). This means that complainants still have to resort to these other remedies if they do not get satisfaction through the charter complaints process. Seen in this light, the informal charter complaints process could in some circumstances become yet one more obstacle to obtaining a legal remedy (for a summary of these issues, see Williams, Goriely 1994).

(The health service ombudsman will probably put store by what the Patient's Charter states. For example, finding against a health board over non-provision of information about waiting times, he included in his criticisms the fact that the board's own charter did not conform with the Patient's Charter for Scotland – and that it should do so (HSC SW.81/92–93)).

FAMILY HEALTH SERVICES AUTHORITY (FHSA) COMPLAINTS PROCEDURES (ABOUT GENERAL PRACTITIONERS, DENTISTS, PHARMACISTS ETC.)

Complaints, both formal and informal, about GPs, dentists and pharmacists are covered by the NHS (Service Committees and Tribunal) Regulations (SI 1992/664 as amended) made under the NHS Act 1977 (various sections). Extensive guidance notes have been issued to health authority managers and community health councils (issued with: FHSL(93)60): the following is based on these notes together with a local FHSA leaflet (Camden and Islington FHSA 1994).

EXTRACTS
Not given here, but see: SI 1992/664.

DISCUSSION
Services Covered
The FHSA complaints procedures covers 'general medical services': that is, general practitioners, general dental practitioners, community pharmacists, ophthalmic opticians, ophthalmic medical practitioners. The FHSA cannot investigate complaints about services provided privately, ie, not on the NHS.

Types of Complainant
The patient, the patient's representative can make a complaint. If the patient has died, anybody can make a complaint.

Form of Complaint
Complaints must be in writing, unless the person cannot make a written complaint on account of disability, illiteracy or a language problem, in which case oral complaints can be accepted. The FHSA must arrange for the oral complaint to be tape-recorded.

Time Limits

Complaints should normally be made within 13 weeks of the event complained about. FHSAs can choose to ignore this time limit if there is a good reason for the delay in making the complaint.

Minor or Major Complaint?

Examples of 'major' complaints more suitable for formal investigation might be, for example, prolonged treatment without seeing the patient, failure to examine, inability to contact the doctor, failure to relieve severe pain in terminal illness.

Informal Procedure

An informal procedure is used for 'minor complaints'. The procedure should be completed within one month. Lay conciliators, appointed by the FHSA, are sometimes involved (with the complainant's consent) to try and resolve the complaint.

Formal Procedure

If a complaint is 'major' or is not resolved at the informal stage, a formal procedure is available. Certain criteria have to be met for progressing a formal complaint: the FHSA Service Committee Chairperson must consider that there are reasonable grounds for believing that the practitioner has broken the terms of his or her service. If so, the FHSA asks the practitioner to make written comments on the complaint within four weeks. The complainant can read and make comments on the practitioner's comments. The Chairperson then decides whether a hearing (conducted under procedural rules) is necessary.

The Service Committee's report is sent to the FHSA which decides what to do about it. This decision, together with the report, is sent to the complainant and practitioner. There are rights of appeal against the decision to an Appeals Unit.

Remedies

If the complaint against the practitioner is upheld, the practitioner could be given a warning, have pay deducted, or be referred to the appropriate professional body (eg. General Medical Council).

Financial compensation cannot be given by the FHSA.

FINDING OUT INFORMATION (LOCAL AUTHORITY)

Sometimes service users and their advisers need to gain access to information in order to assist their case. This might, for example, be personal information about the service user; general information about what happens to other service users; or information about an authority's policies.

There are a number of relevant pieces of legislation relevant to obtaining local authority information.

EXTRACTS
Legislation: this is referred to in the following paragraphs.

DISCUSSION
Access to Personal Files
Relevant legislation is the Access to Personal Files Act 1987 and the Access to Personal Files (Social Services) Regulations 1989 (SI 1989/206).

Local authorities have a duty to inform individuals if they hold 'accessible personal information' about him or her – and to give the person access to it for a small fee. If any other individual (other than a health professional or a local authority employee) is identifiable in the information, then that other person's consent must be asked for.

The authority must give the person access to the information within 40 days of the request or of the consent received from another person. The quickest way for advisers to get information is to include with the request a letter of authority signed by the service user and anybody else known to be mentioned in the information; and to include the current fee of £10.00.

The definition of personal information includes an expression of opinion about someone – but does not include an indication of the intentions of the authority towards that person. Information recorded before the 1st April 1989 is not regarded as accessible. Authorities do not have to supply information if to do so would cause serious harm to the physical or mental health of the applicant or anybody else. They do not have to supply it if to do so would disclose the identity of the person who was the source of the information – if that person has not consented. Legal professional privilege, which could be maintained in legal proceedings, is another reason why authorities do not have to supply information.

Authorities can rectify inaccurate information if requested by the individual concerned – and a local authority committee can look into disputes about access to, rectification or erasure of information.

Information About Other People
The access which people have to personal records does not entitle a particular user to information about how other service users have been treated. Their consent would be needed, and probably each of them would have to make a separate application. Therefore, from the point of view of service users and their advisers, there is a need to pool local knowledge so that radically dissimilar decisions can be identified in similar cases. Such information might be useful, for example, in challenging an authority's assessment that somebody is not 'in need' and in bringing some objectivity to the concept of need.

From authorities' point of view, they should be able to argue that no two cases are ever exactly the same because individuals' circumstances vary greatly, even where people's conditions or disabilities are apparently similar.

Attendance at Meetings

Relevant legislation is the Public Bodies (Admission to Meetings) Act 1960 and the Local Government Act 1972 (ss.110A-K). These give the public the right to attend local authority meetings (with some exceptions) including some social services committee meetings. Access is denied if confidential information is at issue, but confidential information in this context does not include information about other service users. However, access can be denied if exempt information is to be discussed. Exempt information covers past recipients or applicants for any council service or financial assistance. It also covers information about legal proceedings.

Access to agendas, reports and background documents must be given three days before a meeting, but items can be excluded if they relate to parts of the meeting which will not be open to the public.

CHAPTER 24

LEGAL REMEDIES

KEY ISSUES

This chapter outlines when and how legal remedies involving the law courts are used. As explained already, most community care disputes which reach the courts will involve public law (judicial review), rather than private law. However, there are some advantages in using private law (such as not having to seek permission of a judge to bring the case, and the possibility of damages/financial compensation).

The principles and uncertainties underlying public and private law remedies have been explained in Chapter 7 and are not repeated here. In addition, this chapter briefly describes some of the factors involved in judges' decisions — awareness of which might be useful both to authorities and service users.

PUBLIC LAW (JUDICIAL REVIEW)

Public law procedures mostly involve judicial review which examines whether authorities have acted *unreasonably, illegally or unfairly* (see Chapter 7). Essentially, judicial review is used to regulate the way in which local authorities exercise their discretion in making administrative decisions. **Judicial review is not about people's direct rights to service, but is about ensuring that authorities make decisions properly and legally.** For example, a court might find that an authority had decided unreasonably that a person needed only one hour of home help a week instead of ten. The court cannot order that the person receive ten hours of home help but can rule that the authority's decision is invalid, and that it must take the decision again. The authority might still reach the same conclusion as it did before — that the person should only receive one hour — but this time around, would have to so on different, reasonable grounds (eg. because other people have greater needs).

This section summarises the main hurdles which have to be overcome in judicial review; and comments on both advantages and disadvantages of the procedure. Judicial review is a complicated area of law and is by no means cheap, efficient and quick. However, in the community care field, it remains the main ground of legal challenge to authorities.

DISCUSSION

What Can Be Challenged

In the context of community care, judicial review could be used to challenge, for example:

- policies and procedures concerning priorities, criteria of eligibility, means-testing/charging for services;
- decisions about people's qualifying/legal status (eg. whether they are 'ordinarily resident' or whether they are disabled);
- consultation and information-giving procedures;
- operation of complaints procedure;
- lack of reasons for decisions.

Further explanation is given in Chapter 7 about the legal principles involved.

Expense

Judicial review is a specialised legal procedure, and without legal aid, can be expensive.

Leave/Permission of the Court

Unlike private law actions (for example, for negligence), judicial review cannot be pursued without the 'leave' (permission) of the High Court. When leave has been given, the case can proceed to a full and final hearing.

Time Limits for Bringing the Case

A judicial review must be begun within three months of the dispute arising – unless there are good reasons why the case has been brought later.

Because of these time limits, and because of the possible requirement that alternative remedies (such as the complaints procedure) be used first, an application for judicial review could be made but then adjourned until the outcome of the complaints procedure is known. If this were not done, then it might be too late to make the application.

Length of Time Taken for Judicial Review

Judicial review can take up to 18 months to come to court – unless urgency is pleaded and the case is 'expedited' (speeded up), in which case it might not take more than a few weeks.

However, even where the case is going to take a long time to come to court, an *interim injunction* ('interim relief') is possible. For example, in a sufficiently serious case the court could order that services be provided until the dispute finally comes to court and is resolved. This might be one argument for using the judicial review system directly in some circumstances, rather than going through the complaints procedure. For example, although local authorities have the power to provide services urgently for people in need, it would generally be illogical for them to do so if they do not recognise that a person qualifies for services in the first place (Gordon 1993,p.62).

Status of the Applicant

The applicant must have a certain level of interest in the case (known as 'locus standi'). For example, service users themselves or carers clearly have such an interest. Sometimes established advisory organisations, representing particular groups of people, will be recognised by courts as having such an interest in relevant cases; for example, a voluntary organisation challenged (unsuccessfully) government's failure to consult it over grant policy for community care alcohol and drugs services (*R v Secretary of State for Health, ex p. Alcohol Recovery Project 1993*).

Alternative Remedies Precluding or Delaying Judicial Review

If the courts believe that there are appropriate 'alternative remedies' then they are likely to insist that those remedies be used first – before judicial review can be applied for. The obvious alternative remedies in the community care field are the complaints procedure; and the powers of the Secretary of State to declare authorities in default of their duties (see Chapter 23).

However, there are circumstances and reasons why the courts might not insist on these two remedies being 'exhausted' first – because the remedy at issue must be an adequate alternative to judicial review

Complaints Procedure

As far as the community care complaints procedure goes, it is unclear what approach the courts will take. However, service users could argue that a hearing before a panel of non-lawyers without legal representation is inadequate to deal with questions of *illegality* on the part of an authority. The need for authoritative guidance from judges is a basis for an application to proceed directly to a court of law (see eg. *R v Huntingdon DC, ex p. Cowan 1984*, in the context of licensing functions). In addition, it is possible that if a complaints procedure review panel's powers were perceived to be inadequate to solve a dispute, then the judges might step in. This might occur, for example, if a particular panel were unable to call for documents or insist on reasons for decisions from an authority's employees. (All this always supposes that a user wishes to go to judicial review: the complaints procedure might anyway be more advantageous in terms of time, expense, likelihood of a favourable outcome).

On the other hand, it is possible that where *procedural fairness* is at stake, the courts might be inclined to view the complaints procedure as an appropriate alternative remedy.

Default Powers

Although there is a temptation for the courts to argue that the Secretary of State's default powers are an adequate alternative remedy, they will not always do so. For example, in a case about an authority's failure to consult properly with the residents of a home before closing it, the judge held that it was unclear whether the duty was a social services function falling under the complaints procedure. He also stated that the issue was 'entirely one of law in a developing field...appropriate for decision by the courts, rather than the Secretary of State' (*R v Durham CC, ex p. Curtis and Broxson 1992*).

In addition, it might be argued that the default powers are scarcely an adequate alternative remedy since they (under s.7D of LASSA 1970) and their direct predecessors (under s.36 of the NAA 1948) have *never been used*. Furthermore, the Department of Health can take months if not years even when deciding not to use those powers. Also, the default powers apply only to the 'duties' and not to the powers or general functions of authorities; and therefore do not apply to the provision of discretionary services (ie services which an authority can provide but does not have to). It is also quite possible that where *illegality* or *procedural impropriety* (unfairness) is concerned, the courts will wish to retain control of such concepts. However, if *unreasonableness* were involved, then it is possible that the courts would see the default powers as the suitable remedy – because the legislation covering those powers mentions the words 'reasonable excuse' (see p.366). This might imply that it is for the Secretary of State to decide what was reasonable; and in any case the courts might be reluctant to substitute their opinion about reasonableness for that of the Secretary of State (see: *Secretary of State for Education and Science v Tameside MBC 1976, Lord Diplock*).

Full Disclosure of Facts

The applicant must make a full disclosure of all relevant facts. Not to do so could jeopardise an applicant's case (*R v Leeds City Council, ex p. Hendry 1993*).

Judicial Review as a Bargaining Tool

In some circumstances, the threat of judicial review can be a useful bargaining tool for service users against local authorities. For example, it is possible that their budgets might be more strained defending high-profile litigation than by reconsidering services for individual applicants. In addition, an authority might be unwilling to accept the risk of the courts' establishing an unwelcome precedent. Such a precedent might in the future cost the authority a great deal more (in relation to the many applicants who might rely on the precedent) than an out-of court-settlement with the present, single applicant.

Remedies: Court Orders

The court can make the following types of order in judicial review, which have the effect of:

- overturning a decision and ordering the authority to take the decision again (*certiorari:* eg. quashing a decision not to provide services and then ordering the authority to decide again);

- obliging an authority to take a positive action (*mandamus:* eg. to undertake a community care assessment);
- an *injunction:* similar to mandamus, but in its interim form (ie, until the hearing and resolution of the dispute) obliging an authority not to do something (eg. not withdrawing services);
- forbidding an authority from doing something which is contrary to its legal powers (*prohibition:* rarely used now);
- making a statement about rights, remedies and the general legal position of the parties (*declaration:* eg. about whether a person is 'ordinarily resident').

Limits to Remedies of Judicial Review

It should again be emphasised that none of these orders can directly ensure that a service user gets services; even if the user wins the judicial review case, the authority then has to come to a decision a second time. The outcome will sometimes still be unfavourable to the service user and the second decision will stand so long as it has been made legally and properly.

It should also be noted that unless there are private law rights as well as public law issues present, judicial review is generally not a remedy through which financial *damages* are obtainable.

Lastly, the court does not have to award a remedy at all, even if the claimant has 'won' the judicial review case in principle. For example, the court might make a *declaration* (eg. an acknowledgement of what should have happened) that the government should have consulted properly a local authority association about proposed housing benefit regulations – but by the time court heard the case, it was impracticable and pointless to consider striking down the regulations (*R v Secretary of State for Social Services, ex p. AMA 1986*). Similarly there would be no point ordering an authority to re-investigate the needs of a homeless person – if the person was no longer homeless (Emery,Smythe 1986,p.282). And a judge found himself unable to do more than suggest a declaration when he found that a social services department had not acted in accordance with the law (the CSDPA 1970) when it had refused (nearly two years previously) to consider assisting a person with a holiday (*R v London Borough of Ealing, ex p. Leaman 1984*).

PRIVATE LAW

The principles of private law claims have already been explained in Chapter 7. Apart from the common law of negligence in the health service field, private law remedies are generally not – *at present* – established in the community care (social services) field. This means that neither claims for negligence nor for breach of statutory duty are likely to succeed in the community care field. In addition, declarations about, for example, people's qualifying status (such as ordinary residence) are more likely to be sought and considered in public rather than private law.

However, it should be noted that this general situation concerning private law remedies cannot be stated in terms of absolute certainty, since the decisions of the courts are never entirely predictable.

DISCUSSION
Potential Advantages of Private Law Remedies

The existence of private law remedies is, or would be significant (if they were more commonly available), because there are a number of differences between private and public law procedures.

For example:

(1) **(no permission needed)** in private law a claimant does not, at the outset, have to gain the permission of a judge to pursue the case; and cases can be brought in courts all over the country, such as County Courts, District Registries, the High Court (whereas judicial review cases can only be heard in the High Court in London);

(2) **(final decision possible)** the court can actually make a final decision about the matter in dispute. For example, the court could rule that a person should actually receive, or have received, home help – not, as in public law cases, just rule that the authority must decide all over again, albeit according to legal and proper procedures (see above);

(3) **(compulsory remedy)** where a claimant 'wins' the case, the judge in private law cases must grant a remedy of some sort; whereas in public law cases, the judge does not have to do this. Where a remedy is granted, then in private law, but not usually in public law, it can be in the form of monetary compensation – that is, damages.

Breach of Statutory Duty

As explained elsewhere (see Chapter 7), private law remedies only arise where definite, potentially enforceable, individual rights can be identified. Such rights are difficult to identify in welfare legislation for a number of reasons – and so private law actions in this field for breach of statutory duty do not seem, at present, to be generally viable.

Negligence

The bringing of a claim for negligence does not depend on locating rights in legislation, but lies in the common law *duty of care* which professionals and practitioners have towards service users. The principles of proving negligence are summarised elsewhere (p.87).

Negligence is well-established in the health care field (for example, medical negligence) but not, at present, in the community care (social services) field (see p.84).

JUDGES' DECISIONS

The principles – and uncertainties – of public and private remedies have already been covered in Chapter 7. In addition to those uncertainties, there is yet one more dimension of uncertainty. This relates to the workings of the law courts.

It might be useful for authorities and users (and their advisers) to realise that the law, as interpreted by judges, is not easy to predict in any individual case. Much can depend on how judges react to the particular facts and circumstances of cases. A case can be decided one way in one court, but then be decided the other way on appeal; and sometimes judges disagree with each other (there might be three judges in a Court of Appeal and five in a House of Lords case). Furthermore, over a period of time, the courts' general approach to particular types of situation – and general application of particular legal principles – can change.

DISCUSSION

Judges' Reasoning

The reasoning which different judges employ in particular cases is not always predictable; and it is important for both authorities and service users to realise that this judicial reasoning, though often sophisticated and impressive, is not necessarily a simple, logical exercise. Part of the reason for this is that apart from the difficulty of dealing logically with ambiguous and imprecise terms in legislation, other factors are present. For example, judges will bear in mind questions of public policy; and will be wary of intruding on some issues (such as the resources available to health authorities) which they perceive to be the province of Parliament rather than the law courts.

Therefore, for example, part of the judicial approach might be to interfere little in welfare matters and simply state that a particular issue is not for the judges to rule on. For example, this is what the courts said in a case against a health authority about the postponement of an operation on a baby with a hole in his heart (*Re Walker's Application 1987*). Similarly, when considering how far public bodies should have a duty of care in the law of negligence (see p.74), eminent judges have stated that it was a question of public policy as to whether they would or would not find a duty of care in a particular situation (*Dorset Yacht Co v Home Office 1969/1970* (Lord Denning): see Jones 1991,p.33). Such statements are frank admissions that a 'duty of care' in negligence does not exist independently and objectively of the judges; instead its very existence in particular situations can depend on their decisions.

The judges might therefore employ a variety of arguments designed to reach particular conclusions – for example, to avoid identifying clear duties and enforceable private law rights (see Chapter 7). This approach generally assists authorities. Alternatively, judges might, after all, become involved in community care cases and interpret the law so as to assist service users. For example, they might state that the duty to provide after-care under the Mental Health Act

1983 is a very strong duty towards individuals (*R v Ealing DHA, ex p. Fox 1993*); or that the duty to assess people's apparent community care needs extends to possible future needs (*R v Mid Glamorgan CC, ex p. Miles 1993*).

It has been suggested that instead of marshalling the facts, applying the principles to those facts and then reaching the conclusion, judges sometimes might start with the conclusion and *then* seek the reasoning and evidence to support it (see eg. Lee 1989, p.42).

Facts and Circumstances of Individual Cases

In addition still, it should be remembered that the outcome of a case can depend on its particular facts and circumstances; on how well arguments are put by each side; and on the particular approach and sympathies of the judge(s).

Overruling of Decisions and Precedents

In addition, the 'lower' courts can always be overruled by decisions in 'higher' courts – so that even when a precedent is established by, for example, the Court of Appeal, it could be overturned by the House of Lords. This might occur either when the same case is referred to the House of Lords – or at a later date when a similar case reaches the higher court. (For the purposes of public law cases, the hierarchy is: High Court, Court of Appeal, House of Lords.)

In addition, sometimes the decisions of the higher courts might be far from clear-cut; for example, even within a single court the judges might disagree with each other and the decision might be a majority, rather than a unanimous, one. The outcome of cases can be far from predictable; for example, a case could be decided one way in the High Court; the other way in the Court of Appeal; only for the House of Lords to reinstate the original decision.

Changing Law

Although there is an increasing amount of legislation (Acts of Parliament and statutory instruments), judges still 'make law' to some extent by interpreting legislation or by developing the 'common law' (ie. principles derived from law court judgements over the centuries, rather than from legislation. Eg the 'duty of care' in negligence is a common law principle). This means that through judge-made precedents, judges to some extent make, modify, vary and reject interpretations and applications of the law.

Once the Court of Appeal or House of Lords has reached a decision, then a precedent is set for similar cases. For example, the ruling of the Court of Appeal in the case of *Wyatt v Hillingdon LBC 1978* was that a private law claim for *breach of statutory duty* (see p.87) under the National Assistance Act 1948 and the CSDPA 1970 (involving community care services) was out of the question. This followed another Court of Appeal case (*Southwark LBC v Williams 1970*) and thus confirmed the courts' reluctance to recognise (a remedy for) breach of statutory duty in the NAA 1948. However, it is possible in theory (though unlikely in practice at the moment), that if a similar case were to reach the House of Lords, then the precedent in the *Wyatt* case could be overturned or at least thrown into doubt. (For example, the House of Lords is due to consider comparable cases from the local authority education field late in 1994 – although it is not expected to reach any radical conclusions).

Another example of how judges can develop the law has occurred in the law of negligence (see Jones 1991,pp.51–55). At one time, the judges seemed to be broadening the scope of negligence, and possibly increasing the liability of local authorities (eg. *Anns v Merton LBC 1978*). A reaction then took place against this development when the House of Lords put a brake on such development (see eg. *Murphy v Brentwood DC 1990*; *Rowling v Takaro Properties 1988*). Nevertheless, the issue of whether local authorities and their staff can be found to be negligent continues to be debated by the courts. For instance, in 1994 the Court of Appeal has debated the issue in local authority education and child-care field; and the House of Lords will be considering the principle later in 1994.

GLOSSARY

Alternative remedies: judges might sometimes insist that 'other remedies' (such as the social services complaints procedure, or the Secretary of State's powers to declare an authority in default) be used before a case is brought to a court of law

Approvals: a form of delegated legislation made under an Act of Parliament. Approvals give authorities powers, though not duties: that is authorities can do what the Approvals allow them to, but do not have to. (For example, under the Health Service and Public Health Act 1968, Approvals contained in a Circular give authorities the power to provide certain services for old people)

Bias (freedom from): an aspect of fairness: authorities' decisions must be, and be seen to be, free from bias

Breach of statutory duty: when an authority doesn't do its duty towards an individual to whom it owes that duty. In the community care field, a private law claim against an authority for breach of statutory duty seems unlikely to succeed (though it has been established under homelessness law)

Case law: the (interpretation of) law derived from particular cases which have been through the law courts – as opposed to what the legislation (Act of Parliament) or statute law states

Causation: an important and sometimes complicated part of proving negligence; ie proving not just that an act was negligent but that it caused the harm which has occurred

Certiorari: a court order overturns an authority's decision

Charters: for example, the Patient's Charter (or expected Community Care Charters). Potentially useful tools for users to put pressure on authorities to meet specified standards of service, charters are thought not to confer legal rights on individual service users

Circular: used, for the purposes of this book, to refer generally to a range of communications issued by government departments

Commission for Local Administration: office of the local ombudsman (there are several local ombudsmen covering different parts of the country)

Common law: ie. aspects of law which do not derive from statute law.

Community care services: formally defined in s.46 of the NHS and Community Care Act 1990

Consultation: an aspect of fairness. The right to consultation (and the nature of the consultation) might be based on particular legislation; but it is also a concept which the judges might define and develop in some contexts, irrespective of legislation

Court of Appeal: the second-highest UK court (next only to the House of Lords) which receives appeals from the High Court (or from the County Court)

Criteria of eligibility: devices employed by authorities to control and ration access to assessment and to service provision: basically a setting of conditions which individuals have to meet before qualifying for services

Declaration: a judge can make a declaration about the legal position in particular situations: for example, about whether a person satisfies certain conditions (such as ordinary residence) and so qualifies for services. Declarations are in principle available in both public law and private law; in practice, in the context of community care, most declarations are likely to be in public law

Default powers: the powers of the Secretary of State to declare authorities 'in default' of their duties. Neither the community care default powers, nor their predecessors, have ever been used

Delegated legislation: an Act of Parliament can give the government the power to make, for example, regulations (statutory instruments) or directions

Directions: a form of delegated legislation which impose duties on authorities; eg. under the NHS and Community Care Act 1990, Directions have been issued about community care plans

Disability: an uncertain concept, crucial to community care. Circular guidance gives some indication of how authorities should define it. The concept is sometimes contrasted with impairment and handicap. For example, a double leg amputation is the impairment; consequent inability to walk the disability; and consequent inability to get in and out of a 2nd floor flat in a wheelchair a handicap (caused by the environment: there is, for example, no lift).

Disability can be physical or sensory; and affect daily living functions such as moving, getting up, dressing, bathing, cooking, eating, drinking, mobility, writing, speaking, hearing, seeing – and so on. Some disability is obviously more severe than other – for example, a person with a high level spinal injury and who has only head movement, compared to an elderly person with severe arthritis in one wrist. Nevertheless, the effects of disability can depend on the environment, a person's individual needs, way of life, expectations, carers, the person's attitude, the amount of money available to that person to overcome the disability etc.

Disability equipment: includes a wide range of medical and daily living equipment, eg. wheelchairs, walking aids, calipers, car hoists; environmental controls for severely disabled people; electronic speech equipment; home adaptations; bed and bath equipment; household equipment; eating, drinking and cooking equipment – and so on.

Equipment and adaptations are available, depending on the perceived purpose of the equipment through five statutory services: health, social services, housing, education and employment. Voluntary organisations can sometimes assist in the loan or purchase of equipment; specialist shops and some pharmacies carry a range of equipment; equipment is available through mail order; and a number of disabled living centres demonstrate equipment and give advice about it

Disabled facilities grants: available as part of the renovation grants system

Discretion: 'freedom or authority to make judgements and act as one sees fit' (Collins English Dictionary, 1989). In public law, authorities have discretion when making decisions about how to implement their duties. For example, health authorities have a duty to provide services, but only so far as is 'necessary to meet all reasonable requirements'. Therefore authorities have discretion in deciding what this phrase means and in deciding local policies, priorities and resource allocation

Duties: when authorities must provide certain services (although it should be noted that few duties are 'absolute')

Duty of care: an essential element required in a claim for negligence: for example, the common law duty of care which a doctor owes a patient

Fairness (procedural impropriety): a public law (judicial review) concept, to which there a number of different aspects, including legitimate expectation, consultation, information, reasons for a decision, freedom from bias

Fettering of discretion: a legal concept, which requires that authorities do not adopt absolutely rigid policies. According to this principle, policies must be capable of allowing for exceptions; eg. an authority might fetter its discretion if it stated that it would never consider assisting a person with a privately arranged holiday under section 2 of the CSDPA 1970

General medical services: refers to community medical services such as general practitioners, dentists, ophthalmologists, pharacists

Guidance: general term used to cover a variety of guidance issued by government departments (see chapter 6); even when the language of obligation (eg. 'must', 'should') is used, the legal import of such guidance is not always clear

Hansard: the written record of proceedings/debates in the House of Commons and the House of Lords

Health authorities: in this book, district health authorities which purchase health services from hospital and community NHS Trusts

Health Service Commissioner: the health service ombudsman

Health service ombudsman: investigates failure in a service, failure to provide a service which a health authority has a duty to provide, and maladministration

High Court: where public law/judicial review cases are heard (with the possibility of appeal to the Court of Appeal)

House of Lords: the highest UK court, which receives appeals from the Court of Appeal

Illegality: one of the principles by which the courts judicially review the decisions and acts of public authorities: an authority might draw up a policy which is not consistent with the relevant legislation, eg. a health authority might begin charging for equipment (such as walking aids) which the NHS Act 1977 gives it no power to charge for

Independent sector: refers to voluntary and private organisations – as opposed to public bodies

Injunction: a court order directing a person/body either to do something or not to do something. Injunctions can be final or be interim (or interlocutory); the latter is a temporary order to be followed until the dispute is finally settled. For example, in some circumstances a court might rule that an authority provide home help until the case is finally heard and resolved. Injunctions are available in both private and public law; in the community care context, most are likely to be in public law.

Irrationality: (see Unreasonableness)

Judicial review: a public law procedure which reviews whether a public body has made a decision improperly (ie. based on unreasonableness, illegality or unfairness). Judicial review does not directly enforce service users' rights to services but rather ensures that authorities act properly and within the law

Leave: in this book, applying for the permission of a judge to bring a judicial review case

Legitimate expectation: a legal concept associated with fairness (procedural impropriety) which is basically about people's expectations of receiving what authorities have led them to believe that they would get.

Litigant: a party in a law case

Local authorities: for the purpose of this book, means social services departments. (In metropolitan areas, social services and housing department are within the same authority. Otherwise, social services departments are organised county-wide, whereas housing departments are organised at district council level. Thus, within one social services authority, there might be several housing authorities)

Local ombudsman: investigates maladministration in local authorities

Locus standi: in order to bring a judicial review case, a person or organisation must be deemed by the courts to have sufficient interest in the case. This interest is known as 'locus standi' (this literally means 'place of standing')

Maladministration: grounds for investigation by the local ombudsmen and the health service ombudsman. Is about the way in which authorities behave and reach decisions, rather than what those decisions ultimately are. The courts will not in principle investigate maladministration, since bad administration is not of itself unlawful.

Under the umbrella of maladministration, the ombudsmen investigate aspects of services such as consultation, information-giving, giving reasons for decisions, consistent application of local policies and priorities, timely services (ie. regarding waiting times)

Mandamus: a court order which compels an authority to perform its duty

Mandatory: obligatory: for example, referring to services which an authority must (has a duty) to provide, as opposed to services which it has only a power to provide

Means-test: tests of people's resources. Depending on the service involved, the test might be either specified in legislation (for example, for residential/nursing home care) or not so specified (eg. non-residential care services) and instead left for authorities to develop and apply

Minor works assistance: scheme whereby housing authorities can assist people with money or in kind (ie materials); eg. assist elderly people to remain in their own homes

Natural justice: term used by the courts to indicate their concern with procedural fairness

Need: a term central to community care, since 'need' is a necessary (though not always sufficient) condition for service provision. The term is often highly nebulous; and varying local definitions and applications make it even more difficult to understand

Negligence: used in private law cases where a person or organisation has a duty of care to people (eg. to patients); breaches that duty through carelessness; and causes harm to those people as a result. The principle of negligence seems well-established in the health care field but not in the community care (personal social services) field

NHS Trusts: both hospital and community health services trusts: provide services which have been purchased by health authorities

Nursing homes: differentiated from residential homes, in principle, in that nursing care is provided by nursing homes

Ombudsmen: for the purposes of this book, the local ombudsman, health service ombudsman (a few references are also made to the Parliamentary ombudsman who investigates government department administration)

Ordinarily resident: refers to whether an individual is to be deemed a resident of an authority's area. The duty to provide certain services is determined by this qualifying condition, and so legal disputes sometimes arise

Placement: used in this book to refer to local authorities' placing of people in residential and nursing homes

Powers: when local authorities can provide certain services if they wish – but they don't have to (as opposed to duties)

Private law: is about people's identifiable, enforceable rights to services (as opposed to public law): for the purposes of this book it involves negligence and breach of statutory duty

Private sector: refers to private companies and firms, as opposed to voluntary organisations and public authorities

Procedural impropriety: (see Fairness)

Public law: for the purpose of this book, involves judicial review cases, in which the courts ensure that authorities have made decisions properly and legally. Most community care disputes which reach the courts are likely to be public law cases

Reasonableness: (see Unreasonableness)

Reasons for (adverse) decisions: an aspect of the legal concept of fairness

Regulations: (see Statutory instrument)

Residential homes: differentiated from nursing homes, in principle, in that nursing care is not provided by residential homes (although district nurses might visit individual residents)

Secondary legislation: (see Delegated legislation)

Statute law: ie. the law contained in Acts of Parliament – as opposed to case law or common law

Statutory: relating to legislation

Statutory instrument: a form of delegated legislation: Acts of Parliament give the government power to pass these. For example, under the NHS Act 1977 health service prescription charges are altered by statutory instrument on a more or less annual basis

Ultra vires: when an authority has acted outside its powers; ie it has not adhered to the terms of the legislation under which it acts and makes decisions – and acts illegally (see: Illegality)

Unreasonableness: one of the principles by which the courts judicially review the decisions and acts of public authorities. In principle, authorities would have to act very waywardly before the courts deem them unreasonable; in practice authorities are sometimes found to be unreasonable

Usual cost: refers to the maximum amounts which local authorities are prepared to pay for nursing and residential home care

Vicarious liability: for example, where an employer is responsible for the negligence of an employee

Voluntary sector: voluntary organisations, as opposed to private firms and companies and to public authorities

APPENDIX

ACTS

Access to Personal Files Act 1987. London: HMSO.

Chronically Sick and Disabled Persons Act 1970. London: HMSO.

Chronically Sick and Disabled Persons (Northern Ireland) Act 1978. London: HMSO.

Commissioner for Complaints Act (Northern Ireland) 1968. London: HMSO.

Community Care (Residential Accommodation) Act 1992. London: HMSO.

Disabled Persons (Services, Consultation and Representation) Act 1986. London: HMSO.

Health and Medicines Act 1988. London: HMSO.

Health and Social Services and Social Security Adjudications Act 1983. London: HMSO.

Health Service and Public Health Act 1968. London: HMSO.

Health Service Commissioners Act 1993. London: HMSO.

Hospital Complaints Procedure Act 1985. London: HMSO.

Housing Act 1985. London: HMSO.

Local Authority Social Services Act 1970. London: HMSO.

Local Government Act 1972. London: HMSO.

Local Government Act 1974. London: HMSO.

Local Government and Housing Act 1989. London: HMSO.

Leasehold Renewal and Urban Development Act 1993. London: HMSO.

Mental Health Act 1983. London: HMSO.

National Assistance Act 1948. London: HMSO.

National Health Service Act 1977. London: HMSO.

National Health Service and Community Care Act 1990. London: HMSO.

Registered Homes Act 1984. London: HMSO.

BILLS

Chronically Sick and Disabled Persons Bill 1969. London: HMSO.

Chronically Sick and Disabled Persons Bill 1970 (as amended by Standing Committee C). London: HMSO.

Chronically Sick and Disabled Persons (Amendment) Bill 1978 (Jack Ashley). London: HMSO.

Chronically Sick and Disabled Persons (Amendment) Bill 1979 (Edwin Wainwright). London: HMSO.

Chronically Sick and Disabled Persons (Amendment) Bill 1983 (Robert Wareing). London: HMSO.

Chronically Sick and Disabled Persons (Amendment) (No.2) Bill 1983 (Earl of Longford). London: HMSO.

NHS (Supply of Medical Equipment) Bill 1991. London: HMSO.

Registration of Domiciliary Care Agencies Bill 1993. London: HMSO.

STATUTORY INSTRUMENTS

SI 1984/1345. Residential Care Homes Regulations 1984. London: HMSO.

SI 1984/1578. Nursing Home and Mental Nursing Homes Regulations 1984. London: HMSO.

SI 1988/551. National Health Service (Travelling Expenses and Remission of Charges) Regulations 1988. London: HMSO.

SI 1989/206. Access to Personal Files (Social Services) Regulations 1989. London: HMSO.

SI 1989/394. National Health Service (Dental Charges) Regulations 1989. London: HMSO.

SI 1989/396. National Health Service (Optical Charges and Payments) Regulations 1989. London: HMSO.

SI 1989/419. National Health Service (Charges for Drugs and Appliances) Regulations 1989. London: HMSO.

SI 1991/554. NHS Functions Regulations 1991. London: HMSO, 1991.

SI 1992/563. National Assistance (Charges for Accommodation) Regulations. London; HMSO, 1992.

SI 1992/635. National Health Service (General Medical Services) Regulations 1992. London: HMSO.

SI 1992/664. NHS (Service Committees and Tribunal) Regulations 1992. London: HMSO, 1992.

SI 1992/2244. Local Authority Social Services (Complaints Procedure) Order 1990. London: HMSO.

SI 1992/2977. National Assistance (Assessment of Resources) Regulations 1992. London: HMSO. (includes SI 1993/964).

SI 1993/462. National Assistance (Sums for Personal Requirements) Regulations 1991. London: HMSO, 1993.

SI 1992/3182. Residential Accommodation (Determination of District Health Authority) Regulations 1992. London: HMSO, 1992.

SI 1993/553. Housing Renovation etc. Grants (Grant Limit) Order 1993. London: HMSO, 1993.

SI 1993/2711. Housing Renovation etc. Grants (Grant Limit) (Amendment) Order 1993. London: HMSO, 1993.

SI 1993/554. Assistance for Minor Works to Dwellings (Amendment) Regulations 1993. London: HMSO.

SI 1993/582. Residential Accommodation (Determination of District Health Authority) (Amendment) Regulations 1993. London: HMSO, 1993.

SI 1993/2711. Housing Renovation etc. Grants (Grant Limit) (Amendment) Order 1993. London: HMSO.

SI 1994/42. Housing (Welfare Services) Order 1994. London: HMSO.

SI 1994/648. Housing Renovation etc. Grants (Reduction of Grant) Regulations 1994. London: HMSO.

SI 1994/690. National Health Service (Charges for Drugs and Appliances) Amendment Regulations 1994. London: HMSO.

SI 1994/826. National Assistance (Sums for Personal Requirements) Regulations 1994. London: HMSO.

DIRECTIONS

Community Care Plans Direction 1991 (with LAC(91)6)

Community Care Plans (Consultation) Directions 1993. (with LAC(93)4); made under the LASSA 1970,s.7A and NHSCCA 1990,s.46(2)(f))

Community Care Plans (Independent) Sector Non-Residential Care) Direction 1994: with LAC(94)12; made under the LASSA 1970,s.7A)

Complaints Procedure Directions 1990

Inspection Units Directions 1994 (with LAC(94)16; made under the LASSA 1970,s.7A)

CIRCULARS

(Note. As explained in Chapter 6, there is sometimes confusion about the status of Circulars. Even when a Circular has formally been cancelled, it may remain a useful indication of government policy if neither the Circular nor the message it contains have been superseded.

ELs (executive letters) are normally of short duration, having a life often of no more than a year. However, the messages they contain may remain valid; for example, an EL, explaining that the NHS Act 1977 prevents health authorities and NHS Trusts from charging for all but specified equipment, may be cancelled – but its interpretation of the law clearly remains valid.

Other circulars thought (the Department of Health does not publish a list of valid Circulars) to be formally cancelled are marked with an asterisk – they have been nevertheless been mentioned in the book by way of historical/contextual explanation.

*CI(92)34. Social Services Inspectorate. Implementing caring for people: assessment. London: Department of Health, 1992.
(This letter from the Social Services Inspectorate was cancelled on 31st March 1994. However, the policy and practice advice which it contained has not been explicitly replaced or rejected by the Department of Health and so the letter remains useful evidence of government policy.

CI(93)7. Social Services Inspectorate. Health of the Nation: mental illness key area handbook. London: Department of Health, 1993.

DENI 1987/21. Department of Education for Northern Ireland. Education of children with special educational needs. Bangor: DENI, 1987.

DES (1992). Department of Education and Science. Addendum to Circular 22/89: assessments and statements of special educational needs: procedures within the education, health and social services. London: DES.

DHSS (12/70), DES 13/70, MHLG 65/70, ROADS 20/70. Department of Health and Social Security; Department of Education and Science; Ministry of Housing and Local Government; Ministry of Transport. The Chronically Sick and Disabled Persons Act 1970. London: DHSS.

DHSS (19/71). Department of Health and Social Security. Welfare of the elderly: implementation of s.45 of the Health and Public Health Act 1968. London: DHSS.

DHSS (45/71). Department of Health and Social Security. Services for handicapped people living in the community: the Chronically Sick and Disabled Persons Act 1970. London: DHSS, 1971.

*DHSS (53/71). Department of Health and Social Security. Help in the home: section 13 of the Health Services and Public Health Act 1968. London: DHSS, 1971.

*DoE 59/78, LAC(78)14, WO 104/78. Department of Environment; Department of Health and Social Security; Welsh Office. Adaptations for people who physically handicapped. London: HMSO. (*Superseded by DoE 10/90*)

DoE 4/90. Department of Environment. Assistance with minor works to dwellings. London: HMSO, 1990.

DoE 10/90; LAC(90)7. Department of Environment; Department of Health. House adaptations for people with disabilities. London: HMSO, 1990.

DoE 10/92; LAC(92)12. Department of Environment; Department of Health. Housing and community care. London: HMSO, 1992.

EL(90)M5/LAC(90)12. Department of Health. Community care – policy guidance. London: DH, 1990.

EL(90)MB/45. Community care.

EL(91)28. NHS Management Executive. Continence services and the supply of incontinence aids. London: DH, 1991.

EL(91)129. NHS Management Executive. Charging NHS patients. London: DH, 1991.

EL(92)20. NHS Management Executive. Provision of equipment by the NHS. London: Department of Health.

EL(93)18; CI(93)12. NHS Management Executive; Social Services Inspectorate. Implementing caring for people. London: Department of Health, 1993.

EL(93)21. NHS Management Executive. Community care: arrangements for people who are in independent sector residential care and nursing homes on 31 March 1993: LAC(93)6. London: DH, 1993.

EL(93)22. NHS Management Executive. Implementation of caring for people: communications. Leeds: Department of Health.

EL(93)119, CI(93)33. NHS Management Executive; Social Services Inspectorate. Community care: September SSI/RHA monitoring. London: Department of Health, 1993.

EL(94)3. NHS Management Executive. Pressure sores – a key quality indicator. Leeds: Department of Health, 1994.

EL(94)8. NHS Management Executive. Hospital admission and discharge procedures. London: Department of Health, 1994.

EL(94)55. NHS Executive. Priorities and planned guidance for the NHS: 1995/96. Leeds: DH.

FHSL(93)60. NHS Management Executive. Guidance notes for FHSAs on the National Health Service (Service Committees and Tribunal) Regulations 1992. Leeds: Department of Health, 1992.

HC(77)9. Department of Health and Social Security. Organisation and management of NHS chiropody services. London: DHSS, 1977.

HC(78)16. Department of Health and Social Security. NHS chiropody services. London: DHSS, 1978.

HC(81)1. Department of Health and Social Security. Contractual arrangements with independent hospitals and nursing homes and other forms of co-operation between the NHS and the independent medical sector. London: DHSS, 1981.

HC(81)5. Department of Health and Social Security. Health services complaints procedure. London: DHSS, 1981.

HC(84)21. Department of Health and Social Security. Registration and inspection of private nursing homes and mental nursing homes (including private hospitals). London: DHSS, 1984.

HC(88)37; HN(FP)(88)18. Department of Health and Social Security. Hospital Complaints Procedure Act 1985. London: DHSS, 1988.

HC(89)5. Department of Health. Discharge of patients from hospital. London: DH, 1989.

HC(90)23; LASSL(90)11. Department of Health. Care programme approach for people with a mental illness referred to the specialist psychiatric services. London: Department of Health, 1990.

HN(89)7,HN(FP)(89)9. Department of Health. Health care in local authority residential care homes for elderly people. London: DH, 1989.

HN(84)12. Department of Health and Social Security.Communication aids centres (CACs): procedures for out of district referrals. London: DHSS, 1984.

HN(88)26; HN(FP)(88)(25); LASSL(88)8. Health service development: the development of services with people with physical or sensory disabilities. London: DH.

HN(90)5, HN(FP)(90)1, LASSL(90)1. Department of Health. Certification of blind and partially sighted people: revised form BD8 and procedures. London: DH, 1990.

HRC(74)16. Department of Health and Social Security. Statutory provisions: charges under section 2(2) of the National Health Service Reorganisation Act 1973. London: DHSS, 1974.

HRC(74)33. Department of Health and Social Security. Chiropody. London: DHSS, 1974.

HSC(IS)11. Department of Health and Social Security. Services for chronic renal failure. London: DHSS, 1974.

HSG(92)4. Implementing the Patient's Charter. London: NHS Management Executive, Department of Health, 1992.

HSG(92)10. Department of Health. Charges for drugs, appliances, oxygen concentrators and wigs and fabric supports. London: DH.

HSG(92)21. Implementation of the health information services. London: NHS Management Executive, Department of Health, 1992.

HSG(92)36. NHS Management Executive. Patient's Charter: monitoring and publishing information on performance. London: Department of Health, 1992.

HSG(92)42. NHS Management Executive. Health services for people with learning disabilities (mental handicap). London: Department of Health, 1992.

HSG(92)43. NHS Management Executive. Health authority payments in respect of social services functions. London: Department of Health, 1992.

HSG(92)50. NHS Management Executive. Local authority contracts for residential and nursing home care: NHS related aspects. London: Department of Health, 1992.

HSG(93)27. NHS Management Executive. Patient's Charter and primary health care. London: Department of Health, 1993.

HSG(93)30. NHS Management Executive. Provision of haemophilia treatment and care. London: DH, 1993.

HSG(93)45. NHS Management Executive. Code of practice: section 118 of the Mental Health Act 1983. London: Department of Health, 1993.

HSG(93)48. NHS Management Executive. Home dialysis patients: costs of metered water used for home dialysis. London: DH.

HSG(94)5. NHS Management Executive. Introduction of supervision registers for mentally ill people from 1 April 1994. London: Department of Health, 1994.

HSG(94)12. NHS Management Executive. Charges for drugs, appliances and wigs and fabric supports. London: DH, 1994.

HSG(94)27. Department of Health. Guidance on the discharge of mentally disordered people and their continuing care in the community. London: DH.

LAC(84)15. Department of Health and Social Security. Registration of residential homes and Registered Homes Tribunal. London: DHSS, 1984.

LAC(86)6. Department of Health and Social Security. Registration of residential homes. London: DHSS, 1986.

LAC(87)6. Department of Health and Social Security. Disabled Persons (Services, Consultation and Representation) Act 1986: implementation of sections 4, 8(1), 9 & 10. London: DHSS, 1987.

LAC(88)2. Department of Health and Social Security. Disabled Persons (Services, Consultation and Representation) Act 1986: implementation of s.5 and s.6. London: DHSS, 1988.

LAC(89)2; HN(89)3; HN(FP)(89)3. Department of Health. I. Access to Personal Files Act 1987: Access to Personal Files (Social Services) Regulations; II. Local Authority Social Services Designation of Functions Order 1989. London: DH.

LAC(89)7. Department of Health. Discharge of patients from hospital. London: DH, 1989.

LAC(91)6. Department of Health. Secretary of State's Direction – s.46 of the NHS and Community Care Act 1990: community care plans. London: DH.

LAC(91)8. Department of Health. Employment by local authorities of chiropodists, occupational therapists, dieticians, physiotherapists, radiographers, medical laboratory scientific officers and orthoptists. London: DH, 1991.

LAC(91)14. Department of Health. Health-related social work: NHS and local authority collaboration: provision of NHS services to local authorities and of health-related social work services to the NHS. London: DH.

LAC(92)15. Department of Health. Social care for adults with learning disabilities (mental handicap). London: DH, 1992.

LAC(92)17. Department of Health. Health authority payments in respect of social services functions. London: DH, 1992.

LAC(92)19. Department of Health. Charges for residential accommodation. London: DH, 1992.

LAC(92)24. Department of Health. Local authority contracts for residential and nursing home care: NHS related aspects. London: DH, 1992.

LAC(92)27. Department of Health. National Assistance Act 1948 (Choice of Accommodation) Directions 1992. London: DH, 1992.

LAC(93)2. Department of Health. Alcohol and drug misusers within community care. London: DH, 1993.

LAC(93)3. Department of Health. AIDS support grant 1993/94. London: DH, 1993.

LAC(93)4. Department of Health. Community care consultation directions. London: DH, 1993..

LAC(93)6. Department of Health. Local authorities' powers to make arrangements for people who are in independent sector residential care and nursing homes on 31 March 1993. London: DH.

LAC(93)7. Department of Health. Ordinary residence. London: DH.

LAC(93)8. Department of Health. National Assistance (Sums for Personal Requirements) Regulations 1993. London: DH, 1993.

LAC(93)10. Department of Health. Approvals and directions for arrangements from 1 April 1993 made under schedule 8 to the National Health Service Act 1977 and sections 21 and 29 of the National Assistance Act 1948. London: DH.

LAC(93)12. Department of Health. Further and Higher Education Act 1992: implications for sections 5 and 6 of the Disabled Persons (Services, Consultation and Representation) Act 1986. London: DH, 1993.

LAC(93)18. National Assistance Act 1948 (Choice of Accommodation) (Amendment) Directions 1993: amendment to the statutory direction on 'choice'. London: Department of Health, 1993.

LAC(93)19. Department of Health. Code of practice: section 118 of the Mental Health Act 1983. London: DH, 1993.

LAC(94)1. Department of Health. Charges for residential accommodation: CRAG amendment no. 2. Charges for non-residential adult services under section 17 of the Health and Social Services and Social Security Adjudication Act 1983. London: DH, 1994.

LAC(94)6. Department of Health. Specific grant for the development of social care services for people with a mental illness. London: DH, 1994.

LAC(94)12. Department of Health. Community care plans (independent sector non-residential care) direction 1994. London: DH.

LAC(94)14. Department of Health. National Assistance (Sums for Personal Requirements) Regulations 1994. London: DH, 1994.

LAC(94)16. Department of Health. Inspecting social services. London: DH, 1994.

LASSL(94)16. Department of Health. Precondition on the 1994/1995 community care special transitional grant.

LASSL(94)1. Department of Health. Community care: special transitional grant allocations and conditions 1994/95. London: DH, 1994.

NHS 1989(GEN)39. Scottish Home and Health Department. Private nursing homes: entitlement of patients to NHS supplies and services. Edinburgh: Scottish Office, 1989.

PL/CNO(89)3. Department of Health and Social Security. Social Services Inspectorate report: 'Health care in local authority residential homes for elderly people'. London: DHSS, 1989.

CASES

Anns v Merton LBC [1978] AC 728

Associated Provincial Picture Houses Ltd v Wednesbury Corporation (CA) [1947] 2 All ER 680

Barnett v Chelsea & Kensington Hospital Management Committee [1969] 1 QB 428

Bradbury v Enfield [1967] 1 WLR 1311

Bromley London Borough Council v Greater London Council (HL) [1983] 1 AC 768

Cocks v Thanet District Council [1983] 2 AC 286

Council of Civil Service Unions v Minister for the Civil Service [1984] 3 All ER 935

De Falco v Crawley Council (CA) [1980] QB 460

Dorset Yacht Co. v Home Office [1969] 2 QB 412, [1970] AC 1004

E (a minor) v Dorset County Council; Christmas v Hampshire County Council; Keating v Bromley Borough Council (CA) [1994] 3 WLR 853

Ettridge v Morrell (1986) 150 LGRev 627

Gillick v West Norfolk Area Health Authority [1986] 1 AC 112

Harrison v Cornwall County Council (CA) (1992) 156 LGRev 703.

Hague v Deputy Governor of Parkhurst Prison [1991] 3 All ER 733

Hill v Chief Constable of West Yorkshire [1988] 2 All ER 238

Hong Kong v Ng Yuen Shiu [1983] 2 All ER 346

In re Walker's Application 1987 (High Court, November 24th 1987; Court of Appeal, November 25th 1987). Times, 26th November 1987

Jones v Department of Employment (CA) [1988] 2 WLR 493

Levene v Inland Revenue Commissioner (HL) [1928] AC 217

M (a minor) and another v Newham London Borough Council and Others, P and Others v Bedfordshire County Council (CA) [1994] 2 WLR 554

Mallinson v Secretary of State for Social Security (1994) 144 NLJ 604

Meade v Haringey [1979] 1 WLR 637

Murphy v Brentwood DC [1990] 2 All ER 908

Pepper (Inspector of Taxes) v Hart (1992), NLJ 1993; 143(6582), pp.17–19.

R v Avon County Council, ex p. M [1994] 2 FCR 259

R v Birmingham City Council, ex p. Kaur (1990) Times, 11 July 1990

R v Brent London Borough Council, ex p. Gunning (1985), Times 30 April 1985

R v Central Birmingham Health Authority, ex p. Collier (1988), Times 6 January 1988; Lexis, 6 January 1988

R v Cleveland County Council, ex p. Cleveland Care Homes Association and Others (1994) 158 LGRev 641

R v Department of Health and Social Security and Kent County Council, ex p. Bruce (QBD) 1986, Times 8 February 1986; Lexis, 5 February 1986

R v Dorset County Council, ex p. Rolls (1994) 26 HLR 381

R v Durham County Council, ex p. Curtis and Broxson (CA) (1992) 6 Admin LR 113

R v Ealing District Health Authority, ex p. Fox (QBD) [1993] 1 WLR 373

R v Governors of Small Heath School, ex p. Birmingham City Council (1989) Independent, 30 June 1989; affirmed 1990 COD 23 (CA)

R v Hereford and Worcester County Council, ex p. Chandler (1991) CO/1759/91 (discussed by Luke Clements in Legal Action, September 1992, pp.15–16)

R v Hereford and Worcester LEA, ex p. Jones [1981] 1 WLR 768

R v Hertfordshire County Council, ex p. Three Rivers District Council (1993) 157 LGR 526

R v Higher Education Funding Council, ex p. Institute of Dental Surgery [1994] 1 WLR 242

R v Home Secretary, ex p. Khawaja [1984] AC 74

R v Home Secretary, ex p. Phansopkar [1976] QB 606

R v Huntingdon District Council, ex p. Cowan [1984] 1 WLR 501

R v Inner London Education Authority, ex p. Ali and Murshid [1990] COD 317, Lexis 14 February 1990

R v Inland Revenue Commissioners, ex p. National Federation of Self-Employed and Small Businesses Ltd [1982] AC 617

R v Islington London Borough Council, ex p. Trail (1993) Independent, 14 June 1993

R v Knowsley Borough Council, ex p. Maguire (1992) 90 LGR 653

R v Lancashire County Council, ex p. Huddleston [1986] 2 All ER 941

R v Leeds City Council, ex p. Hendry (QBD) (1994) 158 Local Government Review Reports 621; Lexis, December 14 1993

R v Liverpool Corporation, ex p. Liverpool Taxi Fleet Operators' Association [1972] 2 All ER 589

R v London Borough of Brent, ex p. Macwan (CA) (1994), Independent, 15 April 1994; Lexis 23 March 1994

R v London Borough of Ealing, ex p. Jennifer Lewis [1992] 224 HLR 484 (CA)

R v London Borough of Ealing, ex p. Leaman (QBD) (1984), Times, 10th February 1984; Lexis 6 February 1984

R v London Borough of Lambeth, ex p. Carroll (1988) 20 HLR 142

R v London Borough of Lambeth, ex p. Walters (1994) 26 HLR 170

R v London Borough of Redbridge ex p. East Sussex County Council 1992

R v London Borough of Sutton, ex p. Hamlet (1986), Lexis 26 March 1986

R v London Borough of Tower Hamlets, ex p. Begum [1993] 2 All ER 65 (heard with: R v Oldham Metropolitan Borough Council, ex p. Garlick; R v London Borough of Bexley, ex p. B)

R v Manchester City Council, ex p. Donald King (1991), Times April 3 1991

R v Mid-Glamorgan County Council, ex p. Greig (1988) Independent, 1 June 1988; Lexis 20 April 1988

R v Mid-Glamorgan County Council ex p Miles (1993) (comment on: Legal Action, January 1994, p.21)

R v National Insurance Commissioners, ex p. Secretary of State for Social Services [1981] 2 All ER 738

R v North Yorkshire County Council, ex p. Hargreaves (1994) (CO/878/94: transcript)

R v Northavon District Council, ex p. Palmer (1994), Independent 22 February 1994

R v Northavon District Council, ex p. Smith (1994) 144 NLJ 1010

R v Secretary of State for Education and Science, ex p. E [1992] 1 FLR 377

R v Secretary of State for Health, ex p. Alcohol Recovery Project [1993] COD 344

R v Secretary of State for Health, ex p. U.S. Tobacco International Inc. (QBD) [1992] QB 353

R v Secretary of State for the Home Department, ex p. Doody [1993] 3 WLR 154

R v Secretary of State for the Home Department, ex p. Khan [1984] 1 WLR 1337 (CA)

R v Secretary of State for the Home Department, ex p. Rofathullah [1989] QB 219

R v Secretary of State for Social Services, ex p. Hincks (QBD) 123 Sol Jo 436; Lexis 18 March 1980

R v Secretary of State for Social Services, ex p. Association of Metropolitan Authorities [1986] 1 All ER 164

R v Sheffield Health Authority, ex p. Seale (1994) (article in the Independent, 18 October 1994)

R v South Hams District Council, ex p. Gibb (1994) 26 HLR 307 (heard together with R v Gloucestershire County Council, ex p. Davies; R v Warwickshire County Council, ex p. Waller)

R v Torbay Borough Council, ex p. Cleasby (CA) [1991] COD 142

R v Waltham Forest London Borough Council, ex p. Vale (1985) Shah v London Borough of Barnet (1983)

R v Wandsworth Borough Council, ex p. Banbury (1987) 19 HLR 76

Re Findlay [1985] AC 318

Re J [1992] 4 All ER 614

Re Walker's Application (1987) (CA), Times 26 November 1988 (Court of Appeal and first instance); Lexis 25 November 1987; (at first instance, November 24 1987

Ridge v Baldwin [1963] 2 All ER 66

Rowling v Takaro Properties [1988] AC 473

Secretary of State for Education and Science v Tameside Metropolitan Borough Council [1977] AC 1014

Smith v Brighton and Lewes HMC (1955), Times, 21 June 1955

Southwark London Borough Council v Williams [1971] Ch 734

Sutton London Borough Council v Davis 1994. Guardian, 21 March 1993.

T v Surrey County Council and Others (QBD) (1994) 144 NLJ 319

Thornton v Kirklees Metropolitan Borough Council [1979] QB 626

Vicar of Writtle v Essex County Council (1979) 77 LGR 656

White and Others v Chief Adjudication Officer and Another (CA) 1993. Times Law Reports, August 2nd 1993

Woodling v Secretary of State for Social Services (HL) [1984] 1 All ER 593

Wyatt v Hillingdon Borough Council (CA) [1979] 76 LGR 727

LOCAL OMBUDSMAN INVESTIGATIONS

CLAE (194/A/86). Commission for Local Administration in England. Report on investigation against Gravesham Borough Council and Kent County Council. London: CLAE, 1987.

CLAE (88/A/0303). Commission for Local Administration in England. Investigation: complaint against the London Borough of Islington. London: CLAE, 1988.

CLAE (88/C/0814). Commission for Local Administration in England. Report on an investigation into complaint against the Northumberland County Council. York: CLAE, 1989.

CLAE (88/C/1048). Commission for Local Administration in England. Report on an investigation into complaint against the Sheffield City Council. London: CLAE, 1989.

CLAE (89/C/1114, 89/C/1130, 89/C/1151, 89/C/1387, 89/C/1852, 89/C/2288). Commission for Local Administration in England. Report on an investigation into complaints against Wirral Metropolitan District Council. York: CLAE, 1991. [Complaint by Legal Advice Centre].

CLAE (90/A/2675, 2075, 1702, 1273, 1228, 1172). Commission for Local Administration in England. Report on investigation into complaint against Essex County Council. London: CLAE, 1991.

CLAE (90/B/1676). Commission for Local Administration in England. Report on an investigation into complaint against Hertfordshire County Council. Coventry: CLAE, 1992.

CLAE (90/C/2203). Commission for Local Administration in England. Discontinuation report on an investigation into complaint against Wakefield Metropolitan District Council. York: CLAE, 1992.

CLAE (90/C/2413). Commission for Local Administration in England. Report on an investigation into complaint against Wirral Metropolitan Borough Council. York: CLAE, 1992.

CLAE (90/C/2438). Commission for Local Administration in England. Report on an investigation into complaint against Cumbria County Council. York: CLAE, 1992.

CLAE (91/A/0482). Commission for Local Administration in England. Report on investigation against the London Borough of Hackney. London: CLAE, 1993.

CLAE (91/A/1481). Commission for Local Administration in England. Report on investigation against the London Borough of Camden. London: CLAE, 1993.

CLAE (91/A/2523). Commission for Local Administration in England. Report on investigation against London Borough of Barking and Dagenham. London: CLAE, 1993.

CLAE (91/A/3466). Commission for Local Administration in England. Report on investigation against the London Borough of Ealing. London: CLAE, 1993.

CLAE (91/A/3602). Commission for Local Administration in England. Report on investigation against the London Borough of Newham. London: CLAE, 1993.

CLAE (91/A/3782). Commission for Local Administration in England. Discontinuation report on investigation against London Borough of Greenwich. London: CLAE, 1993.

CLAE (91/B/0254 & 91/B/0380). Commission for Local Administration in England. Report on investigation into complaint against Leicester City Council and Leicestershire County Council. Coventry: CLAE, 1992.

CLAE (91/B/2154 & 91/B/2155). Commission for Local Administration in England. Report on investigation against Leicester City Council and Leicestershire County Council. Coventry: CLAE, 1992.

CLAE (91/C/0121). Commission for Local Administration in England. Report on an investigation into complaint against Liverpool City Council. York: CLAE, 1993.

CLAE (91/C/0553). Commission for Local Administration in England. Report on an investigation into complaint against Manchester City Council. York: CLAE, 1992.

CLAE (91/C/0565 & 92/C/1400). Commission for Local Administration in England. Report on investigation into a complaint against North Yorkshire County Council & Harrogate Borough Council. York: CLAE, 1993.

CLAE (91/C/0729). Commission for Local Administration in England. Report on investigation into complaint against Wirral Metropolitan Borough Council. York: CLAE, 1992.

CLAE (91/C/0774). Commission for Local Administration in England. Investigation into complaint against Humberside County Council. York: CLAE, 1992.

CLAE (91/C/0831). Commission for Local Administration in England. Report on investigation into complaint against Wirral Metropolitan Borough Council. York: CLAE, 1993.

CLAE (91/C/1246). Commission for Local Administration in England. Report on investigation into a complaint against Wakefield Metropolitan District Council. York: CLAE, 1993.

CLAE (91/C/1254). Commission for Local Administration in England. Report on an investigation into a complaint against Wirral Metropolitan Borough Council. York: CLAE, 1993.

CLAE (91/C/1970). Commission for Local Administration in England. Report on investigation into a complaint against Liverpool City Council. York: CLAE, 1993.

CLAE (91/C/1972). Commission for Local Administration in England. Report on investigation against Salford City Council. York: CLAE, 1993.

CLAE (91/C/1852). Commission for Local Administration in England. Report on investigation into complaint against Wirral Metropolitan Borough Council. York: CLAE, 1993.

CLAE (91/C/2038). Commission for Local Administration in England. Report on investigation into complaint against Wirral Metropolitan Borough Council. York: CLAE, 1992.

CLAE (91/C/3210). Commission for Local Administration in England. Report on investigation into complaint against Wirral Metropolitan Borough Council. York: CLAE, 1992.

CLAE (91/C/3108). Commission for Local Administration in England. Report on investigation against Wirral Metropolitan Borough Council. London: CLAE, 1993.

CLAE (91/C/3811). Commission for Local Administration in England. Report on investigation into a complaint against Wirral Metropolitan Borough Council. London: CLAE, 1993.

CLAE (91/A/3911). Commission for Local Administration in England. Report on investigation against the London Borough of Newham. London: CLAE, 1993.

CLAE (92/A/1173). Commission for Local Administration in England. Report on investigation against the London Borough of Redbridge. London: CLAE, 1993.

CLAE (92/A/1374). Commission for Local Administration in England. Report on investigation against London Borough of Tower Hamlets. London: CLAE, 1993.

CLAE (92/A/1693). Commission for Local Administration in England. Report on investigation against London Borough of Lewisham. London: CLAE, 1993.

CLAE (92/A/3725. Commission for Local Administration in England. Report on investigation against the London Borough of Haringey. London: CLAE, 1993.

CLAE (92/A/4104). Commission for Local Administration in England. Report on investigation against the London Borough of Islington. London: CLAE, 1994.

CLAE (92/A/4108). Commission for Local Administration in England. Report on investigation against the London Borough of Redbridge. London: CLAE, 1993.

CLAE (92/C/0298). Commission for Local Administration in England. Report on an investigation into complaint against Wirral Metropolitan Borough Council. York: CLAE, 1994.

CLAE (92/C/0579). Commission for Local Administration in England. Report on investigation into a complaint against Pendle Borough Council Borough Council. York: CLAE, 1994.

CLAE (92/C/0670). Commission for Local Administration in England. Report on investigation into a complaint against Bolton Metropolitan Borough Council. York: CLAE, 1992.

CLAE (92/C/1042). Commission for Local Administration in England. Report on investigation into a complaint against Cleveland County Council. York: CLAE, 1994

CLAE (92/C/1381). Commission for Local Administration in England. Report on investigation into a complaint against North Tyneside Metropolitan Borough Council. York CLAE, 1994

CLAE (92/C/1403). Commission for Local Administration in England. Report on investigation into a complaint against Wirral Metropolitan Borough Council. York CLAE, 1994

CLAE (92/C/2376). Commission for Local Administration in England. Investigation into complaint against Wirral Metropolitan Borough Council. York: CLAE, 1994.

CLAE (92/C/2413). Commission for Local Administration in England. Report on investigation against Wirral Metropolitan Borough Council. York: CLAE, 1992.

CLAE (92/C/2438). Commission for Local Administration in England. Report on an investigation into complaint against Cumbria County Council. York: CLAE, 1992.

CLAE (92/C/2753 & 92/C/2754). Commission for Local Administration in England. Report on investigation into a complaint against Durham City Council and Durham County Council. York: CLAE, 1993.

CLAE (92/C/3402). Commission for Local Administration in England. Report on investigation into a complaint against Holderness Borough Council. York: CLAE, 1994.

CLAE (93/A/0523). Commission for Local Administration in England. Report on investigation into a complaint against the London Borough of Brent. London: CLAE, 1994.

CLAE (93/A/2071). Commission for Local Administration in England. Report on investigation into a complaint against the London Borough of Tower Hamlets. London: CLAE, 1994.

CLAE (93/C/0005). Commission for Local Administration in England. Report on investigation into a complaint against Sheffield City Council. York: CLAE, 1994.

CLAS (101/81). Commission for Local Administration in Scotland. Report of investigation of a complaint against Renfrew District Council. Edinburgh: CLAS, 1982.

CLAW (92/741). Commission for Local Administration for Wales. Investigation into complaint against Lliw Borough Council. CLAW, 1992.

HEALTH SERVICE OMBUDSMAN INVESTIGATIONS

HSC (W.111/75–76). Health Service Commissioner. NHS patient in private nursing home: refusal to refund charges. 3rd report for session 1976–1977. HC 321. London: HMSO, 1977.

HSC (W.68/77–78). Health service commissioner. Use of 'means test' by NHS. 2nd report 1977–1978. HC 343. London: HMSO, 1978.

HSC (W.360/77–78). Health Service Commissioner. Failure to provide a community nursing service. 1st report 1979–1980. London: HMSO, 1979.

HSC (W.194/78–79). Health Service Commissioner. Refusal of NHS treatment after private consultation. 1st report 1980–1981. London: HMSO, 1980.

HSC (W.224/78–79). Health Service Commissioner. Waiting time for orthopaedic treatment. 1st report 1978–1979. London: HMSO, 1979.

HSC (WW.3/79–80). Health Service Commissioner. Refusal to provide crutches. 1st report 1981–1982. HC 9. London: HMSO, 1981.

HSC (W.340/80–81). Health Service Commissioner. Care and treatment provided for a paralysed patient at home. 2nd report 1981–1982. HC 372. London: HMSO, 1982.

HSC (W.263/83–84). Health Service Commissioner. Reimbursement of cost of privately purchased medical equipment. 1st report 1984–1985. HC 33. London: HMSO, 1984.

HSC (W.371/83–84). Health Service Commissioner. Delay in providing hearing aid. 4th report 1983–1984. HC 476. London: HMSO, 1984.

HSC (W.420/83–84). Health Service Commissioner. Discharge arrangements for an elderly, immobile patient. London: HMSO.

HSC (SW.28.84/85). Health Service Commissioner. Care of an elderly patient. 1st report 1985–1986. HC 27. London: HMSO, 1985.

HSC (W.24 and 56/84–85). Health Service Commissioner. Failure in care and communication about discharged patient. 2nd report 1984–1985. HC 418. London: HMSO, 1985.

HSC (W.40/84–85). Health Service Commissioner. Proposals to discharge younger chronic sick patient. 2nd report 1984–1985. HC 418. London: HMSO, 1985.

HSC (W.113/84–85). Health Service Commissioner. Failures in care and communication. 2nd report 1984–1985. HC 418. London: HMSO, 1985.

HSC (W.707/85–86). Health Service Commissioner. Provision by hospital eye service (HES) of NHS contact lenses. 3rd report 1987–1988. HC 232. London: HMSO, 1988.

HSC (W.783/85–86). Health Services Commissioner. Failures in speech therapy service. 3rd report 1987–1988. HC 232. London: HMSO, 1988.

HSC (SW.82/86–87). Health Services Commissioner. Unsatisfactory discharge arrangements. 4th report 1987–1988. HC 511. London: HMSO, 1988.

HSC (W.286/86–87). Health Services Commissioner. Discharge arrangements made for domiciliary care. 4th report 1987–1988. HC 511. London: HMSO, 1988.

HSC (W.533/87–88). Referred to in: HSC(1990). Health Service Commissioner. Annual report for 1989–1990. HC 538. London: HMSO.

HSC (W.254/88–89). Health Services Commissioner. Discharge of patient and attitude to bereaved relatives. 1st report 1989–1990. HC 199. London: HMSO, 1990.

HSC (W.421/89–89). Health Services Commissioner. Discharge of an elderly patient. 1st report 1989–1990. HC 199. London: HMSO, 1990.

HSC (W.194/89–90). Health Services Commissioner. Inability to provide NHS care for man in need of a hospital bed. 2nd report 1990–1991. HC 482. London: HMSO, 1991.

HSC (W.478/89–90). Health Services Commissioner. Provision of long-term care. 2nd report 1990–1991. HC 482. London: HMSO, 1991.

HSC (W.599/89–90). Health Services Commissioner. Provision within the NHS of long-term care. 2nd report 1990–1991. HC 482. London: HMSO, 1991.

HSC (W.226/91–92). Health Service Commissioner. Refusal to provide prescribed orthoses free of charge. First report 1991–1992. HC 32. London: HMSO, 1992. (Also summary attached to: EL(92(73)).

HSC (W.547/92–93). Health Services Commissioner. Care of a patient at risk of developing pressure sores. 1st report 1993–1994. HC 30. London: HMSO, 1993.

HSC (SW.81/92–93). Health Service Commissioner. Rights under the Patient's Charter. 1st report 1993–1994. HC 30. London: HMSO, 1993.

HSC (W.256/92–93; W.579/92–93). Health Service Commissioner. Discharge to a nursing home where fees were payable. Third report 1993–94. HC 498. London: HMSO, 1994.

HSC (W.524/92–93). Health Service Commissioner. Unexpected costs after transfer to a nursing home. Third report 1993–94. HC 498. London: HMSO, 1994.

HSC (E.62/93–94). Health Service Commissioner. Failure to provide long term NHS care for a brain damaged patient. 2nd report 1993–1994. HC 197. London: HMSO, 1994.

PARLIAMENTARY OMBUDSMAN INVESTIGATIONS

PCA (C.12/K 1975–1976). Parliamentary Commissioner for Administration. 6th report 1975–1976. Departmental advice to local authorities about the Chronically Sick and Disabled Persons Act 1970. London: HMSO, 1976.

PCA (5/325/77, 1977–1978). Parliamentary Commissioner for Administration. Third Report 1978–1979. Provision of batteries for a hearing aid. London: HMSO, 1978.

PCA (5/915/78, 1978–1979). Parliamentary Commissioner for Administration. Fourth Report 1978–1979. Failure to provide a suitable hearing aid. HC 302. London: HMSO, 1979.

PCA (C.799/81, 1981–1982). Parliamentary Commissioner for Administration. Assistance under Chronically Sick and Disabled Persons Act 1970. 5th report 1981–1982. London: HMSO, 1972.

PCA (C656/87,1987–1988). Parliamentary Commissioner for Administration. Delay in investigating a local authority's duty to provide a 'Vistel' telephone aid. 6th report 1987–1988. HC 672. London: HMSO, 1988.

HANSARD REFERENCES

1. House of Commons, Written Answers, 19 April 1994, col.474, Dr. Mawhinney.

2. House of Commons, Written Answers, 9 March 1994, col.308, Dr. Mawhinney

3. House of Commons, Written Answers, 3 May 1994, col.455, Mr. Bowis

4. House of Lords, 10 May 1990, col. 1513, Baroness Blatch

5. House of Lords, 14 June 1990, cols 480–482, Baroness Blatch.

6. House of Commons, Written Answers, 25 May 1993, col.506, Alfred Morris

7. House of Lords, 28 June 1990, col.1754

8. House of Commons, Standing Committee E, 13 Feb 1990, cols 919–936

9. House of Commons, Written Answers, 11th July 1988, col.54, Mr. Scott

10. House of Commons Debates, 20 March 1970, cols.876–833

11. House of Lords Debates, 30 April 1970, cols.1115–1123

12. House of Commons Debates, 27 May 1970, cols.2004–2006, Alfred Morris

13. House of Commons, Written Answers, 18 July 1988, col.481, Mr. Scott.

14. House of Commons, Written Answers, 11 July 1988, col.54, Mr. Scott

15. House of Commons, Written Answers, 16 December 1982, col.241, Mr. Rossi.

16. House of Commons Debates, 20 March 1970, cols.876–881, Dr. John Dunwoody

17. House of Lords, 10 May 1990, cols. 1553–1554, Baroness Blatch

18. House of Lords, June 14 1990, col.519, Baroness Blatch

19. House of Commons, Standing Committee E, 13 Feb 1990, col.969, Virginia Bottomley

20. House of Lords, 10 May 1990, cols 1552–1553, Baroness Blatch

21. House of Lords, 14 June 1990, col.519, Baroness Blatch

22. House of Lords, 19 July 1978, col.391, Baroness Phillips

23. House of Lords, 27 July 1978, col.984, Baroness Phillips

24. House of Commons, Written Answers, 24 November 1983, col.281, Mr. Newton

25. House of Lords, 14 June 1990, col.520, Baroness Blatch

26. House of Commons, Standing Committee E, 15 Feb 1990, col.1020, Mrs. Virginia Bottomley

27. House of Commons, Standing Committee E, 15 Feb 1990, col.1061, Mrs. Virginia Bottomley.

28. House of Lords, 10 May 1990, cols 1580–1584

29. House of Commons, Standing Committee E, 15 Feb 1990, cols.1040–1042, Mr. Grist

30. House of Lords, 10 May 1990, col.1589

31. House of Lords, 25 June 1990, col.1390, Baroness Hooper

32. House of Commons, Standing Committee E, 22 Feb 1990, cols.1229–1230, Virginia Bottomley

33. House of Lords, 10 May 1990, col.1561, Baroness Hooper

34. House of Lords, 14 June 1990, cols.520–2

35. House of Commons, Oral answers, 5th August 1975, cols. 219–220, Barbara Castle

36. House of Commons, Oral answers, 13 December 1984, col.1206, Prime Minister

37. House of Commons, Written answers, 31 January 1985, col.294, Prime Minister

38. House of Commons, Oral answers, 5th August 1975, cols 219–220, Barbara Castle

39. House of Commons, Written answers, 16 Feb 1993, col.160, Mr.Yeo

40. House of Lords, 10 May 1990, cols 1533–1539, Baroness Blatch

41. House of Lords, 14 June 1990, col.492, Baroness Hooper

42. House of Commons, Written answers, 9 March 1994, col.268, Mr. Stewart

43. House of Commons, Written answers, 3 March 1994, col.855, Mr. Bowis

44. House of Lords, 8 May 1990, cols 1285–1287, Baroness Hooper

45. House of Commons, Written answers, 22nd November 1990, col 32, Mr. Dorrell

46. House of Commons, Written answers, 20 December 1990, cols.347–8, Mr. Dorrell

47. House of Lords, 24th April 1990, cols.546–550, Baroness Masham and Baroness Hooper

48. House of Commons, Written Answers, 4th March 1991, col.22, Mr. Dorrell.

49. House of Commons, Written Answers, 3 December 1991, col.116, Mrs. Virginia Bottomley

50. House of Commons, Written answers, 16 February 1993, col.160, Mr. Yeo

51. House of Commons, Written answers, 16 July 1992, col.900, Mr. Yeo

52. House of Lords, 3 April 1990, col.1342, Baroness Masham

53. House of Commons, Written answers, 22 May 1992, col.301, Mr. Yeo

54. House of Commons, Written answers,22 May 1992, col.303, Mr. Yeo

55. House of Commons, Written answers, 22 May 1992, col.303, Mr. Yeo

56. House of Commons Debates, July 12th 1989, col.980, Kenneth Clarke

57. House of Lords, 14 May 1986, col.1227, Baroness Masham

58. House of Commons, Written answers, 25 January 1994, col.232, Dr. Mawhinney

59. House of Lords, 10 May 1990, cols 1538–9, Baroness Blatch

60. House of Commons, Written answers, 8 Feb 1994, col.188, Mr.Gwilym Jones

61. House of Commons Debates, 5th December 1969, col.1856, Alfred Morris

62. House of Commons, Standing Committee 'C', 4 February 1970, col.153, Alfred Morris

63. House of Commons, Written answers, 26 July 1983, col.410, Mr. Newton

64. House of Commons Debates, 10 June 1985, col.651, Mr. Newton

65. House of Lords, 10 May 1990, vol.518, cols.1563–1564, Baroness Hooper

66. House of Commons, Standing Committee 'E', 15 Feb 1990, col.1026, Virginia Bottomley

67. House of Commons, Standing Committee 'E', 15 Feb 1990, col.1070, Michael Forsyth

68. House of Commons, Written answers, 14 April 1993, col.613, Mr. Yeo

69. House of Commons, Oral answers, 23 March 1993, col.748, Mr. Yeo

70. House of Lords, 25 June 1990, col.1379, Baroness Blatch

71. House of Commons, Standing Committee 'E', 15 Feb 1990, col.1038, Mr. Grist

72. House of Commons, Oral answers, 24th June 1991, col.667, Ann Widdecombe

73. House of Commons, Written answers, 28 Oct 1992, col.670, Mr. Baldry

74. House of Lords, 14 June 1990, col.466, Lord Henley

75. House of Commons Debates, 21 October 1991, col.662, Secretary of State for Health.

76. House of Lords, 25 June 1990, col.1396–7, Baroness Blatch

77. House of Commons, Standing Committee 'E', 15 Feb 1990, cols.1055–1059, Mrs. Bottomley

78. House of Commons, Standing Committee 'E', 20 February 1990, col.1086–1089, Mr.Freeman

79. House of Commons Debates, 2 Feb 1979, col.1909, Mr. Jack Ashley

80. House of Commons, Standing Committee 'E', 20 February 1990, col.1091, Mr. Freeeman

81. House of Commons, Written answers, 23 July 1985, col.534, Mr. Newton

82. House of Commons, Written answers, 14 May 1987, cols 354–355, Mr. Major

83. House of Commons, Written answers, 9 July 1986, col.170, Mr. Newton

84. House of Commons, Standing Committee 'E', 20 Feb 1990, cols.1088–1091, Under-Secretary of State for Health

85. House of Lords, 10 May 1990, col.1571, Baroness Hooper; see also House of Lords, vol.520, 1990, col.483, Baroness Blatch

86. House of Lords, col.492, 14 June 1990, Baroness Hooper

87. House of Lords, 7 June 1990, cols.1588–1596, Baroness Blatch

88. House of Lords, 24 April 1990, col.551, Baronesss Masham of Ilton

89. House of Commons, Standing Committee 'E', 20 February 1990, col.1088, Under Secretary of State for Health

90. House of Commons Debates, 12 December 1991, col.1013, Mr. Alfred Morris

91. House of Lords, 10 May 1990, vol.518, cols 1590–1591, Baroness Hooper

92. House of Lords, 9 April 1970,, col.242, Earl of Longford

93. House of Commons, Standing Committee 'E', 13 Feb 1990, col.969, Virginia Bottomley

94. House of Commons, Written Answers, 5 Feb 1991, col.96, Mr. Dorrell

95. House of Commons, Standing Committee E, 15 Feb 1990, cols. 1055–1070

96. House of Commons Debates, 4th February 1970, col. 153, Alfred Morris

97. House of Lords, 9th April 1970, col.241, Earl of Longford

98. House of Lords, 10 May 1990, col.1564, Lord Reston

99. House of Commons Debates, 1 July 1992, col.874, Mr. Yeo

REFERENCES

ADSS News (1994). Status of guidance should be clarified. ADSS News: April 1994,p.4.

Age Concern (1991). Meredith, B. Issues in continuing care of older people relating to findings by the Health Service Commissioner: submission to the House of Commons Select Committee on the Parliamentary Commissioner for Administration. London: Age Concern.

Age Concern England (1992). *Home help and care: rights, charging and reality.* London: Age Concern England.

Age Concern England (1993). *No time to lose: first impressions of community care reforms.* London: Age Concern England, 1993.

Age Concern England (1993a). *Provision of welfare services by council housing departments.* London: Age Concern England.

Age Concern England (1994). *Preserved and protected? A report and recommendations about the community care reforms and people with preserved rights to Income Support.* London: Age Concern England.

Age Concern England (1994a). *The next steps: lessons for the future of community care.* London: Age Concern England.

Alzheimer's Disease Society (1993). *NHS psychogeriatric continuing care beds.* London: Alzheimer's Disease Society.

AMA; LGIU (1991). *Too high a price? Examining the cost of charging policies.* London: Association of Metropolitan Authorities; Local Government Information Unit.

AMA; LGIU (1992). *Review of issues relating to charging for community care services.* London: Association of Metropolitan Authorities; Local Government Information Unit.

AMA (1993). *DoH advice on assessment: AMA trawl on authorities' response to that advice.* London: Association of Metropolitan Authorities.

Arnold,P; Bochel,H; Brodhurst,S; Page,D (1993). *Community care: the housing dimension.* York: Joseph Rowntree Foundation; Community Care.

Arnold,P; Bochel,H; Page,D (1994). Involving housing agencies. In: *The next key tasks.* Sutton: Community Care.

Audit Commission (1992). *Community revolution: personal social services and community care.* London: HMSO.

Audit Commission (1993). Progress with care in the community. *Bulletin.* London: Audit Commission, 1993.

Audit Commission (1994). *Finding a place: a review of mental health services.* London: Audit Commission.

Balen,P (1994). Causation problems: difficulties of proving causation in medical negligence cases. *Solicitors Journal:* 22 July 1994; 138(28),pp.742–743.

Balloch,S (1993). *AMA/ACC survey of social services charging policies 1992–1994.* London: Association of Metropolitan Authorities. (Draft version).

Balloch, S (1994). *A survey of social services charging policies 1992–1994.* London: AMA. (Published version).

Barron,A; Scott,C (1992). Citizen's Charter Programme. *Modern Law Review* 1992; 55(4), 526–546.

Beardshaw, V. (1988). *Last on the list: community services for people with physical disabilities.* London: King's Fund Institute.

Berry, Lynne (1990). *Information for users of social services departments.* London: National Consumer Council; National Institute for Social Work.

Bewley,C; Glendinning,C (1994). *Involving disabled people in community care planning.* York: Joseph Rowntree Foundation.

Bhuttarcharji,S (1992). Misleading statements: the art of 'statementing' for children with special educational needs. *Therapy Weekly* 1992; 19(6), p.7.

Bottomley,V (1994). National health, local dynamic. *Independent,* 22 August 1994, p.14.

Brazier,M (1992). *Medicine, patients and the law.* 2nd edition. London: Penguin.

British Medical Association (1968). *Aids for the disabled.* London: BMA.

British Medical Association (1993). *British Medical Association. Survey on the impact of the implementation of the community care reforms.* London: BMA.

Buckley,R.A (1993). *Modern law of negligence.* 2nd edition. Butterworths: London.

Calabresi G; Bobbitt,P (1978). *Tragic choices.* New York: Norton.

Carey, S (1993). (Office of Population Censuses and Surveys). *Older people and community care: an examination of information sources in relation to levels of dependency and care in the community.* London: OPCS.

Centre for Policy on Ageing (1984). *Home life: a code of practice for residential care.* London: CPA.

Challis,L; Henwood,M (1994). Equity in community care. *British Medical Journal:* 4 June 1994; 308, pp.1496–1499.

Chartered Society of Physiotherapy (1993). *Survey of physiotherapy services to older people resident in private nursing homes.* London: CSP.

Child Poverty Action Group (1994). *National welfare benefits handbook.* London: CPAG.

CLAE (1990). *Local government ombudsmen: annual report 1989/1990.* London: Commission for Local Administration in England.

CLAE (1993). *How to complain to the Local Government Ombudsman.* London: Commission for Local Administration in England.

CLAE (1993a). *Good administrative practice.* London: Commission for Local Administration in England.

CLAE (1994). *Local government ombudsmen: annual report 1993/1994.* London: Commission for Local Administration in England.

Clements, L (1992). Duties of social services departments. *Legal Action Journal,* September 1992.

Clements, L (1994). Community care: definition of 'need'. *Legal Action Journal* 1994; January, p.21.

Clements (1994a). Shifting sands: the NHS could have tranche of its responsibilities subtly shifted on to social services. *Community Care:* 29th September – 5th October 1994, pp.24–25.

Collyer,M; Hanson-Kahn,C (1989). *Feet first: a reappraisal of footcare services in London.* London: Age Concern London.

Collyer,M (1992). *Swept under the carpet: a report on domestic services for older people in London.* London: Age Concern Greater London.

Committee of Public Accounts, House of Commons (1993). *Health services for physically disabled people aged 16 to 64.* HC 538. London: HMSO.

Cook,J; Mitchell,P (1982). *Putting teeth in the Act: a history of attempts to enforce section of the Chronically Sick and Disabled Persons Act.* RADAR: London.

Cooper,M (1992). Charging for local authority services. *Local Government Review.* 29th February 1992; 56, pp.161,179.

Coopers and Lybrand (1988). *Information needs of disabled people, their carers and service providers: final report.* London: Department of Health and Social Security, Priority Care Division.

Cox,B (1993). Community care: top-up funding: R v Avon CC ex p Hazell (1993) 5 July QBD. *Legal Action Journal,* October 1993, p.22.

Devon SSD (1989). *Disabled Persons (Services, Consultation and Representation) Act 1986: code of practice.* Devon SSD: Exeter, 1989.

DH (1989). *Discharge of patients from hospital.* London: Department of Health.

DH (1989a). *Income generation: a guide to local initiative.* London: Department of Health.

DH (1990). *Community care in the next decade and beyond: policy guidance.* HMSO, London.

DH (1990a). *The care of children: principles and practice in regulations and guidance.* Third impression. London: HMSO.

DH (1991) *Patient's Charter.* London: Department of Health.

DH (1992). *Equipped for independence? Meeting the equipment needs of disabled people.* London: Department of Health.

DH (1992a). *Correspondence with the College of Occupational Therapists, 9 June 1992. 'Provision of equipment by the NHS:* EL(92)20. London: Department of Health.

DH (1993). *Implementing community care: population needs assessment: good practice guidance.* London: Department of Health.

DH (1994). *Hospital discharge workbook.* London: Department of Health.

DH (1994a). *Pressure sores – a key quality indicator.* London: Department of Health.

DH (1994b). *Monitoring and development: first impressions April-September 1993 [community care].* London: Department of Health.

DH (1994c). *A framework for local community care charters in England: consultation document.* London: Department of Health.

DH; KPMG (1992). *Improving independent sector involvement in community care planning.* London: Department of Health; KPMG Management Consultants.

DH; SHHD; WO (1989). *National Health Service and Community Care Bill: notes on clauses: House of Commons.* Department of Health; Scottish Home and Health Department; Welsh Office.

DH; WO (1993). Department of Health; Welsh Office. *Code of practice: Mental Health Act 1983.* London: HMSO.

DHSS (1986). *Management of private practice in health services hospitals in England and Wales.* London: Department of Health and Social Security.

Dimond, B (1994). How far can you go? [Boundaries of NHS responsibilities to pay for long-term care]. *Health Service Journal,* 14th April 1994, pp.24–25.

Disability Alliance (1994). *Disability Rights Handbook April 1994 – April 1995.* London: Disability Alliance.

Disabled Living Foundation (1994). *Handling people.* London: DLF.

DoE (1993). Consultation paper by the Department of Environment: Local Government and Housing Act 1989, Housing and Urban Development Bill, Clauses 112 to 114: housing welfare services and the Housing Revenue Account. London: Department of Environment.

DoE (1993a). The future of private housing renewal programmes: a consultation document. London: Department of Environment.

DoE; DH; WO (1991). Department of Environment; Department of Health; Welsh Office. *Homelessness: code of guidance for local authorities.* 3rd edition. London; HMSO.

DSS/DH (1991). Memorandum submitted by the Department of Social Security and Department of Health. Fourth Report of the Social Security Committee. Financing of private residential and nursing fees. Volume 2. Minutes of evidence and appendices, p.92. HC 421–II. London: HMSO, 1991. Quoted in Age Concern England (1993). *Hospital discharge procedures.* Ref: Briefings, 2493. London: Age Concern England, 1993.

Dugdale,A.M; Stanton,K.M (1989). *Professional negligence.* London: Butterworths.

Edwards,F.C; Warren,M.D (1990). *Health services for adults with physical disabilities: a survey of district health authorities.* London: Royal College of Physicians.

Ellis, Kathryn (1993). *Squaring the circle: user and carer participation in needs assessment.* York: Joseph Rowntree Foundation.

Emery,C.T; Smythe,B (1986). *Judicial review.* London: Sweet & Maxwell.

Encyclopaedia of Social Services and Child Care Law. (Jones, R). London: Sweet and Maxwell (looseleaf: December 1993 release).

Fiedler,B. (1994). *Living options lottery: housing and support services for people with severe physical disabilities:* 1986/88. London: Prince of Wales' Advisory Group on Disability.

Finch, J (1994). *Speller's law relating to hospitals.* 7th edition. London: Chapman & Hall Medical

Fordham,M (1994). *Judicial review handbook.* London: Wiley Chancery Law Publishing.

Francis,J (1994). The waiting game [About housing and community care]. In: *The next key tasks.* Sutton: Community Care.

Garden, B (1990). *Information on disability: final report of the Lothian Project.* Edinburgh: Disability Scotland.

George,M (1994). Paying direct. *Community Care:* 25–31 August 1994.

Gordon,R (1993). *Community care assessments.* London: Longman.

Gould,J (1994). *Not just fine tuning: a review of shire county community care plans for rural areas.* London: National Council for Voluntary Organisations.

Griffiths (Chairman) (1988). *Community care: agenda for action: a report to the Secretary of State for Social Services.* London: HMSO.

Hardy,B; Wistow,G; Leedham,I (1994). (Community Care Division, Nuffield Institute for Health). *Analysis of a sample of English community care plans 1993/94.* London: Department of Health.

Health Committee (House of Commons) (1993). *Community care: the way forward.* 6th report 1992–1993. 2 vols. London: HMSO.

Health Committee (House of Commons) (1994). *Better off in the community? The care of people who are seriously mentally ill.* London: HMSO.

Health Service Ombudsman for England (1991). *How the health service ombudsman can help you.* London: HMSO.

Henwood,M; Wistow,G (1994). Social Services Inspectorate; NHS Management Executive; Nuffield Institute for Health Care Studies. *Hospital discharge and community care: early days.* London: Department of Health.

Henwood,M (1994a). *Fit for change? Snapshots of the community care reforms one year on.* Nuffield Institute for Health; King's Fund Centre.

Heywood,F (1994). *Adaptations: finding ways to say yes.* Bristol: University of Bristol, School for Advanced Urban Studies.

Hinchcliffe,D (1994). *Incontinence: suffering in silence.* London: Labour Party.

HSC(1990). Health Service Commissioner. Annual report for 1989–1990. HC 538. London: HMSO.

HSC (1991). Health Service Commissioner. Annual report for 1990–91. London: HMSO.

HSC (1993). Health Service Commissioner for England, Scotland and for Wales. Annual report for 1992–93. London: HMSO.

HSC (1994). Health Service Commissioner for England, Scotland and for Wales. Annual report for 1993–94. Fourth report 1993–94. HC 499. London: HMSO.

Hunt,L (1994). Pensioner in pain says age and cost influenced care. *Independent,* 15th April 1994.

Hunter,C; McGrath,S (1992). *Homeless persons: Arden's guide to the Housing Act 1985, Part III.* London: Legal Action Group.

Jeffrey,J (1994). Rise of the broker: care management is a new phenomenon for social workers: how are social services departments interpreting it? *Care Weekly,* 9 June 1994, pp.10–11.

Jones,M.A (1991). *Textbook on torts. 3rd edition.* London: Blackstone Press.

Judge,K; Mays,N (1994). Allocating resources for health and social care in England. *British Medical Journal,* 21 May 1994, pp.1363–1366.

Kenny,D; Edwards,P; Stanton,R (1994). *From social security to community care: the impact of the transfer of funding on local authorities.* Luton: Local Government Management Board.

Kent County Council Social Services (1993). *Summary community care plan for Kent (adult and children's services) 1993/94–1995/96.* Maidstone: Kent County Council.

KPMG Peat Marwick (1993). *Informing users and carers.* London: Department of Health.

Laing,W (1993). *Financing long-term care: the crucial debate.* London: Age Concern.

LBOTMG (1988). *Occupational therapists' criteria for the provision of adaptations in the homes of people with disabilities.* London: London Boroughs Occupational Therapy Managers Group.

LBOTMG (1992). *Occupational therapists' criteria for the loan of equipment to people with disabilities.* London: London Boroughs Occupational Therapy Managers Group.

Lee, S (1989). *Judging judges.* London: Faber and Faber.

Leedham,I; Wistow G (1992). *Community care and general practitioners: the role of GPs in the assessment process with special reference to the perspectives of social services departments.* Leeds: Nuffield Institute for Health Care Studies, University of Leeds.

London Borough of Barnet Directorate of Social Services (1987). *Serving people with disabilities.* London: London Borough of Barnet.

Macintosh,S; Leather,P (1993). *Minor works: a major step: minor works assistance in practice.* Nottingham: Care and Repair, 1993.

Macintosh,S; Leather,P; McCafferty,P (1993). *The role of housing agency services in helping disabled people.* London: HMSO.

Mair, A (1972). *Medical rehabilitation: the pattern for the future.* Edinburgh: HMSO. 25.

Mandelstam,M (1993). *How to get equipment for disability.* 3rd edition. London: Jessica Kingsley and Kogan Page (for the Disabled Living Foundation).

Marks, L (1994). Seamless care or patchwork quilt: discharging patients from acute hospital care. *Research Report 17.* London: King's Fund Institute.

McColl (Chairman) (1986). *Review of artificial limb and appliance centres.* London: Department of Health and Social Security.

McLeod,I (1993). *Judicial review.* Chichester: Barry Rose.

Means,R; Lart,R (1994). *Involving older people in community care planning.* In: More power to our elders. London: Counsel and Care, 1994.

Mental Health Foundation (1994). *Creating community care: report of the Mental Health Foundation into community care for people with severe mental illness.* London: Mental Health Foundation.

Ministry of Health; Department of Health for Scotland (1944). *A National Health Service.* London: HMSO.

NAHA (1984). *Registration and inspection of nursing home: a handbook for health authorities.* Birmingham: National Association of Health Authorities and Trusts.

NAHA (1988). *Registration and inspection of nursing home: a handbook for health authorities: 1988 supplement.* Birmingham: National Association of Health Authorities and Trusts.

NAHA (1988a). *Health authority concerns for children with special needs: a report on a survey of health authorities on the implementation of the Education Act 1981.* Birmingham: National Association of Health Authorities.

NAHAT (1991). National Association of Health Authorities and Trusts. *Care in the community: definitions of health and social care: developing an approach: a West Midlands study.* Birmingham: NAHAT.

NAHAT (1991). National Association of Health Authorities and Trusts. *NHS Handbook.* London: Macmillan, 1991.

NAO (1992). National Audit Office. *Health services for physically disabled people aged 16–64.* London: HMSO.

National Federation of Housing Federations (1993). *Community care hotline: housing and community care: the loose connection?* London: NFHA.

Neate,P (1994). Under pressure: care managers are on the front line between clients and service providers. In: *The next key tasks.* Sutton: Community Care.

Neill,J; Williams,J (1992). National Institute for Social Work Research Unit for the Department of Health. *Leaving hospital: elderly people and their discharge to community care.* London: HMSO.

Nelson-Jones,R (1990). *Medical negligence case law.* London: Fourmat.

NHSE (1994). NHS Executive. *NHS responsibilities for meeting long term health care needs.* Leeds: Department of Health.

North, C; Ritchie,J; Ward,K (1993). *Factors influencing the care implementation of the Care Programme Approach: a research study carried out for the Department of Health.* London: HMSO.

NWTROTAG (1993) *Statement on EL(92)20 [charging for equipment].* Stanmore: North West Thames Regional Occupational Therapy Advisory Group, 1993.

O'Brien,C; Wurr,J (1993). *Community care plans 1993/94: alcohol and drug use.* London: Alcohol Concern; Standing Conference on Drug Abuse.

RADAR (1993). *Disabled people have rights: a two year project to enforce section 2 of the Chronically Sick and Disabled Persons Act 1970: interim report.* Sponsored by the Nuffield Provincial Hospitals Trust. London: Royal Association for Disability and Rehabilitation.

RADAR (1994). (Keep,J; Clarkson,J). *Disabled people have rights: final report on a two year project funded by the Nuffield Provincial Hospitals Trust.* London: Royal Association for Disability and Rehabilitation.

Redmayne,S; Klein,R; Day,P (1993). *Sharing out resources: purchasing and priority in the NHS.* Birmingham: National Association of Health Authorities and Trusts.

Ritchie,J.H (chair) (1994). Report of the inquiry into the care and treatment of Christopher Clunis: presented to the Chairman of North East Thames and South East Thames Regional Health Authorities, February 1994. London: HMSO.

Roberts,S; Steele,J; Moore,N (1991). *Finding out about residential care: results of a survey of users.* London: Policy Studies Institute.

Ross,F; Campbell,F (1992). 'if it wasn't for this wheelchair – I might as well be dead': a study of equipment and aids for daily living in the community: a district nurse and consumer perspective. London: Department of Nursing Studies, King's College London.

RCN (1992). A scandal waiting to happen? Elderly people and nursing care in residential and nursing homes. London: Royal College of Nursing.

RCN; Spastics Society (1992). Day in, day out: a survey of views of respite care. London: Royal College of Nursing; Spastics Society, Spastics Society.

RCP (1994). Ensuring equity and quality of care for elderly people: the interface between geriatric medicine and general (internal) medicine. London: Royal College of Physicians.

Sanderson, J (1991). An agenda for action on incontinence services. London: Department of Health.

Secretaries of State (1989). Secretary of State for Health; Secretary of State for Social Security; Secretary of State for Wales; Secretary of State for Scotland. Caring for people: community care in the next decade and beyond. London: HMSO.

Secretary of State for Health (1991). The health of the nation: a consultative document for health in England. London: HMSO.

SHHD/DGM (1991)67. National Health Service in Scotland Management Executive. Private nursing homes: entitlement of patients to NHS supplies and services. Edinburgh: Scottish Office, 1991.

Smale G; Tuson,G; Biehal,N; Marsh,P (1993). National Institute for Social Work. Empowerment, assessment, care management and the skilled worker. London: HMSO.

Smith,J (1994). Power, older people and being care for. In: More power to our elders. London: Counsel and Care, 1994.

Social Services Committee (House of Commons) (1990). Community care: choice for service users. Sixth report. London: HMSO, 1990.

Social Services Committee (House of Commons) (1990a). Community care: planning and cooperation. London: HMSO.

SSI (1988). Social Services Inspectorate. Health in homes: a review of arrangements for health care in 54 local authority homes for elderly people. London: Department of Health.

SSI (1988a). Social Services Inspectorate. Services for people with a physical disability. London: Department of Health.

SSI (1988b). Social Services Inspectorate. A wider vision: report of an inspection of the management and organisation of services for people who are blind or partially sighted. London: Department of Health.

SSI (1989). Social Services Inspectorate. Sign posts: leading to better social services for deaf–blind people. London: Department of Health. London: Department of Health.

SSI (1990). Social Services Inspectorate. Developing services for disabled people: results of an inspection to monitor the operation of the Disabled Persons (Services, Consultation and Representation) Act 1986. London: Department of Health.

SSI (1991). Social Services Inspectorate. Getting the message across: a guide to developing and communicating policies, principles and procedures on assessment. London: HMSO.

SSI (1991a). Social Services Inspectorate. Report of an inspection of occupational therapy services in Dudley. Birmingham: Department of Health.

SSI (1991b). Social Services Inspectorate. Inspection of the occupational therapy services in Devon. Bristol: Department of Health.

SSI (1991c). Social Services Inspectorate. Assessment systems and community care. London: Department of Health.

SSI (1991d). Social Services Inspectorate. *Right to complain: practice guidance on complaints procedures in social services departments.* London: HMSO.

SSI (1991e). Social Services Inspectorate. *HIV and AIDS service provision in social services departments.* London: Department of Health.

SSI (1991f). Social Services Inspectorate. *Managing aids to daily living.* Bristol: Department of Health.

SSI (1991g). Social Services Inspectorate. *Hear me: see me: an inspection of services from three agencies to disabled people in Gloucestershire.* Bristol: Department of Health.

SSI (1992). Social Services Inspectorate. *Social services for hospital patients 1: working at the interface: a report of the findings in five social services departments.* London: Department of Health.

SSI (1992b). Social Services Inspectorate. *Mental illness specific grants: monitoring of proposals for use 1991/92.* London: Department of Health.

SSI (1993). Social Services Inspectorate. *Social services for hospital patients III: users and carers perspective.* London: Department of Health.

SSI (1993a). Social Services Inspectorate. *Whose life it anyway? A report of an inspection of services for people with multiple impairments.* London: Department of Health.

SSI (1993b). Social Services Inspectorate. *Social services department inspection units: the first eighteen months: report of an inspection of the work of inspection units in ten local authorities.* London: HMSO, 1993.

SSI (1993c). Social Services Inspectorate. *Progress on the right to complain: monitoring social services complaints procedures 1992/3.* London: Department of Health.

SSI (1993d). Social Services Inspectorate. *Inspection of complaints procedures in local authority social services departments.* London: HMSO.

SSI (1993e). Social Services Inspectorate. *Inspection of assessment and care management arrangements in social services departments: interim overview report.* London: Department of Health.

SSI (1993f). Social Services Inspectorate. *Social services for hospital patients III: users and carers perspective.* London: Department of Health.

SSI (1993g). Social Services Inspectorate. *Raising the standard: the second annual report of the Chief Inspector, Social Services Inspectorate 1992/93.* London: HMSO.

SSI (1993h). Social Services Inspectorate. *Achieving the change in SSI Central Region: fifth report on the implementation of Caring for People.* Birmingham: Department of Health.

SSI (1993j). Social Services Inspectorate (1993j). *Community care implementation: monitoring report for London.* London: Department of Health.

SSI (1993k). Social Services Inspectorate. *Caring for people progress review: North of England region.* Leeds: Department of Health.

SSI (1993m). Social Services Inspectorate; KPMG Peat Marwick. *Diversification and the independent residential care sector.* London: HMSO.

SSI (1993n). Social Services Inspectorate (Southern England Region, Policy and Business Division). *Caring for people: progress on implementation.* London: Department of Health.

SSI (1993o). Social Services Inspectorate. *Health of the Nation: key area handbook: mental illness.* London: Department of Health.

SSI (1994a). Social Services Inspectorate. *Occupational therapy: the community contribution.* London: Department of Health.

SSI (1994b). Social Services Inspectorate. *Advice note for use by Social Services Inspectorate: discretionary charges for adult social services (section 17 of Health and Social Services and Social Security Adjudications Act 1983).* London: Department of Health.

SSI (1994c). Social Services Inspectorate. *Inspection of the complaints procedure: North Yorkshire County Council.* Leeds: Department of Health, 1994.

SSI (1994d). Social Services Inspectorate. *Inspection of assessment and care management arrangements in social services departments:* London Borough of Tower Hamlets. London: Department of Health.

SSI (1994e). Social Services Inspectorate. *Report of an inspection of assessment and care management arrangements in social services departments:* London Borough of Harrow, 1–10 December 1993. London: Department of Health.

SSI (1994f). Social Services Inspectorate. *Report of the inspection of complaints procedures in West Sussex Social Services Department, November 1993.* London: Department of Health.

SSI (1994g). Social Services Inspectorate. *Inspection of assessment and care management arrangements in social services departments: October 1993 – March 1994: second overview report.* London: Department of Health.

SSI (1994h). Social Services Inspectorate. *Inspection of social services department arrangements for the discharge of elderly people from hospital to residential and nursing home care:* Northumberland. Gateshead: Department of Health.

SSI (1994j). Social Services Inspectorate. *Lambeth Social Services Department: arrangements for the discharge of elderly people from hospital to nursing home care: 8th/18th March 1994.* London: Department of Health.

SSI/DLF (1992). (Brearley,P; Mandelstam,M). Social Services Inspectorate; Disabled Living Foundation. *Review of literature 1986–1991 on day care services for adults.* London: HMSO.

SSI/NHSME (1993). Social Services Inspectorate; National Health Service Management Executive. *SSI/RHA community care monitoring, September 1993: national summary.* London: Department of Health. (attached to joint Circular EL(93)119, CI(93)35).

SSI/NHSME (1994). Social Services Inspectorate; NHS Management Executive. *Implementing community care for younger people with physical and sensory disabilities.* London: Department of Health.

SSI/NHSME (1994a). Social Services Inspectorate; NHS Management Executive. *Assessment special study: a joint SSI/NHSME study of assessment procedures in five local authority areas.* London: Department of Health.

SSI/NHSME (1994b). Social Services Inspectorate; NHS Management Executive. *31 December agreements: reviewing the implementation.* London: Department of Health.

SSI/NHSME (1994c). Social Services Inspectorate; NHS Management Executive. *Community care monitoring: special study: mental health services.* London: Department of Health.

SSI/NHSE (1994d). Social Services Inspectorate; NHS Executive. *Role of the GP and primary healthcare team.* London: Department of Health.

SSI/NHSE (1994e). Social Services Inspectorate; NHS Executive. *Care management.* London: Department of Health.

SSI/NHSE (1994f). Social Services Inspectorate; NHS Executive. *'It's our lives': community care for people with learning disabilities.* London: Department of Health.

SSI/NHSME (1994g). Social Services Inspectorate; NHS Management Executive. *Special study of purchasing and contracting.* London: Department of Health.

SSI/NHSE (1994h). Social Services Inspectorate; NHS Executive. *Community care for people with HIV and AIDS.* London: Department of Health.

SSI/NHSE (1994j). Social Services Inspectorate, NHS Executive. *Community care packages for older people.* London: Department of Health.

SSI/SIS (1991). Social Services Inspectorate; Social Information Systems. *Assessment systems and community care.* London: Department of Health.

SSI/SWSG (MG) (1991). Social Services Inspectorate; Social Work Services Group. *Care management and assessment: managers' guide.* London: HMSO.

SSI/SWSG,PG (1991). Social Services Inspectorate; Social Work Services Group. *Care management and assessment: practitioners' guide.* London: HMSO.

Stanton,K.M (1986). *Breach of statutory duty in tort.* London: Sweet & Maxwell.

Steele,J; Hinkley,P; Rowlands,I; Moore,N (1993). *Informing people about social services.* London: Policy Studies Institute.

Tarling,C (1992). Developing safe handling policies. *Nursing Standard* 1992; 6(47), pp.33–36.

Therapy Weekly (1992). Patients charged illegally. *Therapy Weekly,* March 12 1992; 18(34),p.1.

Therapy Weekly (1994). Victory for PT arthritis patient. *Therapy Weekly:* April 28 1994; 20(41),p.1.

Therapy Weekly (1994a). Outcry over PT age bar. *Therapy Weekly:* April 21 1994; 20(40),p.1.

Thomas,M (1994). *Charging older people for care: 1993/94 update.* Edinburgh: Age Concern Scotland.

Thomas, P (1994). The maladministration business: what the Local Government Ombudsman can and cannot do. *Solicitor's Journal;* 138(7),178–179.

Timmins,N (1994). Sick woman must pay for long-term care: dispute over who should pay for a patient's continuing care. *The Independent,* 6th May 1994,p.4.

Timmins,N (1994a). Insecurely into old age. *Independent,* 15 August 1994, p.15.

Tinker,A; McCreadie,C; Salvage,A (1993). *Information needs of elderly people – an exploratory study.* London: Age Concern Institute of Gerontology.

Tomkin,Z (1991). Footing the bill: the orthopaedic service at Guy's Hospital is trying to cut costs by offering patients stock shoes where possible, or inviting them to go private. *Therapy Weekly* 1991; 18(9),p.4.

Topliss,E; Gould,B (1981). *A charter for the disabled.* Oxford: Blackwell.

Wade,H.W.R (1988). *Administrative Law.* 6th edition. Oxford: Oxford University Press.

Warner,N (1994). *Community care: just a fairy tale?* London: National Carers' Association.

Whelan,J (1993). *Priority setting in the NHS: the drugs budget.* London: Age Concern England. (Letter of 2nd November 1993, to the Department of Health).

Which? (1994). Who should live and who should die? *Which?:* July 1994, pp.50–53.

Whitehead,M (1994). Is it fair?: evaluating the equity implications for the NHS reforms. In: Robinson,R; Le Grand,J. *Evaluating the NHS reforms.* London: King''s Fund Institute, 1994.

Whitehead, M. (1994a). Who cares about equity in the NHS? British Medical Journal: 14 May 1994; 308, pp.1284–1287.

Wiggin,C; Carpenter,G (1994). Going it alone: user control over resources. *Community Care:* 8–14th September 1994.

Wignall, G (1994). Legitimate expectation and the abuse of power. *New Law Journal* 1994; 144(6658), pp.1038–1039.

Williams,T; Goriely,T (1994). Big idea – any effect: the Charter complaints system as an alternative to statutory rights. *New Law Journal* 1994; 144(6661), pp.1164–1165.

Wilson,A (1994) (Chairman). *Being heard.* London: HMSO.

Wistow,G (1989). Planning and collaboration in a mixed economy. In: Wolstenholme,L; Wistow,G; Gilroy,D (eds). *Community care in a mixed economy: meeting the challenge.* Leeds: Nuffield Institute for Health Services Studies, University of Leeds.

Wistow,G; Leedham,I; Hardy,B (1993). *Community care plans: a preliminary analysis of a sample of English community care plans.* (Undertaken by the Nuffield Institute (Health Service Studies) for the Social Services Inspectorate). London: Department of Health, Social Services Inspectorate.

Wistow,G; Henwood,M (1994). *Residential care: will social security pay?* Leeds: Nuffield Institue for Health Care, Community Care Division.

Worth, A (1994). Quicker and sicker: how much do social workers really know about the discharge of elderly patients from hospital? *Care Weekly:* 28 July 1994.

Wyatt,J (1992). U-turn by health authority after three-year battle. *Caring Times* 1992; 4(8),p.1.

INDEX

In addition to this index, a detailed A–Z list of services and types of equipment, referenced to the legislation under which they might be provided, is given on pages 53–57.